VIOLENCE

IN
INTIMATE
RELATIONSHIPS

VIOLENCE
IN
INTIMATE
RELATIONSHIPS

Edited by
Gordon W. Russell, Ph.D.
Department of Psychology
University of Lethbridge
Lethbridge, Canada

PMA PUBLISHING CORP.
NEW YORK

Copyright © 1988 by PMA Publishing Corp.

NOTICE: The editors, contributors, and publisher of this work have made every effort to ensure that the drug dosage schedules and/or procedures are accurate and in accord with the standards accepted at the time of publications. Readers are cautioned, however, to check the product information sheet included in the package of each drug they plan to administer. This is particularly important in regard to new or infrequently used drugs. The publisher is not responsible for any errors of fact or omissions in this book.

Library of Congress Cataloging in Publication Data

Violence in intimate relationships / [edited by] Gordon W. Russell.
   p. cm
   Bibliography: p.
   Includes index.
   ISBN 0-89335-305-1 : $45.00
   1. Family violence – Congresses . 2. Violence – Congresses.
3. Interpersonal conflict – Congresses   4. Agressiveness
(Psychology) – Congresses.   5. Intimacy (Psychology) – Congresses.
I. Russell, Gordon W.
HQ809.V55   1988
362.8'2 – dc 19   88-318
                                                                       CIP

Printed in the United States of America

Dedicated to Cameron and Shelley

Contributors

DR. AFESA M. ADAMS
Office of Academic Affairs
University of Utah
Salt Lake City, Utah

SUSAN A. BARTON
Department of Psychology
University of Manitoba
Winnipeg, Manitoba, Canada

DR. CAROL BAUER
Department of History
Long Island University
C.W. Post Center
Greenvale, New York

DR. J. EDWIN BOYD
Department of Psychology
University of Calgary
Calgary, Alberta, Canada

DR. JAMES J. BROWNING
Department of Psychology
University of British Columbia
Vancouver, British Columbia, Canada

DR. BARRY R. BURKHART
Department of Psychology
Auburn University
Auburn, Alabama

DR. JAMES V.P. CHECK
Department of Psychology
York University
Downsview, Ontario, Canada

DR. CAROLIE J. COATES
Faculty of Education
University of Lethbridge
Lethbridge, Alberta, Canada

DR. BARRY S. CORENBLUM
Department of Psychology
Brandon University
Brandon, Manitoba, Canada

MOREEN C. CORSON
Department of Psychology
University of Lethbridge
Lethbridge, Alberta, Canada

DR. DONALD G. DUTTON
Department of Psychology
University of British Columbia
Vancouver, British Columbia, Canada

BARBARA ELIAS
Department of Psychology
University of Manitoba
Winnipeg, Manitoba, Canada

DR. AUB EVERETT
Department of Education
University of Newcastle
New South Wales, Australia

DR. BEVERLY I. FAGOT
Oregon Social Learning Center
Eugene, Oregon

DR. THOMAS FERA
Communication Studies
University of California at Los Angeles
Los Angeles, California

DR. SEYMOUR FESHBACH
Department of Psychology
University of California at Los Angeles
Los Angeles, California

MARY T. HUDDLE
Department of Psychology
University of Lethbridge
Lethbridge, Alberta, Canada

DR. JOHN F. KNUTSON
Department of Psychology
University of Iowa
Iowa City, Iowa

JAMES KUNATH
Communication Studies
University of California at Los Angeles
Los Angeles, California

DR. DEBORAH J. LEONG
Department of Teacher Education
Metropolitan State College
Denver, Colorado

DR. SONJA PETERSON-LEWIS
Department of African-American Studies
Temple University
Philadelphia, Pennsylvania

DR. ROLF LOEBER
Western Psychiatric Institute
Pittsburgh, Pennsylvania

DR. NEIL M. MALAMUTH
Communication Studies/Psychology
University of California at Los Angeles
Los Angeles, California

DR. JOHN G. MEHM
Capital Region Mental Health Center
Hartford, Connecticut

DR. JOHN B. REID
Oregon Social Learning Center
Eugene, Oregon

DR. LAWRENCE RITT
Professor Emeritus of History
Long Island University
C.W. Post Center
Greenvale, New York

PROF. GORDON W. RUSSELL
Department of Psychology
University of Lethbridge
Lethbridge, Alberta, Canada

DR. ANNETTE L. STANTON
Department of Psychology
Auburn University
Auburn, Alabama

DR. LEAH S. SUBOTNIK
St. Cloud, Minnesota

DR. CHARLES W. TURNER
Department of Psychology
University of Utah
Salt Lake City, Utah

Contents

Preface   xi

Introduction   xiii

Section I: Historical Antecedents and Origins

Chapter

1   The Work of Frances Power Cobbe: A Victorian Indictment
    of Wife-Beating   7
    Carol Bauer & Lawrence Ritt

2   Hostility Toward Women: Some Theoretical Considerations   29
    James V. P. Check

3   Sexual Aggression in Acquaintance Relationships   43
    Barry R. Burkhart & Annette L. Stanton

4   Transgenerational Patterns of Coercion in Families
    and Intimate Relationships   67
    John F. Knutson & John G. Mehm

5   Developmental Determinants of Male-to- Female Aggression   91
    Beverly I. Fagot, Rolf Loeber, & John B. Reid

6   Attribution Processes in Repeatedly Abused Women   107
    Sonja Peterson-Lewis, Charles W. Turner,
    & Afesa M. Adams

Section II: Personality

7   The Role of Personality in Violent Relationships   135
    Aub Everett

8   Hostility Toward Men in Female Victims of
    Male Sexual Aggression   149
    James V. P. Check, Barbara Elias,
    & Susan A. Barton

9   Power Struggles and Intimacy Anxieties as
    Causative Factors of Wife Assault   163
    Donald G. Dutton & James J. Browning

10   A Psychosocial Approach to Family Violence:
Application of Conceptual Systems Theory   177
Carolie J. Coates & Deborah J. Leong

11   Men Who Batter Women: From Overcontrolled
to Undercontrolled in Anger Expression   203
Leah S. Subotnik

Section III: Situational/External Determinants

12   Alcohol and Spouse Abuse: A Social Cognition Perspective   217
Barry Corenblum

13   Aggressive Cues and Sexual Arousal to Erotica   239
*Neil M. Malamuth, Seymour Feshbach,
Thomas Fera, & James Kunath*

14   At Close Quarters: Personal Space Requirements
of Men in Intimate Heterosexual Dyads   253
*Gordon W. Russell, Mary J. Huddle,
& Moreen C. Corson*

15   Intra-Familial Violence: Training Police
for Effective Interventions   269
J. Edwin Boyd

Index   291

Preface

The present volume had its origin in the program of the North American meetings of the International Society for Research on Aggression (ISRA) held in Victoria, British Columbia, during the summer of 1983. The conference attracted well over 100 delegates from 6 nations, a majority of whom are active investigators and experts in their respective areas of aggression research. Approximately a half dozen papers in the program reported on the results of research investigating aggression between persons involved in intimate relationships, for example, wife-battering and rape. These papers formed the nucleus and, to a degree, dictated the organizational framework of the book. A further set of invited chapters is intended to complement and extend the topics treated at the ISRA meetings.

One of the special features of ISRA, in addition to its international character, is the multidisciplinary composition of its membership. That diversity is reflected in the original set of conference presentations; it has been maintained, even increased, in the set of invited chapters. Thus, another aim of this volume is to provide the reader with a selected sample of the ongoing research programs and theoretical views of scholars actively investigating questions within this multidisciplinary field.

It would be folly to attempt an understanding or to hope to achieve solutions to the phenomenon of violence between intimates from the limiting perspective of any single discipline. Important contributions have been made and continue to be made by a range of social scientists, each with his or her own specialized research strategies, theoretical models, and levels of analyses. Only by bringing the diverse talents of sociologists, psychologists, educators, criminologists, and others to bear on questions of interpersonal conflict can we hope to realize major gains in our understanding and a comprehensive empirical base from which to derive enlightened and effective solutions.

Introduction

A s recently as 1976, one listing of the books written by social scientists addressing the topic of human aggression totaled 432 entries (Russell, 1976). Each book in the bibliography represents a scholarly attempt to explain or provide fresh insights into the complexities of interpersonal aggression. Since that time, the running total has easily surpassed 600 volumes. If one were to characterize the recent growth in books on aggression, the trend has been towards increased specialization. Topical categories such as rape, wife-battering, and child abuse have emerged in the past 10 to 15 years largely in response to widely publicized "discoveries" of the unacceptably high incidence of these phenomena.* The present volume continues this trend in presenting recent developments in theory and empirical investigations of many of the central issues associated with violence between adults involved in intimate relationships.

However, to gain some perspective on this welcome surge of interest, one should additionally note that scientific attention and widespread public concern has so far been confined to a mere handful of nations (Campbell, 1985). For example, in a recent survey (Goldstein & Segall, 1983) of the aggression occurring in 17 countries, each written by academics indigenous to the culture he or she reviewed, spousal abuse is scarcely mentioned as a significant category of violence. Thus, "wife-battering" warrants only two entries in the subject index, one from Brazil and the other from Turkey. Both authors simply note an absence of official statistics in their homelands and further comment that wife- beating appears to be more prevalent among the lower socioeconomic levels.

It is further notable that even in countries where there is a general awareness and official concern over violence between intimates, the legal system may not respond effectively to the needs of victims. For example, Ford (1983) investigated

---

* see, for example, one recent estimate (Koss, Gidycz & Wisniewski, 1987) of the scope of rape in the US.

the processing and eventual disposition of 325 cases involving victims of spousal violence in Marion County, Indiana, who sought a redress of their grievances through the criminal justice system. Not only did a mere 30 of the original 325 complaints ever reach court, but the victim's conjugal status was found to be an important determinant of whether or not she was encouraged by authorities to pursue her case. This is not to say that the legal system need necessarily be ineffectual in dealing with domestic violence cases. Prosecutions notwithstanding, other options open to law enforcement officials show promise of reducing spousal violence, at least in the short run. For example, Sherman and Berk (1984) have recently reported fewer recurrences of assaults in instances where the police exercise an arrest option rather than giving the accused "advice" or ordering an 8-hour separation from the victim (see also Berk & Newton, 1985).

While scholars have shown an increasing interest in various facets of violence between intimates in recent years, many basic questions surprisingly remain unanswered. Indeed, in a thoughtful and provocative article, Loseke and Cahill (1984) express serious doubts regarding both the quality and depth of evidence found to underlie the assumptions of many "experts" and others actively working in the area of wife-battering (see also, Hatty, 1987). Admittedly, a sense of urgency is associated with this and similar phenomena. However, in the long-term interest of minimizing the occurrence of such phenomena, it behooves us to continually reassess current assumptions and extend our data base with regard to programs and practices. It is in this spirit that the contributors to this volume have been brought together. The work of several of the present researchers can be seen to challenge a number of our working assumptions; others have broken entirely new ground in exploring the roles of variables not previously associated with violence between intimates. Still other authors have proposed original models or extended existing theory to account for violence occurring in particular categories of close relationships.

An overview of the chapters reveals considerable diversity in the levels of analyses and approaches that the authors have chosen to employ in the investigation of their respective topics. Some have provided theory (Chapter 2) where little original theory exists, while others treat important specific issues such as why Black women remain in abusive relationships (Chapter 6). Still others have chosen to trace the origins of spousal violence transgenerationally (see Chapter 4), others to examine the role of variables predictive of acquaintance rape (Chapter 3). A concluding set of chapters investigates external-situational influences including the role of alcohol (Chapter 12) and applied questions such as the best means to train police officers to effectively and safely intervene in domestic disputes (Chapter 15). As with most research, the relatively few questions that are answered in an investigation almost invariably prompt yet a further set of questions. I believe I reflect the collective wish of the present researchers in expressing my hope that others will build upon and pursue the questions and directions set by the work of the contributors to this volume. The editing of a collection such as this is only possible through the concerted efforts and cooperation of a large number of individual scholars. To the present contributors I express my thanks for their patience, responsiveness, and attention to deadlines. Thanks also to Punch Publications Ltd. for allowing me to reproduce their illustration in the Introduction to the first section. *The Toronto Star* also kindly granted permission to reprint a political cartoon by John Larter in the same section. The efforts of Carol Bauer and Wendy C. Fox in locating the respective illustrations is greatly appreciated. The *International Journal of Women's Studies* generously permitted publication of a combined version of two papers by Bauer and Ritt (Chapter 1). The patience and guidance in my efforts shown me by Maurice Ancharoff and Sharon Hird of PMA Publishing Corporation is appreciated. Finally, I wish to express my gratitude to Audrey M. Russell, whose tireless efforts and support helped bring this volume to fruition.

REFERENCES

Berk, R.A., & Newton, P.J. (1985). Does arrest really deter wife battery? An effort to replicate the findings of the Minneapolis spouse abuse experiment. *American Sociological Review, 50,* 253-262.

Campbell, J.C. (1985). Beating of wives: A cross- cultural perspective. *Victimology, 10,* 174-185.

Ford, D.A. (1983). Wife battery and criminal justice: A study of victim decision-making. *Family Relations, 32,* 463-475.

Goldstein, A.P., & Segall, M.H. (Eds.) (1983). *Aggression in global perspective.* New York: Pergamon.

Hatty, S. (1987). Woman battering as a social problem: The denial of injury. *The Australian and New Zealand Journal of Sociology, 23,* 36-46.

Koss, M.P., Gidycz, C.A., & Wisniewski, M. (1987). The scope of rape: Incidence and prevalence of sexual aggression and victimization in a national sample of higher education students. *Journal of Consulting and Clinical Psychology, 55,* 162-170.

Loseke, D.R., & Cahill, S.E. (1984). The social construction of deviance: Experts on battered women. *Social Problems, 31,* 296-310.

Russell, G.W. (1976). A bibliography of human aggression and violence. Research Bulletin #76-01, Department of Psychology, University of Lethbridge, Canada.

Sherman, L.W., & Berk, R.A. (1984). The specific deterrent effects of arrest for domestic assault. *American Sociological Review, 49,* 261-272.

VIOLENCE
IN
INTIMATE
RELATIONSHIPS

Part One
Historical Antecedents and Origins

INTRODUCTION

Two strikingly similar debates took place in the parliaments of two of the world's leading democracies. Neither their common topic nor even the reaction to its being raised is as remarkable as the fact that these two events were separated by over a century of modern history. The lessons to be drawn with regard to legislative inaction and the resilience of certain deeply entrenched attitudes require little by way of elaboration.

A debate in the British Parliament in 1874 occasioned the cartoon in Figure 1. Figure 2 was prompted by a similar debate more than a hundred years later. Below we can find excerpts from debate in the Canadian House of Commons, May 12, 1982 on the "Status of women: Parliamentary report on battered wives — Government action."

> *Mrs. Margaret Mitchell (Vancouver East):* Madam Speaker, I have an upbeat question for the minister responsible for the Status of Women. The minister knows that the parliamentary report on battered wives was tabled in the House yesterday. It states that one in ten husbands beat their wives regularly.

> *Some Hon. Members:* Oh, oh!

> *Mrs. Mitchell:* These women —

> *Some Hon. Members:* Oh, oh!

> *Mrs. Mitchell:* I do not think it is very much of a laughing matter, Madam Speaker.

> *An Hon. Member:* I don't beat my wife.

> *Mrs. Mitchell:* Madam Speaker, I do not think it is a laughing matter. I would like to say that the battered wives in these cases rarely have any refuge. They have no safe place to go with their children. Police who are

1

PUNCH, OR THE LONDON CHARIVARI.—May 30, 1874.

"WOMAN'S WRONGS."

BRUTAL HUSBAND. "AH! YOU 'D BETTER GO SNIVELLIN' TO THE 'OUSE O' COMMONS, *YOU* HAD! MUCH THEY 'RE LIKELY TO DO FOR YER! YAH! READ THAT!"

"MR. DISRAELI.—There can be but one feeling in the House on the subject of these dastardly attacks—not upon the weaker but the fairer sex. (*A laugh.*) I am sure the House shares the indignation of my hon. friend who will, I hope, consider he has secured the object he had in view by raising, the question. * * * Assuring my hon. friend that Her Majesty's Government will not lose sight of the question, I must ask him not to press his Motion further on the present occasion."—*Parliamentary Report, Monday, May* 18.

Figure 1   Reprinted with permission of Punch Publications, Ltd.

Figure 2 Response of parliamentarians. Reprinted with permission of The Toronto Star Syndicate.

called on an emergency basis rarely respond to domestic calls. Charges are not laid in the courts, and there are very few instances of prosecutions in our judicial system.

I want to ask the minister responsible for the status of women what she intends to do immediately in a major way—we do not want just reports, research and conferences—at the federal level to protect battered women.

Some Hon. Members: Hear, hear!

Hon. Judy Erola (Minister of State (Mines)): Madam Speaker, I too am not amused by the derision which greeted the statement that one in ten women is beaten. I do not find that amusing, and neither do the women of Canada.

Some Hon. Members: Hear, hear!

The debate continued on May 13, 1982 – "Status of women – Call for apology by House of Commons – Motion under S.O. 43."

Mrs. Margaret Mitchell (Vancouver East): Madam Speaker, I rise under the provisions of Standing Order 43 on a matter of urgent and pressing necessity. I ask for support of this motion by all parties in the House. Yesterday many male members of the House laughed uproariously when they were told that one out of every ten men in Canada beat their wives repeatedly. As a result, there has been a public outcry against the appalling attitude expressed by these honorable members. Therefore I move, seconded by the honorable member for Beaches (Mr.Young):

That all members of this House apologize to the women of   Canada for the shameful and disgusting display of   discrimination and ignorance by members who degraded this House   yesterday with their performance.

Madam Speaker: Is there unanimous consent for this motion?

Some Hon. Members: Agreed.

Some Hon. Members: No.

The debate continued in the Canadian House of Commons on May 14, 1982 – "Status of women: Gravity of family violence issue – Motion under S.O. 43."

Mrs. Ursula Appolloni (York South-Weston): Madam Speaker, under the provisions of Standing Order 43 I would like to move, seconded by the honorable member for Don Valley East (Mr. Smith):

That this House assure the women of Canada that the issue of family violence, and especially of wife battering, is considered by all members of this House to be an extremely grave and alarming one; and that the Report on Violence in the Family, tabled in this House last Tuesday as a result of deliberations in committee by members from all sides of this House, will be given serious consideration by all members in recognition of the fact that wife battering takes place in every constituency across Canada, and affects one out of every ten women.

Some Hon. Members: Hear, hear!

Madam Speaker: Is there unanimous consent for this motion?

Some Hon. Members: Agreed.

Hon. James A. McGrath (St. John's East): Madam Speaker, in rising to support this motion I want to say on behalf of my party that we very much regret what happened in the House yesterday, or at least the way in which the incident was reported yesterday, because I do not believe the House intended, yesterday or at any time, to belittle this report or the importance of it.

I want to say we commend the committee for its excellent report. We believe it is a very serious problem in the country, probably more widespread than is generally believed. We feel very strongly that not only should the House address itself to the report in this way but that the government, through the Minister of Justice (Mr. Chretien) and the Solicitor General (Mr. Kaplan), should address itself to this report so that the people who are the subject of the report, namely, battered wives, can receive the same protection of the laws of Canada as all other groups.

Mr. Neil Young (Beaches): Madam Speaker, I too join with other members in this House in congratulating the committee for bringing forth such a report, and would urge the government to take immediate action on its implementation.

Madam Speaker: Does the House agree to adopt the motion?

Some Hon. Members: Agreed.

Motion agreed to. — *(Commons Debates, 1st Session, 32nd Parliament)*

The chapters in Part One of this book are set against the background of male reactions on two occasions, mentioned above, when concern over one form of violence between intimates, wife- abuse, was brought before senior legislators. In Chapter 1, Bauer and Ritt provide a sobering insight into the desperate plight of British women throughout the latter half of the 19th century in their historical account of the work and time of Frances Power Cobbe. Those attitudes so vividly revealed in Chapter 1 have a disturbingly current ring to them. In Chapter 2, James Check presents an overview of those models that have attempted to account for male aggression, specifically that directed against women. Burkhart and Stanton (Chapter 3) then present important basic data on an equally troubling form of violence between intimates, acquaintance rape. Next, Knutson and Mehm examine transgenerational influences on wife-battering and in so doing pose important questions to conventional wisdom on the issue (Chapter 4). In Chapter 5, Fagot, Loeber, and Reid trace the origins of developmental factors associated with the formative years of abusive men. The concluding chapter in this part, Chapter 6, provides a comprehensive examination of the perplexing question of why some women remain in abusive relationships.

Chapter 1
The Work of Frances Power Cobbe: A Victorian Indictment of Wife-Beating

Carol Bauer and Lawrence Ritt

The interest in wife-beating displayed by some modern defenders of women's rights has its antecedents in the activities of a few nineteenth-century English feminists, who perceived that the apparently random wife-abuse of the period was in fact the symptom of a condition—the distorted relationship of the sexes—which must first be corrected if wife-beating were to cease. To most Victorian reformers concerned with the Woman Question, it seemed that they could gain more by concentrating their energies on such popular objectives as education, employment, property rights, and the vote (Bauer & Ritt, 1979; Pratt, 1897). That, however, was not the case as Frances Power Cobbe—and a handful of similarly motivated women—saw it. To them, a significant change in the average woman's position was out of the question while her husband had the generally accepted right to beat her into a state of cringing submissiveness, as he did his horse or dog. Until she was liberated from this domestic tyranny, no meaningful improvement in her status was possible.

Although current scholarship has shed light on various facets of feminist activity in Victorian England, there are no historical studies that focus on the concern of nineteenth-century English feminists with wife-beating. Over the course of the last decade, however, a number of sociological studies on various aspects of domestic violence has emerged (Dobash & Dobash, 1980; Langley & Levy, 1977; Martin, 1976; Steinmetz & Straus, 1974). Understandably, very few of these studies consider wife-beating in its historical context. Regrettably, in the works that do, the efforts of Frances Power Cobbe—if they are mentioned at all—are

7

viewed merely as an interesting but somewhat isolated attempt to examine the question of wife-abuse. In addition, such studies occasionally suggest that the link between wife-beating and conventional notions of woman's inferiority has only recently been "discovered."

But Cobbe's interest in wife-beating and her subsequent attempt to publicize the horrors to which women were daily subjected was not an aberration. It was, in fact, the natural development of her broad interest in all questions that affected women. Cobbe lived according to a precept that she urged on others: to share the burdens that were uniquely feminine. Paraphrasing the Latin poet Terence, she advocated a view that could be construed as a challenge to her sex: "I am a *woman*. Nothing concerning the interests of women is alien to me" (Cobbe, 1894, vol. 2, p. 554). Cobbe's concern for abused wives, consequently, was an integral part of her passionate commitment to further the interests of women, economically, politically, and socially; this commitment was, in turn, a logical outcome of the feminist philosophy that won for Cobbe the accolade, "excepting John Stuart Mill, she has done more than anyone to give the dignity of principle to the woman's movement" (Lewin, 1894, p. 321).

In her concern for victims of wife-abuse, Cobbe did not stand alone. Other less well known feminists followed her lead, and published in the 1880s and 1890s a number of articles and books demonstrating the fact that this topic was not irrelevant to the interest of late Victorian feminists. Furthermore, despite the contrary opinions of present-day commentators, Cobbe and her successors clearly recognized that wife-beating could be understood only in the light of conventional attitudes toward the female sex. In short, the animal-like existence that was the lot of so many women was, in the minds of these feminists, deeply rooted in the traditional views of what constituted woman's place, her role, and her relation to man.

This chapter is an attempt to place Cobbe's interest in wife- beating within the broad framework of her feminist philosophy. In doing so, it will correct the impression that Victorian reformers failed to view the problem on its most fundamental level, that is, as an expression of the distorted relationship of the sexes.

THE WIFE-BEATING PROBLEM IN VICTORIAN ENGLAND

That domestic brutality was a widespread and serious problem in Victorian England is undoubtedly true (Kaye, 1856; Pulling, 1876). In the late nineteenth century, English court records attested to a daily average of four cases of aggravated assaults of husbands on wives, a figure of course, that represented only those relatively few cases of assault which appeared before the courts (Brittain, 1953, p. 24). The pervasiveness of wife-beating is also reflected in the popular literature of the period, particularly the novels of Charles Dickens. While Dickens sometimes treated the subject with levity, as in the *Pickwick Papers,* where one of his characters refers to wife-beating as an "amiable weakness," in *Great Expectations* and *Oliver Twist* he provided a grim picture of domestic tyranny— even murder.

Although it may have been the boast of Englishmen that Englishwomen were protected by the law, that claim was nowhere less justified than in cases of wive abuse. The socially prominent Caroline Norton, herself a battered wife, went so far as to maintain that in no other country of Europe were women so *little* protected and that it constituted "a national disgrace" (Norton, 1854, 1855). On this subject, of course, she was speaking from bitter experience. Her marriage to the volatile Mr. Norton was punctuated by his frequent wild outbursts, during which for example, he flung the inkstand at his bride of a few weeks, and later and periodically over the course of their marital life kicked her, dashed her down to the floor, and burned her hand by deliberately placing a scalding tea kettle on it. In short, Mrs. Norton suffered what she described as "seventeen years of torment, sorrow, and shame," but nevertheless discovered that she had no grounds on which to divorce her husband. When she was writing in 1854 and 1855, marital cruelty was defined only as "cruelty that endangers life or limb." If a woman had once forgiven or "condoned" her husband's offenses, there was no longer any legal possibility of redress (Harrison, 1886, pp. 128- 129; Norton, 1854, 1855).

Mrs. Norton's case was perhaps exceptional, but, as one reviewer maintained, "*only* in degree"; actually, he continued, her experience could be considered common (Kaye, 1855, p. 537). The fact of the matter was that public opinion sanctioned the physical abuse of wives. The marital bond was such that, as John Stuart Mill observed, "the vilest malefactor" had "some wretched woman tied to him, against whom he [could] commit any atrocity except killing her, and, if tolerably cautious, [could] do that without much danger of the legal penalty" (Mill, 1970, p. 35). Mill observed, in addition, that even men who "without being in a legal sense malefactors in any other respect," nevertheless habitually brutalized their wives, encouraged by the belief that the law had "delivered [their mates] to them as their thing, to be used at their pleasure" (Mill, 1970, p. 35). It was no wonder to him then, that the numbers who abused the institution of marriage were "appalling." These facts, Mill insisted, made a mockery both of the oft expressed assurance that men were the "natural protectors" of women, and of the claim that women's interests were more than adequately looked after by men.

In a speech to the House of Commons, May 20, 1867, on behalf of female suffrage, Mill, emphasizing the fallacy of the argument that the interests of women "are safe in the hands of their fathers, husbands, and brothers," made it clear that physical tyranny might be inflicted on women almost with impunity. "I should like," Mill said,

> to have a return laid before this House of the number of women who are annually beaten to death, kicked to death, or trampled to death by their

male protectors; and, in an opposite column, the amount of the sentences passed, in those cases in which the dastardly criminals did not get off altogether. I should also like to have, in a third column, the amount of property, the unlawful taking of which was, at the same sessions or assizes, by the same judge, thought worthy of the same amount of punishment. We should then have an arithmetical estimate of the value set by a male legislator and male tribunals on the murder of a woman, often by torture continued through years, which, if there is any shame in us, would make us hang our heads. (Mill, 1867, pp. 14- 15)

Wife-beating was not, of course, a peculiarly nineteenth- century English phenomenon.* In fact, it could be argued that the traditional patriarchal notions of family life were nowhere better illustrated than in the time worn idea of the power of the husband to compel wifely obedience to his authority by kicks, blows, and stomps. The long and dishonorable history of wife- beating serves as a bleak reminder that the right of personal chastisement not only had the sanction of the major religious, political, and philosophical thinkers in the Western tradition, but also was a frequently exercised and jealously guarded prerogative of the husband. It spanned both time and place and cut across cultural and social distinctions. Numerous adages attest to this fact: for example, in the Russian proverb, "A wife isn't a jug...she won't crack if you hit her ten times"; the African proverb, "Those whom we marry are those whom we fight"; and the old English proverb, "A spaniel, a woman, and a walnut tree, the more they're beaten, the better they be." Indeed, it is impossible to find any historical period in which there were no rules governing wife- beating and "specifying the conditions under which a wife was deserving of a good clout" (Dobash & Dobash, 1980, p. 31).

WIFE-BEATING AND ENGLISH LAW

The law of England mirrored the public acceptance of wife-beating and in turn, reinforced it. The root of the English law dealing with the relations between husband and wife was frequently alleged to be the notion of the unity of the spouses, a legal rendering of the Christian concept of marriage, whereby a man shall "leave father and mother, and shall cleave to his wife: and they twain shall be one flesh" (Matthew xix, 5). Whether or not his notion did indeed constitute the basis of the law, it is undeniably true that it was continually put forward by civil and religious authorities as a justification for the power of the husband over his wife (Birrell, 1896; *Gottliffe v. Edelston,* 1930; Morrison, 1957; Pollock & Maitland, 1898, vol. 2, p. 406).

---

* The use of the term *"le vice Anglais"* to describe wife-battering as peculiarly English (see e.g., Freeman, 1977) is incorrect. Specifically, the term *the English vice* is a code word for either homosexuality (as given in the *Dictionary of Foreign Words and Phrases*) or flagellation (as used in Gibson, 1978), but not for wife- battering.

The fiction that a man and a woman were, through marriage, merged into a single legal identity, or as Blackstone phrased it, that the husband and wife were "one person in law," demanded the "suspension" of a wife's legal existence. A woman after marriage became a *"femme couverte,"* a term which meant in practice that her services, her property, and her children were placed under the protection of her husband. She was his inferior, his servant or vassal. The analogy between the husband-wife relationship and the lord-vassal relationship is illustrated by the fact that in the medieval era, the murder of a wife by a husband was an ordinary felony, punishable with death by hanging, but the murder of a husband by his wife was considered petty treason, punishable with death by burning (Browne, 1891; Burr, 1889; Cleveland, 1896; Cornwallis, 1856; Hecker, 1914; Pike, 1876; Reiss, 1934).

The legal sanction of wife-beating derived from the husband's authority to correct his wife by physical force if necessary. An early example of the use of the right to correct is found in an ecclesiastical court case in 1395, when Margaret Neffield of York produced witnesses who testified that her husband had wounded her arm and broken a bone when he attacked her on a number of occasions with a knife and a dagger. Her husband defended his behavior by asserting that his action was motivated solely by the desire to preserve her from error. Despite evidence of physical harm, the court ruled that the couple must continue to live together (Helmholz, 1974, p. 105). Other examples of physical cruelty in the medieval era make it clear that wifely disobedience carried penalties ranging from kicks and blows to burning at the stake (Davis, 1971).

The common law sanctioned only the right of "reasonable chastisement," as illustrated for example, in Bacon's statement that by law, a husband had "Power and Dominion over his Wife"; he might "keep her by Force within the Bonds of Duty," and might "beat her, but not in a violent or cruel Manner" (Bacon, 1786; Hecker, 1914, pp. 174-175; Pollock & Maitland, 1898,vol. 2, p. 406). But in practice, the courts interpreted very freely the extent to which a husband's authority might reasonably extend. The popular maxim that the husband could beat his wife with a rod no thicker than his thumb was most likely a "gloss" (as one scholar terms it) put on by the common people to acknowledge their understanding of "reasonable" chastisement (Dunning, 1953, p. 79; Prosser, 1971, p. 136). (Although the seventeenth-century English law did not explicitly sanction the idea of the thumb as a standard, two nineteenth-century court cases in the United States popularized that notion. In 1824, *[Bradley v. State]* a Mississippi judge commented on the right of a husband to chastise his wife with a "whip or rattan no bigger than my thumb, in order to enforce the salutary restraints of domestic discipline." Similarly, in a case that came before a North Carolina judge in 1868 *[State v. Rhodes]*, it was asserted that the defendant "had a right to whip his wife with a switch no bigger than his thumb.")

Blackstone, writing in the 1760s, confirmed the medieval law's sanction of "moderate correction," noting that, since the husband was responsible for his wife's misbehavior, the law entrusted him with the power of "restraining her, by domestic chastisement." Blackstone pointed out, however, that the "power of correction" had been "confined within reasonable bounds" (Ehrlich, 1959, p. 85). After observing that the civil law also provided for chastisement, and occasionally even to a greater degree than that provided by English common law (Bryce, 1968; Minton-Senhouse, 1889, pp. 355-358), Blackstone noted that among the higher ranks of society, "the power of correction began to be doubted" in the latter half of the seventeenth century (in the reign of Charles II); nevertheless, "the lower rank of people," Blackstone asserted, still claimed and exerted "their ancient privilege" (Ehrlich, 1959, p.85).

In 1840, seventy-five years after Blackstone's *Commentaries* were published, an English judge confirmed the legality of the ancient privilege: "There can be no doubt of the general dominion which the law of England attributes to the husband over the wife" (Cochrane, 1840). The "general dominion" to which the judge referred included the husband's right to correct his wife through physical chastisement, as well as his right to restrict her personal freedom. In fact, as late as 1946, an English court actually held that a husband's assault on his wife was justified because she had disobeyed his orders to refrain from visiting her relations. Although the decision in this case, *Meacher v. Meacher* (1946), was later overruled on appeal, it illustrates clearly the tenacity of the belief that English law permitted the husband to chastise his wife.

COBBE TACKLES THE PROBLEM

The obstacles confronting anyone who aspired to challenge Victorian attitudes toward wife-beating were formidable: the courts, the church, and Parliament were overwhelmingly hostile, and their institutional opposition was reinforced by the indifference of the public at large. Nevertheless, a talented woman, Frances Power Cobbe, was equal to the challenge.

Surveying Cobbe's productivity, a modern student of the Victorian era would be justified in concluding, as the *New York Times* put it almost ninety years ago, that her career was "decidedly unique" (*New York Times,* 1894, p. 23). Born into the Anglo- Irish aristocracy (she counted five archbishops and a bishop among her ancestors), Cobbe was considered "one of the most remarkable women of the Victorian era" (Review of Reviews, 1894, p. 562) — a successful journalist, essayist, critic, philanthropist, theologian, and moralist. She was also a practical, down-to-earth worker and organizer in such areas as workhouse reform and Poor Law administration, and her interest in these areas in turn furthered philanthropic reform (Chadwick, 1867; Cobbe, 1860, 1861a, 1861b, 1861c, 1861d, 1864c, 1866a). Although she has been described as "happily married" (Davidson, 1977,

p. 17), Cobbe was actually a lifelong spinster and a member of a type – the single woman concerned with social reform – with which England seemed to be peculiarly blessed in the nineteenth century (Schupf, 1974, pp. 301-317).

Cobbe's influence on her contemporaries was great, and in some respects, lasting; her accomplishments were impressive enough to win her an international reputation as a reformer (*The Times*, 1904; *New York Times*, 1904; Verschoyle, 1904). During the course of her long life (1822-1904), she met and corresponded with a number of the outstanding figures of the time: Darwin, Lyell, Shaftesbury, Mill, Tennyson, Manning, Colenso, and many others (Cobbe, 1894). Her impact, however, derives not from her associations with the intellectual luminaries of the period, but rather, from her indictment of contemporary social evils.

She was a prolific writer. Speaking of her achievement in ethical studies, Frances Willard, the noted American temperance leader, wrote: "She has no peer among women, and but few equals among men" (Willard, 1888, p. 8). Although the bulk of her output was concerned with theological and philosophical topics, her most widely read works were polemics dealing with the Woman Question. Among her most popular articles and pamphlets were "What Shall We Do With Our Old Maids?," "Celibacy vs. Marriage," "Criminals, Idiots, Women and Minors," "The Little Health of Ladies," and her well known *Duties of Women*, which went to eight editions.*

A highly effective propagandist, Cobbe is entitled to recognition as one of the few dedicated champions of the rights of English women. To that end, she labored incessantly and passionately in the literary and intellectual circles in which she moved. She brought to the feminist movement her keen wit and acerbic style, and was active in many women's causes. Although in her busy career as a reformer she was involved in most of the major concerns of the day, it was the status of women in general and the plight of working class wives in particular that evoked all of Cobbe's eloquence, indignation, and anger.

Each of these qualities was displayed in a seminal article, "Wife-Torture in England," which appeared in the April issue of *Contemporary Review* in 1878. Intent on arousing public opinion to the problem of wife-beating, Cobbe asked:

> How does it happen that the same generous-hearted gentlemen, who would themselves fly to render succour to a lady in distress, yet read of the beatings, burnings, kickings, and "cloggings" of *poor* women well-nigh every morning in their newspapers without once setting their teeth, and saying, "This must be stopped! We can stand it no longer!" (Cobbe, 1878b, p. 56)

---

* The most important of Cobbe's philosophical writings include: Cobbe, 1855, 1864a, 1864b, 1865, 1866b, 1867, 1868b, 1870, 1872, 1874b, 1882, 1883, 1884, 1890. Cobbe's most important works dealing with the Woman Question include: Cobbe, 1862a, 1862b, 1868a, 1878a, 1881. All subsequent references in this chapter to *The Duties of Women* are taken from the eighth American edition (Cobbe, 1888).

It was Cobbe's hope that her article, by giving the subject the attention it deserved, would succeed in marshaling public opinion.

Cobbe deliberately chose the term "wife-torture" as the title of her article instead of the more conventional "wife-beating," a rubric which she felt understated the savagery and cruelty of the treatment to which women were subjected. She was not primarily concerned with what she termed "the mere preliminary canter before the race" – the occasional black eye, the bruises, the hair pulled from the scalp, or the spittle in the face. It was the wife-beating that became wife-torture, leading to wife-maiming, or wife-blinding, and culminating in wife-murder, which caused Cobbe to vow: "I will never rest till I have tried what I can do to stop this" (Cobbe, 1878b, p. 72; Cobbe, 1894).

SOME PRACTITIONERS OF DOMESTIC TORTURE

What Cobbe could do – and she did it superbly – was to document the horrors that lay about her. Women, she charged, were not only beaten with closed fists, but kicked and jumped upon. The nineteenth-century wife-beaters used their clogs, hobnailed shoes (certain parts of Liverpool and London were called "kicking districts"), and a variety of objects connected with their livelihood, such as hammers, hatchets, and corrosive chemicals like vitriol. Women were savaged by bulldogs, thrust into burning fireplaces, and thrown out of windows or down flights of stairs. The evidence assembled by Cobbe is chilling, particularly since it is drawn from the police reports of only three or four months, and she was at pains to exclude cases that were merely "sensational." Those listed below can be considered typical:

James Mills cut his wife's throat as she lay in bed. He was quite sober at the time. On a previous occasion he had nearly torn away her left breast.

John Mills poured out vitriol deliberately, and threw it in his wife's face, because she asked him to give her some of his wages. He had said previously that he would blind her.

James Lawrence...who had been supported by his wife's industry for years, struck her on the face with a poker, leaving traces of the most dreadful kind when she appeared in court.

Frederick Knight jumped on the face of his wife (who had only been confined a month) with a pair of boots studded with hobnails.

Richard Mountain beat his wife on the back and mouth, and turned her out of her bed and out of their room one hour after she had been confined.

John Harris, a shoemaker at Sheffield, found his wife and children in bed, dragged her out, and, after vainly attempting to force her into the oven, tore off her night-dress and turned her round before the fire "like a piece of beef," while the children stood on the stairs listening to their mother's agonized screams.

Richard Scully knocked in the frontal bone of his wife's forehead.

William White, stonemason, threw a burning paraffin lamp at his wife, and stood quietly watching her enveloped in flames, from the effects of which she died.

William Hussell, a butcher, ran a knife into his wife several times and killed her. He had threatened to do so often before.

Robert Kelly, engine-driver, bit a piece out of his wife's cheek.

William James, an operative boilermaker, stabbed his wife badly in the arm and mouth, observing afterwards, "I am sorry I did not kill both" (his wife and her mother).

Thomas Richards, a smith, threw his wife down a flight of fourteen steps, when she came to entreat him to give her some money for her maintenance.

James Frickett, a ratcatcher. His wife was found dying with broken ribs and a cut and bruised face, a walking-stick with blood on it lying by.

James Styles beat his wife about the head when he met her in the City Road. She had supported him for years by char-work, and during the whole time he had been in the habit of beating her, and on one occasion so assaulted her that the sight of one of her eyes was destroyed. He got drunk habitually with the money she earned.

John Harley, a compositor, [was] committed for trial for causing the death of his wife by striking her with an iron instrument on the head.

George Ralph Smith, oilman, cut his wife, as the doctor expressed it, "to pieces," with a hatchet, in their back parlour. She died afterwards, but he was found Not Guilty, as it was not certain that her death resulted from the wounds (Cobbe, 1878b, p.74).

The abuses Cobbe described were not confined wholly to the lower classes. Even if it was true, as she asserted, that "the better sort of Englishmen," compared to their continental counterparts, were "exceptionally humane and considerate to women," many individuals of this class practiced wife-abuse, but they did it discreetly, usually in the form of "an occasional blow or two of a not dangerous kind" (Cobbe, 1878b, pp. 56, 58). Going beyond this would have caused comment. A wife's black eye or broken arm, particularly if such injuries were to recur, might be embarrassing to her respectable spouse. Because of the possibility of disgrace and scandal, the middle- or upper-class wife-beater made sure to direct his blows or kicks to those parts of the female anatomy—the abdomen, for example—that were less likely to exhibit telltale scars or bruises.

Such inhibitions, however, did not trouble Englishmen of the lower classes, who, according to Cobbe (1878b), were "proverbial for their unparalleled brutality" (p. 56). These were the "dangerous" wife-beaters, men who belonged "almost exclusively to the artisan and labouring classes" — colliers, weavers, shoemakers, butchers, tailors, stonemasons, and large numbers of unskilled laborers. According to one London magistrate, in one of the worst districts in London, four-fifths of the wife-beating cases that came before the courts occurred among the lowest classes of Irish laborers (Cobbe, 1878b, p. 58). Cobbe, who had lived in Ireland on the family estate during the potato famine of the 1840s, had been struck by the fact that during that period, when customary social observances might have been expected to lapse, Irishmen of all classes remained kind and compassionate. When transported to an English slum, however, they too apparently became wife-abusers (Cobbe, 1894, vol. 1, pp. 138-139; Pulling, 1876, p. 345).

Drawing on a parliamentary study published in 1875, *Reports to the Secretary of State for the Home Department on the State of the Law Relating To Brutal Assaults,* Cobbe (1878b) pointed out that there were, in a single year, "nearly five times as many wife-beaters of the more brutal kind, in proportion to the population, in Durham [an industrial town] as in London" (p. 59). What sort of lives, Cobbe asked, did the inhabitants of such a town lead?

> They are lives out of which almost every softening and ennobling element has been withdrawn, and into which enter brutalizing influences almost unknown elsewhere. They are lives of hard, ugly, mechanical toil in dark pits and hideous factories, amid the grinding and clanging of engines and the fierce heat of furnaces, in that Black Country where the green sod of earth is replaced by mounds of slag and shale, where no flower grows, no fruit ripens, scarcely a bird sings; where the morning has no freshness, the evening no dews; where the spring sunshine cannot pierce the foul curtain of smoke which overhangs these modern Cities of the Plain, and where the very streams and rivers run discoloured and steaming with stench, like Styx and Phlegethon, through their banks of ashes. (p. 59)

Accurate figures were hard to come by; those used by Cobbe were taken from *Judicial Statistics for England and Wales* (1877). According to her estimates (Cobbe, 1878b), the number of cases of aggravated assault on women and children that came before the courts in 1876 was probably less than a third of the total of such offenses. More than half of the individuals executed in 1876 were guilty of wife-murder, or what Cobbe termed *"quasi* wife murder" (pp. 70-71). In making use of the abstracts of the Reports of Chief Constables for the years 1870 through 1874 (included in the *Report... on the State of the Law Relating to Brutal Assaults),* she noted that the reports from some districts were "obviously imperfect." For example, the chief constables in four counties — Rutland, Salop, Radnor, and Cardiganshire—reported that "there were no brutal assaults in their jurisdictions over a five-year period," a state of affairs which, Cobbe acidly observed, bordered on the "miraculous" (p. 72). Despite her reservations as to the value of the available statistics, Cobbe felt that she could "fairly estimate the number of brutal assaults (*brutal* be it remembered, not ordinary) committed on women in England and Wales and actually brought to justice at about 1,500 a year, or more than four per diem; and of these the great majority [were] of husbands on wives" (p. 72).

CAUSES OF WIFE-BEATING

Cobbe (1878b) noted in particular four distinct incitements to wife-beating. First, she indicated drink—specifically, "poisoned drink." Although the "seas of brandy and gin, and the oceans of beer imbibed annually" were "bad enough," she noted, it was the "vile adulterations introduced into them" that made drink an even worse hazard, an addition that could "literally *sting* the wretched drinkers into cruelty" (p. 65). It seemed only reasonable to Cobbe that as long as Englishmen continued to swallow "millions' worth yearly of brain poison," society could expect "brutality the most hideous and grotesque." Cobbe's conclusion then, that the "makers and vendors of these devil's philtres" were "responsible for an amount of crime and ruin which some of the worst tyrants in history might have trembled to bear on their consciences" (p. 65), seems plausible.

A second incitement to wife-beating Cobbe related to the existence of "the great sin of great cities"—prostitution—which, she maintained, aroused jealousy and, in turn, precipitated violence. A passion that was the converse of sympathy, which Cobbe had earlier termed "heteropathy" (Cobbe, 1874a, 1874b), consisting of anger and cruelty which manifested themselves in an impulse to hurt and destroy, was especially prevalent among the lower classes and acted as a third factor tending to violence. Cobbe (1878b) illustrated the effect of this passion by her comment: "If the baby cry in the cradle, [the husband] stamps on it. If his wife wring her hands in despair, he fells her to the ground" (pp. 65-66).

Finally, Cobbe asserted that the friction engendered by living together in unbearably close quarters played a role in instigating brutal assaults. Men in the working-class districts of London and other large towns, living at an intolerable level of degradation and brutality, plagued by disease, crime, and filth, literally with not enough space in which to move about freely, were likely to vent their rage and frustration on the nearest convenient human objects, who happened most often to be members of their own families, particularly their wives. Unlike the rich, who enjoyed sufficient breathing space, the poor suffered "interminable inevitable propinquity," with a consequent increase in brutality (p. 66).

However, not even these incitements to violence, taken singly or collectively, provided an adequate explanation of the problem. On this point, Cobbe was emphatic. The fundamental cause of wife- abuse, she insisted, could be understood only in a broad social context that focused not merely on specific conditions, but took into account as well, a more general and profound relationship— the elemental one between men and women (pp. 62-63). A society in which half of its members were deemed inferior to the other half, and in which women were routinely lumped together with criminals, idiots, and minors, Cobbe maintained, was almost certain to erupt in domestic violence (Cobbe, 1888, pp. 20-21).

Cobbe (1878b) alleged that women, as individuals and as a sex, were generally depreciated with "sacred" phrases such as "the virtues of motherhood," employed to conceal the brutal facts of the female condition. She indignantly pointed out the contradiction between the ideal of womanhood to which so much lip service was given and the systematic degradation that was actually woman's lot:

> I consider that it is a very great misfortune to both sexes that women should be thus depreciated in the opinion of that very class of men whom it would be most desirable to impress with respect and tenderness for them; who are most prone to despise physical infirmity and to undervalue the moral qualities wherein women excel. All the softening and refining influences which women exert in happier conditions are thus lost to those who most need them, — to their husbands and still more emphatically to their children; and the women themselves are degraded and brutified in their own eyes by the contempt of their companions…Why are not mothers allowed to respect themselves, that they may fitly claim the respect of their sons? How is a lad to learn to reverence a woman whom he sees daily scoffed at, beaten, and abused, and when he knows that the laws of his country forbid her, ever and under any circumstances, to exercise the rights of citizenship; nay, which deny to her the guardianship of *himself* — of the very child of her bosom — should her husband choose to hand him over to her rival out of the street? (Cobbe, 1878b, p. 62)

Women in Victorian England were, in general, treated with contempt, but working-class wives were especially degraded, Cobbe asserted, because of the prevailing belief (still held by some of today's wife-beaters) that a man literally owned his wife. "The notion that a man's wife is his PROPERTY, in the sense in which a horse is his property…is the fatal root of incalculable evil and misery," she claimed (1878b, p. 62). Men took it so much for granted that they had property rights in their wives that they protested when arrested for abusing them: "May I not do what I will *with my own?*" (1878b, p. 62). There were even those who, Cobbe observed, regarded this claim with sympathy: "It is even sometimes pleaded on behalf of poor men, that they possess *nothing else* but their wives, and that, consequently, it seems doubly hard to meddle with the exercise of their power in that narrow sphere!" (pp. 62-63).

One can understand Cobbe's insistence that a wife regarded as nothing but a thing was in fact no better than a slave. It was in the so-called industrial "kicking districts" that the status of women most closely approximated that of slaves in the antebellum American South. But, while the condition of those slaves had been somewhat improved by emancipation, that of English working-class wives in the nineteenth century had not changed appreciably. Their lack of power — political and economic — confined them to a miserable existence, characterized by "utter contempt and lack of consideration." Such women, Cobbe maintained, were condemned by society "to an order of insults and wrongs which are never inflicted by equals upon an equal, and can only be paralleled by the oppressions of a dominant caste or race over their helots..." (p. 61). Consequently, when Cobbe charged that the relationship between working-class husbands and their wives in Victorian England was little better than "one of master and slave," she was only partly indulging in hyperbole. Despite some improvement in the laws relating to women (the Married Women's Property Act of 1870, for example), English working-class women and, in particular, working-class wives, were still subject to the "marital tyranny" of their husbands. The ultimate cause of wife-abuse, according to Cobbe, was the fact that the position of a woman "before the law as wife, mother, and citizen" remained "so much below that of a man as husband, father, and citizen" that she inevitably was "regarded by him as an inferior," and thus failed "to obtain from him such a modicum of respect as her mental and moral qualities might win did he see her placed by the State on an equal footing" (p. 61). The law, in sum, taught women that they were inferior beings, a doctrine that ultimately resulted in "wives [being] trampled on by husbands" (Cobbe, 1888, pp. 20-21).

Because Cobbe was so explicit on the cause-and-effect relationship between the inferior status of women and wife- beating, it is difficult to understand how some present-day writers have found it possible to present her views (or what purport to be her views) in a way that fails to do her justice. For example, one of them summarizes Cobbe's four incitements to violence, but he inexplicably fails to mention her fundamental explanation for wife-battering (Gayford, 1977, p. 125). So, too, does another writer in this field, who further compounds his error by declaring that *no* nineteenth-century reformer understood that violence against wives was a function of woman's subordinate position (Freeman, 1979, pp. 128-129). According to that reading, Victorian reformers (including Cobbe) viewed the wife-beating problem as "the product of the degradation of working-class life...and the unequal legal status of wives"; they sought, therefore, to "eliminate" the problem by social reform measures that would "improve the material conditions of existence, legal reform to remove inequalities and legal remedies to deal with men who, for pathological reasons, persisted in brutal attacks on their wives" (Freeman, 1979, p. 128). Freeman continues (italics ours): *"What they failed to understand is that violence is endemic in any society which treats women as unequal."* That blanket statement is, of course, erroneous. Frances Power Cobbe understood only too clearly the connection between violence and the social subjugation of women. This theme, in fact, permeates her writings on the Woman Question in general, as well as on the wife-beating problem in particular, and is evident in, for example, her statement that, while "the general depreciation of women *as a sex*" was "bad enough," the "special depreciation of *wives* [was] more directly responsible for the outrages they endure" (p. 55). In a similar vein, Cobbe wrote: "I conceive then, that the common idea of the inferiority of women, and the special notion of the rights of husbands, form the undercurrent of feeling which induces a man, when for any reason he is infuriated, to wreak his violence on his wife" (p. 65). By such unequivocal assertions Cobbe hammered away at her conviction that the question of marital brutality was inseparable from the negative view of the female sex that was at the heart of the Woman Question.

WIFE-BEATING SANCTIONED BY PUBLIC OPINION

Turning from the fundamental cause of domestic violence to a consideration of society's view of the wife-beating problem, Cobbe (1878b) pointed out the fact that the wife-beater was unique in nineteenth-century England because, unlike other practitioners of violence (criminals, for example), he could count on the tolerance — even the sanction — of society, which found it easy to condone his offense. Legal safeguards against assault and battery were in effect ignored for the wife-beater's benefit. In fact, claimed Cobbe, "in no other instance save that of the wife-beater [was] excuse made for a man taking the law into his own hands" (1878b, p. 63). To allow a man to be his own "judge, jury, and executioner" was tantamount to flouting the constitutional safeguards against tyranny, yet the average English magistrate apparently saw nothing objectionable in a husband's tormenting his wife because of her allegedly "improper" behavior. A wife's drunkenness or obscenity, Cobbe suggested, was regarded "as if it not only furnished an excuse for outrage upon her, but made it quite fit and proper for the Queen's peace to be broken and the woman's bones along with it" (1878b, p. 64).

The fact was that society willingly sanctioned brutality and degradation as long as its victims were simply wives. In order to illustrate this attitude, Cobbe divided violent crimes into three categories: assaults of men on other men, assaults of men on women who were not their wives, and finally, assaults of men on their wives. Cobbe pointed out, that of the three categories public opinion regarded most seriously, and the law dealt with most severely, were the offenses in the first class — assaults of men on other men. Those in the second were judged considerably "less heinous" than the former, and the offenses in the last category were so far from being judged criminal acts that the public, Cobbe observed, considered them "minimum offenses," marked by "a certain halo of jocosity which inclines people to smile whenever they hear of a case of it" (1878b, pp. 56-57). Thus, Cobbe continued, "the abstract idea of a strong man hitting or kicking a weak woman – per se, so revolting – [had] somehow got softened into a jovial kind of domestic lynching" (p. 58). In short, the English thought wife-beating was funny. This attitude reminded Cobbe of that peculiarly English institution, the Punch and Judy show, and made her marvel that "so much enjoyment should concentrate about the thwacking of poor Judy, and the flinging of the baby out of the window" (p. 57).

Society's sanction of domestic brutality had consequences that tended to aggravate the problem. For example, the tacit sympathy for wife-beaters encouraged further violence. According to Cobbe and other observers, wives were so conditioned to regard their husbands as "beating animals" with a vested right to abuse them that maltreated women frequently feared to testify against their mates in a court of law (Pulling, 1876). Some clergymen perceived society's acceptance of wife-abuse as consistent with Christian teachings. Cobbe recalled that one of them, the Rev. F.W. Harper, asserted that if he were to turn into a wife, he would "choose to be beaten by [his] husband to any extent (short of being slain outright) rather than it should be said a stranger [the magistrate] came between us" (Cobbe, 1878b, p. 64n). Harper's further comment that linked wife-beating and religious duty Cobbe found particularly shocking. As she phrased it, "after thus bringing to our minds the beatings, the kickings, and blindings, and burnings, and 'cloggings' which sicken us, he bids us remember that the true idea of marriage is 'the relation of Christ to his Church!'" (p. 64n). Such a perversion was appalling to Cobbe, and she said so: "I should have expected that a minister of the Christian religion would have shuddered at the possibility of suggesting such a connection of ideas as these notions involve. Heaven help the poor women of Durham and Lancashire if their clergy lead them to picture a Christ resembling their husbands" (pp. 64n-65n).

FAILURE TO PASS EFFECTIVE LEGISLATION

The efforts that had been made in the past to alleviate the problem of wife-beating were, Cobbe pointed out, total failures. Her terse recounting of the few sporadic attempts to deal with the matter served primarily to highlight a fact that appeared to her undeniable: Parliament had consistently failed to secure protection for wives victimized by their husbands' brutality. There had been, of course, a few half-hearted attempts at remedial legislation, like the one in 1853, for example, when Parliament passed "An Act for the Better Prevention and Punishment of Aggravated Assaults Upon Women and Children, and for Preventing Delay and Expense in the Administration of the Criminal Law" (Criminal Procedure Act). The Act called for assaults resulting in actual bodily harm to women or children to be punished before two Justices of the Peace in Petty Sessions, or before any Police or Stipendiary Magistrate, with the penalty not to exceed six months' imprisonment or a 20 pound fine. This Act was, however, totally ineffective, and in the twenty-five year interim following its passage, Parliament had produced no new legislation that might possibly provide relief to battered wives, Cobbe emphasized. The Offences Against the Person Act [24 & 25 Vict., c. 100] had simply confirmed the provisions of the 1853 Act, nor did the Divorce Act of 1857 (the Matrimonial Causes Act, 20 & 21 Vict., c. 85) offer any real protection for such women. Although Section 16 of that Act provided for judicial separation on proof of cruelty, protection was in practice "unattainable," Cobbe charged, particularly for "ignorant, friendless, and penniless women, who [were] the chief victims of wife-torture" (1878b, p. 77).

Cobbe was willing to concede that the promoters of these legislative reforms acted from the highest motives, and might have sincerely believed that they would stem the tide of domestic violence. But one fact remained evident, she noted: "The offense [appeared] to have diminished very little, if at all, during the twenty years which have since intervened" (p. 78).

It was to redress this failure, Cobbe recalled, that Colonel Egerton Leigh spoke out in 1874 on the subject of wife-abuse to his fellow members of the House of Commons. Leigh's highly emotional speech referred to England's reputation as "the Paradise of women," but, he predicted, if Parliament chose to ignore this matter of domestic brutality, England would become "a Hell of women" (Hansard's Parliamentary Debates, 1874). His subsequent motion, that Parliament alleviate the wife-beating problem by imposing a stiffer punishment for aggravated assaults, apparently met with uniform sympathy. Prime Minister Disraeli pointed out in his brief response to Leigh that there could be no other reaction, for indeed, this was a subject which defied "any differences of opinion." Thanking Leigh for devoting attention to the subject, Disraeli assured the Commons that the Secretary of State for the Home Department would address the subject at the proper time. This assurance apparently satisfied Leigh, who immediately withdrew his motion (although to Cobbe's disgust, he dismissed the subject with one of the little jokes that seemed to her "so inexpressibly sickening") (Hansard's Parliamentary Debates, 1874).

Six months after Leigh's speech, the Home Office did indeed initiate an inquiry of various judges, recorders, and magistrates of police courts on the subject of brutal assaults. The results, published in the previously mentioned parliamentary Blue Book (*Reports to the Secretary of State for the Home Department on the State of the Law Relating to Brutal Assaults,* 1875) (British Parliamentary Papers, 1849-1879, 1971), confirmed the fact that the existing law on brutal assaults was deficient. But, despite the impressive agreement on the subject (by a panel which included several distinguished jurists and recorders, and one Lord Chief Justice), no practical use was made of the panel's work. Cobbe, writing her article three years after the appearance of this Blue Book inquiry, was furious that such testimony, collected at the public expense, was simply ignored; she was nevertheless not surprised. Only "the uninitiated," she observed wryly, would think that Parliament would respond promptly to a measure carrying "such weighty recommendation." Its failure to do so could have been anticipated, she observed, when one considered that in the three years since the publication of that particular Blue Book,

> scores of Bills, on every sort and kind of question *interesting to the represented sex,* have passed through Parliament; but this question on which the lives of women literally hang, has never been even mooted since [Disraeli] so completely assured its solitary champion [Leigh] that "Her Majesty's Government would bear in mind the evident feeling of the House on the subject. (Cobbe, 1878b, p. 79)

Cobbe's disgust with this state of affairs was undisguised: "Something like 6,000 women...have been in the intervening years 'brutally assaulted' – that is, maimed, blinded, trampled, burned, and in no inconsiderable number of instances murdered outright" (p. 79).

And why did such outrages persist? The answer to that question was clear to Cobbe. Parliament did not act because Parliament did not choose to act. Consequently, the conclusion was inescapable: the oft-expressed assurance "year after year by smiling senators" that women might "absolutely and always rely on men to provide deepest and tenderest concern for everything which concerns the welfare of women," was, in reality, a lie (p. 80). The "long neglected wrongs of our trampled sisters," Cobbe charged, made that fact only too clear. Nevertheless, despite that pessimistic conclusion, Cobbe was determined to secure action.

COBBE'S PROPOSAL AND PARLIAMENT'S RESPONSE

Although Cobbe believed that the complete cessation of wife- torture was impossible – at least for the time – she hoped that her focusing attention on the problem would spur Parliament to provide some measure of relief to the wretched victims of marital brutality. What Cobbe specifically proposed was the passage of a bill that would protect wives from husbands convicted of brutal assaults. The means by which this was to be secured was a Protection Order (to be issued either by the police magistrate or by the petty sessions court) that would have the effect of a judicial separation. Such a measure, by making available to working-class wives the legal remedies that had long been enjoyed by upper-class women, would end, Cobbe believed, the anomaly of "one law for the rich and one for the poor."

Cobbe's proposal reflected her awareness of the difficulties frequently encountered in securing prosecution for a wife-beater, including the overwhelming reluctance of wives who feared to bring testimony against their husbands. Even those women who, in the immediate aftermath of violence, *were* willing to tell their stories to constables, Cobbe pointed out, were a week or month later sufficiently intimidated to dread the consequences of bearing testimony. Instead of telling her true story, the fearful victim was "constantly found to narrate some poor little fable whereby the husband [was] quite exonerated, and perhaps the blame taken on herself" (1878b, p. 81). The case cited by Egerton Leigh in the House of Commons in 1875 serves as an example: a woman appeared with a badly injured nose before the magistrate, and informed him that she had bitten it herself (Hansard's Parliamentary Debates, 1874). In short, Cobbe maintained, the current procedure served not to repress crime, but merely to discourage complaints. The measure that Cobbe proposed, by providing the injured wife with protection against further violence, would she believed, encourage victims of repeated aggravated assaults to come forward to testify.

In addition, Cobbe advocated awarding custody of the children to the wife and requiring the husband to pay a weekly sum that would be determined by the courts for the maintenance of his family. By this suggestion, she made clear her conviction that "the man who was capable of kicking, maiming, and mutilating his wife" was "even less fit to be the guardian of the bodies and souls of children than the lord and master of a woman." Children, Cobbe asserted, were no more safe under a wife-beater's roof than they were "in the cage of a wild beast" (1878b, p. 85).

Cobbe closed her appeal with a dual request: addressing the gentlemen of England, she pleaded that they not "leave these helpless women to be trampled to death under their very eyes." As for the ladies of England, Cobbe urged them "to take to heart the wrongs and agonies of our miserable sisters, and to lift up on their behalf a cry which must make Parliament either hasten to deal with the matter, or renounce for very shame the vain pretense that it takes care of the interests of women" (1878b, p. 87).

Cobbe's determination to extend "the privilege of rich women to their poorer sisters" through a parliamentary act that would effect a separation from a husband convicted of an aggravated assault won parliamentary support. Meeting no opposition in either House, a bill became law on May 27, 1878, under the title "An Act to Amend the Matrimonial Causes Act" (Geary, 1892). The new law paved the way for separation orders to be granted in applicable cases, and the possibility was opened that some women would henceforth be spared the effects of their husbands' violence.

The passage of this Act afforded immense satisfaction to Cobbe. Indeed, toward the end of her long and active career as a feminist reformer, it was to this particular effort, "to obtain protection for unhappy wives, beaten, mangled, mutilated, or trampled on by brutal husbands," that Cobbe looked back "with the most satisfaction" (Cobbe, 1894, vol. 2, pp. 534-535). Her crucial role in winning public support to alleviate the wife- beating problem was acknowledged by her contemporaries as a significant achievement (Verschoyle, 1904; "Women's newspapers," 1878) and certainly, her efforts to rouse Parliament to action cannot be overestimated.

CONCLUSION

The Act of 1878, however important it was both in enunciating the notion that abused wives should be protected, and in providing specific relief to some wives, did not unfortunately become a Magna Carta for women victimized by tyrannical husbands. Nor was this suprising to those who, like Cobbe, saw wife-beating in the broader context of a feminist philosophy. Cobbe understood that this Act could be no more than a palliative; she recognized that wife-beating on its most fundamental level reflected the underlying disparity between the sexes, and therefore, a solution to the problem of domestic brutality was impossible as long as society failed to revise the prevailing modes of thought and feeling. Men must be made to understand that their monopoly of power was unjustifiable and immoral, and that in order for them to be "truly civilized," they must help to raise women to positions of dignity and respect (Cobbe, 1888, p. 55).

Because Cobbe so clearly perceived the organic relationship between wife-beating and the fundamental biases of a patriarchal society, it is surprising to read that modern scholars believe they have only recently "discovered" the extent of that relationship (Combo, 1979, pp. 181-182; Freeman, 1977, p. 250; Freeman, 1980, p. 220, pp. 240-241; Fromson, 1977, p. 142; O'Brien, 1974, p. 65; Straus, 1978, p. 61). Such a claim is unwarranted; it does a disservice to nineteenth-century feminists because it creates the impression that they failed to get to the heart of the problem and were therefore willing to settle for no more than a limited degree of reform. From that point of view, the activities of Victorian reformers were confined to working for specific, isolated measures that were useful enough as far as they went, but stopped short of dealing with the basic issue – the unequal position of the sexes (Freeman, 1979, p. 128). On the contrary, the interests of nineteenth-century feminists were not at all limited. No one who has read what Cobbe, for example, had to say on the subject is likely to commit the error of assuming that she was unaware of the fundamental cause of wife-abuse: the widely accepted belief that women were inferior to men. If that notion can be called a "discovery" (a term she would have been too modest to use), the credit for it must go to those nineteenth-century feminists who clearly recognized that if real reforms were to be accomplished, it was necessary to free society from its sexist bias.

Cobbe, and those of her contemporaries who thought as she did, recognized a century ago that wife-beating was a symptom of what was wrong with society in general. Men who would never have lifted a hand to strike a woman, and who would have indignantly denied the charge that they had anything to do with wife-beating, nevertheless, as Cobbe pointed out, by being aware of widespread and chronic crimes against wives and tacitly refusing to do anything about them, were in effect sanctioning the evil. The problem of wife-beating, as a number of Victorian feminists made clear, sprang from the failure of English society to correct the distorted relationship between men and women. Only if that were done, they insisted, would there be significant progress toward a solution of the wife-beating problem.

REFERENCES

An Act to Amend the Matrimonial Causes Acts, 41 & 42 Vict., c. 19, 1878.

Bacon, M. (1786). *A new abridgment of the law* (5th ed.). Dublin: Luke White.

Bauer, C., & Ritt, L. (1979). *Free and ennobled: Source readings in the development of Victorian feminism.* Oxford: Pergamon Press.

Birrell, A. (1896). Woman under the English law. *Edinburgh Review, 184*, 322-340.

Bradley v. State, Walker 156, Miss. (1824).

British Parliamentary Papers, 1849-1879. Legal Administration, Criminal Law (1971), 6, rpt: Irish University Press, 195- 367.

Brittain, V. (1953). *Lady into woman.* London: Andrew Dakers.

Browne, I. (1891). Wife-beating and imprisonment. *American Law Review, 25*, 551-568.

Bryce, J. (1968). Marriage and divorce under Roman and English law. In J. Bryce (Ed), *Studies in history and jurisprudence* (pp. 784-814). Freeport, NY: Books for Libraries Press.

Burr, G. L. (1889). English woman-burning, *Nation, 49*, 169.

Chadwick, J. W. (1867). Frances Power Cobbe, *Christian Examiner, 83*, 265-286.

Cleveland, A. R. (1896). *Woman under the English law.* London: Hurst and Blackett.

Cobbe, F. P. (1855). *An essay on intuitive morals.* London: Longman, Brown, Green, and Longmans.

Cobbe, F. P. (1860, September). *Destitute incurables in workhouses.* Paper presented at the meeting of the Social Science Association, Glasgow, Scotland.

Cobbe, F. P. (1861a). *Friendless girls, and how to help them.* London: Emily Faithfull & Co.

Cobbe, F. P. (1861b). *The sick in workhouses.* London: James Nisbet & Co.

Cobbe, F. P. (1861c). *The workhouse as a hospital.* London: Emily Faithfull & Co.

Cobbe, F. P. (1861d). Workhouse sketches. *Macmillan's Magazine, 3*, 448-461.

Cobbe, F. P. (1862a). Celibacy v. marriage. *Fraser's Magazine, 65*, 228-234.

Cobbe, F. P. (1862b). What shall we do with our old maids? *Fraser's Magazine, 66*, 594-610.

Cobbe, F. P. (1864a). *Broken lights.* London: Trubner & Co.

Cobbe, F. P. (1864b). Christian ethics and the ethics of Christ. *Theological Review, 1*, 396-423.

Cobbe, F. P. (1864c). The philosophy of the poor laws and the report of the committee on poor relief. *Fraser's Magazine, 70*, 373-394.,

Cobbe, F. P. (1864d). *Religious duty.* London: Trubner & Co.

Cobbe, F. P. (1865). Self-development, and self-abnegation. In F. P. Cobbe, *Studies new and old of ethical and social subjects* (pp. 49-85). London: Trubner & Co.

Cobbe, F. P. (1866a). The indigent class. *Fraser's Magazine, 73*, 143-160.

Cobbe, F. P. (1866b). The religion of childhood. *Theological Review, 3*, 317-341.

Cobbe, F. P. (1867). Public morality and its teachers. In F. P. Cobbe, *Hours of work and play* (pp. 1-19). Philadelphia: J. B. Lippincott & Co.

Cobbe, F. P. (1868a). Criminals, idiots, women, and minors. *Fraser's Magazine, 78*, 774-794.

Cobbe, F. P. (1868b). *Dawning lights.* London: E.T. Whitfield.

Cobbe, F. P. (1870). Hereditary piety. *Theological Review, 7*, 211-234.

Cobbe, F. P. (1872). *Darwinism in morals, and other essays.* London: Williams & Norgate.

Cobbe, F. P. (1874a). Heteropathy, aversion, sympathy. *Theological Review, 11*, 1-35.

Cobbe, F. P. (1874b). *The hopes of the human race.* London: Williams & Norgate.

Cobbe, F. P. (1878a). The little health of ladies. *Contemporary Review, 31,* 275-296.

Cobbe, F. P. (1878b). Wife-torture in England. *Contemporary Review, 32,* 55-87.

Cobbe, F. P. (1881). *The duties of women.* London: Williams & Norgate.

Cobbe, F. P. (1882). *The peak in Darien.* London: Williams & Norgate.

Cobbe, F. P. (1883). Agnostic morality. *Contemporary Review, 43,* 783-794.

Cobbe, F. P. (1884). A faithless world. *Contemporary Review, 46,* 795-810.

Cobbe, F. P. (1888). *The duties of women* (8th. Am. ed.), London: Williams & Norgate.

Cobbe, F. P. (1890). The two religions. *Contemporary Review, 58,* 839-848.

Cobbe, F. P. (1894). *Life of Frances Power Cobbe.* (2 vols.) Boston: Houghton Mifflin & Co.

Cochrane, 8 Dowling 630, at 633 (K.B. 1840).

Combo, M. E. (1979). Wife beating: Law and society confront the castle door. *Gonzaga Law Review, 15,* 171-202.

Cornwallis, C. F. (1856). The property of married women. *Westminster Review, 66,* 331-360.

Criminal Procedure Act, 16 Vict., c. 30, (1853).

Davidson, T. (1977). Wifebeating: A recurring phenomenon throughout history. In M. Roy (Ed.), *Battered women: A psychosociological study of domestic violence.* New York: Van Nostrand Reinhold.

Davidson, T. (1978). *Conjugal crime: Understanding and changing the wife-beating pattern.* New York: Hawthorn Books.

Davis, E. G. (1971). *The first sex.* New York: G. P. Putnam's Sons.

Dobash, R. E., & Dobash, R. P. (1980). *Violence against wives: A case against the patriarchy.* New York: The Free Press.

Dunning, A. (1953). *The changing law.* London: Stevens and Sons.

Ehrlich, J. W. (1959). *Ehrlich's Blackstone.* San Carlos, CA: Nourse Publishing Co.

Freeman, M. D. A. (1977). Le vice Anglais? — Wife-battering in English and American law. *Family Law Quarterly, 11,* 199- 251.

Freeman, M. D. A. (1979). *Violence in the home: A socio- legal study.* Farnborough, England: Saxon House.

Freeman, M. D. A. (1980). Violence against women: Does the legal system provide solutions or itself constitute the problem. *British Journal of Law and Society, 7,* 215-241.

Fromson, T. L. (1977). The case for legal remedies for abused wives. *New York University Review of Law and Social Change, 6,* 135-174.

Gayford, J. J. (1977). Battered wives one hundred years ago. *The Practitioner, 219,* 122-128.

Geary, N. (1892). *The law of marriage and family relations.* London: Adam and Charles Black.

Gibson, I. (1978). *The English vice: Beating, sex and shame in Victorian England and after.* London: Duckworth.

Gottliffe v. Edelston, 2 K. B. 378 (1930).

Hansard's Parliamentary Debates, 3rd series, 219 (May 18, 1874).

Harrison, J. C. (1886). *An epitome of the laws of probate and divorce.* (3rd ed.). London: Stevens and Haynes.

Hecker, E. A. (1914). *A short history of women's rights* (2nd ed.). New York: G. P. Putnam's Sons.

Helmholz, R. H. (1974). *Medieval litigation.* Cambridge: Cambridge University Press.

Hooper, W. (1913). *The Englishwoman's legal guide.* London: David Nutt.

Kaye, J.W. (1855). The "non-existence" of women. *North British Review, 23,* 536-562.

Kaye, J. W. (1856). Outrages on women. *North British Review, 25,* 233-256.

Langley, R., & Levy, R. C. (1977). *Wife beating: The silent crisis.* New York: F. P. Dutton.

Lewin, W. (1894, October). Life of Frances Power Cobbe. *Academy, 46,* 321-322.

Manson, E. (1891). Marital authority. *Law Quarterly Review, 7,* 244-255.

Martin, D. (1976). *Battered wives.* San Francisco: Glide Publications.

Meacher v. Meacher, P. 216, C.A. (1946).

Meriwether, L. (1889). Is divorce a remedy? *Westminster Review, 131,* 676-685.

Mill, J. S. (1867). *The admission of women to the electoral franchise.* London: Trubner & Co.

28 A Victorian Indictment

Mill, J. S. (1970). *The subjection of women.* Cambridge, MA: MIT Press.

Minton-Senhouse, R. M. (1889). Married women: An historical sketch. *Westminster Review, 131,* 355-366.

Morrison, C. A. (1957). Tort. In R. H. Graveson and F. R. Crane (Eds.) *A century of family law* (pp. 88-115). London: Sweet & Maxwell.

New York Times (Oct. 7, 1894). Life of Frances Power Cobbe, p. 23.

New York Times (April 6, 1904). Frances Power Cobbe dead, p. 5.

Norton, C. (1854). *English laws for women.* London: n.p.

Norton, the Hon. Mrs. (1855). *A letter to the Queen on Lord Chancellor Cranworth's marriage and divorce bill* (3rd ed.). London: Longman, Brown, Green and Longmans.

O'Brien, J. E. (1974). Violence in divorce-prone families. In S. K. Steinmetz & M. A. Straus (Eds.), *Violence in the family* (pp. 65-73). New York: Harper & Row.

Owens, D. (1975). Battered wives: Some social and legal problems. *British Journal of Law and Society, 2,* 201-211.

Pike, L. O. (1876). *A history of crime in England* (2 vols). London: Smith, Elder & Co.

Pollock, F., & Maitland, F. W. (1898). *The history of English law* (2 vols., 2nd ed.). Cambridge: Cambridge University Press.

Pratt, E. A. (1897). *Pioneer women in Victoria's reign.* London: G. Newnes.

Prosser, W. L. (1971). *Handbook of the law of torts* (4th ed.). St. Paul, MN: West Publishing Co.

Pulling, S. A. (1876). Crimes of violence. *Transactions of the National Association for the Promotion of Social Science,* 345-361.

Reiss, E. (1934). *Rights and duties of Englishwomen.* Manchester: Sherratt & Hughes.

Review of Reviews (1894). Autobiography of Frances Power Cobbe, *10,* 562-569.

Schupf, H. W. (1974). Single women and social reform in mid-nineteenth century England: The case of Mary Carpenter. *Victorian Studies, 17,* 301-317.

State v. Rhodes, 61, N.C. 453 (1868).

Steinmetz, S. K., & Straus, M. A. (Eds.). (1974). *Violence in the family.* New York: Harper and Row.

Straus, M. A. (1978). Sexual inequality, cultural norms, and wife-beating. In J. R. Chapman and M. Gates (Eds.), *Women into wives: The legal and economic impact of marriage* (pp. 59-74). Beverly Hills, CA: Sage Publications.

The Times (London) (April 7, 1904). Miss Frances Power Cobbe, p 7.

Verschoyle, J. (1904). Frances Power Cobbe. *Contemporary Review, 85,* 829-840.

Willard, F. (1888). Introduction. In. F. P. Cobbe, *The duties of women* (8th American ed.). London: Williams & Norgate.

Women's newspapers. (Oct. 15, 1878). *Englishwomen's Review, 66,* 433-440.

Chapter 2
Hostility Toward Women: Some Theoretical Considerations

James V. P. Check

Until recently, the literature on hostility and aggression has largely ignored the issue of male hostility and aggression toward women. Aggression theorists (e.g., Bandura, 1973; Baron, 1977; Berkowitz, 1962; Buss, 1961; Feshbach, 1964; Kaufman, 1970; Zillmann, 1979) have generally conceptualized hostility as a general trait measure, primarily relevant to male-to-male aggressivity. As a consequence, researchers and theorists have made few attempts to assess the extent to which their theories can be generalized to male hostility and aggression against women.

An apparent explanation for this lack of attention would seem to be the agreement among researchers that males in Western culture are generally taught to behave relatively nonaggressively toward females, even when provoked (Bandura, 1962; Buss, 1971; Clausen & Williams, 1963; Kagan, 1964; Taylor & Epstein, 1967; Whiting, 1963). This conclusion is based to a large extent on the behavioral aggression literature employing laboratory-assessed measures of aggression (delivery of electric shock or aversive noise). A review of this literature reveals that the majority of studies does in fact find males to be less aggressive toward females than toward other males (Baron & Bell, 1973; Buss, 1961, 1963, 1966b, 1971; Donnerstein & Berkowitz, 1981, Experiment 1, neutral film condition; Hedges, 1970; Shortell & Biller, 1970; Taylor & Epstein, 1967; Taylor & Smith, 1974; Youssef, 1968), although there have been a number of exceptions to this finding (Buss, 1966a; Check, 1985; Donnerstein & Barrett, 1978; Donnerstein & Hallam, 1978; Hynan & Esselman, 1980; Larsen, Coleman, Forbes, & Johnson, 1972; Silverman, 1971), and in fact two studies reported *more* aggression against opposite-sexed targets than against same-sexed targets (Jaffe, Malamuth, Feingold, & Feshbach, 1974; Titley & Viney, 1969).

While laboratory-assessed male-to-female aggression may be less likely to occur than male-to-male aggression, in the real world there is clear evidence of at least two forms of male aggression against women; rape and wife-battering. Gager and Schurr (1976) for example, have referred to rape as the number-one crime against women in the United States and estimate that 265,000 rapes are committed (but often not reported) each year. Similarly, based upon victimization data from a 13-city survey, Johnson (1980) has estimated that a woman living out her life in a large U.S. city has a 16% chance of being the victim of a completed or attempted rape. Further, the rate of reported rape has been steadily climbing for a number of years (see Court, 1984, for a review).

In terms of domestic violence, Russell (1982) found that 21% of her sample of 644 San Francisco women who had ever been married reported "being subjected to physical violence by a husband at some time in their lives" (p. 96). Similarly, Straus, Gelles, and Steinmetz (1980) found that 22% of their U.S. national sample of 2,143 couples reported husband violence against the wife. In terms of the more extreme forms of violence, Straus et al. found that 3.8% of husbands had engaged in kicking, biting, or punching, hitting with some object, beating up the wife, threatening the wife with a gun or knife, or actually using a gun or knife. And finally, Langley and Levy (1977) conducted an extensive review of the existing literature on family violence and estimated that "there are between 26 and 30 million abused spouses in the U.S. today" (p. 12).

Partially due to this increasing rate of violent crimes against women, and partially due to the rise of the women's movement, a growing number of writers has begun to theorize about the role of hostility toward women in rape and other aggressive acts against women (e.g., Brownmiller, 1975; Check & Malamuth, 1983, 1986; Cohen, Garofalo, Boucher, & Seghorn, 1977; Dworkin, 1974; Gager & Schurr, 1976; Greer, 1970; Griffin, 1971; Groth, Burgess, & Holmstrom, 1977; Henley & Freeman, 1981; Leidig, 1981; Macdonald, 1971; Malamuth, 1981; Millet, 1970; Moreland, 1977; Rada, 1978; Russell, 1975; Stark-Adamec & Adamec, 1982; Walker, 1981). (As detailed further below, "hostility" is used here to refer to an underlying, covert trait or disposition, and is to be distinguished from rape and other forms of overt, aggressive behavior against women.) A number of writers, for example, argue that hostility toward women is one of the primary motivating factors in rape (e.g., Brownmiller, 1975).

Despite the theoretical significance of hostility toward women in these works on rape and other acts of aggression against women, there have to date been no *empirical* investigations of the role that hostility toward women plays in such acts. While this is partially due to the generally accepted belief that aggression against women is rare, a second major reason for this dearth of empirical work has been the lack of a reliable and valid trait measure of hostility toward women. The purpose of this paper is to take some preliminary theoretical steps toward defining hostility toward women, so that it may be measured. Let us now turn to a consideration of the construct of general hostility as it currently exists in the literature.

THE CONSTRUCT OF HOSTILITY

As was previously noted, many researchers consider hostility to be simply a measure of the likelihood of exhibiting aggressive behavior, which is typically defined as behavior intended to inflict harm or injury on another person (Baron, 1977; Berkowitz, 1974; Feshbach, 1970). While some theorists (e.g., Feshbach, 1964) distinguish between the different immediate motivations for a given aggressive response (e.g., hostile or angry motivations versus instrumental motivations), the focus of most aggression theorizing and research has been on the situational, social, and environmental determinants of these motivations rather than exploring the potential underlying dispositional causes of the aggressive response. (As Check, 1985, has noted, this lack of attention to dispositions is most likely due to the literature showing that dispositional measures of hostility/aggressiveness do not predict actual aggressive behavior very well, thus raising doubt as to their utility in testing theory).

In contrast to most aggression theorists, however, Buss (1961) and Kaufman (1970) distinguish between the underlying trait of "hostility" on the one hand, and characteristic "aggressiveness" on the other. According to these authors, characteristic aggressiveness is simply the habit or behavioral tendency to engage in aggressive acts. (Note that, according to this analysis, a person who never actually engages in aggression is by definition not a characteristically aggressive person.) Hostility, on the other hand, is more of an underlying, enduring personal attitude or disposition toward others, and may or may not be accompanied by overt aggressive behavior. Thus, a person may have an extremely hostile disposition toward others throughout his/her life and yet never actually harm anyone. In Buss' oft-quoted words, hostility "is usually not verbalized openly as part of an aggressive response. Typically, it is implicit, consisting of mulling over of past attacks on oneself, rejections, and deprivations...[and]...may be inferred when the attack is reinforced more by injury than attaining some extrinsic reinforcer." (Buss, 1961, p. 12). For example, a juvenile delinquent may be constantly involved in fights with other delinquents, intentionally inflicting considerable harm upon his or her opponents. At the same time, however, he or she may harbor no ill will toward his or her opponents, fighting with them simply to gain respect from his or her peers, or even because that is what he or she was taught to do. On the other hand, a similarly aggressive person may feel a good deal of hostility toward others, and thus get into fights for the sole purpose of harming others (perhaps, as Buss implies in the above quotation, in return for real or imagined past attacks, deprivations, etc. from others).

On the basis of this distinction between hostility and aggressiveness, Buss and Durkee (1957) developed several subscales purportedly measuring these two personality dimensions. The hostility dimension was measured using subscales of resentment, suspicion, and guilt, whereas aggressiveness was measured on subscales of assault, indirect aggression, irritability, negativism, and verbal aggression. Thus, as Buss and Durkee put it, the hostility/aggressiveness construct has two distinct components: an "emotional" or attitudinal component ("People are no damn good") and a "motor" component that involves various aggressive behaviors (p. 348).

Factor-analytic studies have confirmed the existence of these two relatively independent dimensions (Bendig, 1962; Buss & Durkee, 1957; Edmunds & Kendrick, 1980), although Bendig (1962) preferred to refer to Buss' hostility and aggression factors as "covert hostility" and "overt hostility", respectively. This factor-analytic research also supports Buss' contentions that a hostile person may or may not express his or her hostility in overt aggressive behavior, and that a characteristically aggressive person may or may not behave aggressively as a result of his or her hostile feelings toward others. As will become apparent in the following pages, the focus of this paper will be on the construct of hostility (as opposed to aggressiveness) toward women, i.e., the emotional, attitudinal component delineated by Buss and Durkee.

THE CONSTRUCT OF HOSTILITY TOWARD WOMEN

In contrast to the construct of general hostility, there appears to be very little discussion of the construct of hostility toward women in the social psychological literature on aggression. Rather, discussions of both hostility and aggressiveness toward women are found almost exclusively in the literature on rape and wife abuse. However, even those theorists who do talk about hostility toward women frequently fail to define it independently of its behavioral manifestations, a distinction which is important, since as noted earlier the notion of hostility as a personality trait implies that such hostility can exist even though it may not be expressed in overt aggressive behavior. Instead, such discussions typically avoid the issue, focusing on either (a) the sources of hostility and aggressiveness toward women, or (b) its presumed behavioral effect (e.g., rape and wife abuse).

The Sources of Hostility/Aggressiveness Toward Women

There are two main sources of theory regarding the causes of hostility and aggressiveness toward women; psychiatric theory (stemming primarily from the psychoanalytic tradition) and feminist theory. Both of these are found primarily in the literature on rape, and to a much lesser extent in the literature on non-sexual aggression against women (e.g., wife-abuse).

According to psychiatric theorists, rapists' hostility toward women is caused by a history of rejection, cruelty, domination/overprotection, and sexual seduction from important women in the rapist's early life (Cohen et al., 1977; Groth & Birnbaum, 1980; Groth et al., 1977; Karpman, 1954; Macdonald, 1971; Rada, 1978). Rada (1978) posits that in general cruel, sadistic parents are an important factor in determining a child's subsequent aggressivity. However, "when the father is cruel and hostile to the son, the boy may develop an excessive aggressive posture that could become characteristic of all of his relationships" (p. 33), whereas hostility directed specifically toward women is seen by Rada as caused primarily by maternal cruelty. Most other psychiatric theorists are in agreement on this latter point. Groth and Birnbaum (1980) describe Groth et al.'s (1977) anger-motivated rapist as raping in retaliation for "what he perceives or what he has experienced as wrongs suffered at the hands of important women in his life, such as his mother or his wife" (Groth & Birnbaum, 1980, p. 21). Similarly, Cohen et al. (1977) suggest that with respect to mature women, "aggressive-aim" rapists (characterized as motivated primarily by hostility toward women) "tend to experience women negatively as hostile, demanding, ungiving, and unfaithful" (p. 299). With respect to maternal seduction, Macdonald (1971) suggests that "the seductive mother arouses overwhelming anxiety in her son, with great anger which may be expressed directly toward her but more often is displaced on to other women" (p. 136). The Oedipal conflict is frequently brought into this maternal seduction theme, although it is not clearly explained how this can result in hostility toward women. This vagueness is exemplified by Karpman's (1954) statement that "rape may be related unconsciously to early incestuous desires and the fury aroused by the Oedipus complex. The victim may be a substitute for the criminal's mother" (Karpman, 1954, as cited in Gager & Schurr, 1976, p. 235).

In sum, most psychiatric theorists are in substantial agreement on two major theoretical points; (a) hostility toward women as a factor in rape is a consequence of the rapist having been abused by women, and (b) hostility toward women is therefore not just a manifestation of a generally hostile/aggressive personality. The problem is that while these theorists have a clear position on the specific origins of hostility toward women, they do not present a clear conceptualization of hostility toward women itself.

A somewhat different approach to the question of the origins of hostility toward women is the work of Robert Stoller (1970, 1976, 1979). Stoller argues that hostility generally stems from one's need to overcome or undo the childhood frustrations and trauma that originally threatened one's masculinity or femininity. These frustrations, according to Stoller, are essential for normal development, since such development

...demands that infants be increasingly frustrated in order to permit the separation that will result in the ego functions and identity necessary for coping with the external world. This process, using frustration as an essential tool, creates a reservoir of unconscious hatred, coping with which helps to determine successful or maladaptive personality development (1970, p. 498).

For males, Stoller claims, it is especially difficult to develop a distinct identity, since most children are dependent upon and extremely close to their mothers during early childhood. Thus, female children can simply continue to identify with their mother, whereas male children must surmount their feminine identifications. They do this not only by identifying with their father, but also by symbolically overpowering their mother in their fantasies and/or in their later overt behavior with other women. This process can be seen most clearly, says Stoller, in the male fantasy world of pornography:

Very popular are descriptions of a woman who starts out cool, superior, sophisticated, and uninterested but is swept away by the precisely described activities of the man into a state of lust with monumental loss of control. One sees easily therein a power struggle disguised as sexuality: the dangerous woman who is reduced to a victim and the boy who, by means of the pornography, becomes a man (1970, p. 498).

Note that Stoller, while arguing that most men express their hostility in these fantasized power struggles with women, does state that there may be a few cases of men with very little hostility, i.e., those who, in childhood, were treated less cruelly by their mothers. Thus, Stoller conceptualizes hostility toward women as part of all men's psychological makeup to a greater or lesser degree, but does suggest that this hostility lies along a continuum, from the "normal" range (where men for the most part enjoy loving, nonhostile relationships) all the way to the bizarre or psychotic range (Stoller, 1976, pp. 908-909). Finally, Stoller, like other psychiatric theorists, sees hostility toward women as a product of conflict with important women in the individual's early childhood (in this case, the mother).

In sharp contrast to the psychoanalytic view of the causes of hostility toward women is the feminist view. Feminists seem to conceptualize hostility toward women as indistinguishable from aggressivity toward women, arguing that hostility/aggressiveness is a socially learned phenomenon. In fact, they forcefully argue that the psychoanalytic tradition fosters the "myth" that male aggression against women is due to mental illness, for which women themselves are presumably to blame (e.g., Brownmiller, 1975; Clark & Lewis, 1977; Gager & Schurr, 1976; Griffin, 1971; Melani & Fodaski, 1974; Russell, 1975). Thus for feminists hostility/aggressiveness toward women is primarily caused by a patriarchal, male-dominant, violence-prone culture, and in fact they rarely refer to anything resembling an underlying affective or attitudinal component to this construct. Clark and Lewis

(1977), for example, have provided a detailed socio-historical account of the way in which rape is rooted in the historical role of women as forms of private property. Clark and Lewis argue that, because of the fact that women were the property of their male owners, and because their value was in part determined by their sexual and reproductive desirability, an unmarried woman was encouraged to protect her sexual desirability (virginity), and to hold it "in trust" for her father, so that he could give it to her future husband. The important point to be remembered is that, while in contemporary society women are no longer the legal property of men, women still often define themselves in terms of their value as sexual and reproductive commodities. As a result, they are encouraged to (a) "bargain" with men, trading their sexuality for the security of marriage to a man with a good income, and (b) protect themselves from those who would take sex by force and thus (especially in the case of virgins) "damage the goods." Those who would take sex by force, according to Clark and Lewis, are men who (a) do not have the "buying power" (e.g., financial security) or are unwilling to bargain for sex "legitimately," and (b) most strongly identify masculinity with sexual dominance and aggression (i.e., those who hold the most traditional, stereotyped view of man as the conqueror, the aggressor, the powerful). As can be seen from the following quotations, this theme of identifying sexual aggression with natural masculinity is a consistent one, especially with respect to the feminist analyses of rape:

> [We are talking about] physical aggression as "a demonstration of masculinity and toughness" [which is] the prime tenet of the subculture of violence. Sexual aggression is a major part of *machismo*. (Brownmiller, 1975, p. 197)

> Whatever the motivation, male sexuality and violence in our culture seem to be inseparable...in the spectrum of male behavior, rape, the perfect combination of sex and violence, is the penultimate act. (Griffin, 1971, p. 3)

> Rape may be understood as an extreme acting out of the qualities that are regarded as supermasculine in this and many other societies: aggression, force, power, strength, toughness, dominance, competitiveness...i.e., the *masculine mystique*. (Russell, 1975, p. 260)

It can be seen from the above quotations that the dominant theme in feminist analyses of aggression against women is that it is a result of the fact that men are generally aggressive creatures (as a result of male sex-typing and socialization), with some men (those who are more male sex-typed) being more so than others. Thus, in contrast to psychoanalytic theory, the feminist analysis suggests that individual differences in male aggressiveness toward women may be *primarily* accounted for by individual differences in general aggressivity. At an intuitive level, this would seem to negate the construct of hostility specifically directed toward women (at least as Buss and Durkee, 1957, have defined hostility). However, there are some indirect indications in feminist writings that feminists see hostility toward women as also stemming from factors other than learned general aggressivity. Clark and Lewis (1977), for example, suggest that hostility toward women (or what is often termed "misogyny") can also be a byproduct of the way in which men and women bargain with each other in sexual interactions:

> Women are seen as the hoarders and miserly dispensers of a much desired commodity (sex)...and men must constantly wheedle, bargain, and pay a price for what they want. Men naturally come to resent and dislike women because they see them as having something which they want and have a perfect right to, but which women are unwilling to give them freely. (pp. 128-129)

Melani and Fodaski (1974) make much the same argument as Clark and Lewis, suggesting that "the male is aware, apparently, at some level of consciousness, of the hostility that exists between the sexes, a hostility that arises inevitably when men have power and women do not" (p. 90). Similarly, Russell (1975) has suggested that, "with these basic incompatibilities in socialized needs and expected behavior, it is not surprising that there is often hatred between the sexes" (p. 274). Leidig (1981) also claims that men's "hatred" of women is in general socially sanctioned, and accepts Greer's (1970) suggestion that men basically hate women, arguing that "an analysis of violence against women would certainly lead one to consider the veracity of this idea seriously" (Leidig, 1981, p. 204).

There are a number of other, less frequently mentioned hypothesized causes of hostility (as distinguished from aggressivity) toward women in the feminist literature. Stark-Adamec and Adamec (1982) postulate a "fear and loathing" hypothesis. According to this hypothesis, hostility toward women stems from men's fear of menstruation, pregnancy, female sexuality (because female sexuality implies closeness, which men fear), and the feeling that sex is dirty, all of these being coupled with a need for women's emotional support (which is threatening because it implies weakness). Along with Russell (1975), Stark-Adamec and Adamec also suggest that women's increasing "invasion" into traditional male occupations is threatening to many men. This is a variant of what has come to be called the "male backlash to the Women's Liberation Movement," (Russell & Lederer, 1980, p. 27).

In summary, like the psychiatric literature, the feminist literature on the causes of hostility toward women leaves us with a somewhat ambiguous picture. While in general the causative factors implied seem to center around sex roles and "maleness" vis a vis aggressivity, these are not useful concepts for definitional purposes (considering the need to distinguish hostility and aggressivity). The male sex role cannot be considered to be the essence of hostility toward women, because it is postulated as a *cause* of hostility toward women. In fact, feminist writers seem to avoid the use of the term "hostility toward women" except as a label for actual aggressive behavior toward women. When outright "hatred" of women is mentioned, it is postulated as a basic characteristic of *all* men (e.g., Greer, 1970). The only time that hostility toward women is clearly mentioned as something resembling an individual difference variable other than general aggressivity is in reference to sexual interactions.

Thus, in sexual interactions the hostile, sexually aggressive male is seen by feminists as a byproduct of sex roles which he in his position of power has created for himself. Even here, however, no indication is given as to what this hostility "looks like." That is, we are again left without a conceptual definition which distinguishes hostility toward women from other constructs such as aggressivity, masculinity, or sex roles. Let us now direct our search for such a definition to the literature on the consequence or *manifestations* of hostility toward women.

The Manifestations of Hostility Toward Women

There is almost universal agreement amongst theorists that hostility/aggressiveness (especially toward women) plays a causal role in rape, and possibly also in wife-abuse. From the traditional psychiatric point of view, hostility toward women is seen as a motivating factor in rape, but it is not seen as the only factor or even the primary factor. For example, most psychiatric theorists divide rapists into several different types, primarily according to the rapist's "aggressive" versus "sexual" motivations. Cohen et al., (1977), for example, divide rapists into: (a) those with an "aggressive aim," in which "the sexual behavior is not the expression of a sexual wish but is in the service of the aggression, serving to humiliate, dirty, and defile the victim" (p. 299), and whose victims are always complete strangers; (b) rapists with a "sexual aim," for whom "the act is clearly motivated by sexual wishes, and the aggression is primarily in the service of this aim" (p. 303); and (c) those with a "sex-aggression diffusion," who are basically sadists and became sexually aroused primarily by violence. Guttmacher and Weihofen (1952) postulate three categories: (a) those "whose assault is the explosive expression of pent-up sexual impulse," or who have "strong latent homosexual components" (p. 116); (b) sadistic rapists, who "have their deep seated hatred focused particularly on women" (p. 117); and (c) the "predatory" type of rapist, who "like the soldier of the conquering army, is out to pillage and rob" (p. 117) and who is described as the basic "criminal" subtype. Gebhard, Gagnon, Pomeroy, and Christenson (1965) classify rapists into seven categories. However, all but their "drunken" and "mental defective" categories can be subsumed under Guttmacher and Weihofen's three categories. Similarly, Gebhard et al. suggest that it is primarily the sadistic type of rapist who feels "pronounced hostility toward women" (p. 197).

One apparent exception to the traditional psychiatric typological approach is the work of Groth and Birnbaum (1980). These authors suggest that rape is in general a "pseudosexual act, a pattern of sexual behavior that is concerned more with status, hostility, control, and dominance than with sexual pleasure or sexual satisfaction. It is sexual behavior in the service of primarily nonsexual needs" (p. 21). Nonetheless, Groth and Birnbaum postulate three basic types of rape (anger rape, power rape, and sadistic rape), and suggest that only the anger rapist is clearly motivated primarily by hostility toward women: "He is seeking to hurt, punish, degrade, and humiliate his victim, and he sees sex as a weapon to be used to this end" (p. 21). (Sadistic rape is viewed as other psychiatric theorists view it, i.e., as sexually motivated, where "aggression itself is eroticized," p. 22.)

Thus the psychiatric literature seems to distinguish aggressive acts toward women from the hypothesized underlying hostility which purportedly causes such acts, and again they see this hostility as directed specifically toward women.

Feminist theorists differ from traditional psychiatric theorists in that: (a) they see hostility (which they do not distinguish from aggressiveness) as *the* primary motivating factor in rape and wife-abuse, and (b) they tend not to clearly distinguish the construct of hostility toward women from the construct of general hostility. This is most clearly exemplified by Germaine Greer's (1970) statement that the act of rape "is one of murderous aggression, spawned in self-loathing and enacted upon the hated other" (p. 265). Similarly, Brownmiller (1975), who was heavily influenced by Amir's (1971) finding that the rapists he studied were generally violence-prone individuals, states that "the single most important contribution of Amir's Philadelphia study was to place the rapist squarely within the subculture of violence," (p. 197), but at the same time claims that war "provides men with the perfect psychologic backdrop to give vent to their contempt *for women*" (p. 24, emphasis added), and that "rape is nothing more or less than a conscious process of intimidation by which *all men* keep *all women* in a state of fear" (p. 5). Similarly, Clark and Lewis (1977) contend that "virtually all studies have found the rapist to manifest great hostility towards women" (p. 135). (Note that Clark and Lewis do not cite these studies.) At the same time, however, Clark and Lewis suggest that "in varying measure, all men accept sexual aggression as part of their masculine identity" (p. 145). Finally, Griffin (1971) simply states that "rape is a classic act of domination, where, in the words of Kate Millet, 'the emotions of hatred, contempt, and a desire to break or violate personality,' takes place" (p. 8).

In summary, a review of the psychiatric and feminist literature on both the causes and consequences of hostility toward women reveals no clear consensus on the basic nature of this construct. For psychiatric theorists, there seems to be some agreement that hostility toward women is an underlying trait that is (a) different from behavioral aggressiveness toward women, and (b) distinguishable from general hostility/aggressiveness. Feminists, on the other hand, are less clear on these points. They discuss hostility in more general terms, arguing that it is a socially learned characteristic of all men to a greater or lesser degree (depending upon their identification with the traditional masculine stereotype), and suggest that this hostility is the primary causal factor in aggressive behavior against both men and women. There is, however, some indication that feminists at least recognize the possibility that hostility specifically directed toward women can take the form of an underlying, motivational disposition, even though some feminists claim that all men have this disposition to an equal extent (e.g., Greer, 1970). All of these problems notwithstanding, however, the most problematic aspect of this literature is that no one appears to suggest anything resembling a definition of hostility toward women. This chapter will conclude, therefore, by suggesting the definition that has guided our subsequent research on the development and validation of a scale to measure hostility toward women.

Defining Hostility Toward Women

If the literature on aggression against women does not clearly suggest a definition of hostility toward women that is conceptually distinguishable from general hostility (except that it is directed toward women), there is no reason to believe that it will "look" any different from general hostility, *except that it is directed toward women.* On the basis of this assumption, the working definition that was adopted for our own research program was as follows: Hostility toward women is the same trait that existing hostility tests measure, except for the fact this hostility is directed specifically toward women rather than toward people in general. Thus, we can simply rework Buss' (1961, p. 12) description of general hostility to read, "Hostility *toward women* is typically implicit, consisting of the mulling over of past attacks *from women,* rejections *from women,* and deprivations *from women,* and may be inferred when aggression *against a woman* is motivated by a desire to hurt rather than by a desire to attain some extrinsic reinforcer."

The empirical advantage of this approach was of course the fact that items could be written for the Hostility Toward Women Scale which had a good deal of face validity (because they all referred specifically to women) as well as a good deal of content validity (because they all came from existing hostility scales). However, it is also important to note that this definition does not assume that men who score high on a measure of hostility toward women are not hostile toward other men as well. All the above definition implies is that such individuals will *at least* possess some degree of hostility toward women. Thus, our validation research on the Hostility Toward Women Scale required: (a) the usual multitrait-multimethod approach (Campbell & Fiske, 1959) of employing several different types of criterion variables (including variables hypothesized to be related to hostility toward women *and* variables hypothesized to be unrelated to hostility toward women); and (b) the use of a general hostility measure, so that its validity in predicting the criterion variables could be compared to that of the Hostility Toward Women Scale. Such scale-development and validation research, of course, is a long-term undertaking. However, the initial stages of our research program have proved quite encouraging, resulting in the development of a reasonably useful 30-item trait measure of hostility toward women (Check, 1985; Check, Malamuth, Elias, & Barton, 1985).

ACKNOWLEDGMENTS

The author was supported by the Social Sciences and Humanities Research Council of Canada Doctoral Fellowship #453-82-0118 while writing this paper. The author would like to thank Neil M. Malamuth and Ted Guloien for their thoughtful suggestions on earlier drafts of this paper.

REFERENCES

Amir, M. (1971). *Patterns in forcible rape.* Chicago: University of Chicago Press.
Bandura, A. (1962). Social learning through imitation. In M. Jones (Ed.), *Nebraska symposium on motivation.* Lincoln, NE: University of Nebraska Press.
Bandura, A. (1973). *Aggression: A social learning analysis.* Englewood Cliffs, NJ: Prentice-Hall.
Baron, R. A. (1977). *Human aggression.* New York: Plenum Press.
Baron, R. A., & Bell, P. A. (1973). Effects of heightened sexual arousal on physical aggression. *Proceedings of the 81st Annual Convention of the American Psychological Association, 8,* 171-172.
Bendig, A. W. (1962). Factor-analytic scales of covert and overt hostility. *Journal of Consulting Psychology, 26,* 200.
Berkowitz, L. (1962). *Aggression: A social psychological analysis.* New York: McGraw-Hill.
Berkowitz, L. (1974). Some determinants of impulsive aggression: The role of mediated associations with reinforcements for aggression. *Psychological Review, 81,* 165-176.
Brownmiller, S. (1975). *Against our will: Men, women, and rape.* New York: Bantam Books.
Buss, A. H. (1961). *The psychology of aggression.* New York: Wiley.
Buss, A. H. (1963). Physical aggression in relation to different frustrations. *Journal of Abnormal and Social Psychology, 67,* 1-7.
Buss, A. H. (1966a). The effect of harm on subsequent aggression. *Journal of Experimental Research in Personality, 1,* 249-255.
Buss, A. H. (1966b). Instrumentality of aggression, feedback, and frustration as determinants of physical aggression. *Journal of Personality and Social Psychology, 3,* 153-162.
Buss, A. H. (1971). Aggression pays. In J. L. Singer (Ed.), *The control of aggression and violence.* New York: Academic Press.
Buss, A. H., & Durkee, A. (1957). An inventory for assessing different kinds of hostility. *Journal of Consulting Psychology, 21,* 343-349.
Campbell, D. T., & Fiske, D. W. (1959). Convergent and discriminant validation by the multitrait-multimethod matrix. *Psychological Bulletin, 56,* 81-105.
Check, J. V. P. (1985). The Hostility Toward Women scale. *Dissertation Abstracts International, 45(12).*
Check, J. V. P., & Malamuth, N. M. (1983). Sex role stereotyping and reactions to depictions of stranger versus acquaintance rape. *Journal of Personality and Social Psychology, 45,* 344-356.
Check, J. V. P., & Malamuth, N. M. (1986). Pornography and sexual aggression: A social learning theory analysis. *Communications Yearbook, 9,* 181-213.
Check, J. V. P., Malamuth, N. M., Elias, B., & Barton, S. A. (1985, April). On hostile ground. *Psychology Today,* pp. 56-58, 60-61.
Clark, L., & Lewis, D. (1977). *Rape: The price of coercive sexuality.* Toronto: The Women's Press.
Clausen, J. A., & Williams, J. R. (1963). Sociological correlates of child behavior. In H. W. Stevens (Ed.), *Child psychology.* Chicago: University of Chicago Press.

Cohen, M. L., Garofolo, R., Boucher,R. B., & Seghorn, T. (1977). The psychology of rapists. In D. Chappell, R. Geis, & G. Geis (Eds.), *Forcible rape: The crime, the victim, and the offender.* New York: Columbia University Press.

Court, J. H. (1984). Sex and violence: A ripple effect. In N. M. Malamuth & E. Donnerstein (Eds.), *Pornography and sexual aggression.* New York: Academic Press.

Donnerstein, E., & Barrett, G. (1978). Effects of erotic stimuli on male aggression toward females. *Journal of Personality and Social Psychology, 36,* 180-188.

Donnerstein, E., & Berkowitz, L. (1981). Victim reactions in aggressive erotic films as a factor in violence against women. *Journal of Personality and Social Psychology, 41,* 710-724.

Donnerstein, E., & Hallam, J. (1978). The facilitating effects of erotica on aggression against women. *Journal of Personality and Social Psychology, 36,* 1270-1277.

Dworkin, A. (1974). *Woman hating.* New York: Dutton.

Edmunds, G., & Kendrick, D. C. (1980). *The measurement of human aggressiveness.* Chichester, England: Ellis Horwood Ltd.

Feshbach, S. (1964). The function of aggression and the regulation of aggressive drive. *Psychological Review, 71,* 257-272.

Feshbach, S. (1970). Aggression. In P. H. Mussen (Ed.), *Carmichael's manual of child psychology,* New York: Wiley.

Gager, N., & Schurr, C. (1976). *Sexual assault: Confronting rape in America.* New York: Grosset & Dunlap.

Gebhard, P. H., Gagnon, J. H., Pomeroy, W. B., & Christenson, C. V. (1965). *Sex offenders.* New York: Harper & Row.

Greer, G. (1970). *The female eunuch.* New York: Bantam Books.

Griffin, S. (1971). *Rape: The all-American crime.* Andover, MA: Warner Modular Publications. (Reprinted from *Ramparts, 10*(3).)

Groth, A. N., & Birnbaum, H. J. (1980). The rapist: Motivations for sexual violence. In S. L. McCombie (Ed.), *The rape crisis intervention handbook.* New York: Plenum Press.

Groth, A. N., Burgess, A. W., & Holmstrom, L. L. (1977). Rape: Power, anger, and sexuality. *American Journal of Psychiatry, 134,* 1239-1243.

Guttmacher, M. S., & Weihofen, H. (1952). *Psychiatry and the law.* New York: Norton.

Hedges, L. E. (1970). Aggressive responses as a function of target cues and the possibility of retaliation. *Dissertation Abstracts International, 30,* 3385B-3386B.

Henley, N., & Freeman, J. (1981). Violence against women: A feminist-psychological analysis. In S. Cox (Ed.), *Female psychology* (2nd ed.). New York: St. Martin's Press.

Hynan, M. T., & Esselman, J. A. (1980). Victims and aggression. Unpublished manuscript, University of Wisconsin-Milwaukee.

Jaffe, Y., Malamuth, N. M., Feingold, J., & Feshbach, S. (1974). Sexual arousal and behavioral aggression. *Journal of Personality and Social Psychology, 30,* 759-764.

Johnson, A. G. (1980). On the prevalence of rape in the United States. *Signs: Journal of Women and Culture in Society, 6,* 136-146.

Kagan, J. (1964). Acquisition and significance of sex typing and sex role identity. In M. Hoffman & L. Hoffman (Eds.), *Review of child development research.* New York: Russell Sage Foundation.

Karpman, B. (1954). *The sexual offender and his offences.* New York: Julian Press.

Kaufman, H. (1970). *Aggression and altruism.* New York: Holt, Rinehart, and Winston.

Langley, R., & Levy, R. C. (1977). *Wife beating: The silent crisis.* New York: Dutton.

Larsen, K. S., Coleman, D., Forbes, J., & Johnson, R. (1972). Is the subject's personality or the experimental situation a better predictor of the subject's willingness to administer shock to a victim? *Journal of Personality and Social Psychology, 22,* 287-295.

Leidig, M. W. (1981). Violence against women: A feminist- psychological analysis. In S. Cox (Ed.), *Female psychology* (2nd edition). New York: St. Martin's Press.

Macdonald, J. M. (1971). *Rape: Offenders and their victims.* Springfield, IL: Charles C. Thomas.

Malamuth, N. M. (1981). Rape proclivity among males. *Journal of Social Issues, 37,* 138-157.

42   Hostility Toward Women

Melani, L., & Fodaski, L. (1974). The psychology of the rapist and his victim. In N. Connell & C. Wilson (Eds.), *Rape: The first sourcebook for women.* New York: The New American Library.

Millet, K. (1970). *Sexual politics.* Garden City, NY: Doubleday.

Moreland, D. (1977, September). Why are men angry at women? Paper presented at the Conference on Battered Women, American Friends Service Committee, New York.

Rada, R. T. (Ed.). (1978). *Clinical aspects of the rapist.* New York: Grune & Stratton.

Russell, D. E. H. (1975). *The politics of rape.* New York: Stein & Day.

Russell, D. E. H. (1982). *Rape in marriage.* New York: MacMillan.

Russell, D. E. H., & Lederer, L. (1980). Questions we get asked most often. In L. Lederer (Ed.), *Take back the night: Women on pornography.* New York: William Morrow and Co.

Shortell, J. R., & Biller, H. B. (1970). Aggression in children as a function of sex of subject and sex of opponent. *Developmental Psychology, 3,* 143-144.

Silverman, W. H. (1971). The effects of social contact, provocation, and sex of opponent upon instrumental aggression. *Journal of Experimental Research in Personality, 5,* 310-316.

Stark-Adamec, C., & Adamec, R. E. (1982). Aggression by men against women: Adaptation or aberration? *International Journal of Women's Studies, 5,* 1-21.

Stoller, R. J. (1970). Pornography and perversion. *Archives of General Psychiatry, 22,* 490-499.

Stoller, R. J. (1976). Sexual excitement. *Archives of General Psychiatry, 33,* 899-909.

Stoller, R. J. (1979). *Sexual excitement.* New York: Pantheon.

Straus, M. A., Gelles, R. J., & Steinmetz, S. K. (1980). *Behind closed doors.* Garden City, NY: Doubleday.

Taylor, S. P., & Epstein, S. (1967). Aggression as a function of the sex of the aggressor and the sex of the victim. *Journal of Personality, 35,* 474-486.

Taylor, S. P., & Smith, I. (1974). Aggression as a function of sex of victim and male subjects' attitude toward women. *Psychological Reports, 35,* 1095-1098.

Titley, R. W., & Viney, W. (1969). Expression of aggression toward the physically handicapped. *Perceptual and Motor Skills, 29,* 51-56.

Walker, L. E. (1981). A feminist perspective on domestic violence. In R. B. Stuart (Ed.), *Violent behavior: Social learning approaches to prediction, management, and treatment.* New York: Brunner-Mazel.

Whiting, B. B. (Ed.). (1963). *Six cultures: Studies of child rearing.* New York: Wiley.

Youssef, Z. I. (1968). The role of race, sex, hostility and verbal stimulus in inflicting punishment. *Psychonomic Science, 12,* 285-286.

Zillmann, D. (1979). *Hostility and aggression.* Hillsdale, NJ: Erlbaum.

Chapter 3

Sexual Aggression in Acquaintance Relationships

Barry R. Burkhart and Annette L. Stanton

In 1981, the number of forcible rapes reported to police in the United States was 81,536 (U. S. Department of Justice, 1983). In the same year, the National Crime Survey, based on a victimization survey of 60,000 households, estimated the number of rapes at 178,000 (U. S. Department of Justice, 1983). There is widespread agreement among researchers that such figures represent only a fraction of a true annual incidence rate. Rape is the most underreported of the major crimes, particularly if the sexually aggressive event does not correspond to the social stereotype of rape (Skelton & Burkhart, 1980).

The legal definition of rape varies by jurisdiction, but the basic dimensions are relatively constant and include three major elements: (a) carnal knowledge of a woman, defined as sexual penetration, (b) lack of consent to this carnal knowledge, and (c) use of force or threat of force to accomplish the act. The legal definition, despite its apparent simplicity, is operationalized only through a complex, restrictive social definition of rape. Based on extensive data (Burt, 1980; Burt & Albin, 1981; Klemmack & Klemmack, 1976; Weis & Borges, 1973) it is evident that the social definition of rape is quite incongruous with the legal definition and displays a characteristic set of biases primarily reflecting what Burt (1980) has labeled the rape-supportive belief system. Thus the question "What is a rape?" is not answered by a powerful legal litmus test but through a system of beliefs that derive from a misogynistic social content, the "rape culture" (Brownmiller, 1975). Pertinent to this chapter is the consistent finding that relationship status is a very powerful component of the social definition of rape (Burt, 1980; Klemmack & Klemmack, 1976; Koss & Oros, 1982; Skelton & Burkhart, 1980), with the degree of acquaintance being negatively correlated with an attribution of rape by victims, offenders, and other citizens. Even the legal statutes reflect this in at least one relationship circumstance, as many states restrict the definition of rape to a victim who is not the spouse of the offender.

The effects of this bias are many and frequently malevolent. Methodologically, a critical effect is that acquaintance rapes are very much less likely to be perceived as deviant, even by the participants. Koss and her associates (Koss, 1985; Koss & Oros, 1982) have found that most college-aged women forced into intercourse by acquaintances do not define themselves as being raped. Likewise, offenders do not define themselves as rapists (Rapaport & Burkhart, 1984). Thus, epidemiological work assessing the incidence of "rapes" between acquaintances will inevitably underestimate the true number of sexually coercive events, because for most people the phrase "acquaintance rape" is an oxymoron.

In order to develop a more accurate estimate of the magnitude of this problem, researchers have developed measures based on a behaviorally anchored set of questions. This procedure allows a researcher to obtain reports of events via behavioral descriptions, which can then be matched to a criterion definition of rape and thus bypass the subjective bias introduced by using the word "rape." Such research allows a glimpse into those sexually aggressive events that otherwise would be "hidden rapes" (Koss, 1984). The key feature in most hidden rape is that it occurs between people who know each other and often, in fact, are involved in a courtship relationship. This chapter focuses on acquaintance rapes: their incidence, characteristics of participants, and dynamics.

EPIDEMIOLOGY — WOMEN

In their pioneering work, Kirkpatrick and Kanin (1957) found that 55.7% of a sample (N = 291) of college women surveyed by questionnaire reported being offended at some level of erotic intimacy during the previous academic year. Of the women who reported having been offended, 20.9% had experienced forceful attempts at intercourse and 6.2% had experienced "aggressively forceful attempts at sex [sic] intercourse in the course of which menacing threats or coercive infliction of physical pain were employed" (p. 53). Furthermore, these experiences were not isolated incidents, the offended women had experienced a mean of 6.3 sexually aggressive episodes each.

In their replication of this research 20 years after the original studies, Kanin and Parcell (1977) found that approximately 83% of college women had experienced sexually offensive male aggression during their dating history. During the immediately preceding year, 50.7% indicated that they had experienced "offensive and displeasing" sexual aggression. On the average, 5.1 aggressive episodes were reported by offended women. These researchers, comparing the rates 20 years apart, concluded that "the incidence and frequency of sexually offensive male conduct in dating courtship relations, according to our data, appear to have remained relatively unchanged" (p. 75).

Skelton (1982) obtained data roughly equivalent to those reported above. Surveying 263 single undergraduate women students, she found that only 4% reported no aggressive episodes during their courtship history and 25% had experienced at least one instance of coerced, nonconsensual intercourse. In this research, women were requested to provide more detailed information about the three most "offensive and displeasing" sexually aggressive events ever experienced. Of the 789 possible events, 706 incidents were described. Of these, only 31 involved strangers, representing about 4% of the total victimization episodes. Acquaintances or first dates accounted for approximately 36% of the episodes, occasional dates for 26%, and regular or steady dates accounted for 31% of the sexually aggressive events. Clearly, among college students, sexual aggression is relatively rare between strangers and more common between men and women who know each other, particularly if there is some minimal level of courtship relationship between them.

In order to better define the quality of these events, Skelton asked subjects to describe the types of coercive methods utilized in the aggressive incidents. By far the most common method, accounting for 48% of the aggressive incidents, was simply ignoring the victim's protests and requests to stop. Next most common was verbal coercion, accounting for 32% of the total of the offensive or displeasing events. Physical restraint was used in approximately 15% of the episodes. Various kinds of threats or physical aggression were used in 6% of the episodes.

Koss and her colleagues (Koss, 1985; Koss & Oros, 1982) employed a behaviorally anchored scale (the Sexual Experiences Survey) and reported that 13% of a large (N = 2016) sample of women students at a midwestern state university reported having experienced sexual victimization that involved threat or use of physical force which resulted in a nonconsenting act of intercourse. An additional 24% of the women sampled reported an experience of sexual victimization which involved attempted rape. Thus, over a third of the women sampled had had at least one victimization experience meeting the legal definition of rape or attempted rape. Furthermore, 33% of women reported that at least one experience of nonconsenting intercourse had occurred because the woman "felt it was useless to stop him."

Relevant to the previous discussion of the impact of the social belief system on defining sexually aggressive events as rape, Koss and Oros (1982) included an item on the Sexual Experiences Survey directly asking women if they had ever been raped. In a follow-up with women who agreed to be interviewed, Koss (1984) found that only 57% of the women who had had intercourse against their will through use of or threat of force acknowledged that they had been raped. All of those women (43%) who did not acknowledge that rape had occurred knew their assailants; none of them reported the experience to police, and only

13% went to a hospital or rape crisis center. Koss (1985) estimated from her data that at least ten times more rapes occurred in her population of women students than would be noted in official statistics. Furthermore, the confounding effect of relationship status on reporting rates is evident. These results have been replicated by several other studies (Korman & Leslie, 1982; Wilson & Durrenberger, 1982). Taken together these data reveal that sexual aggression and dating appear to go hand in hand.

EPIDEMIOLOGY — MEN

Kanin (1967, 1969) also attempted to obtain data about the prevalence of male sexual aggression by using the self-report of randomly selected male undergraduates. In order to be defined as sexually aggressive, the male had to acknowledge that he had made a forceful attempt at coitus and that his attempt had caused observable distress (e.g., fighting, screaming, crying) in the woman. Of the 341 men for whom completed surveys were obtained, 87 (25.5%) reported at least one such episode.

Rapaport and Burkhart (1984) also have collected epidemiological data on the prevalence of sexually aggressive behavior using males' self-reports. In a survey of 201 male undergraduates, they found that only 29% of the sample denied any form of sexually aggressive behavior and 15% had had intercourse with a woman against her will. Further, 61% of the men admitted that they had fondled a woman's breast against her will, 42% had removed or disarranged a woman's outer garments, 32% had removed or disarranged a woman's underclothing, and 37% had touched a woman's genitals against her will.

Additionally, information about the methods used by the men in coercing sexual behavior was obtained. By far the most common method was attempting to verbally convince a woman, with 70% of the sample reporting having used this method. Ignoring a woman's protest was also a relatively common practice, with 35% of the men acknowledging use of this method. Directly aggressive methods were less common, but still in evidence, with 11% of the men using physical restraint, 6% using threats, and 3% employing physical violence to coerce sexual contact.

Finally, Koss and Oros (1982) administered the Sexual Experiences Survey to 1,846 male undergraduate students. Consistent with previous research, they found a relatively high frequency of self-reported sexual aggression. Fifteen percent of the males reported obtaining sex by coercive verbal pressure and 19% acknowledged saying things that were not true to obtain sex. In her survey, 2.4% of the subjects reported forcing intercourse through threats or physical aggression.

In summary, research relevant to the prevalence and incidence of acquaintance rape demonstrates that, above all, this and other forms of sexual aggression are common. Sexual aggression, at least by count, is normative; it is embedded in the social structure of courtship. Perhaps the only caveat to this summary is the almost exclusive reliance on college samples. However, studies not using college samples (e.g., Russell, 1982) support the data obtained with college students; therefore, this conclusion appears robust.

Given this conclusion, how can we understand it? From our perspective, it is clear that prevalence rates of this magnitude rule out total reliance on either the "sick person" or the "victim precipitation" models. Instead, situational and individual differences may interact with normative social controls in determining aggressive sexual interaction. In the next sections of this chapter, we will try to frame an understanding of the prevalence of acquaintance rape that accounts for the person, the social context, and the immediate situation.

VICTIM AND OFFENDER CHARACTERISTICS

In this section, we will review research addressed to the characteristics of the victims and offenders involved in acquaintance rape as a beginning of a conceptual account of this phenomenon. Prior to reviewing these empirical data, it is necessary to address a troublesome conceptual issue. Research on sexual aggression, like research on other socially embedded behaviors, can be limited by its theoretical and cultural perspective. Rape is an event surrounded by myths (Brownmiller, 1975; Burt, 1980; Clark & Lewis, 1977; Feild, 1978; Griffin, 1971; Weis & Borges, 1973), most of which have pernicious attributions of responsibility for victims and exculpatory effects for offenders. Thus, it is critical that researchers and reviewers be bound by data, not myth. Perhaps the difficulty of this process can be appreciated by the observation, well-known to contemporary researchers in the area of sexual aggression, that *victims themselves, are very likely to blame themselves for their victimization, reality to the contrary.* Thus, self-report data are likely to be biased at the source. Researchers unaware of this bias may not be able to identify the full dimensions or dynamics of coercive sexual behavior. Further, researchers who do not understand how these cultural myths may contaminate data collection may be unwitting participants in the process of "blaming the victim" (Ryan, 1971).

Victim Characteristics

Kanin, in his early prevalence studies, was the first to investigate the characteristics of victims (Kanin, 1957) and offending men (Kanin, 1969). In his early study, Kanin (1957) examined a number of demographic and situational variables to determine those that differentiated between offended and nonoffended women undergraduates. Dating frequency, number of different men dated, and church attendance did not significantly differentiate offended from nonoffended women. Certain other characteristics of the women's families did appear to have some relevance; for example, having an older brother and having parents who warned their daughters about male sexual aggression were found to be more characteristic of nonoffended women. Several features of the relationship also were associated with offended status. In general, Kanin (1957) suggested that offending pair relationships were heterogamous in terms of social status, age, etc. Surprisingly, sexual aggression at more advanced levels was associated more with long-term relationships than with casual pairings. Most (59%) of the sexually aggressive episodes were preceded by some level of consensual sexual activity, particularly in long-term relationships; sexual aggression that occurred with no preceding consensual sexual activity was confined largely to casual dating relationships.

In their follow-up study, Kanin and Parcell (1977) again examined situational and social characteristics of offended women. Contrary to Kanin's earlier research, no support was found for the significance of demographic variables. Thus, Kanin's original interpretation of the offending episodes reflecting a pattern of "male exploitation of females possessing 'inferior' or heterogamous characteristics" (p. 75) was not viable (Kanin & Parcell, 1977). Instead, Kanin and Parcell observed that male sexual aggression had changed in that the aggression occurred earlier and without regard for the quality of the relationship. They interpreted this finding to mean that "all females appear to have become suitable targets regardless of the stage of premarital intimacy, including the most casual and impersonal" (p. 76). The researchers found that, overall, there were few powerful differences between offended and nonoffended women, with the exception that women who had been victimized within the last year had an overall history of being sexually victimized more frequently than nonoffended women.

This pattern of victimization predicting more victimization has been found in several other studies. Wilson and Durrenberger (1982) found that half of the rape victims in their study had experienced at least one other rape attempt. Kirkpatrick and Kanin (1957) also noted that the frequency of offending episodes, repeated by the same man with the victimized woman, ranged from no repetitions to an average of two depending on the level of offensive behavior. This tolerance of sexual abuse, which the authors interpreted as being due to the woman's emotional involvement with the male, was postulated to increase a woman's vulnerability to victimization.

The results of a study by Korman and Leslie (1982) also suggest that being victimized is rarely an isolated instance. In their sample, offended college women had a mean of 5.7 episodes since their senior year of high school and 74% had experienced multiple types of offensive behavior. Korman and Leslie hypothesized that adherence to a feminist ideology and willingness to share date expenses would be associated with fewer episodes of sexual aggression. However, they found no support for either hypothesis.

The failure to demonstrate consistent personality or attitudinal differences between offended and nonoffended women was supported in Koss' (1985) research about hidden rape victims. In her study, Koss attempted to determine whether the variables associated with three major models of rape victimization – social control, victim precipitation, and situational blame – were predictive of victimization status. To test these different models, a large sample of undergraduate students was screened with the Sexual Experiences Survey and all subjects were invited to participate in an in-depth interview. Approximately 25% of the total sample were willing to be interviewed. From these subjects, five groups at four levels of victimization and one with no victimization history were interviewed and completed questionnaires selected to measure variables relevant to the three models of rape victimization. Results indicated that, generally, attitudinal or personality variables did not significantly discriminate between groups, although several demographic and situational variables did. Nonvictimized women, compared to the four victimized groups, had fewer sexual partners, were older at the time of their first intercourse, and had more conservative sexual values. Additionally, situational features specific to the assault experience differed among the four sexually victimized groups. The low-victimized women reported that they were exposed to less coercion than the other offended groups, resisted less, and were not further victimized. The moderately victimized women experienced less physical coercion than the highly victimized groups, but exhibited equivalently intense resistance that apparently had greater impact on their offenders. Koss suggested that these findings could reflect offender characteristics, with the highly victimized group being paired with men less responsive to the women's resistance.

Skelton (1982) also investigated correlates of victimization experiences. She surveyed 263 undergraduate women via a questionnaire designed to elicit detailed information about sexual victimization experiences. Also administered were measures of demographic variables, dating history, sexual history, sexual communication style, Burt's (1980) rape belief measures, locus of control, self-esteem, assertiveness, and ratings by subjects of their usual and ideal dating partners on the Bem Sex Role Inventory. All of these measures were used in several regression procedures as predictors of the two criteria of sexual victimization: (a) the number of victimization experiences within the previous six months, and (b) the maximum level of sexual aggression sustained during the dating history.

Although there was a number of significant zero-order correlations between the predictors and the two criteria, no single variable or set of variables generated very large correlation coefficients. However, it did appear that the two criteria were related to different sets of predictors. A stepwise regression procedure indicated that the significant predictors of the number of victimization experiences were, in order: (a) the victim's score on the Adversarial Sexual Beliefs Scale, (b) the number of dating partners, (c) the Bem Sex Role Inventory masculinity scale score for usual dating partner, (d) self- esteem, and (e) the victim's score on the assertion inventory. Both self-esteem and assertion levels were negatively correlated with the number of victimizations. Although all the above variables were significant, it should be noted that the total multiple R for these five predictors was only .36. Thus, the prediction model accounted for less than 14% of the variance before cross-validation.

The significant predictors of the maximum level of sexual aggression sustained were, in order of magnitude: (a) the number of sexual partners in the previous six months, (b) the number of dating partners in the previous six months, (c) the score on Burt's Sex Role Stereotyping Scale, (d) the number of dates in the previous month, and (e) reliance on nonverbal means of communication for sexual consent. Again, however, the multiple R for these five significant predictors was only .42, which accounted for less than 18% of the criterion variance.

Victimization status of women, then, does not seem very predictable, and significant predictors appear to relate to enhancing vulnerability by increasing the risk of exposure to a sexually aggressive dating partner. However, there is also some evidence that less assertive styles of communication in both general and sexual situations may be relevant. The notion that the sex role socialization of women heightens their vulnerability is suggested in the literature (Weis & Borges, 1973); however, to this point, there is little empirical evidence for this hypothesis. Nonetheless, the ready assumption of blame by victims for their victimization experience does support the importance of the sex role socialization process. A powerful illustration of this process and how it might operate is revealed in the example of one of our subjects. She had been raped by her date at a fraternity party. It was an unambiguous, forceful sexual assault, obviously planned by her date. It had been a very traumatic event for her and she was still having emotional problems as a result. During the interview, she was asked about how the assailant had responded to her resistance. She hesitated before replying and said:

> Even as I say this now it sounds crazy to me, after what he did to me...but I didn't scream, not because I didn't think to scream. I remember thinking about screaming as I tried to fight him off, but I decided not to scream...I can't believe I even thought this...I decided not to scream because *I didn't want to embarrass him*...

This poignant statement clearly illuminates the bind of the feminine sex-role socialization process. Adhering to her role of being nurturant and kind compromised her ability to be powerful and self-determining. Such acceptance of emotional responsibility in the relationship may be critical to the vulnerability of women. We are currently examining this in our research.

Before turning our attention to the characteristics of sexually aggressive males, the effects of the sexual victimization of women by acquaintances will be reviewed. While there are many studies examining victim reactions to rapes reported to crisis centers or police (see Ellis (1984) for a review), there is very little research addressed specifically to the reactions of victims of sexual assault perpetrated by acquaintances. To remedy this deficiency, Rogers (1984) assessed the effects of coercive sexual experiences occurring within dating relationships on the social and psychological adjustment of college women. Subjects were 260 undergraduate women, who provided specific information about their most offensive experience with sexually aggressive behavior. Three comprehensive sets of effect measures, reflecting psychiatric symptomatology, social adjustment, and personality functioning were developed. Results of her analyses revealed significant overall relationships between the levels of the offense sustained by the victim and each of the three sets of effect measures. Specifically, exposure to a greater degree of sexual aggression was associated with significantly higher levels of anxiety, greater guilt associated with sexual behavior, and poorer overall social and family adjustment. Exposure to more aggressive methods of coercive sexual behavior was associated with generally poorer overall social adjustment. It is surprising that the relationships between the recency of offense and all three sets of effect measures were nonsignificant. Thus, there was no support for the notion that the intensity of the victim's response dissipated with time.

Sexual aggression in courtship situations appears anything but benign. Such negative effects, in conjunction with the high incidence rates, suggest that sexual aggression is a pathogen whose impact on women's lives is seriously underestimated. It is curious and discouraging that it has taken so long to recognize this fact.

Offender Characteristics

Women's personality and attitudinal variables generally do not predict victimization status of women. Moreover, the variability in victimization status associated with features involving the characteristics of male offenders clearly implicates the need for research with sexually coercive men. Kanin (1967, 1969) was the first researcher to investigate the characteristics of male sexual aggression in the courtship setting. In a survey study of 341 college men, supplemented with case material obtained via direct interview or anonymous biography from approximately 60 other university men, Kanin found that 87 (25.5%) reported at least one sexually aggressive episode since entering college. The most compelling finding was that "the sexually aggressive male, in contrast to his non-aggressive peers, has not only had considerably more sexual experience but is persistently seeking new sexual involvements and utilizing more surreptitious techniques with greater frequency in order to obtain sexual activity" (Kanin, 1967, p. 429). Despite their greater sexual experience, sexually aggressive males were more dissatisfied with their sexual activity than nonaggressive males (Kanin, 1967, 1983). In part, Kanin (1969) attributed this to the pressure for sexual activity experienced by sexually aggressive males as a consequence of a strong peer-group emphasis on sexual conquest, although he also noted that the interpersonal style of these men in their relationships with women "may be characterized as predatory" (Kanin, 1967, p. 432).

Recent theorizing about sexual aggression has broadened considerably from a focus on a peer-group process to a conception of sexual aggression "as an instrument of male dominance, embedded in and supported by the social structure" (Rapaport & Burkhart, 1984, p. 216). Thus, attention has turned to an examination of the "rape culture" (Brownmiller, 1975; Clark & Lewis, 1977; Weis & Borges, 1973). The rape culture is distinguished by beliefs, attitudes, and social patterns that legitimize and support forms of sexual aggression against women as a way of maintaining the inequitable distribution of power in society. In its extreme form, this model would assert that rape "is nothing more or less than a conscious process of intimidation by which all men keep all women in a state of fear" (Brownmiller, 1975, p. 15). This conceptual framework, emphasizing the rape- supportive cultural context, has often been contrasted to the psychopathological model, which holds that rape is an individually determined behavior reflecting personal dynamics of the rapist. The extreme form of the psychopathological model holds that rape is a sexual aberration engaged in by deviant men. Relevant to this section is that these two models form the base for much of the contemporary research about the dynamics of male involvement in acquaintance rape (Koss, 1985; Rapaport & Burkhart, 1984).

In a study directly assessing the adequacy of these two models, Koss, Leonard, Beezley, and Oros (1985) identified sexually aggressive males by surveying a large sample of male undergraduate students (N = 1,846). Based on their responses to the Sexual Experiences Survey, subjects were designated into four groups varying from sexually nonaggressive to sexually assaultive at the level of rape. After responding to the survey, willing subjects participated in further assessment procedures, which included measures chosen to reflect the two conceptual domains of social conflict and individual psychopathology. Using a discriminant-analysis procedure, Koss et al. found that the four groups were significantly discriminated by biographical items, number of sexual partners, and six attitude scales. Men who were more sexually aggressive had more sexual partners and had higher scores on measures reflecting belief in rape-supportive attitudes. The measures derived from the individual psychopathology model did not discriminate between the groups.

The research of Burkhart and his students also has been guided by the conceptual distinction between psychopathological and social- conflict models (Rapaport & Burkhart, 1984; Rapaport, 1984). This program of research has been oriented toward identifying men who display varying levels of sexual aggression and determining what factors predict their level of aggressive sexual behavior. Like Koss et al., (1985), they reasoned that the personality variables found to distinguish convicted rapists (Armentrout & Hauer, 1978; Groth, 1979; Rada,

1978; Rader, 1977) would be useful in identifying the types of personality characteristics that sexually coercive males might possess. Furthermore, they hypothesized that sexually aggressive men would endorse a pattern of beliefs characterized by sex role stereotypes of women, an adversarial heterosexual stance, an acceptance of interpersonal violence, and a disinhibition to the use of force as a way of resolving conflict.

The methodology used in the Rapaport and Burkhart study differed from Koss et al. (1985). Koss' procedure was to administer a screening instrument and then invite further extended participation from subjects to extract predictor or further criterion data, while our procedure was to administer all instruments to all subjects in the initial contact. This avoided the problem of differential rates of participation across the different levels of sexual aggression and was intended to reduce the impact of volunteerism biases in the data. Additionally, because subjects did not have to be recontacted, the data collection procedures were conducted under conditions of complete anonymity.

In the first study (Rapaport & Burkhart, 1984), 201 male undergraduates completed a battery of measures selected to reflect conceptually relevant dimensions of coercive sexuality. These included: (a) Responsibility, Socialization, and Empathy scales from the California Psychological Inventory (CPI); (b) Burt's (1980) scales, including Own Sex Role Satisfaction, Sex Role Stereotyping, Adversarial Sexual Beliefs, Sexual Conversation, and Acceptance of Interpersonal Violence; (c) the Attitudes Toward Women Scale; (d) the Endorsement of Force Scale, developed specifically for this study to assess the degree to which subjects endorsed the use of force by the male to obtain sexual acts; and (e) the Coercive Sexuality Scale (CSS), the criterion measure developed to define a continuum of coercive sexual behavior.

Data were analyzed with correlation and regression procedures using the total CSS score as a criterion and the other measures as predictors. Regression analyses indicated that the CSS score was predictable; for the equation combining all predictors, the multiple $R = .45$, ($p < .0001$). The significant variables were: Responsibility and Socialization from the CPI, Adversarial Sexual Beliefs and Acceptance of Interpersonal Violence from Burt's (1980) scales, and the Endorsement of Force Scale. Thus, unlike the Koss et al. findings (1985), characterological as well as attitudinal variables were significant predictors of sexual aggression.

It appears, then, that in addition to the social conflict dynamics, there is support for characterological mediation of sexual aggression. Such support also was found in a follow-up study (Rapaport, 1984). Reasoning that if sexual aggression was part of a general antisocial style, Rapaport predicted that sexually coercive men should evidence more frequent and more intense nonsexual antisocial conduct. This is just what she found: sexually aggressive males were much more likely to have histories of antisocial conduct of all types. Therefore it seems that sexually aggressive males are, in fact, characterized by both a general antisocial stance and a misogynistic attitudinal structure. As Rapaport and Burkhart (1984) state:

> It appears then, that sexually coercive males act on a system of values wherein females are perceived as adversaries, and that this value system is potentiated by the characterological dimensions of irresponsibility and poor socialization. Sexual encounters become the setting for the behavioral expression of this combination of values and personality traits. (p. 220)

Additionally, Rapaport (1984) was interested in determining whether other characteristics of incarcerated rapists would be found in acquaintance rapists. Recent research with rapists found that they evidenced higher sexual arousal than nonrapists controls to aggressive sexual stimuli (Abel, Barlow, Blanchard, & Guild, 1977). In fact, the average sexual arousal of rapists was as high to aggressive sexual stimuli as it was to presentations of consensual sexual activity. Postulating a continuity between convicted rapists and acquaintance rapists, Rapaport presented groups of acquaintance rapists, sexually coercive men who had not coerced intercourse, and noncoercive men with three types of sexual stimuli: (a) consenting intercourse; (b) rape, with the woman victim experiencing orgasm, and (c) rape with the victim response being disgust. She found that both the acquaintance rape and sexually coercive groups were more sexually aroused to all three types of sexual stimuli. Thus, sexually aggressive males responded with significantly more sexual arousal to rape presentations as well as to depictions of consenting intercourse. These data are consistent with the notion that heterosexual relationships among sexually aggressive males are motivationally overdetermined (Kanin, 1969, 1983). It appears characteristic of such men to define heterosexual relationships by reference to both sexual and hostile, power-oriented criteria. Thus, sexual activity comes to serve not just sexual motives, but needs for power and anger expression. The combination of these motives may be responsible for the great significance that sexually aggressive men place on their sexual conquest. Sexual activity is doubly reinforced by its ability to gratify both sexual and power needs.

One other line of research should be mentioned in reference to male involvement in sexual violence. Malamuth and his colleagues have systematically examined characteristics of men who acknowledge some likelihood of raping a woman given an assurance of not being caught or punished (Malamuth, 1981, 1983; Malamuth & Check, 1983; Tieger, 1981). The basic hypothesis of their program of research is that many "normal" men possess a proclivity to rape which can be assessed by their self-reported likelihood of raping in circumstances assuring freedom from punishment. Their research has supported an association between the characteristics of convicted rapists and men who report a high likelihood of raping in terms of acceptance of rape myths and sexual arousal to rape stimuli. Further, higher likelihood of raping did predict greater aggression against women within a laboratory context (Malamuth, 1983).

Summarizing the data about personality, attitudinal, and situational variables involved in acquaintance rape is difficult. However, two overall trends emerge. First, male involvement in sexual aggression is strongly related to a set of misogynistic and rape-supportive beliefs and attitudes, a tendency to define heterosexual relationships in an overdetermined motivational manner, and a personality style characterized by interpersonal irresponsibility, hostility (particularly toward women) and a deficit in basic socialization. Second, it appears that women's involvement in sexually aggressive episodes, though not well predicted by their personality or attitudinal characteristics, may be associated with sex role demands, although the evidence is indirect at this point. However, situational features, all of which appear to enhance vulnerability by increasing the woman's chance of exposure to a sexually aggressive male, do predict victimization.

ACQUAINTANCE RAPE AS A SOCIAL PHENOMENON

Perhaps the most prominent theme running through writings regarding rape (e.g., Brownmiller, 1975; Klemmack & Klemmack, 1976; Weis & Borges, 1973) is that coercive sexuality represents a natural consequence of the firmly embedded cultural tradition of male dominance coupled with an acceptance of interpersonal violence toward women. According to this thesis, differential gender-role socialization acts to normalize rape and promote its occurrence through the promulgation of a constellation of rape- supportive beliefs and patterns of interaction between males and females that are conducive to sexual aggression. We will first examine culturally transmitted beliefs that may serve to condone rape and go on to review the literature regarding characteristic communication patterns that may promote sexual aggression.

Rape-Supportive Beliefs

Brownmiller (1975) pointed to the importance of a culturally transmitted belief system in condoning rape, among which are: "All women want to be raped." "No woman can be raped against her will." "She was asking for it." "If you're going to be raped, you might as well relax and enjoy it." She noted, "These are the deadly male myths of rape, the distorted proverbs that govern female sexuality" (pp. 311-312). Empirical demonstration of the existence of such beliefs would provide preliminary support for Brownmiller's thesis.

The endorsement by the general public of rape myths has been demonstrated by several researchers (Barnett & Feild, 1977; Burt, 1978, 1980; Feild, 1978). Burt (1980) found a substantial degree of agreement with rape myths, with over half her adult sample endorsing statements such as: "In the majority of rapes, the victim was promiscuous or had a bad reputation" and "A woman who goes to the home or apartment of a man on the first date implies she is willing to have sex." Feild (1978) found that the degree of rape myth acceptance differed among respondent groups (e.g., police officers, rape-crisis counselors, citizens, convicted rapists), with citizens and the police being more similar to rapists than to rape-crisis counselors in their attitudes toward rape. Adherence to such beliefs has been found to occur in the absence of substantial knowledge regarding the actualities of rape (Feild, 1978) and to appear more prominent in men than in women (Ashton, 1982; Barnett & Feild, 1977; Check & Malamuth, 1983; Feild, 1978; Malamuth & Check, 1981). For example, Barnett and Feild (1977) found that 33% of male undergraduate subjects endorsed the belief that it would do some women good to get raped, as compared with only 8% of female subjects.

Indirect evidence for the prominence of rape myths comes from the substantial literature regarding attribution of causality in cases of rape. Primarily, this body of research relies on assessing subjects' perceptions regarding who is "at fault" in hypothetical descriptions of rape, which typically vary the characterological or descriptive characteristics of the victim, assailant, or environmental cues. Of primary interest here is the obtained gender difference in attribution of responsibility to the assailant or the rape victim. As in studies directly assessing rape myths, females generally find greater fault with the rapist, while males often place greater responsibility with the victim than do females (Calhoun, Selby, & Warring, 1976; Cann, Calhoun, & Selby, 1979; Kanekar & Kolsawalla, 1980; Thornton, Robbins, & Johnson, 1981; Thornton & Ryckman, 1983).

These studies often demonstrate that male subjects more often endorse such beliefs as "the female victim had an 'unconscious' desire to be raped" (Cann et al., 1979) and also demonstrate that subjects often assign blame based on rather superficial descriptive characteristics of the victim. This lends credence to the hypothesis that rape myths are embedded in a characteristic belief structure, although it should be noted that in some of the studies (e.g., Thornton & Ryckman, 1983), the more general finding was of lesser responsibility attributed to the victim than to the rapist.

One possible explanation of the tendency of men to assign greater responsibility to the victim than do women lies in the hypothesized differences in empathy. In attribution studies, females are often found to identify more with the victim (Smith, Keating, Hester, & Mitchell, 1976), whereas males tend to identify with the rapist (Krulewitz, 1981). Deitz, Blackwell, Daley, and Bentley (1982) constructed the Rape Empathy Scale in order to assess the tendency to assume the psychological perspective of the characters involved in the rape incident. As predicted, they found that females possessed greater empathy toward the rape victim than males and that the degree of empathy toward the victim was a better predictor of causal rape attributions than was a measure of traditionality of attitudes toward women. Subjects scoring high on the Rape Empathy Scale were more likely to assume the victim's perspective and assigned a harsher punishment to a hypothetical rapist. Thus, Deitz et al. argued that women's greater ability to identify with the victim contributes to obtained sex differences in attribution of responsibility. This argument is bolstered by a study by Tieger (1981), in which feminine subjects (as measured by the Bem Sex Role Inventory), regardless of their gender, had greater empathy toward the victim.

Another relevant finding from the attribution literature is the demonstration that the greater the acquaintance between victim and assailant, the less "serious" the rape is judged (L'Armand & Pepitone, 1982) and the less likely the incident is to be defined as "rape" (Klemmack & Klemmack, 1976; Oros, Leonard, & Koss, 1980). Employing a female subject sample, Klemmack and Klemmack (1976) found that the likelihood of defining a situation as rape varied directly with the perceived degree of acquaintance between victim and assailant: "If any relationship is known to exist between the victim and the accused, no matter how casual, the proportion of those who consider the event rape drops to less than 50 percent" (p. 144).

Noting this reluctance on the part of observers and actors to view rape between acquaintances as "real" rape, Shotland and Goodstein (1983) examined subjects' decision processes regarding rape-attribution in a situation involving moderate acquaintance (i.e., a hypothetical couple who had been dating for approximately two months). Undergraduate subjects were presented with descriptions of a date in which the level of force used by the male to obtain intercourse and levels of timing and type of protest against sexual activity used by the female were manipulated. These researchers found that subjects were more likely to blame the female and to perceive her as desiring sex when the male was portrayed as using little force and the female was portrayed as protesting late during sexual foreplay. The hypothetical incident was more likely to be defined by subjects as rape when there was more force used by the male and more intense protest by the female that occurred early during sexual activity. Further, those with more egalitarian attitudes toward women were less likely to perceive the female as desiring sex, less likely to blame the victim, and more likely to define the incident as rape. From these data, it is clear that many individuals hold particular beliefs about the definitional components of rape, which diverge from legal definitions.

How do these beliefs about rape develop? Again, a feminist analysis would place the onus of responsibility on the cultural milieu. Thus, an examination of the antecedents of rape-myth acceptance is instructive. Burt (1980) attempted such an investigation and found that rape-myth acceptance was predicted by an acceptance of interpersonal violence (particularly directed by men toward women), traditional sex-role stereotyping (see also Acock & Ireland, 1983; Feild, 1978), and an expectancy that sexual relationships are fundamentally exploitative. Thus, it appears that more general attitudes regarding male-female relationships may precipitate rape-supportive beliefs.

After marshalling support for the importance of a broader attitudinal constellation in engendering rape-supportive beliefs, Burt and Albin (1981) went on to the next conceptual link, that of demonstrating the consequences of rape-myth acceptance. They found that greater acceptance of interpersonal violence renders one less willing to convict a hypothetical rapist and that stronger rape-myth acceptance leads to a more restrictive definition of rape, potentially engendering a denial of the reality of many rapes. Thus, the hypothesized connection between adherence to rape-supportive beliefs and the normalization of rape was obtained. It is more difficult to demonstrate a direct link between the existence of rape-supportive beliefs and the actual occurrence of rape, although the work of Malamuth (Check & Malamuth, 1983; Malamuth, 1981) and Burkhart (Rapaport & Burkhart, 1984) suggests that males who are rated as likely to commit rape and males who do rape acquaintances are also likely to accept rape myths, interpersonal violence, adversarial sexual beliefs, and to engage in sex-role stereotyping.

In summary, we have seen that many individuals, particularly males, hold rape-supportive beliefs, that these beliefs tend to occur within a broader constellation of attitudes that include sex-role stereotyping, adversarial sexual beliefs, and acceptance of interpersonal violence. This attitudinal structure is believed to be firmly embedded in a cultural tradition which serves to legitimize sexual aggression and to minimize its consequences. Much of the empirical literature thus far reviewed, however, has not been specific to coercive sexuality between acquaintances. We now examine the process by which cultural messages translate to behaviors among dating couples that eventually lead to forcible sexual contact.

COERCIVE SEXUALITY AMONG DATING COUPLES: THE INTERACTIONAL CONTEXT

In itself, the finding that acquaintance rape occurs with such frequency on the college campus lends support to the thesis that sexual aggression is a culturally sanctioned phenomenon. Many writers (e.g., Check & Malamuth, 1983; Klemmack & Klemmack, 1976; Weis & Borges, 1973) agree that the American dating system provides a stage conducive to rape. Weis and Borges (1973) asserted: "The dating system can easily lead to rape. It places actors with highly socialized but differing expectations into a socially approved but ambiguous situation in which there is maximum privacy" (p. 89).

What are these "highly socialized expectations?" Gagnon and Simon (1973) suggest that all sexual behavior involves social scripts which "define the situation, name the actors, and plot the behavior" (p. 19). For the dating couple, these scripts provide guidelines for initiating and participating in sexual interaction in novel situations. We have already found that individuals, particularly males, may include in their sexual scripts general rape-supportive beliefs, which they bring into the dating situation. Additional evidence that dating couples adhere to specific beliefs that may promote coercive sexuality is derived from several sources. One such belief was postulated by Brownmiller (1975), who pointed to the underlying cultural assumption that it is the natural masculine role to proceed aggressively toward a sexual goal, while the natural feminine role is to "resist" or "submit" (p. 385). Studies that examine the normal dating behaviors of university students lend credence to this hypothesis. In their two-year longitudinal study of couples who were "going together," Peplau, Rubin, and Hill (1977) found that although 95% of their subjects advocated identical sexual standards for males and females in a love relationship, couples' actual behaviors reflected beliefs consistent with Brownmiller's hypothesis. The authors concluded, "Men continue to exert positive control; they play the role of sexual initiator. This does not mean, of course, that women have no part in initiating sex. Women may indeed communicate, often subtly, that they are interested and willing. Women continue to hold negative control, however; they can reject the man's advances or slow the pace of increasing sexual intimacy" (p. 96).

Further, McCormick and her colleagues (LaPlante, McCormick, & Brannigan, 1980; McCormick, 1979), in examining college students' views of influence in sexual encounters, found that subjects stereotyped all strategies for having sex as masculine and all strategies for avoiding sex as feminine. When asked the extent to which they personally employed each strategy, male students reported using a greater number of strategies for having sex than women, while females employed more strategies for avoiding sex (LaPlante et al., 1980).

It is thus clear that both men and women are likely to enter the dating situation with the expectation that the male will be the aggressor and the female the limit-setter with regard to sexual interaction. This in itself may set the stage for sexual aggression. The problem is exacerbated, however, when other expectations and beliefs held by the partners are at odds, leading to differential interpretation of interpersonal and contextual cues. To illustrate, Knox and Wilson (1981) found that less than 15 percent of their male and female undergraduate subjects reported that their dates always shared their understanding regarding how long couples should wait before engaging in three sexual activities (kissing, petting, intercourse). Large discrepancies were obtained between males and females regarding the degree of acceptable sexual conduct, with half of the males but only one-quarter of the females reporting that intercourse was appropriate by the fifth date.

These differing beliefs regarding appropriate sexual interaction may be coupled with differential beliefs regarding what constitutes consent to engage in intercourse. For example, Brodyaga and colleagues (Brodyaga, Gates, Singer, Tucker, & White, 1975) suggested that males come to believe that although females' initial stance may be resistance to sexual contact, this reluctance belies an underlying willingness and desire to engage in sex, thus, "boys are taught that girls say 'no' when they mean 'yes'" (p. 149). This may contribute to an interaction in which initial consensual sexual contact is perceived by the female as producing stabilization and partial gratification, whereas the male views the acts as an invitation to sexual intercourse (Kanin, 1969). Support that this may be the case is provided by Schultz and DeSavage (1975), who reported that a substantially smaller percentage of females than males agreed that fondling of the male's genitals by the female invited sexual intercourse.

As the couple approaches the sexual encounter with varying standards regarding what constitutes both appropriate sexual contact and communication of consent, yet other conflicting expectations may be operative. The female, for example, may believe that increasing levels of sexual contact come only with increasing levels of emotional intimacy (Knox & Wilson, 1981; Peplau et al., 1977), that rape cannot occur among dating partners (Koss & Oros, 1980), or that the male will stop whenever she requests it (Brodyaga et al., 1975). Perhaps sexual aggression would be less likely if the above expectations and standards were clearly communicated and negotiated by the members of the dating pair early in their interaction, but this is unlikely. Couples, regardless of their levels of intimacy, are often reluctant to communicate clearly their expectations and desires. Additionally, individual partners may believe that they are sending and receiving veridical interpersonal cues when, in fact, misperception may be more the norm.

That males tend to view interpersonal interactions as carrying more sexual intent than females provides one basis for misinterpretation in the dating encounter. This tendency has been elegantly demonstrated by Abbey (1982) in a study ostensibly concerned with the acquaintance process. Here, unacquainted male-female pairs engaged in a brief conversation, while another undergraduate pair looked on. At the conversation's end, both male actors and male observers rated the female actor as being more seductive and promiscuous than did female actors and observers. Males were also more sexually attracted to the opposite-sex actor than were the females to the male actor. In addition, male observers attributed more sexual intent to the male actor than did females. These findings led Abbey to conclude that men are more likely to perceive the world in sexual terms and to make sexual judgments than are females. Providing additional evidence, Burkhart, Rogers, and Aldred (1984) found that males assigned greater sexual intent than females to the actors in written descriptions of heterosexual social situations, as did Hendrick (1976, cited in Abbey, 1982). Even younger adolescent males (i.e., ages 14-18) were found to be more likely than females to interpret various cues in a dating context as conveying sexual intent (Zellman, Johnson, Giarrusso, & Goodchilds, 1979). This tendency to sexualize, coupled with sexually aggressive males' tendency to be relatively deficient in interpersonal responsibility (Rapaport & Burkhart, 1984) may contribute to a sexual context where misinterpretation is likely. Such misunderstanding of interpersonal and environmental cues may eventuate in forced sexual contact, which both partners may be reluctant to define as rape, yet which may carry similar negative emotional consequences for the women.

COMMENTS ON METHODOLOGY AND SUGGESTIONS FOR FUTURE RESEARCH

Thus far we have concentrated on presenting and integrating the findings from studies pertinent to sexual aggression among acquaintances as they stand, without extensive focus on methodological strengths and shortcomings. Our decision to do so stems from the opinion that the early research in this area, although not without flaws, serves to illuminate a significant social problem, identify its likely determinants, and provide potential directions for its amelioration. Nonetheless, there are methodological issues which we wish to address, our aim being to suggest refinements and directions for future research which may prove beneficial in extending our knowledge about sexual aggression between acquaintances.

First, it must be noted that the empirical study of aggressive sexual behavior in the dating relationship is in its infancy. The incidence research conducted thus far suggests that sexual aggression between acquaintances is rather common. It appears from the reports of both college men and women that between 13 and 25 percent of undergraduate females may be unwilling participants in at least one instance of coerced sexual intercourse. However, few incidence studies have assessed the level of acquaintance involved between the victim and assailant for each type of sexual behavior experienced. Assessment of the extent of acquaintance is important in all self-report research regarding nonconsensual sexual behavior. A dichotomous assessment of stranger- versus nonstranger-committed sexual aggression is not sufficient, however. For example, the personality attributes of a male who forces intercourse with a female he has just met at a party might be very different from those of a male who coerces intercourse with his fiancee, just as the interactional contexts in which the sexual aggression occurs might differ. Further, the emotional consequences for both the male and female partners may vary greatly, depending on the level of acquaintance. Clearly, research also needs to be extended to populations other than undergraduate samples. Further research on younger adolescents and on adults who do not attend college would be instructive. Also, assessment of sexual aggression among acquaintances which permits cross-study comparison would be beneficial.

The literature has reached the stage in which research must move beyond examining incidence. Investigation of hypothesized determinants of sexual aggression among acquaintances should be a central area of focus for researchers. For example, little research has been directed toward examining the specific mechanisms responsible for the transmission of belief structures and personality characteristics that promote coercive sexual interactions. Research (Giarrusso, Johnson, Goodchilds, & Zellman, 1978; Zellman et al., 1979) indicates that, by middle adolescence, values which may promote coercive sexuality have coalesced. A suggestive investigation by Malamuth and Check (1981) indicated that males exposed to films portraying violence against women as having positive consequences evidenced an increased acceptance of interpersonal violence against women and a tendency toward future acceptance of rape myths. For females, however, a significant trend in the opposite direction on both scales was found. Clearly, further research regarding socialization processes that eventuate in such an early development of these values and behaviors is necessary. In this regard, an in-depth examination of characteristics of males who *do not* engage in aggressive sexual conduct may be helpful in elucidating the processes in socialization that discourage coercive sexuality.

A fertile issue for future research regarding sexual aggression among acquaintances involves the interactional and situational contexts conducive to such activity. Much of the pertinent literature reviewed herein investigated the attitudes and behaviors involved in the typical dating processes of college students. Although these processes are relevant, a closer look at the coercive sexual interaction itself is warranted. Do males who admit to sexual aggression, as compared with other males, believe that females say "no" but mean "yes"? Do they sexualize their female partners' actions? Do they hold extreme expectations regarding appropriate sexual behaviors? How are women's resistances neutralized or ignored? These and many other questions remain to be answered.

With regard to research on the incidence and determinants of sexual aggression among acquaintances, it is necessary that investigators address an additional methodological issue. Research regarding private sexual behavior necessitates a reliance on self-report data. Careful questionnaire construction is essential, and in-depth structured interviews such as those conducted by Koss (1985) and

Russell (1982) may provide a more complete picture of coercive sexual behavior. Further, experimental investigations such as those of Malamuth and Check (Check & Malamuth, 1983; Malamuth & Check, 1981) and Abbey (1982) will also extend our knowledge of this phenomenon.

We conclude our discussion of sexual aggression among acquaintances by calling for investigation in an additional area, that of prevention and intervention. It has been suggested that acquaintance rape may have serious emotional consequences for females, although further substantiation of this finding is necessary. Negative consequences for males and for adaptive male- female relationships also are likely. However, the majority of intervention programs regarding sexual aggression concentrate on stranger rape, a focus which may be misplaced, given the relative incidence rates for acquaintance and stranger rapes. We are currently investigating the effects of educational and systems- level interventions regarding coercive sexual behavior on attitudes and behavioral intentions of an entering college sample.

By themselves, these levels of intervention will probably be insufficient to prevent aggressive sexual activities, although nonetheless necessary and worthy of attention. In Burt's (1980) view, "it appears that the task of preventing rape is tantamount to revamping a significant proportion of our social values" (p. 229). This chapter is dedicted to that end. Sexual violence between men and women violates the basic premise of relationships and until such violence is truly an anomalous rather than a common event, many relationships between men and women will include elements of distrust and deception.

REFERENCES

Abbey, A. (1982). Sex differences in attributions for friendly behavior: Do males misperceive females' friendliness? *Journal of Personality and Social Psychology, 42,* 830-838.

Abel, G. G., Barlow, D. H., Blanchard, E., & Guild, D. (1977). The components of rapists' sexual arousal. *Archives of General Psychiatry, 34,* 895-903.

Acock, A. C., & Ireland, N. K. (1983). Attribution of blame in rape cases: The impact of norm violation, gender, and sex-role attitude. *Sex Roles, 9,* 179-193.

Armentrout, J. A., & Hauer, A. L. (1978). MMPI's of rapists of adults, rapists of children, and nonrapist sex offenders. *Journal of Clinical Psychology, 34,* 330-332.

Ashton, N. L. (1982). Validation of rape myth acceptance scale. *Psychological Reports, 50,* 252.

Barnett, N. J., & Feild, H. S. (1977). Sex differences in university students' attitudes toward rape. *Journal of College Student Personnel, 18,* 93-96.

Brodyaga, L., Gates, M., Singer, S., Tucker, M., & White, R. (1975). *Rape and its victims: A report for citizens, health facilities, and criminal justice agencies.* National Institute of Law Enforcement and Criminal Justice, Law Enforcement Assistance Administration, U. S. Department of Justice. Washington, DC: U. S. Government Printing Office.

Brownmiller, S. (1975). *Against our will: Men, women and rape.* New York: Simon and Schuster.

Burkhart, B. R., Rogers, L. C., & Aldred, L. A. (1984). *When is a behavior a sexual behavior: Gender and situational determinants of sexual attributions.* Unpublished manuscript.

Burt, M. R. (1978). Attitudes supportive of rape in the American culture. In House Committee on Science and Technology, Subcommittee on Domestic and International Scientific Planning, Analysis, and Corporation (Ed.), *Research into violent behavior: Sexual assault* (Hearing, 95th Congress, Second session, January 10-12, 1978, pp. 277-322). Washington, DC: Government Printing Office.

Burt, M. R. (1980). Cultural myths and support for rape. *Journal of Personality and Social Psychology, 38,* 217-230.

Burt, M. R., & Albin, R. S. (1981). Rape myths, rape definitions, and probability of conviction. *Journal of Applied Social Psychology, 11,* 212-230.

Calhoun, L. G., Selby, J. W., & Warring, L. J. (1976). Social perception of the victim's causal role in rape: An exploratory examination of four factors. *Human Relations, 29,* 517-526.

Cann, A., Calhoun, L. G., & Selby, J. W. (1979). Attributing responsibility to the victim of rape: Influence of information regarding past sexual experience. *Human Relations, 32,* 57- 67.

Check, J. V. P., & Malamuth, N. M. (1983). Sex role stereotyping and reactions to depictions of stranger vs. acquaintance rape. *Journal of Personality and Social Psychology, 45,* 344-356.

Clark, L., & Lewis, D. (1977). *Rape: The price of coercive sexuality.* Toronto: The Women's Press.

Deitz, S. R., Blackwell, K. T., Daley, P. C., & Bentley, B. J. (1982). Measurement of empathy toward rape victims and rapists. *Journal of Personality and Social Psychology, 43,* 372-384.

Ellis, E. M. (1984). A review of empirical rape research: Victim reactions and response to treatment. *Clinical Psychology Review, 3,* 473-490.

Feild, H. S. (1978). Attitudes toward rape: A comparative analysis of police, rapists, crisis counselors, and citizens. *Journal of Personality and Social Psychology, 36,* 156-179.

Gagnon, J., & Simon, W. (1973). *Sexual conduct: The social sources of human sexuality.* Chicago: Aldine.

64　Sexual Aggression in Acquaintance Relationships

Giarrusso, R., Johnson, P., Goodchilds, J., & Zellman, G. (1978). Adolescents' cues & signals: Sex & assault. Paper presented at the meeting of the Western Psychological Association, San Diego.

Groth, A. N. (1979). *Men who rape*. New York: Plenum Press.

Griffin, S. (1971). Rape: The all-American crime. *Ramparts*, September, 26-35.

Kanekar, S., & Kolsawalla, M. B. (1980). Responsibility of a rape victim due to her respectability, attractiveness, and provocativeness. *Journal of Social Psychology, 112*, 153- 154.

Kanin, E. J. (1957). Male aggression in dating-courtship relations. *American Journal of Sociology, 10*, 197-204.

Kanin, E. J. (1967). An examination of sexual aggression as a response to sexual frustration. *Journal of Marriage and Family, 29*, 428-433.

Kanin, E. J. (1969). Selected dyadic aspects of males sex aggression. *Journal of Sex Research 5*, 12-28.

Kanin, E. J. (1983). Rape as a function of relative sexual frustration. *Psychological Reports, 52*, 133-134.

Kanin, E. J., & Parcell, S. R. (1977). Sexual aggression: A second look at the offended female. *Archives of Sexual Behavior, 6*, 67-76.

Klemmack, S. H., & Klemmack, D. L. (1976). The social definition of rape. In M. J. Walker & S. L. Brodsky (Eds.), *Sexual assault* (pp. 135-147). Lexington, MA: D. C. Heath & Company.

Kirkpatrick, C., & Kanin, E. J. (1957). Male sexual aggression on a university campus. *American Sociological Review, 22*, 52-58.

Knox, D., & Wilson, K. (1981). Dating behaviors of university students. *Family Relations, 30*, 255-258.

Korman, S. K., & Leslie, G. R. (1982). The relationship of feminist ideology and date expense sharing to perception of sexual aggression in dating. *Journal of Sex Research, 18*, 114-129.

Koss, M. P. (1985). The hidden rape victim: Personality, attitudinal, and situational characteristics. *Psychology of Women Quarterly, 9*, 193-212.

Koss, M. P., Leonard, K. E., Beezley, D. A., & Oros, C. J. (1985). Nonstranger sexual aggression: A discriminant analysis of the psychological characteristics of undetected offenders. *Sex Roles, 12*, 981-992.

Koss, M. P. & Oros, C. J. (1980). The "unacknowledged" rape victim. Paper presented at the meeting of the American Psychological Association, Montreal, Canada.

Koss, M. P., & Oros, C. J. (1982). Sexual experiences survey: A research instrument investigating sexual aggression and victimization. *Journal of Consulting and Clinical Psychology, 80*, 455-457.

Krulewitz, J. E. (1981). Sex differences in evaluations of female and male victims' responses to assault. *Journal of Applied Social Psychology, 11*, 460-474.

LaPlante, M. N., McCormick, N., & Brannigan, G. G. (1980). Living the sexual script: College students' views of influence in sexual encounters. *Journal of Sex Research, 16*, 338-355.

L'Armand, K., & Pepitone, A. (1982). Judgments of rape: A study of victim-rapist relationship and victim sexual history. *Personality and Social Psychology Bulletin, 8*, 134-139.

Malamuth, N. M. (1981). Rape proclivity among males. *Journal of Social Issues, 37*, 138-157.

Malamuth, N. M. (1983). Factors associated with rape as predictors of laboratory aggression against women. *Journal of Personality and Social Psychology, 45*, 432-442.

Malamuth, N. M., & Check, J. V. P. (1981). The effects of mass media exposure on acceptance of violence against women: A field experiment. *Journal of Research in Personality, 15*, 436- 446.

Malamuth, N. M., & Check, J. V. P. (1983). Sexual arousal to rape depictions: Individual differences. *Journal of Abnormal Psychology, 92*, 55-67.

McCormick, N. B. (1979). Come-ons and put-offs: Unmarried students' strategies for having and avoiding sexual intercourse. *Psychology of Women Quarterly, 4*, 194-211.

Oros, C. J., Leonard, K., & Koss, M. P. (1980). Factors related to self attribution of rape by victims. Paper presented at the meeting of the American Psychological Association, Montreal, Canada.

Peplau, L. A., Rubin, Z., & Hill, C. T. (1977). Sexual intimacy in dating relationships. *Journal of Social Issues, 33*, 86- 109.

Rada, R. T. (1978). *Clinical aspects of the rapist.* New York: Grune and Stratton.

Rader, C. M. (1977). MMPI profile types of exposers, rapists, and assaulters in a court services population. *Journal of Consulting and Clinical Psychology, 45,* 61-69.

Rapaport, K. (1984). Sexually aggressive males: Characterological features and sexual responsiveness to rape depictions. Unpublished doctoral dissertation, Auburn University, Alabama.

Rapaport, K., & Burkhart, B. R. (1984). Personality and attitudinal characteristics of sexually coercive college males. *Journal of Abnormal Psychology, 93,* 216-221.

Rogers, L. C. (1984). Sexual victimization: Social and psychological effects in college women. Unpublished doctoral dissertation, Auburn University, Alabama.

Russell, D. E. H. (1982). The prevalence and incidence of rape and attempted rape of females. *Victimology, 7,* 81-93.

Ryan, W. (1971). *Blaming the victim.* New York: Random House.

Schultz, L. G., & DeSavage, J. (1975). Rape and rape attitudes on a college campus. In L. G. Schultz (Ed.), *Rape victimology* (pp. 77-90). Springfield, IL: Charles C. Thomas.

Shotland, R. L., & Goodstein, L. (1983). Just because she doesn't want to doesn't mean it's rape: An experimentally based causal model of the perception of rape in a dating situation. *Social Psychology Quarterly, 46,* 220-232.

Skelton, C. A. (1982). Situational and personological correlates of sexual victimization in college women. Unpublished doctoral dissertation, Auburn University, Alabama.

Skelton, C. A., & Burkhart, B. R. (1980). Sexual assault: Determinants of victim disclosure. *Criminal Justice and Behavior, 7,* 229-236.

Smith, R. E., Keating, J. P., Hester, R. K., & Mitchell, H. E. (1976). Role and justice considerations in the attribution of responsibility to a rape victim. *Journal of Research in Personality, 10,* 346-357.

Thornton, B., Robbins, M. A., & Johnson, J. A. (1981). Social perception of the rape victim's culpability: The influence of respondents' personal-environmental causal attribution tendencies. *Human Relations, 34,* 225-237.

Thornton, B., & Ryckman, R. M. (1983). The influence of a rape victim's physical attractiveness on observers' attributions of responsibility. *Human Relations, 36,* 549-562.

Tieger, T. (1981). Self-rated likelihood of raping and the social perception of rape. *Journal of Research in Personality, 15,* 147-158.

United States Department of Justice, Bureau of Justice Statistics (1983). *Report to the nation on crime and justice: The data* (NCJ-87068). Rockville, Maryland. National Criminal Justice Reference Service.

Walker, M. J. & Brodsky, S. L. (Eds.). (1976). *Sexual assault.* Lexington, MA: D. C. Heath & Company.

Weis, K., & Borges, S. (1973). Victimology and rape: The case of the legitimate victim. *Issues in Criminology, 8,* 71-115.

Wilson, W., & Durrenberger, R. (1982). Comparison of rape and attempted rape victims. *Psychological Reports, 50,* 198.

Zellman, G. L., Johnson, P. B., Giarrusso, R., & Goodchilds, J. D. (1979). Adolescent expectations for dating relationships: Consensus and conflict between the sexes. Paper presented at the meeting of the American Psychological Association, New York.

Chapter 4

Transgenerational Patterns of Coercion in Families and Intimate Relationships

John F. Knutson and John G. Mehm

INTRODUCTION

Injurious acts in intimate relationships, such as spouse abuse, are increasingly being recognized as quite common. Based on interviews with couples, Straus (1978) offered a conservative estimate of the yearly incidence of wife abuse as 3.8% and an estimate of lifetime prevalence as much as five times greater. Based on a national probability sample, Straus, Gelles, and Steinmetz (1980) suggested that 28% of U.S. couples engaged in physically coercive acts. Other evidence for the widespread occurrence of physical abuse of wives is reflected in the records of medical services (e.g., Appleton, 1980; Rounsaville, 1978) and in transcripts of divorce proceedings (e.g., Byles, 1978; Levinger, 1966).

Although the research by Straus et al. (1980) and Steinmetz (1978) suggested little difference between men and women in their use of physically coercive acts, the males were more likely to engage in the more seriously injurious acts. Campbell's (1981) study of homicide provides additional evidence regarding the asymmetry in the fatal consequences of cross-sex aggression. Although the use of physical force in an intimate relationship might well be considered deviant by many lay persons and professionals, some authors (e.g., Straus, 1980) have suggested that physically coercive acts within the family are so embedded in Western culture that they can be considered normative behaviors. For that reason, it has been suggested that marriage licenses are "hitting licenses" (Straus, 1980) and that tissue-damaging coercion is merely part of this physically violent tradition.

67

Although the inference that society condones coercive acts in intimate relationships can be made from survey work designed to establish epidemiological data on domestic violence in the general population (e.g., Straus et al., 1980), most of the evidence regarding violence in intimate relationships has been obtained from samples of deviant families seen in hospitals, mental health facilities, and prisons. Estimates of incidence or prevalence are often seen as compromised by extensive use of such clinical samples. However, recent work completed in this laboratory indicated that estimates of the prevalence of child abuse in clinic and nonclinic populations were remarkably similar (Berger, Knutson, Mehm, & Perkins, 1986; Knutson, & Zaidi, 1986). Such data suggest that similar patterns of spouse abuse could be obtained in both clinic and nonclinic samples.

Variables commonly implicated in violent intimate relationships include: economic stress (e.g., Straus, 1980); alcoholism and personality disorders (e.g., Gayford, 1975; Hilberman & Munson, 1978; Stewart, deBlois & Cummings, 1980); and socioeconomic class (e.g., Stewart & deBlois, 1981). However, the variable about which there seems to be general agreement regarding the emergence of injurious acts in intimate relationships is the punitive and violent history of perpetrators and victims in spouse-abusing interactions (e.g., Gelles, 1983; Straus et al., 1980). Indeed, a history of violent interactions has been seen as a critical variable in some models of spouse abuse (e.g., Straus, 1980), suggesting a transgenerational hypothesis of spouse abuse that is quite similar to transgenerational models of child abuse (e.g., Green, 1979; Helfer, 1980; Scott, 1980; Steele, 1978, 1980).

Since over 90% of the population subscribe to the use of physical punishment of children, it is inevitable that spouse-abusing dyads will report childhood histories of physical punishment. Although the recall of more punitive histories has been associated with spouse-abusing dyads (e.g., Straus et al., 1980), there is little evidence to support the position that coercion in intimate relationships is embedded in a history of coercive or abusive childhood experiences. However, the position is quite consistent with social learning models of aggression (e.g., Bandura, 1973; Patterson, 1982).

As suggested by Patterson (1986), coercive opportunities in the family provide a training ground for aggressive behavior in highly coercive families. Furthermore, recent observational research by the Oregon Social Learning Center suggests that aggression by boys against mothers and sisters provides a training ground for later cross-sex aggression (John B. Reid, personal communication, April 5, 1984). Since it has also been suggested that victims of abuse develop victim characteristics and behave in a manner that maintains victim patterns of behavior, Straus (1980) has argued that women who were repeatedly abused as children may come to expect similar abuse in their adult relationships. Similarly, if women observed their fathers repeatedly using physical force with their mothers, they might develop personal norms that view marital violence as acceptable. An analogous process may result in the development of complementary characteristics of perpetrators of violent intimate relationships. Since the abusive experiences of children have been associated with antisocial aggressive and conduct-disordered behavior (e.g., Cunningham, 1983; George & Main, 1979; Jenkins, 1972; Reidy, 1977), such data are consistent with the notion that abusive environments produce coercive males who might use violence in intimate relationships. Thus, both males and females from abusive backgrounds might develop patterns of victim or aggressor in their adult relationships.

The bulk of support for the notion that abusive or violently punitive childhood experiences are related to the emergence of violence in intimate relationships, including spouse-abusing behavior, rests on theoretical reasoning. However, empirical support does exist for the hypothesis that marital discord is associated with child abuse (Blumberg, 1974; Burgess & Conger, 1977; Flynn, 1970; Gelles, 1973; Herrenkohl & Herrenkohl, 1981). Recently collected data from this laboratory suggested an association between spouse abuse and abusive parenting. Berger et al. (1986) surveyed four large samples of college students and determined that 8.2%-11% of the respondents indicated that their parents used physical force with each other. Knutson and Zaidi (1986) used the same instruments with two samples of parents of children who were consecutive referrals at a tertiary care psychiatry clinic. Approximately 14% of these parents indicated that their own parents used physical force with each other. In these studies, correlations were obtained between family violence and physically punitive experiences that were consistent with a relationship between abusive childhood experiences and the emergence of violence in subsequent family relationships.

GOAL OF THE PRESENT STUDY

The purpose of the present research was to determine whether a severely punitive childhood history was a factor in the emergence of coercive or violent interactions in intimate adult relationships. The social learning theory hypothesis—that abusive childhood experiences are important in the emergence of violence in intimate relationships—has two components. First, the abusive childhood experiences yield a propensity to respond aggressively in the perpetration of violence in intimate relationships. Second, a history of abuse can yield a pattern of victim behavior that is evidenced in intimate relationships.

The present research was designed to examine the possibility of the existence of both patterns by assessing childhood histories and current violent patterns in intimate relationships in samples from three distinct populations. In a sample of college students, the relationship of an abusive childhood history was examined with respect to the emergence of physically coercive acts in relationships that varied in levels of intimacy. Thus, the research with this sample was designed to determine whether abusive childhood histories were associated with the use or receipt of violence within developing intimate relationships.

Relationships described by college students included a large number of transient relationships as well as ones that developed more permanency. To assess abusive histories and the emergence of violence in intimate relationships, samples from two populations of adults in "permanent" relationships were also studied. One of these samples included single and married women hospitalized at an antepartum facility immediately prior to the birth of a child. All of these women could provide information regarding childhood histories and all were in intimate relationships that, we theorized, would probably differ from those described by university students. The third sample was comprised of parents of children seen for services at a child psychiatry clinic. Wife abuse had been previously identified in a sample from this population (e.g., Stewart & deBlois, 1981) and abusive childhood histories had been described in such a sample previously (Knutson & Zaidi, 1986).

ASSESSING ABUSIVE CHILDHOOD EXPERIENCES OF ADULTS

For a number of years, researchers from our laboratory have been investigating the contribution of abusive childhood experiences to problems in adulthood. When this research was initiated, it became immediately apparent that there were no standard questionnaires or interview schedules designed to assess the punishment histories and abusive childhood experiences of adults. Consequently, a first step in this research was the development of a questionnaire designed to assess punitive and abusive childhood histories, as well as a number of other childhood experiences purported to be associated with child abuse. The Assessing Environments III (AEIII) questionnaire (Berger et al., 1986) was the result of a series of studies designed to assess such childhood histories. The development of this questionnaire followed the rational-statistical approach (see Burisch, 1984) for producing a content-valid (cf. Loevinger, 1957) questionnaire. The AEIII consists of 164 True-False items that assess a range of childhood experiences, personal attitudes, and perceptions, as well as the occurrence of a range of physical punishment acts and parenting activities that are commonly described in the child-abuse literature.

The Physical Punishment Scale of the questionnaire sampled events that ranged from spanking and mild physical discipline to severe physical discipline and punishment acts that are seen as common forms of abusive parenting (e.g., Gil, 1970; Sapp & Carter, 1978; Straus, 1980). Although not included on the Physical Punishment Scale, several additional items were conditionally scored to obtain a more complete description of some of the punitive experiences which respondents endorsed. That is, when respondents indicated on the AEIII that they had been injured by the disciplinary activity of their parents, the injuries which occurred could be identified by endorsing items that included common injurious consequences of excessive parental discipline (e.g., bruises, cuts, fractures, dental injuries, head injuries). Similarly, when respondents indicated that parental discipline necessitated the provision of medical services, the respondent could indicate whether stitches, casts, or hospitalizations were required. Since being struck by some objects is considered within the range of normal parenting, while the use of other objects can be considered abusive (e.g., Sapp & Carter, 1978), when respondents indicated they had been struck by objects on the AEIII, the specific objects used could be identified through the conditional scoring of relevant items on the questionnaire.

The AEIII questionnaire was originally developed for use with young adults sampled from nonclinical populations. In order to evaluate whether the Physical Punishment Scale of the AEIII questionnaire sampled abusive parenting experiences, additional scales were included to assess many family characteristics that had been associated with child abuse in the literature. If the Physical Punishment Scale of the AEIII were assessing abusive childhood experiences, it was expected that these other AEIII scales would be modestly correlated with the Physical Punishment Scale. Recently completed research demonstrated that such correlations between these abuse-related scales and the Physical Punishment Scale were obtained in both nonclinical (Berger et al., 1986) and clinical samples (Knutson & Zaidi, 1984).

The Father Scale is an abuse-related scale that assesses the irritable, aggressive, and antisocial behavior patterns of the respondent's father as well as his cold and unsympathetic temperament; such a pattern was described by Smith and Hanson (1975) in their analysis of fathers from abusive families. The Smith, Hanson, and Noble (1974) research suggested that mothers from abusive families can have depressed or neurotic characteristics, and the Mother Scale was designed to assess such characteristics of the respondent's mother. The Age Inappropriate Demands Scale was developed to assess whether the respondent had been left unattended at an inappropriately early age, was required to be responsible for siblings, or was expected to provide emotional support for one or both parents. The development of this scale was stimulated by the work of Steele (1976), Steele and Pollack (1974), Morris and Gould (1963), Elmer (1977), and Wasserman (1968).

Since it has been suggested that abused youngsters are also rejected by their parents (cf. Friedrich & Boriskin, 1976; Herzberger, Potts, & Dillon, 1981), the Parental Rejection Scale was developed to assess this feeling. Several authors (e.g., Morris & Gould, 1963; Nurse, 1974; Parke & Colmer, 1975; Smith, 1975) have suggested that abusive families are often isolated from family and friends; for this reason, the Family Isolation Scale was developed to assess whether the respondent had a childhood in which isolation was one salient characteristic. The Community Involvement Scale was designed to determine whether the respondent's family engaged in activities outside the home and beyond the extended family, because it has been suggested (e.g., Straus, 1980) that child abuse is more common among families who do not participate in social or religious organizations. The Positive Parental Contact Scale assesses past contact and continuing contact between the respondents and their parents.

Several additional abuse-related scales of the AEIII seem particularly relevant for the purpose of the present research because they have been associated with the emergence of spouse abuse or violence against women. Consistent with descriptors of marital relationships of abusive families (e.g., Blumberg, 1974; Burgess & Conger, 1977; Flynn, 1970; Gelles, 1973; Galdston, 1971; Herrenkohl & Herrenkohl, 1981; Johnson & Morris, 1968; Smith, 1975; Steele & Pollack, 1974), the Marital Discord Scale assesses nonphysical acrimonious interactions between the respondent's parents. This scale assesses the respondent's opportunity to observe discordant marital relationships, which might relate to a tendency to initiate the same pattern later, or to behave as if such interactions were appropriate in intimate relationships. The Family Violence Scale tapped physically coercive imitative opportunities or norm-setting experiences within the family by assessing physically coercive interactions between the respondent's parents and abusive acts directed toward siblings. The Negative Family Atmosphere Scale, composed of items that assess verbal aggression among family members, is the verbal equivalent of the Family Violence Scale.

The Peer Relations Scale was originally designed to assess the absence of childhood friends and whether there was a teasing or victimizing characteristic of the respondent's relationships with childhood peers. Victim characteristics and difficult interactions with peers have been considered in the context of child abuse (see Friedrich & Boriskin, 1976, for a review), but the possibility of poor peer relations evolving into later physically coercive interactions in intimate relationships suggested the possible utility of this scale in the present research as well. The Perception of Discipline Scale of the AEIII was designed to determine whether respondents perceive their discipline as harsh, capricious, or unreasonable, and in a sense provides an index of the personal norms that a respondent applies to the childhood disciplinary acts that he or she had experienced. Such personal norms could be a variable in determining whether violent patterns of interaction are perpetuated.

Gelles (1980) suggested that child abuse is most common in families where power is concentrated in one parent, and consequently the Shared Parenting Scale was developed to assess an asymmetry in the responsibilities of the respondent's parents in making important family decisions. The dominance of one member over another in a dyad could certainly play a role in spouse-abusing families as well. Since lower economic status and economic stress have been implicated as factors in both child abuse (e.g., Kempe & Helfer, 1972; Pelton, 1978) and in spouse abuse (Stewart & deBlois, 1981), the Potential Economic Stress Scale included items that assessed sustained stressful economic circumstances as well as acute economic reversals. The Positive Orientation to Education Scale assesses the educational history of the respondent's family as well as the existence of objects in the home that could be associated with an educationally oriented environment. It is commonly believed in clinical service settings that coercive acts in intimate relationships are more prevalent in poorly educated populations.

Thus, the AEIII questionnaire was incorporated in the present research to assess abusive childhood experiences of adults, as well as a range of childhood experiences that have been associated with child abuse. Since many of these experiences have been implicated in the ontogeny of spouse-abusing relationships, the use of the AEIII questionnaire was seen as a viable tactic for assessing the early life experiences of adults to predict their subsequent coercive experiences in intimate relationships.

Research Samples and Procedures

Young Adults

Subjects. Our subjects were 564 students enrolled in either of two introductory courses offered by the Department of Psychology at the University of Iowa. Participation in this research was among many possibilities that students could select to meet the research participation requirements of the two courses. Since most students who matriculate at the University of Iowa as freshmen enroll in one of these courses during their four years in residence, the sample is representative of the student body as a whole. Columns 1 and 2 of Table 4.1 show the demographic characteristics of the men and women of this sample.

Assessing Coercive Acts and Childhood Histories. To assess the occurrence of coercive acts in intimate relationships, a series of 37 items was randomly inserted in the AEIII Questionnaire for the college students. These items were designed to determine whether respondents had used or received physical force in various relationships characterized by differing levels of intimacy including: dating relationships, steady relationships, intimate relationships, like-sex and opposite-sex relationships, heterosexual and homosexual relationships. Items also assessed whether the respondent had inflicted or received injuries in the context of these relationships. Similarly, whether the physical force or injurious acts occurred in the context of sexual activity was ascertained.

Procedure. Within a one-week period during the first quarter of the semester, students enrolled in the introductory psychology courses were informed that they could receive research participation credit by attending a group testing session, at which they would be administered a number of experimental questionnaires. Included among the research materials was the modified AEIII and a variety of questionnaires. None of the other questionnaires administered to the participants during these sessions was designed to assess aggressive behavior, sexual

Table 4.1. Basic Demographic Characteristics of the College Student, Antepartum
Clinic, and Child Psychiatry Samples

	College males	College females	Antepartum clinic mothers	Child psychiatry mothers
N	237[a]	290[a]	109	99
Age				
Mean	19.1	19.0	21.5[b]	34.7
Range	17-40	18-47	15-31[b]	23-60
Marital status				
Single	97.0	96.9	20.2	2.0
Married	1.7	2.4	71.6	93.9
Divorced/				
separated	1.2	0.7	8.3	4.0
Number of children				
0	97.9	96.9	46.8	0.0
1	0.8	1.4	31.2	10.1
2	0.8	0.3	13.8	36.4
3	0.0	0.3	4.6	27.3
>3	0.4	1.0	3.7	26.3
Number of siblings				
0	5.1	3.4	4.6	0.0
1	21.1	22.8	11.0	21.2
2-5	65.8	65.9	60.6	64.6
6-10	8.0	7.2	19.3	11.1
>10	0.0	0.7	4.6	3.0
Position in family				
First born	39.2	29.7	26.6	34.3
Second born	19.4	23.1	22.9	26.3
Third born	10.5	11.4	12.8	16.2
Last born	20.7	25.5	11.0	9.1
Self-described Socio-economic status				
Lower	6.8	4.1	21.1	32.3
Middle	76.8	83.8	76.1	64.6
Upper	16.0	11.7	1.8	1.0

experiences, or child psychopathology. Experimenters were available to answer
questions; however, self-explanatory instructions were included with each questionnaire and in the appropriate informed-consent materials.

Table 4.1. Basic Demographic Characteristics of the College Student, Antepartum
Clinic, and Child Psychiatry Samples (Continued)

	College males	College females	Antepartum clinic mothers	Child psychiatry mothers
Religion				
Catholic	38.0	41.4	18.3	27.3
Protestant	34.6	39.7	18.3	51.5
Jewish	3.4	4.1	0.0	1.0
Other	14.3	12.1	48.6	16.2
None	9.7	2.8	13.8	4.0
Geographic background				
Rural	26.2	31.0	49.5	50.5
Urban	29.1	31.7	36.7	37.4
Suburban	44.7	36.9	11.0	12.1

a An additional 37 college students did not identify their sex.
b Based on N = 69 women who provided their age.

To assure anonymity and to facilitate candid responding, the modified AEIII questionnaires were administered with a set of instructions and machine-score-able answer sheets that were discriminable from the other research materials. Thus, none of the modified AEIII material was associated with information identifying the research participant. To permit the possibility of follow-up contact with the participants, each modified AEIII questionnaire and answer sheet was precoded with an idiosyncratic identification number. Participants were specifically instructed not to put their social security or university identification number on either the modified AEIII questionnaire or answer sheet. Thus, participants completed the questionnaires anonymously, but each questionnaire was idiosyncratically coded to a particular respondent so additional studies could be conducted with the same sample. For the purposes of the present research, no subsequent sessions were conducted.

Women from an Antepartum Clinic

Subjects. In this research, 109 women temporarily residing in a facility of the University of Iowa Hospitals and Clinics Antepartum Program voluntarily participated. Women seen for obstetrical services in this program are either indigent or their pregnancy is associated with a number of obstetrical risk factors that require prenatal services or delivery at a tertiary care facility. Column 3 of Table 4.1 shows the demographic characteristics of this sample. The present study was part of a larger research program assessing personality characteristics and social history of high-risk mothers. Although an effort was made to include consecutive admissions in the sample, women admitted on weekends or with a delivery

Table 4.2. Endorsement Rates of Physical Punishment Scale Items and Other Abuse-Related Items

	College males	College females	Antepartum clinic mothers	Child psychiatry mothers
Physical Punishment Items				
Physical discipline	62.4	53.8	37.6	52.5
Hit (not spanked,	25.3	21.7	24.1	20.2
Spanked	79.3	83.1	78.7	80.8
Hit with objects	35.4	32.1	43.0	49.5
Punched	5.1	4.1	6.5	4.0
Severely beaten	0.8	0.3	4.6	2.0
Kicked	5.5	3.4	4.6	3.0
Choked	1.5	1.3	1.9	0.0
Locked in closet	1.7	0.0	0.9	1.0
Injured by parents	26.6	27.9	20.2	10.1
Received medical services due to discipline by parents	4.2	1.0	1.8	1.0
Tied up	2.1	0.3	0.9	1.0
Abuse-Related Items				
Sexual abuse by parents	3.0	1.4	5.5	6.1
Sexual abuse by siblings	3.0	4.1	1.8	6.1
Physically abused	1.7	1.7	6.5	7.1
Siblings were abused	3.4	5.9	11.1	7.1
Spouse abuse by parents	8.0	9.0	11.0	13.1

imminent are somewhat underrepresented in the sample. Since both the date of admission and the timing of birth are presumably randomly determined, the sample can be considered a random and representative sample of women seen for services in this clinic.

Procedure. During the afternoon on the first or second day of residence, each potential participant was approached by a research assistant and was asked to complete the AEIII, several other personality and social history questionnaires, and a brief interview regarding her social and medical history. Thus, data regarding coercive acts during childhood, adolescence, and intimate relationships were obtained through interview schedules and questionnaires. The entire procedure involved approximately two hours of the participant's time, and for the most part it fit easily into her rather uneventful days preceding childbirth.

Parents of Children Seen at Child Psychiatry

Subjects and Procedures. As part of an ongoing series of studies regarding abusive childhood histories among parents of children referred for psychiatric services, the AEIII was administered to consecutively referred families seen for services at the Child Psychiatry Service of the University of Iowa Hospitals and Clinics. This clinic is the tertiary care center for the state of Iowa, and the program receives referrals from throughout the state and from western Illinois as well. During an 18-month period, the AEIII was administered to 223 women who were mothers, adoptive mothers, or foster mothers of children referred to the clinic. At the time this research was being conducted, colleagues in the Child Psychiatry Service were using a structured interview schedule to ascertain specific information regarding the referred child's home.

For the purposes of the present research, questions regarding the incidence of physical violence between the parents, and whether such violence required the intervention of law enforcement agencies, was determined. The random sampling procedure used by the Child Psychiatry investigators resulted in complete interview schedule information from 99 women who had also completed the AEIII for the present study. The demographic characteristics of this sample are shown in the fourth column of Table 4.1. An analysis of the characteristics of the 99 women included in this sample and the 124 women for whom interview information was not available indicated there were no differences between the sampled and unsampled mothers in terms of demographic characteristics and their scale scores on the AEIII. Thus, these 99 women can be considered representative of the women seen at this clinic.

Results and Discussion

Prevalence of Punitive Childhood Experiences

The endorsement rates of various punitive activities and a number of abuse-related items from the AEIII are shown in Table 4.2 for each of the samples used in this study. Although drawn from markedly different populations, the endorsement rates of these items by the subjects from the three different samples are remarkably similar. The endorsement rates by male and female college students provide another replication of data described earlier by Berger et al. (1986), in which the endorsement rates were not distinguished on the basis of sex.

As Berger et al. (1986) noted, whether the childhood experiences can be considered abusive is a function of the criterion used. Berger et al. analyzed data

Table 4.3. Relative Frequencies of Group Membership, Based on Three Abuse Criteria and Self-Labeling as Abused

| | | | Self-labeled As: | |
Sample	Criterion	Group Member-ship	Abused	Not abused
College Males	Liberal abuse criterion	Abused	1.7	54.9
		Not abused	0.0	43.5
	Texas abuse criterion	Abused	1.7	32.1
		Not abused	0.0	66.2
	Physical Punishment Scale abuse criterion	Abused	1.3	10.5
		Not abused	0.4	87.8
College Females	Liberal abuse criterion		1.7	51.4
		Abused	0.0	45.9
		Not abused		
	Texas abuse criterion	Abused	1.7	27.9
		Not abused	0.0	69.3
	Physical Punishment Scale abuse criterion	Abused	1.7	6.2
		Not abused	0.0	91.0
Antepartum clinic women	Liberal abuse criterion	Abused	6.4	49.5
		Not abused	0.0	44.1
	Texas abuse criterion	Abused	6.4	22.9
		Not abused	0.0	68.8
	Physical Punishment Scale abuse criterion	Abused	5.5	6.4
		Not abused	0.9	87.2

from college students, using an earlier version of the Assessing Environments Questionnaire (AEIII), with respect to three different criteria for defining abusive childhood experiences. One criterion was based on Straus' (1980) liberal criterion and another was based on the responses of 1,339 Texans surveyed regarding their personal criteria for child abuse (Sapp & Carter, 1978). The third

Table 4.3. Relative Frequencies of Group Membership, Based on Three Abuse
Criteria and Self-Labeling as Abused (Continued)

			Self-labeled As:	
Sample	Criterion	Group Member-ship	Abused	Not abused
Child psychiatry mothers	Liberal abuse criterion	Abused	7.1	48.5
		Not abused	0.0	44.4
	Texas abuse criterion	Abused	7.1	33.3
		Not abused	0.0	59.6
	Physical Punishment Scale abuse criterion	Abused	4.0	2.0
		Not abused	3.0	90.9

was the criterion Berger (1981) used to select abused subjects for an analog parenting task. Table 4.3 shows the relative frequencies for each of the samples used in the present study that met each of the three criteria for having been abused as children and whether they endorsed an item regarding being physically abused by their parents. Interestingly, most persons who met the various behavioral criteria for having been abused failed to describe themselves as being abused. When considered together, the data of Tables 4.2 and 4.3 indicate that each of these samples provides subjects representing a broad range of punitive backgrounds. Regardless of the child abuse criterion used, abuse is represented in all samples and these samples are considered suitable for addressing questions regarding the role of abusive childhood experiences in the emergence of violence in subsequent adult and intimate relationships.

Violence in Intimate Relationships

For the college students, the modified AEIII questionnaire included items that assessed the use and receipt of physical force and injurious acts in relationships that varied with respect to degree of intimacy. Similarly, whether force was used or received in a sexual context was also assessed. All items assessing the use and receipt of force and injury, excluding those pertaining to like-sex or opposite-sex nonintimate relationships, were combined into User and Receiver scales, respectively. The proportion of males and females from the college student sample that used or received force or injury in a relationship at least once was analyzed. Combining data of males and females, 18.8% described using force or injurious acts, and 17.4% described receiving such acts at least once. Females, at 23.4%, are surprisingly more likely than males (11.8%) to report using physical force or injurious acts in this sample, (p < .01). The difference between men (15.2%) and women (19.6%) in the receipt of physical force or injurious acts was not significant, however. An interesting aspect of these data is the apparent reciprocity of the acts. That is, 40% of the female users were also recipients and 57% of the male users were also recipients. Similarly, 56% of the female recipients were users, and 45% of the male recipients were users. However, the lack of available data regarding actual intimate dyads renders any assumptions about the occurrence of reciprocating interactions only speculative. Considering that the notion of reciprocity is consistent with theory and data regarding other coercive acts (e.g., Patterson, 1982), study of young dyads would be appropriate.

As might be expected with this sample of young adults, the degree of intimacy did not generally extend beyond dating or steady relationships. Overall, 9.9% of the sample indicated they had been injured in a relationship, and 9.8% indicated they had been forced to engage in sexual activity through actual or threatened physical force. The use and receipt of physical force in a dating relationship were 14.1% and 9.9%, respectively, while the use and receipt of physical force in steady dating relationships were 7.8% and 11.0%, respectively. Since only a small proportion of these college students were married or living in intimate relationships, the overall endorsement rates of using force (3.4%) and receiving force (5.1%) in a permanent relationship suggest an extremely high base rate of coercive activity in such relationships. The pattern of data suggests that physically coercive and injurious acts are not uncommon in the intimate relationships of these predominantly middle-class young adults. Such a pattern suggests that the emergence of spouse abuse or violence with a live-in partner could be embedded in a history of developing relationships.

Of the women seen at the antepartum clinic, 22% indicated they had been physically abused by their spouse or live-in partner. Since the abuse was defined as injurious or physically coercive acts, the criterion is comparable to the questionnaire items regarding receipt of force or injurious acts used with college students, and the difference between samples is not appreciable. Only 11% of the mothers of children seen for services at the Child Psychiatry Clinic reported that their spouses had used physical force with them, that they had been injured sufficiently to require medical services, or that the police had been contacted because of a violent interaction between them and their spouses.

Predicting Violence in Intimate Relationships
from Violent Childhood Experiences
    The primary goal of the present research was to determine whether there was an association between the reported childhood experiences of adults, with respect to personal abuse and an acrimonious family environment, and the emer-

gence of physically coercive intimate relationships. Implicit in the hypothesis that violence in intimate relationships is an outgrowth of violence in childhood is the notion of temporal continuity. That is, violent intimate relationships that occur as a function of childhood experiences ought to emerge during the development of dating relationships and then continue into steady, intimate, and marital relationships.

To assess whether coercive and acrimonious childhood experiences are related to subsequent violence in intimate relationships, AEIII data were used in discriminant classification functions to predict the occurrence of coercion in adult relationships. Because of the temporal continuity notion, a strategy was adopted to determine whether the AEIII scales that most directly assessed personal abuse and an acrimonious family environment could be used in a linear discriminant classification function to predict the occurrence of coercive acts in intimate relationships in these three samples. The five AEIII scales considered to be most closely related to the hypothesis that violence in intimate relationships reflects childhood experiences were the Physical Punishment, Family Violence, Negative Family Atmosphere, Marital Discord, and Shared Parenting scales.

For the women at the antepartum clinic and the mothers at Child Psychiatry, the classification was primarily directed toward being a victim. Consequently, to conduct comparable analyses in college students, discriminant classifications attempted to identify women who were recipients of coercive acts and males who were users of physical force in a manner consistent with the research of Koss and Oros (1982). The resulting discriminant classifications of male users and female recipients from the college sample and of women from the antepartum clinic and Child Psychiatry Service are shown in Table 4.4. Because group memberships within samples varied widely in size, statistical significance in these discriminant classifications was based on exceeding a maximum chance criterion (cf. Huberty, 1984). As is obvious from Table 4.4, none of the four discriminant classification functions exceeded the maximum chance criterion, suggesting an inability to predict the emergence of coercion in intimate relationships as a function of these specific indices of coercive childhood histories.

The AEIII questionnaire samples a broad range of childhood experiences and perceptions that relate to abusive life events (e.g., Berger et al., 1986; Knutson & Zaidi, 1986). Perhaps the a priori selected AEIII scales are not the best predictors of violent intimate relationships, even though their content is most closely related to the phenomenon of interest. An alternative strategy would be to select variables statistically through a stepwise discriminant procedure, which maximizes the difference between groups as a function of an increase in Rao's V (1973). Those variables selected in the discriminant function by the stepwise procedure would then be combined in a linear discriminant classification procedure. Because of the assumption of temporal continuity in violence in intimate relationships, and because of the larger sample size, the strategy adopted was to

Table 4.4 Discriminant Classifications of Intimate Violence Characteristics Using Pre-

selected AEIII Scale

College males using physical force or injury			Predicted	
			No	Yes
	Actual	No	208	1
		Yes	27	1

College females receiving physical force or injury			Predicted	
			No	Yes
	Actual	No	230	3
		Yes	56	1

Antepartum clinic women receiving physical force			Predicted	
			No	Yes
	Actual	No	78	2
		Yes	21	2

			Predicted	
Child psychiatry mothers			No	Yes
	Actual	No	87	1
		Yes	11	0

select the variables for the discriminant classifications based on an initial discriminant analysis of the college student samples. Because this resulting discriminant classification function would not yield an unbiased estimate of error rates,

Table 4.5. Discriminant Classifications of Users and Recipients of Physical Force Among College Students Using the AEIII Scales Identified in the Stepwise Discriminant Procedure

College females receiving physical force or injury			Predicted	
			No	Yes
	Actual	No	227	6
		Yes	50	7

College males using physical force or injury			Predicted	
			No	Yes
	Actual	No	206	3
		Yes	26	2

selected variables would undergo external tests (cf. Huberty, 1984) in discriminant classifications of the Antepartum Clinic women and the Child Psychiatry clinic mothers. In these external tests, new coefficients weighting the selected variables would be computed because the assumption of identical covariance matrices among samples cannot be made.

Table 4.5 shows the two discriminant classifications of male users and female recipients from the college student sample using variables selected in the stepwise linear discrimination procedures. With respect to predicting whether the men in the college student sample had been users of coercive acts in intimate relationships, the discriminant classification did not exceed the maximum chance criterion. Of the 28 men who used physical force in intimate relationships, only 2 were correctly classified on the basis of the discriminant classification. Similarly, the discriminant classification based on variables selected in the stepwise discriminant function of female recipients correctly identified only 7 of the 57 female recipients of physical force in intimate relationships. Thus, these two discriminant classifications based on a stepwise statistical selection of AEIII variables were quite unsuccessful.

Since the stepwise procedure did not identify a set of AEIII variables that could be effectively used in a discriminant classification function with the college women, the planned external tests of the discriminant classification would be un-

Table 4.6. Discriminant Classifications of Recipients of Physical Force
Among Antepartum and Child Psychiatry Women Using te AEIII Scales
Identified in the Stepwise Discriminant Procedure

Child psychiatry mothers receiving physical force			Predicted	
			No	Yes
	Actual	No	88	0
		Yes	6	5
Antepartum clinic women receiving physical force			Predicted	
			No	Yes
	Actual	No	76	4
		Yes	17	6

reasonable. Consequently, recognizing that it would be impossible to establish an unbiased estimate of error rate, the stepwise procedure was again used with both the women from the Antepartum Clinic and the Child Psychiatry mothers. The results of the two discriminant classification functions using variables selected in the respective stepwise discriminant functions are shown in Table 4.6. Again, neither of these classifications exceeded a maximum chance criterion. Indeed, the correct prediction of group membership using childhood history obtained with the AEIII scales was decidedly unsuccessful.

Because users of physical force also tend to be recipients, it is possible that the discriminant functions were unsuccessful because the criterion groups were not sufficiently distinct. Within the college student sample, it was possible to identify males who had used physical force but were never recipients and women who reported being recipients but never having been users of physical force or injurious acts. These male "pure user" and female "pure recipient" groups were then used in stepwise linear discriminant functions and the selected AEIII scales were used in discriminant classifications. Table 4.7 shows the results of these discriminant classifications to predict membership in the male "pure user" group and in the female "pure recipient" group. Again, the discriminant classification functions could not successfully discriminate those males who only used physical force from those who had neither used nor received physical force. They were also un-

Table 4.7. Discriminant Classifications of Male "Pure User" and
Female "Pure Recipient" Characteristics Using
Stepwise Selected AEIII Scales

College females as pure recipients of physical force			Predicted	
			No	Yes
	Actual	No	193	4
		Yes	22	3
College males as pure users of physical force			Predicted	
			No	Yes
	Actual	No	189	0
		Yes	12	0

successful in discriminating females who had only received physical force from those who had neither received nor used physical force. Thus, even extreme male user and female recipient groups could not be successfully classified using a broad range of adverse childhood history variables.

The results of these discriminant classification functions raise serious doubts about an association between coercive childhood histories or acrimonious family backgrounds and coercive acts in intimate adult relationships. However, given the widespread acceptance, theoretical viability (e.g., Bandura, 1973; Patterson, 1982), and empirical support of this notion (e.g., Straus et al., 1980), some consideration of the basis of these failures seems necessary. One possibility is the inadequacy of the AEIII scales to sample the necessary characteristics of violent childhood backgrounds. However, given the reliability of the AEIII (Berger et al., 1986) and the breadth of acrimonious and violent family experiences that are covered by the questionnaire, that possibility seems unlikely.

It is also possible that the stepwise discriminant function did not yield the best set of variables for use in a discriminant classification function, and that another set of variables would be superior. However, the fact that the discriminant classification functions using the scales that theoretically are most closely related to the ontogeny of coercion in intimate relationships also failed argues against that possibility. A third possibility is that our samples are different than those usually described in the spouse abuse literature. Based on analyses of the retrospective recall of persons already identified as abusive, the literature (e.g., Fagan, Stewart, & Hansen, 1983; Gelles, 1983; Hilberman, 1980) has argued that a violent history is a stable characteristic of spouse abusers. This evidence is almost exclusively related to perpetrators, with little study of the victim characteristics considered in our paper. However, the discriminant classification functions of male perpetrators in the college sample were no more successful than the discriminant classification functions of female victims.

A fourth possible account of the failure of these discriminant classifications involves the fact that violent behavior is necessarily a dyadic exchange, whereas only one member of a dyad was used in the present discriminant analyses. In prior studies using the AEIII scales to predict child abuse and antisocial progeny, predictions from the childhood history of mothers alone or fathers alone were decidedly unsuccessful, but predictions based on the histories of both parents were somewhat successful (Knutson & Zaidi, 1986). It is possible, then, that childhood history data from both members of a dyad are required to predict the occurrence of coercive acts in adult relationships. To test that possibility, a post hoc analysis of identifiable dyads was conducted with the mothers of children seen at Child Psychiatry whose husbands had also completed the AEIII.

There were 76 mother-father dyads available in the Child Psychiatry sample, and 5 provided unambiguous evidence regarding the occurrence of spouse abuse. The discriminant classification function using variables selected in a stepwise discriminant analysis was quite successful, with 98.7% of the cases correctly classified. There were no false positive assignments, and only a single false negative. Although we recognize the lack of an unbiased estimate of error rate, we note that this classification analysis does suggest the possibility that the childhood history of both members of a dyad can predict the emergence of coercion in intimate relationships. The Physical Punishment scale was not included in this classification function; however, the mother AEIII scale of Potential Economic Stress, Peer Rejection, and Perception of Discipline were used, along with the father AEIII scales of Marital Discord, Family Isolation, Community Involvement, Family Violence, and Shared Parenting. The Positive Parental Contact and Negative Family Atmosphere scales for both members of the dyad were also included. If such a pattern were replicated, it would suggest that women who were treated harshly and capriciously within an acrimonious family, and who had poor peer relations and economic disadvantages could be the recipients of spouse abuse when they assortively mated with men whose families were characterized by marital discord, family acrimony, an asymmetry in parenting responsibilities, and lack of involvement in the community.

CONCLUSIONS

Because estimates of the prevalence of violence in intimate relationships vary widely, it would be impossible for any study to be in agreement with all base rate estimates in the spouse abuse literature. However, considering the paucity of research on coercion within relationships of nondeviant samples, it is noteworthy that the present prevalence estimates regarding the occurrence of violence in intimate relationships in a university population closely approximate the prevalence estimates of male use and female receipt of violence in sexual contexts with other samples of university students (e.g., Koss & Oros, 1982; Rapaport & Burkhart, 1984). It is also interesting that the sample from the Antepartum Clinic yields a prevalence estimate of coercion in intimate relationships that is not unlike those estimates based on data from university samples. In contrast to those consistencies, the data from the Child Psychiatry Service are not at all consistent with earlier studies of the same population; Stewart and deBlois (1981) reported prevalence estimates of spouse abuse close to 44%. Although a slightly more liberal criterion had been used by Stewart and deBlois (1981), a sampling difference is more likely to be an accurate account of this difference.

The results of the present discriminant analyses cast doubt on the simple notion that coercive childhood experiences yield coercive and violent patterns in intimate adult relationships. The results do not indicate that these backgrounds are unimportant, but merely that they do not account for enough of the variance to make strong inferences regarding causal relationships. Quite simply, they suggest that the emergence of violent and coercive acts in intimate relationships is likely to be determined by more variables than just punitive or acrimonious childhood histories of victims or perpetrators. Furthermore, since analyses of aggression are increasingly considering dyadic relationships (cf. Patterson, 1982), it is perhaps unreasonably naive to believe that the history of one person will determine the emergence of exchanges that necessarily occur within a dyad.* The modest success of the discriminant classification using data from both parents in the Child Psychiatry sample suggests the importance of considering the childhood backgrounds of both members of a dyad. Of course, replication with an independent sample would be necessary to argue that a specific joint childhood history yields violence in intimate relationships.

While the results of the discriminant classifications of female victims in all three samples did not support the hypothesis that a history of child abuse is a good predictor of violence in intimate relationships, these discriminant analyses could be considered as providing indirect support for a typology of spouse abuse such as that offered by Snyder and Fruchtman (1981). In their five-class typology of victims of spouse abuse, only one class, constituting only slightly more than 9% of the sample, had an *extensive* history of violence in the family of origin. However, Snyder and Fruchtman (1981) also noted that 25% of the victimized women reported being abused by their parents and 50% reported being neglected by their parents. Thus, although not included as a *defining* characteristic

---

* see also, the results of a recent study by Briere (1987) [G.W.R.].

of the other classes, noxious childhood histories were necessarily represented in more than that single class. Moreover, since the criterion for abuse by parents was not specified in that article, and since self-labeling as being physically abused by one's parents tends to be an underestimate of abuse (Berger et al., 1986; Knutson & Zaidi, 1986), it is possible that abusive life events are actually well represented in the other four classes of the Snyder and Fruchtman (1981) typology. A replication of the Snyder and Fruchtman (1981) research, using a more specific behavioral criterion of abuse, would be important for assessing the prevalence of child abuse among possible classes of victims in intimate relationships.

ACKNOWLEDGMENTS

The cooperation and assistance of Susan deBlois, Jane Kelso, Lillian Bullers, and Lisa Zaidi are gratefully acknowledged.

REFERENCES

Appleton, W. (1980). The battered woman syndrome. *Annals of Emergency Medicine, 9,* 84-91.

Bandura, A. (1973). Social learning theory of aggression. In J. F. Knutson (Ed.), *Control of aggression: Implications from basic research.* Chicago: Aldine-Atherton.

Berger, A. M. (1981). An examination of the relationship between harsh discipline in childhood, later punitiveness toward children and later ratings of adjustment. Unpublished doctoral dissertation, The University of Iowa.

Berger, A. M., Knutson, J. F., Mehm, J. G., & Perkins, K. A. (1986). *The self-report of punitive childhood experiences of young adults.* Manuscript submitted for publication.

Blumberg, M. L. (1974). Psychopathology of the abusing parent. *American Journal of Psychotherapy, 28,* 21-29.

Briere, J. (1987). Predicting self-report likelihood of battering: Attitudes and childhood experiences. *Journal of Research in Personality, 21,* 61-69.

Burgess, R. S., & Conger, R. D. (1977). Family interaction patterns related to child abuse and neglect: Some preliminary findings. *Child Abuse and Neglect, 1,* 269-277.

Burisch, M. (1984). Approaches to personality inventory construction: A comparison of merits. *American Psychologist, 39,* 214-227.

Byles, J. A. (1978). Violence, alcohol problems and other problems in disintegrating families. *Journal of Studies of Alcohol, 39,* 551-553.

Campbell, J. (1981). Misogyny and homicide of women. *ANS: Women's Health,* American Nursing Society, 67-85.

Cunningham, S. (1983). Abused children more likely to become teenaged criminals. *The APA Monitor,* 26-27.

Elmer, E. (1977). *Fragile families, troubled children.* Pittsburgh: The University of Pittsburgh Press.

Fagan, J. A., Stewart, D. K., & Hansen, K. V. (1983). Violent men or violent husbands? Background factors and situational correlates. In D. Finkelhor, R. J. Gelles, G. T. Hotaling, & M. A. Straus (Eds.), *The dark side of families.* Beverly Hills, CA: Sage Publications.

Flynn, W. R. (1970). Frontier justice: A contribution to the theory of child battery. *American Journal of Psychiatry, 127*(3), 375-379.

Friedrich, W. N., & Boriskin, J. A. (1976). The role of the child in abuse: A review of the literature. *American Journal of Orthopsychiatry, 46*(4), 580-590.

Galdston, R. (1971). Violence begins at home. *Journal of the American Academy of Child Psychiatry, 10,* 336-350.

Gayford, J. J. (1975). Wife battering: A preliminary survey of 100 cases. *British Medical Journal, 1,* 194-197.

Gelles, R. J. (1973). Child abuse as psychopathology: A sociological critique and reformulation. *American Journal of Orthopsychiatry, 43*(4), 611-621.

Gelles, R. J. (1980). A profile of violence toward children in the United States. In G. Gerbner, C. J. Ross, & E. Zigler (Eds.), *Child abuse: An agenda for action.* New York: Oxford University Press.

Gelles, R. J. (1983). An exchange/social control theory. In D. Finkelhor, R. J. Gelles, G. T. Hotaling, & M. A. Straus (Eds.), *The dark side of families.* Beverly Hills, CA: Sage Publications.

George, C., & Main, M. (1979). Social interactions of young abused children: Approach, avoidance and aggression. *Child Development, 50,* 306-318.

Gil, D. G. (1970). *Violence against children.* Cambridge: Harvard University Press.

Green, A. H. (1979). Child-abusing fathers. *Journal of Child Psychiatry, 18*(2), 270-282.

Helfer, R. E. (1980). Developmental deficits which limit interpersonal skills. In C. H. Kempe & R. E. Helfer (Eds), *The battered child* (3rd edition). Chicago: The University of Chicago Press.

Herrenkohl, R. C., & Herrenkohl, E. C. (1981). Some antecedents and developmental consequences of child maltreatment. *New Directions for Child Development, 11,* 57-76.

Herzberger, S. D., Potts, D. A., & Dillon, M. (1981). Abusive and nonabusive parental treatment from the child's perspective. *Journal of Consulting and Clinical Psychology, 49,* 81-89.

Hilberman, E., & Munson, K. (1978). Sixty battered women. *Victimology, 2,* 460-470.

Hilberman, E. (1980). Overview: The wife beater's wife reconsidered. *American Journal of Psychiatry, 137,* 1336-1347.

Huberty, C. J. (1984). Issues in the use and interpretation of discriminant analysis. *Psychological Bulletin, 95,* 156-171.

Jenkins, R. L. (1972). Varieties of children's behavior problems and family dynamics. *American Journal of Psychiatry, 124,* 1440-1445.

Johnson, B., & Morris, H. A. (1968). Injured children and their parents. *Children, 15*(4), 147-152.

Kempe, C. H., & Helfer, R. E. (1972). *Helping the battered child and his family.* Philadelphia: J.B. Lippincott.

Knutson, J. F., & Zaidi, L. Y. (1986, July). Punitive childhood experiences and adult parenting behavior: Clinical and analog tests of transgenerational coercion. Paper presented at the meeting of the International Society for Research on Aggression, Chicago.

Koss, M. P., & Oros, C. J. (1982). Sexual experiences survey: A research instrument investigating sexual aggression and victimization. *Journal of Consulting and Clinical Psychology, 50,* 455-457.

Levinger, G. (1966). Sources of marital dissatisfaction among applicants for divorce. *American Journal of Orthopsychiatry, 36,* 803-807.

Loevinger, J. (1957). Objective tests as instruments of psychological theory. *Psychological Reports, 3,* 635-694.

Morris, M. G., & Gould, R. W. (1963). Role-reversal: A necessary concept in dealing with the "battered child syndrome." *American Journal of Orthopsychiatry, 33,* 746-749.

Nurse, S. M. (1974). Familial patterns of parents who abuse their children. *Smith College Studies in Social Work, 32,* 11-25.

Parke, R. D., & Colmer, C. W. (1975). Child abuse: An interdisciplinary analysis. In E. M. Hetherington (Ed.), *Review of child development research, Volume 5.* Chicago: The University of Chicago Press.

Patterson, G. R. (1982). *Coercive family process.* Eugene, OR: Castalia Publishing Company.

Patterson, G. R. (1986). The contribution of siblings to training for fighting: A microsocial analysis. In J. Block, D. Olweus, & M. Radke-Yarrow (Eds.), *Development of antisocial and prosocial behavior* (pp. 235-261). New York: Academic Press.

Pelton, L. H. (1978). Child abuse and neglect: The myth of classlessness. *American Journal of Orthopsychiatry, 43,* 608-617.

Rao, C. R. (1973). *Linear statistical inference and its application*. New York: Wiley.

Rapaport, K., & Burkhart, B. R. (1984). Personality and attitudinal characteristics of sexually coercive college males. *Journal of Abnormal Psychology, 93*, 216-221.

Reidy, T. J. (1977). The aggressive characteristics of abused and neglected children. *Journal of Clinical Psychology, 33*, 1140-1145.

Rounsaville, B. J. (1978). Battered wives: Barriers to identification and treatment. *American Journal of Orthopsychiatry, 48*, 487-494.

Sapp, A. D., & Carter, D. L. (1978). *Child abuse in Texas: A descriptive survey of Texas residents' attitudes*. Survey Research Program, College of Criminal Justice, Sam Houston State University, Huntsville, Texas.

Scott, W. J. (1980). Attachment and child abuse: A study of social history indicators among mothers of abused children. In G. J. Williams & J. Money (Eds.), *Traumatic abuse and neglect of children at home*. Baltimore: The Johns Hopkins University Press.

Smith, S. M. (1975). *The battered child syndrome*. London: Butterworths.

Smith, S. M. & Hanson, R. (1975). Interpersonal relationships and child rearing practices in 214 parents of battered children. *British Journal of Psychiatry, 127*, 513-525.

Smith, S. M., Hanson, R., & Noble, S. (1974). Social aspects of the battered baby syndrome. *British Journal of Psychiatry, 125*, 568-582.

Snyder, D. K., & Fruchtman, L. A. (1981). Differential patterns of wife abuse: A data-based typology. *Journal of Consulting and Clinical Psychology, 49*, 878-885.

Steele, B. F. (1976). Violence within the family. In R. E. Helfer & C. H. Kempe (Eds.), *Child abuse and neglect: The family and the community*. Cambridge: Ballinger Publishing Company.

Steele, B. F. (1978). The child abuser. In I. L. Kutash, S. B. Kutash, & L. B. Schlesinger (Eds.), *Violence: Perspectives on murder and aggression*. San Francisco: Jossey-Bass, Inc.

Steele, B. F. (1980). Psychodynamic factors in child abuse. In C. H. Kempe & R. E. Helfer (Eds.), *The battered child*, (3rd edition). Chicago: The University of Chicago Press.

Steele, B. F., & Pollack, C. B. (1974). A psychiatric study of parents who abuse infants and small children. In R. E. Helfer & C. H. Kempe (Eds.), *The battered child* (2nd edition). Chicago: The University of Chicago Press.

Steinmetz, S. K. (1978). The battered husband syndrome. *Victimology, 2*, 499-509.

Stewart, M. A. & deBlois, C. S. (1981). Wife abuse among families attending a child psychiatry clinic. *Journal of the American Academy of Child Psychiatry, 20*, 845-862.

Stewart, M. A., deBlois, C. S., & Cummings, C. (1980). Psychiatric disorder in the parents of hyperactive boys and those with conduct disorder. *Journal of Child Psychology and Psychiatry, 21*, 283-292.

Straus, M. A. (1978). Wife beating: How common and why? *Victimology, 2*, 443-458.

Straus, M. A. (1980). Stress and physical child abuse. *Child Abuse and Neglect, 4*, 75-88.

Straus, M. A., Gelles, R. J., & Steinmetz, S. K. (1980). *Behind closed doors: Violence in the American family*. New York: Anchor Press.

Wasserman, S. (1968). The abused parent of the abused child. *Children, 14*(5), 175-179.

Chapter 5
Developmental Determinants of Male-to-Female Aggression

Beverly I. Fagot, Rolf Loeber, and John B. Reid

In this chapter, we are particularly concerned with the developmental determinants of male-to-female aggression within the family. Why does a small group of males choose female victims? Are there any patterns within their family of origin that would help us predict future problems? First, we report on data from several studies by Patterson, Reid, Fagot, and Loeber at the Oregon Social Learning Center (OSLC) that looked at the general problem of the development of aggression within the family. Second, we discuss the relevant data from studies on sex role development in preschool children done by Fagot and colleagues at the University of Oregon. Finally, we will attempt to bring together the information we have concerning male-to-female aggression within the family and with peers. Because the studies were not designed for this specific purpose, our results should be construed as a basis for the design of a more complete study, rather than as a definitive answer to why or how male-to-female aggression is learned.

First, we will discuss differences in the development of male and female aggression with an emphasis on Patterson's model of coercive families, and we will examine the data specifically related to male-to-female aggression. At the end of the chapter we present a special case of Patterson's model of family coercion, one in which the young boy learns to direct his aggression, not against his male peer group, but against women.

DEVELOPMENTAL DIFFERENCES IN THE PATTERN OF MALE AND FEMALE AGGRESSION

Maccoby and Jacklin (1974, 1980) have argued convincingly that there are sex differences in the way that aggression develops in males and females. They point out that in literally hundreds of studies males are more likely to aggress than females. Their argument is that this pattern of aggression is well set by the time children are six years old. They also point out that we do not have much information concerning the development of aggression in young children.

Fagot and her colleagues have attempted to study aggressive behavior in very young children in several studies involving both home and peer playgroup settings. Young children engage in aggressive acts at high rates compared to older children. For instance, in normal families 3-year-old boys emit an average of one aggressive act every minute and one-half; 13- to 14-year-olds average one aggressive act every 10 minutes. Compared to older children, the assertive acts of preschool children are brief (Patterson, 1982).

Fagot and Hagan (1985) found that sex differences were present by the time children are 18 months old, with boys consistently more physically aggressive than girls. Furthermore, peers act differently toward the aggression of boys and girls. Girls' aggression was ignored more of the time (51%) than boys' aggression (32%). Boys responded more to the acts of other boys than to the acts of girls, while girls responded more equally to acts of boys and girls. This study is in accord with the study of slightly older children by Brindley, Clarke, Hutt, Robinson, and Wethli (1973), who found that boys directed aggression toward other boys and not toward girls, while girls' aggression was directed more equally toward both boys and girls. They found, moreover, that boys produced more aggressive incidents than girls.

Fagot, Hagan, Leinbach, and Kronsberg (1985) looked at a group of infants and followed them for nine months. No sex differences in aggression were found when the children were infants (12 to 16 months old), but the caregivers reacted very differently to the aggressive acts of boys and girls. When girls aggressed, their behavior was ignored 80% of the time, while boys' aggression was attended to 80% of the time. By the time these same children were toddlers, there were sex differences in aggression; this replicated the peer findings from the Fagot and Hagan study.

We became interested in the interplay between the child's construction of gender role and aggression. Leinbach and Fagot (1986) devised a nonverbal task that allowed us to test toddlers' knowledge of gender labels. We found that children first learned adult labels and then labels for boys and girls. The average age at which children learned boy-girl distinction was 30 months, but there were wide variations. Fagot, Leinbach, and Hagan (1986) found that those children who understood boy-girl gender labels showed sex-typical differences in aggression, while children who did not have this classification did not show such differences. This study suggests that the male's use of aggression is built into the child's construction of his gender schema, while aggression is not a part of the girl's gender schema; in fact, the typical female gender schema may include avoidance of the expression of aggression.

We agree with Bem (1983) that, by allowing children to include all kinds of irrelevant information in their gender schema, we teach children to define social behaviors as male and female that in fact have very little to do with their biological sex. For most boys, then, physical aggression becomes one way to obtain their goals, and as young children they use it frequently. Most boys gradually learn that physical aggression is a costly way to obtain goals, and they substitute other, more socially acceptable behaviors; physical aggression is always in the background as a gender-acceptable behavior. Girls learn that aggression is not an acceptable behavior within their gender schema, and they typically drop it out of their behavior repertoire very early.

BOYS WHO DO NOT LEARN TO CONTROL THEIR AGGRESSION

Patterson (1982) has developed a model of the coercive family in which boys learn to be aggressive and then practice that learning on society. Patterson is concerned with the general problem of the development of aggression in boys and gives us a striking picture of these families at work. These families are basically ones in which the parents do not have control of the child. They are deficient in what Patterson (Patterson & Stouthamer-Loeber, 1984) calls family-management skills: they do not know how to effectively discipline the child; they do not do a good job of monitoring his behavior; they do not solve problems well; and they do not provide positive role models for the child. If a child starts to use coercion to obtain his way in such families, the parents do not use efficient family management to bring the child's behavior under control, nor do they teach him more positive ways to achieve his goals. They instead respond to him irritably, but ineffectively, often finally giving in when he is most noxious. The result is a coercive cycle: the next time, the child starts his behavior at a more intense level; the parents again either fail to respond or respond inappropriately. With each incident, the intensity rises, but nothing is learned either by the child or by the parents. Such children are at real risk of becoming social aggressors, for within the family such aggressive behaviors control their interactions. When they go outside the home and use the same techniques, they are quickly in trouble with schools and peers. Patterson (1984) notes that both mothers and siblings in these families practice aggression at high rates, and he points out that mothers are the most likely targets for such aggression. We have, then, a family system that is out of control, resulting in a child who is out of control. However, a large number of these children practice their physical aggression on other boys outside of the home environment. Why does a small percentage select female targets?

STUDIES LOOKING AT MALE-TO-FEMALE AGGRESSION

The studies on male-to-female aggression are perplexing. Studies of normal children show that physical aggression from age three is primarily a male activity directed at other males. This is one of the less controversial findings within developmental psychology, and has been replicated many times in preschool, elementary school, and high school children (Dawe, 1934; Savin-Williams, 1979). As mentioned earlier, Fagot and her colleagues have shown that boys drop in their rate of aggressing against girls in peer playgroups around the age of two. So, some process takes place within the normal population by which most males learn not to aggress against females most of the time. Yet there is also the literature on spouse abuse that suggests that within intimate relationships a reasonably large proportion of the population uses aggression against women. Straus (1980) reported that males were more likely to cause serious injuries to their wives than vice versa. Homicides in families are not typically one-time explosive incidents. Chimbos (1978) reports that in Canadian spousal homicides 70% of the victims reported physical abuse prior to the murder. Gates (1978) reported that 85% of those involved in domestic homicides had been in contact with the police for domestic violence prior to the murder. That male-to-female aggression is more lethal than female-to-male aggression is documented by Campbell (1981), who found that, of women who were murdered, 91% of their assailants were men, contrasted to the finding that of male victims, only 21% of the assailants were women.

It is clear, then, that there is a real need to understand the patterns of development resulting in individuals engaging in male-to-female violence. It is our feeling that such patterns develop within the family of origin, and that we need precise information concerning the actual patterns of interaction within the family.

One family relationship that provides children a chance to practice aggression is their relationship with siblings. Patterson (1984) found that if one child in a family is referred for social aggression, then the rest of the siblings in the family will also have elevated rates of aggression. The survey studies by Dengerink and Covey (1981) showed that subjects who had an early history of violence with their siblings also tended to report more violence toward people outside the family. So there is some indication that in coercive families all members have heightened rates of aggression toward each other. While there is a kind of myth that boy and girl siblings do not physically fight with one another as much as male siblings, recent research data do not consistently support this conclusion. In an observation study, Abramovitch, Corter, and Lando (1979) found that male and female sibling dyads did not differ significantly in terms of total agonistic behavior, though male dyads engaged in significantly more physical aggression than female dyads. Abramovitch, Corter, and Pepler (1980) observed mixed-sex sibling dyads and found no sex differences in agonistic behavior, but girls were more prosocial than boys. Levels of interaction between mixed sex pairs were very similar to those reported in the earlier study with same-sex pairs (Abramovitch et al., 1979). In contradiction to the Abramovitch studies, Dunn and Kendrick (1979) reported that same-sex sibling dyads had higher rates of positive and lower rates of negative behaviors than mixed-sex dyads. Patterson (1984) found that, in coercive families, male and female siblings fight at about the same rates as male-only siblings, providing some training for male-to-female aggression. One important question is, does this generalize to other settings and other relationships?

In our work at the Oregon Social Learning Center (OSLC) with children who are high-rate aggressors, we have observed several hundred families, using codes that allow us to look at targets of aggression within the home setting. These observations have convinced us that the home serves as a rich training ground for male-to-female aggression. Patterson (1980) found that mothers were the primary victims of their sons' aversive behaviors. As it is the mother, even in two-parent families, who does most of the disciplining, she is also the family member who bears the brunt of the child's failure to comply.

Loeber, Weissman, and Reid (1983) looked at 11 assaultive adolescents who had been treated as young children. These children were compared with a normal sample and a sample of children who stole but did not show physical aggression. The home observation data from their earlier contacts with OSLC were examined. It was clear that the assaultive children showed higher rates of negative behaviors than all other members of their family, and much higher rates of negative scores than the children from normal families. The mothers at the time of the observations also said that sibling fighting was a family problem. In addition, the fathers in the assaultive families showed very high rates of negative behaviors, but not as high as their sons. In a post-hoc analysis, it turned out that the assaultive boys averaged fewer male siblings and more female siblings than the normal families. Therefore, these boys whose mothers reported sibling fights as a major family problem were more likely to be fighting with girls rather than with boys. The results of this study, along with Patterson's findings that the mother is most likely to be a victim, prompted Reid (1983) to examine male-to-female aggression in four family types: (1) families with high parent-child conflict and volatile, self-reported physical confrontations between parent and child; (2) child-abusive families with serious, documented instances of physical abuse; (3) high aggressive child families, in which the child was referred for therapy; and (4) non-distressed control families. All families were observed on the Family Interaction Coding System (FICS), which gives a running account of interactions between the target child and other family members (Reid, 1978). Hoffman et al. (in press) had mothers rate the FICS items on a Likert scale and developed three clusters: Negative, Positive, and Neutral. The clusters are presented in Table 5.1.

Reid found that the three family groups differed significantly in the amount of both positive and negative behaviors emitted by the target child. In particular, children in the high parent-child conflict group, and children in the aggressive group emitted significantly more negative behaviors than children in the other two groups. Next, Reid examined the way in which the target boys reacted to the different family members. Reid again confirmed that mothers in all four groups received the most negative behaviors from the child, although this was not sig-

Table 5.1. FICS Code Categories Grouped by Composites

Negative (NEG)	Neutral (NEU)	Positive (POS)
*Command Negative	Command	Approval
Dependency	Cry	Attention
Destroy	No response	Compliance
Disapproval	Receive	Indulgence
High rate	Self-stimulation	Laugh
*Humiliate		Normative
Ignore		Physical positive
Negativism		Play
Noncompliance		Talk
*Physical negative		Touch
Tease		Work
Whine		
*Yell		

Based on Likert scale ratings of the aversiveness of the mothers' sons' behavior. The sons ranged in age from 3 to 12 years, mean age = 8.5 years.

NEG category is composed of behaviors rated "somewhat annoying" to "extremely annoying"; POS category is composed of behaviors rated "somewhat pleasant" to "extremely pleasant"; the remaining behaviors comprise the NEU composite. (Hoffman, in press)

*These four categories make up the Abuse cluster (AC).

nificant in the normal group. Male and female siblings received approximately the same amount of negative behavior from the target child, and much more in the high parent-child conflict families as well as in the aggressive-child families. When Reid examined the conditional probability that the target boy's aversive initiations would be followed by either a positive or negative response, he found that only in the normal families did the child receive more punishment for attacking the mother than for attacking siblings or the father. When he looked at the probability of positive responses, then for all families the aversive behavior toward the mother was more likely to be followed by a positive response than aversive behavior to any other family member, although this was significant only in abusive families. Reid expected that female siblings would also be victims of the target boys, but they were victims no more often than male siblings. However, Reid did find that when the boys in the abusive group aggressed, approximately two-thirds of that aggression was against females, either mothers or sisters. The rates of attack by target children to family members and the probability that the child would be given positive or negative reactions for attack behavior are presented in Tables 5.2, 5.3, and 5.4.

Table 5.2. The Rate per Unit Interaction at which Target Boys in the Four Groups Directed Aversive Behaviors Toward Other Classes of Family Members*

Classes of family members	(1) Child abusive	(2) High parent-child conflict	(3) Highly aggressive	(4) Non-distressed	F/p	m's @ p < .05
Female siblings (A)	.01	.09	.07	.02	10.88 .001	2,3 > 1 > 4
Male siblings (B)	.03	.08	.08	.02	6.81 .001	2,3 > 1, 4
Mothers (C)	.07	.15	.13	.03	19.77 .01	2 > 3,1 > 4
Fathers (D)	.02	.08	.04	.01	7.23 .01	2 > 3,1, 4
F/p	2.20 p<.11	3.11 p.<05	2.46 <.08	.82 p=.49		
m's @ p < .10	C>D,B,A	C>D,B	C>D,A,B	No difference at p<.10		

*The complete data set was analyzed using a group x subject type (i.e., family member) ANOVA. Both main effects were significant at p < .001. The interaction was marginally significant (p < .10).

Table 5.3. The Mean Conditional Probabilities That an Aversive Initiation by the Target Boys to the Various Classes of Family Members was Followed Immediately by a Positive Reaction*

Probability of an immediate positive reaction to a boy's aversive behavior to his:	(1) Child abusive	(2) High parent-child conflict	(3) Highly aggressive	(4) Non-distressed	F/p		m's @ p < .05
Mother (A)	.55	.42	.41	.28	3.93	.02	1 > 4
Sister (B)	.13	.26	.2	.19	1.56	n.s.	– – –
Father (C)	.39	.25	.15	.16	3.41	.03	1 > 4, 3
Brother (D)	.19	.26	.32	.17	1.03	n.s.	– – –
F/p	6.77 p<.01	2.31 p<.10	1.13 n.s.	.81 n.s.			
m's @ p < .05	A > B,D	– – –	– – –	– – –			

*Overall 2 x 2 ANOVA (groups x family member type): Groups, F   = 1.95, p < .15
Family members,F   = 5.00, p < .01
Groups x family members,F   = 2.32, p < .02

Table 5.4. The Mean Conditional Probabilities That an Aversive Initiation by the Target Boys to the Various Classes of Family Members was Followed Immediately by a Negative Reaction*

Probability of an immediate negative reaction to a boy's aversive behavior to his:	(1) Child abusive	(2) High parent-child conflict	(3) Highly aggressive	(4) Non-distressed	F/p		m's @ p < .05
Mother (A)	.15	.24	.28	.14	4.07	.01	3>1,4
Sister (B)	.07	.28	.16	.03	8.97	.001	2>3>1,4
Father (C)	.11	.21	.12	.04	2.78	.05	2>4
Brother (D)	.07	.17	.20	.07	3.44	.02	3>4,1
F/p	1.54 n.s.	.74 n.s.	.80 n.s.	2.31 $p <$ .08			
m's @ $p <$ .05	---	---	---	A>B,C,D			

*Overall two-way ANOVA for these data (groups x family members): the main effect for groups significant, F = 15.23; p < .001.

PLANNING GRANT DATA

In a longitudinal planning study undertaken by Patterson, Loeber, and other OSLC staff, subjects were a total of 210 fourth-, seventh-, and tenth-grade boys and their families, who were assessed on a wide variety of measures. Ninety-nine of these families were observed at home using a modified observation system (Toobert, Patterson, Moore, & Halper, 1982). On the basis of the sibling constellations, the sample was divided in three groups: (a) the only-female sibling group (n = 31), (b) the mixed sibling group (n = 21), and (c) the male sibling group (n = 26). The rest of the children had no siblings (n = 21). The average number of siblings living in the home for the three sibling groups were, respectively: (a) 1.35, (b) 2.76, and (c) 1.38, which was significantly different (F[2,75] = 24.8, p < .001). The target boys within the groups were not significantly different in terms of age, incidence of broken families, and observed Composite Aversive Behavior Score, or CAB score, a summary score of the following behaviors: noncomply, command, command ambiguous, criticize, complain, defend self, get off my back, provoke, threat, refutation-denial, disapproval, yell, cry, restrain, grab, destroy, and physical negative. The number of older and younger female or male siblings (compared to the target boy) was not significantly different among the groups, with the exception of older female siblings, who were about twice as numerous in the mixed sibling groups compared to the only-female group.

Boys were classified by mothers' report as fighters or nonfighters. When fighters and nonfighters who had sisters only were compared with boys who had brothers only, it was clear that fighters do indeed fight more at home, validating the mothers' self-report (F[1,47] = 5.37, p < .025), but boys did not fight significantly more with sisters. Although it was not significant, the mean level of fighting with brothers was higher. The fighting boys had the same proportion of sisters to brothers as did the nonfighters.

Next, we were interested to see if these boys directed more aversive behavior against mothers than fathers. We looked at all two-parent families and did a 2 x 2 ANOVA (fighter vs. nonfighter, mom vs. dad, repeated). We found no significant difference in aggression toward parents in the fighter versus nonfighter group, but significantly more aggression was directed to mothers than fathers (F[1,45] = 5.62, p < .022). This normal teenage sample replicates both Patterson's (1980) and Reid's (1983) findings on victimization of mothers, and also replicates Reid's findings that female siblings are not picked on more than male siblings.

There is another way to identify highly aggressive boys, and that is to use the Combined Aversive Behavior (CAB) scores from the observations and look at boys who score one standard deviation above the mean in terms of aversive behavior in the home. Using this criterion, 13 boys fit our criterion of very aggres-

Table 5.5. Classification of Fighters by Mothers and Aversive Children by
Observation

	Non-fight	Home fight
Non-aversive	51	12
Aversive	7	6

sive vs. 18 boys whom the mothers identified as fighters at home. Six of these boys
had female siblings only, three had both male and female siblings, and four had
male siblings only, which is just what one would expect in terms of the base rate
of boys in each group. Next, we were interested in determining how well our
mother-reported fighters matched our observed aversive children. The match is
not particularly good, as shown in Table 5.5. Mothers are obviously reporting
something different than aversive behavior when they complain about children
who fight, either physically or verbally, at home. Next, we looked at the amount
of aversive behavior directed toward male and female siblings by highly aversive
vs. nonaversive boys. We found that highly aversive boys directed significantly
more aggression toward their siblings (F[1,53] = 38.6, p < .001), but there was
no difference in the amount of aggression directed toward male and female siblings. We looked at all two-parent families and found that highly aversive children direct more aversive behaviors against their parents (F[1,54] = 5.50, p <
.023), and there was also a main effect, with mothers receiving more aversive behavior than fathers (F[1,54] = 4.50, p < .038). So even though the aversive children as identified by observation and fighters identified by mothers do not totally
overlap, their behavior in the home, in terms of aversive behavior directed toward
their siblings or toward their parents, is very similar. We feel that the data we
have presented clearly show that boys have ample opportunity to practice antisocial acts toward females in their families; sisters serve as targets for aggressive
acts as often as brothers.

Unfortunately, in neither Reid's study nor in the longitudinal planning study
was there information concerning aggression toward females outside the home.
Fagot does have some information on the relationship of family patterns and aggression with the play group, but with very young children.

LONGITUDINAL STUDY OF VERY AGGRESSIVE CHILDREN

For a study on social development in young children, Fagot and colleagues at
the University of Oregon observed a total of 240 children. The children involved
were observed in play groups for a study on social development, with 12 to 15
children in each class, equally divided among boys and girls. At least two under-

graduate students served as teachers throughout the term. At the time these data were collected, the children in the play groups ranged from 18 to 44 months of age. The data were collected over a four-year period, during the first and second term of each child's attendance in the play group. The basic procedure was similar to the other studies.

Children who are highly aggressive are quickly labeled by others in the environment. This is reflected in comments made by other parents and by teachers who want methods to control such behaviors. We examined children who were two standard deviations above the mean for aggression in their play group for at least two consecutive terms and tried to document how these children are similar and just what happens to such children in our classrooms. Two terms of high scoring rather than just one were chosen, because we found that a child under temporary stress (i.e., a new sib, a new home) would often show a burst of aggressive behaviors. However, such behavior would quickly subside when the stress was diminished. Nine children fit our criteria.

First of all, one similarity stood out: all of these children are boys—but after this there are no particular family patterns. Some of the children were only children; others had several brothers and sisters. Most came from two-parent families, although two did have only the mother in the home. Parents ranged from professional parents to a welfare mother. What was consistent was what happened to these children in the classroom as they continued their aggression. It was clear that teachers considered them problems and kept their eye on them. While teachers of young children tend to respond to aggression rather mildly, with these children, teacher reaction came faster and was consistently more negative. The boys became more and more isolated from the majority of their peers, with many children fleeing from them in obvious fear. Teachers gave significantly more negative feedback to these boys, even when the children were not being aggressive. However, these aggressive boys did have a group of friends, usually other boys, with whom they played in a positive and constructive fashion, so that overall positive peer behaviors were quite high. These boys received more negative reaction from both peers and teachers, but the amount of positive reaction from both peers and teachers was no different than the class average.

All nine of these boys were from families where parents showed high disagreement on child rearing at times as measured by the Child-Rearing Practices Report (CRPR) (Block, Block, & Morrison, 1981).

Boys Who Choose Girls as Victims

There were nine very aggressive boys, but only three of them chose primarily female victims. All three of these boys had female siblings only and all were younger siblings. This suggested to us that perhaps having a female sibling was important in learning to aggress against girls.

We then went back to the total sample of 127 boys, and compared boys with male siblings only to boys with female siblings only. Thirty-eight of the boys fell into the two categories. We looked at rate of aggression against females in the peer group as a dependent variable. We classified each child as above or below the median of his own class for aggression toward females. Twenty boys had brothers only, and 18 had sisters only. Boys with brothers did not show a difference from chance in aggressing against girls in the play group (12 above median and 8 below). However, for boys with sisters, 15 of the 18 boys were above the median of aggression against females for their class, and this was significant at the .004 level. When one looks at positive interactions with girls, this same pattern is not replicated; boys with sisters do not just play more with girls, but they do fight more with girls. We also found that aggression directed toward boys in the class was unrelated to sex of sibling.

DISCUSSION

We are now at the point where we believe we can extend Patterson's model of coercive families to predict specific aggression against females. We feel that three conditions must be met to produce a child who will be a consistent aggressor against females. First, the family must be out of control, that is, the parents lack disciplining skills, do not monitor the child, fail to problem-solve effectively, and do not provide positive models. They fit the model of the coercive family and the target child gets his way by emitting higher and higher rates of aversive behaviors, directed primarily at the mother. This leads to the second condition: the child must have female models to practice on. As mothers are present in most families, they receive the greatest share of aggression, but female siblings, if available, also are often targets. The boy's aversive behavior toward female models is not effectively punished, so he learns he can aggress without severe punishment, and in effect he gets his way by doing so. We see, then, that not only are females present, but that the boy is allowed to get away with this aggression. This leads us to the third necessary condition to develop a real female victimizer. There must be a system of family attitudes or values that devalues females, values suggesting to the child that females are indeed fair game for male violence and that puts males in a position of dominance over females. We would expect that such values would show up in behavioral and attitude measures in which the target child is allowed to emit aversive acts against the mother or sister, often without punishment and even more often being allowed to obtain his goal. We feel at this time that we have the theoretical model and the technology available to test our ideas.

ACKNOWLEDGMENTS

This report was based on work supported by NIMH, U.S. PHS grants 7 R01 MH 37940, 1 R01 MH 373979, and 1 R01 MH 37911, and a grant from the Center for Study of Women in Society, University of Oregon.

REFERENCES

Abramovitch, R., Corter, C., & Lando, B. (1979). Sibling interaction in the home. *Child Development, 50,* 997-1003.

Abramovitch, R., Corter, C., & Pepler, D. (1980) Observations of mixed sex sibling dyads. *Child Development, 51,* 1268-1271.

Bem, S. L. (1983). Gender schema theory and its implications for child development: Raising gender-aschematic children in a gender-schematic society. *Signs, 8,* 598-611.

Block, J. H., Block, J., & Morrison, A. (1981). Parental agreement-disagreement on child rearing orientations and gender related personality correlates in children. *Child Development, 52,* 965-967.

Brindley, C., Clarke, P., Hutt, C., Robinson, I., & Wethli, E. (1973). Sex differences in the activities and social interactions of nursery school children. In R. P. Michael and J. H. Crook (Eds.), *Comparative ecology and behavior of primates.* London: Academic Press.

Campbell, J. (1981). Misogyny and homicide of women. *ANS: Women's Health.* American Nursing Society.

Chimbos, A. D. (1978). *Marital violence: A study of interspousal homicide.* San Francisco: R & E Research Associates.

Dawe, H. C. (1934). An analysis of 200 quarrels of preschool children. *Child Development, 5,* 139-157.

Dengerink, H. A., & Covey, M. K. (1981). Implications for an escape-avoidance theory of aggressive responses to attack. In R. Geen & E. Donnerstein (Eds.), *Aggression: Theoretical and empirical reviews.* New York: Academic Press.

Dunn, J., & Kendrick, C. (1979). Interaction between young siblings in the context of family relationships. In M. Lewis & L. A. Rosenblum (Eds.), *The child and its family.* New York: Plenum Press.

Fagot, B. I., & Hagan, R. (1985). Assertive behavior in toddlers. *Sex Roles, 12,* 341-351.

Fagot, B.I., Hagan, R., Leinbach, M.B., & Kronsberg, S. (1985). Differential reactions to assertive and communicative acts of toddler boys and girls. *Child Development, 56,* 1499-1505.

Fagot, B. I., Leinbach, M. D., & Hagan, R. (1986). Gender labeling and adoption of gender role behaviors. *Developmental Psychology, 22,* 440-443.

Gates, M. (1978). Introduction. In J. R. Chapman and M. Gates (Eds.), *The victimization of women* (Volume 3). Beverly Hills, CA: Sage Publications.

Hoffman, D. A., Fagot, B. I., Reid, J. B., & Patterson, G. R. (in press). A validation of the Family Interaction Code System using parent ratings. *Behavioral Assessment.*

Leinbach, M. D., & Fagot, B. I. (1986). Acquisition of gender schema: A test for toddlers. *Sex Roles, 15,* 655- 666.

Loeber, R., Weissman, W., & Reid, J. B. (1983). Family interactions of assaultive adolescents, stealers, and nondelinquents. *Journal of Abnormal Child Psychology, 11,* 1-14.

Maccoby, E. E., & Jacklin, C. N. (1974). *The psychology of sex differences.* Stanford, CA: Stanford University Press.

Maccoby, E. E., & Jacklin, C. N. (1980). Sex differences in aggression: A rejoinder and reprise. *Child Development, 51,* 964-980.

Patterson, G. R. (1980). Mothers: The unacknowledged victims. *Monographs of the Society for Research in Child Development,* (Vol. 45, No. 186).

Patterson, G. R. (1982). *A social learning approach. Vol. 3: Coercive family process.* Eugene, OR: Castalia Publishing Co.

Patterson, G. R., & Stouthamer-Loeber, M. (1984). The correlation of family-management practices and delinquency. *Child Development, 55,* 1299-1307.

Patterson, G. R. (1984). Siblings, fellow travellers in the coercive process. In R. J. Blanchard and D. C. Blanchard (Eds.), *Advances in the study of aggression* (Vol. 1, pp. 173-215). New York: Academic Press.

Reid, J. B. (Ed.). (1978). *A social learning approach to family intervention, Vol. 2: Observation in home settings.* Eugene, OR: Castalia Publishing Company.

Reid, J. B. (1983). Final report: Investigation of boys' aggression toward women and girls. Unpublished manuscript. Eugene, OR: Oregon Social Learning Center.

Savin-Williams, H. S., (1979). Dominance hierarchies in groups of early adolescents. *Child Development, 50,* 923-935.

Straus, M. A. (1980). Social stress and marital violence in a national sample of American families. In F. Wright, C. Bain, & R. W. Rieber (Eds.), Forensic psychology and psychiatry, *Annals of the New York Academy of Sciences,* (Vol. 347).

Toobert, D. J., Patterson, G. R., Moore, D. R., & Halper, V. (1982). MOSAIC: A multidimensional description of family interaction. Unpublished manuscript. Eugene, OR: Oregon Social Learning Center.

Chapter 6

Attribution Processes in Repeatedly Abused Women

Sonja Peterson-Lewis, Charles W. Turner, and Afesa M. Adams

Spouse abuse is a multifaceted problem with many antecedent conditions and many consequences (Straus, Gelles, & Steinmetz, 1980). One perplexing feature of spouse abuse is the fact that many women remain in their marriages even though they are abused repeatedly. The present chapter provides an analysis of cognitive and attributional processes (Heider, 1958; Jones & Davis, 1965; Kelley, 1967) that appear to deter battered women from leaving relationships in which they are repeatedly abused.

The chapter provides a theoretical model which examines the combined effects of cultural learning, personality variables, and attributional processes in repeatedly abused women. As a first step in understanding these women's reactions, the model examines women's attributions (or interpretations) of the "causes" of their mate's abusive behavior. These attribution processes can determine whether the woman perceives the cause of the abuse as being either internally or externally motivated.

We propose that attributional processes can determine whether individuals remain in or terminate an abusive relationship. Individuals are assumed to be more likely to remain in an abusive relationship if they perceive their partner's behavior as resulting from causes external to the partner. Presumably, these external causes are perceived as producing uncontrollable or transitory situational forces, which lead to the physical abuse. For example, a woman might perceive her partner's abusive behavior as resulting from an external force which he did not anticipate and could not avoid, or from an external event which he could not control. For example, she might think, "He lost his temper because of something that happened to him," or she might identify her own behavior as the external cause of her spouse's behavior. Regardless of the actual cause of the abuse, the abuser is unlikely to be blamed or be seen as responsible for the abuse when the behavior is attributed to causes external to the abuser (Rule & Ferguson, 1984). Subsequently, the abused woman is unlikely to terminate the relationship.

We also propose that a woman is unlikely to remain in abusive situations if she attributes the cause of the abuse to an internal, stable property of the partner, such as his negative disposition (e.g., if a woman perceives her partner to be a vicious person). In addition, she might perceive him to have a negative attitude toward her. When the cause of the abuse is attributed to something internal to the abuser, he is more likely to be blamed or be seen as responsible for the abuse. Subsequently, the abused individual is more likely to terminate the relationship.

CULTURE, ATTRIBUTION PROCESS, AND ABUSE

A woman's socialization experiences can influence her interpretation of the causes of her spouse's abusive behavior. One important aspect of a woman's socialization is the interpretation her particular culture makes of male/female relationships and the expectations subsequently held by the woman for male behaviors. The woman's culture can make certain explanations highly salient or available to her. Tversky and Kahneman (1974) have demonstrated that highly salient information is viewed as being more probable than less available information.

In a similar manner, the woman's culture can emphasize either internal or external causes of spouse abuse. Consequently, the culture can make these explanations highly salient so that these explanations are also likely to be seen as the most *probable* explanation for the abuser's behavior. Prior research provides support for this reasoning. Researchers have demonstrated that an observer's interpretation of the causes of another person's behavior is influenced by the relative salience or availability of situational (external) or dispositional (internal) labels (Higgins, Rholes, & Jones, 1977; McArthur & Post, 1977).

The socialization experiences and popular culture of low-income and minority women may be especially likely to lead them to make external rather than dispositional attributions for a wide variety of social behaviors. Based on this premise, subsequent sections of the present chapter focus on the popular culture and the socialization experiences of Black women. These sections examine attribution processes that might influence a Black woman's decision to remain in an abusive marital relationship. We do not assume that the experiences of Black women apply to all cultural groups, nor that our analysis applies to all Black women. However, such analyses similar to the one presented in this chapter can be performed for women of other cultural groups. These analyses would help to examine the validity and extent to which one can generalize the attribution processes that are hypothesized to be used by some Black women.

Mass Media Attention to Spouse Abuse

The mass media is one important example of the popular culture of all women. We propose that the media (e.g., newspapers, magazines, and television) can influence a woman's interpretation of the causes of her own and her partner's abusive behavior. Subsequently, by changing the woman's attributions for the causes of the abuse, the media may influence her decision to remain in or leave the relationship. The present section of the chapter reviews some of the themes that have appeared in the media's characterization of spouse abuse.

Tierney (1982) has noted that seven articles addressing the problem of spouse abuse appeared in the *New York Times* in 1976. However, in the five years prior to 1976, only eight articles had even mentioned the problem.

During the late 1970s and continuing into the 1980s, a variety of popular magazine articles addressed issues related to the problems of violence among intimates — whether married, cohabiting, or dating couples. Articles about violence in intimate relationships appeared in women's magazines such as *Good Housekeeping, Vogue,* and *Mademoiselle,* in addition to other general audience magazines.

The media attention to spouse abuse may have had dual effects. On one hand it provided resource information to women in abusive relationships. On the other hand, the media attention could have produced some inadvertent effects of encouraging some women to accept a role in abusive relationships. Popular magazines with high readership among women frequently present articles that reflect research published in scientific journals. Many of the articles appearing in popular magazines have focused upon the presumed causes of a number of social problems. These problems are frequently portrayed as being caused by societal forces rather than being caused by the dispositions of the individuals who are involved in the social problem. Of course, many of these articles' contentions are based on well-documented facts, and societal pressures can be readily linked to a myriad of social problems.

As with other social problems, much of the research in the popular literature on marital violence has been concerned with the social factors or family variables that seem to foster intrafamilial violence. Thus, much of the popularly reported evidence specifies family and situational variables that appear to be related to the occurrence of violent behavior within family units. Some familial/circumstantial variables that have been proposed include: (a) wife's educational level being higher than the husband's; (b) wife's income level exceeding the husband's income (Marshall, 1983a, 1983b); (c) role confusion or role reversal between wife and husband, (d) low socioeconomic status of the family; (e) previous experience with familial violence in family of origin (i.e., either the wife's or husband's parents practiced spouse abuse); and (f) frequent alcohol consumption among husbands (Coleman, Weinman, & Hsi, 1980).

Justified or not, authors in the popular media who emphasize societal (i.e., external) causes of behavior may produce some unintended effects on the audience or reader. The authors' arguments can serve as readily available justifications or rationalizations by the abused for an abuser's behavior. In other words, when the media portrays spouse abuse as being caused by social (external) pressures on the male, the media actually may have played an important role in changing women's attributions about abuse and, subsequently, in convincing some abused women to remain in abusive relationships. These media portrayals imply that the women should not hold the husband responsible for his abusive behavior, since the behavior results from forces over which he has little control.

The next section of this chapter summarizes some of the predominant rationalizations used by abused women for remaining in their marital relationships. We do not assume that these rationalizations are created solely from media characterizations of spouse abuse. Nevertheless, some women might be influenced by the media portrayals.

Attribution Processes and Abusive Relationships

An individual who is confronted with an abusive spouse might be expected to take action to terminate the abuse. One way to terminate the abuse is to leave the abusive relationship. However, many abused individuals remain in the relationship through repeated episodes of abuse. Ferraro and Johnson (1983) have identified six rationalizations or "justifications" which are commonly used by wives who remain in abusive relationships. In each of these rationalizations, the abusive situation is defined so that either the husband's or the wife's behavior is believed to be caused by external events such that both spouses' behavior is perceived as unalterable. After presenting the six rationalizations identified by Ferraro and Johnson (1983), these rationalizations are analyzed according to the attribution theory principles of Kelley (1967), Heider (1958), and Jones and Davis (1965).

Rationalization of Women Remaining in Abusive Relationships

Ferraro and Johnson (1983) interviewed women who were confined to spouse-abuse shelters. The researchers found that the women were likely to resort to one or more of the following rationalizations for staying in the relationship if they had remained with their husbands for long periods of time after the abuse began.

1. Appeal to the Salvation Ethic

By staying in the relationship, the abused wife perceives herself as helping to cure the husband of the "illness" that leads him to abuse her. She may perceive him as acting out against his will — as being possessed by some strange and alien ailment that causes him to behave with hostility toward her. She differentiates between the "real" husband and the abusive one, rationalizing that the two are distinctly different entities. If she remains in the relationship, she hopes that she will be able to *save* the real husband from his "illness."

2. Denial of the Victimizer

The abused partner identifies the abuser's behaviors as entities other than the partner's. She may perceive the frustrations he suffers on his job or in other aspects of his life as the real source of his anger and aggression. If the wife is able to perceive the husband as society's victim (either rightly or through distorted rationalizations), she can attribute his behavior to his position in life rather than to a negative disposition toward her.

3. Denial of Injury

The abused may actually underestimate the seriousness of her injuries. For example, she may choose to interpret a slap as only a playful pat, and a fractured or broken limb as only a sprain. She may reason that she is reasonably or even extraordinarily strong and healthy, and is therefore able to take a "few minor" bruises. Some women may continue in this mode of perception even when the abusiveness becomes quite frequent and quite serious.

4. Denial of Victimization

The victim denies that the partner's abusive behavior toward her was spontaneous or unprovoked. In thinking back or recounting the events that led up to the abusive episode, she may perceive herself as having motivated the abuse by some provocative behavior. For example, she may reason that her "unladylike" behavior or utterances provoked the husband to slap her. If only she had behaved in a more feminine manner, he would not have needed to react so violently. In the process of denying victimization, the abused individual not only avoids blaming her partner for his abusive behavior, but she also may begin to assign the blame for her abuse to herself.

5. Denial of Options

One of the most common reasons that women give for remaining in an abusive relationship is their dependency upon the relationship for economic support. Many believe that they would not be able to survive without the financial rewards that come from the relationship. In addition to economic incentives for remaining in the relationship, many women concede that they receive important emotional rewards from the relationship when the abuse is absent. Many women resorting to this rationalization are afraid that they will not be able to find other persons with whom they can develop a rewarding emotional relationship. This fear can deter an abused individual from leaving the abusive relationship.

6. Appeal to Higher Loyalties

Some women, because of variables related to socialization or religion, may believe that there are entities that are of higher value or more significance than themselves. Essentially, the abused partner reasons that factors such as the legal bond between herself and the partner deserve more consideration than her own complaints or dissatisfactions with the relationship. In giving priority to the state of matrimony, the abused individual removes her option of leaving the relationship. When individuals are socialized to assign great value to marriage and partnership, they may be particularly susceptible to this line of reasoning.

The appeal to higher loyalties may also entail the victim's contending that endurance of difficulties in the present will result in vast rewards in the afterlife. Thus, women using this rationalization believe that they will be compensated in heaven for the abuse they endure on earth so that they, as victims, do not need to take any corrective action.

According to Ferraro and Johnson (1983), women with strong religious affiliations are frequently advised by their clergymen to stay in the relationship and to "try to work things out," or to "try to be a better partner." In giving such advice, the clergy may implicitly remove responsibility from the abuser and place it upon the abused; that is, the abused individual becomes responsible for improving the relationship. If she/he leaves the relationship, then she/he becomes responsible for the failure of the relationship.

SUMMARY

In a previous section, we briefly proposed attribution processes in women that should influence their decision to continue or to terminate a relationship. We hypothesized that a woman would be motivated to leave her relationship if she perceived her partner's stable, negative disposition as the "cause" of his injurious behavior toward her. The six rationalizations described by Ferraro and Johnson (1983) permit abused women to attribute either their own or their partner's behavior to "external" causes.

The first four rationalizations permit an abused woman to avoid blaming her partner for the abusive behavior. These rationalizations define his behavior either as being noninjurious (rationalization 3) or as being due to some cause outside the relationship (rationalizations 1 and 2) or as being due to the woman's own behavior (rationalization 4). In short, the woman does not need to blame the male for the abuse if she uses any of these four rationalizations.

The next two rationalizations permit the woman to avoid blaming herself for remaining in an abusive relationship. The woman can attribute her inability to leave an abusive relationship either to environmental (i.e., external) causes that she cannot control (rationalization 5) or to an external moral force which she cannot resist (rationalization 6).

Women experiencing repeated abuse apparently are highly motivated to understand their spouse's behavior. If causal responsibility is assigned to the provocateur, then the harmed individual is likely to blame the harmdoer for the injury. In addition, the assignment of blame is likely to lead to anger. Anger can lead to an increased desire to retaliate against the harmdoer (Berkowitz & Turner, 1974). Moreover, the victim is likely to believe that she might be harmed again in the future. If she does not think that she can control the harmdoer's behavior in the future, she may attempt to withdraw from the relationship (Turner, Fenn, & Cole, 1981). Thus, principles that influence a woman's attribution processes can influence a woman's decision to remain in a relationship that involves repeated abuse.

In the course of moving toward a final decision about the relationship, the abuse victim would be likely to think about many aspects of her abuser's behavior. She might consider the frequency of his abusive behavior (i.e., whether it occurs on a stable weekly basis or whether there are long spans of time between violent episodes). In addition, she might consider whether her situation and experience is unique or whether violence is normal in a marriage. Thus, she may engage in social comparison, using acquaintances or even media persons as gauges for the "normality" of her experiences.

The abused woman also might consider the degree to which the abusive behavior affects her personal functioning. From such assessments, she can better decide her appropriate course of action — whether she should remain in the relationship or seek a separation and divorce. Perhaps, she might even decide to retaliate through the use of violence. Her decision is likely to depend upon the outcome of the attributional analysis she applies to her relationship.

ATTRIBUTION THEORIES

To some extent, all attribution theories examine the process by which individuals identify the sources of their own or other's behaviors. These theories also give some clues as to how an individual's responses might be affected by his or her attributional analysis of another's behavior. These theories can help to predict and to explain responses to marital violence. The following section presents some of the major principles which govern attribution processes.

One important determinant of an individual's anger and aggressive retaliation for being harmed is the severity of the harm. However, the severity of injury may not be as important as the attributional processes in determining an individual's reactions to being harmed (Averill, 1982; Dyck & Rule, 1978; Novaco, 1979; Rule & Ferguson, 1984). The injured individual could attribute the harmful behavior to a personal characteristic of the harmdoer (e.g., "he is a bully" or "he hates me"). Alternatively, an attribution could be made to a feature of the environment (e.g., "he did not mean to harm me, it was an accident" or "he just lost his temper").

Heider's Attributional Theory

Heider (1958) described some of the major processes by which observers assign causal responsibility to an actor (the individual performing the behavior) or to the environment (the setting in which the behavior takes place). The observer may be particularly likely to attribute the cause of the actor's behavior to the actor's disposition in certain situations. For example, when the observer has a personal interest in the outcome of the actor's behavior, she or he may be more likely to interpret the behaviors in terms of outcomes (e.g., how much injury occurred) rather than in terms of the environmental forces impacting the actor. In other situations, the actor's disposition may be ignored while the environment is highlighted as the cause of the actor's behavior. The assignment of responsibility to harmdoers depends upon: (a) whether they could or did foresee the harmful consequences; (b) whether they tried to produce or tried to avoid the harm; and (c) whether their behavior was socially appropriate or inappropriate (Rule & Ferguson, 1984).

Kelley's Attributional Model

In his analysis of attributional processes, Kelley (1967) proposed that observers use three factors in their consideration of whether to place causality or blame for an act with the actor (internal attribution) or with the circumstances (external attribution). These three factors are consistency, distinctiveness, and consensus. Consistency occurs when an actor displays the same behavior across time, situations, and modalities. Distinctiveness occurs when the actor's behavior is directed toward one specific target or object as opposed to being generalized across targets. Consensus occurs when the actor's behavior appears to be widely practiced by the population at large rather than being unique to the actor.

An internal attribution is likely to occur when consistency is high, distinctiveness is low, and consensus is low (Kelley, 1967; McArthur, 1972). Thus, an internal attribution for an abusive behavior would occur: (1) if the individual was abusive at many different times and across many different situations (high consistency); (2) if the individual behaved abusively toward many people (low distinctiveness); and (3) if the abusive behavior was not a common characteristic of most people (low consensus). When the actor's behavior can be characterized by these three factors, the actor's behavior will be perceived as resulting from his or her disposition, and the observer is then likely to infer that the abuse will occur repeatedly. In addition, the observer is likely to assign blame to the actor for any harm that occurs in the abusive situation.

However, even repeated abusive situations may not lead to dispositional attributions about the abuser. When abuse recurs in families, the abusive behavior is likely to be interspersed with extensive nonabusive behavior (Gelles, 1979). In short, abuse may not be perceived as being high in consistency. In addition, the abuse may be directed primarily or solely toward the spouse; thus the behavior is perceived as high in distinctiveness. Finally, abused women may believe that many men commit abuse; these women may have experienced abuse from their fathers or witnessed the abuse of their mothers or other adult females they have known. These experiences would lead to the perception of high consensus for males' abusive behavior and to the perception that violence in intimate relationships is inevitable.

When consistency is low, distinctiveness is high, and consensus is high, an external attribution is likely to be made to explain the actor's abusive behavior (McArthur, 1972; Pryor & Kriss, 1977). Under these conditions, the actor is not likely to be blamed for any harm that his behavior has caused. In addition, the actor's behavior is assumed to be the result of some specific situational constraint. Hence, the actor is perceived as being unlikely to display the same behavior again unless the specific situation recurs.

One additional factor must be considered in determining whether the target of a behavior would make an internal attribution about the actor's behavior. In a given situation, all of the necessary conditions for making an internal or dispositional attribution could be present. That is, the actor could be highly consistent across time or situations in his abusiveness. In addition, his targets could be general rather than distinct individuals. Finally, his abusiveness could be perceived as not being a general, consensual characteristic of other comparable males. Even though all of the necessary conditions exist, the observer may use the discounting principle (Kelley, 1967), which proposes that when there are several possible causes of an actor's behavior, the observer may discount some causes in favor of others. For example, the target may believe that the actor was under the influence of some external force (e.g., alcohol or drugs) during his abusive episodes. The target may therefore assume that the actor's behavior was the product of a temporary and transitory state rather than the product of a permanent dispositional characteristic. Hence, the observer has disregarded or *discounted* the role of the dispositional attribute as a cause of the actor's behavior.

In Kelley's (1967) and Heider's (1958) attributional models, the observer is not assumed to have a strong preexisting motivation to perceive either the actor or the circumstances as being more responsible for the act under consideration. The observer is assumed to be relatively unbiased in terms of attributional preference. One important feature of the attributional process in spouse abuse is that the observer is also the target of the actor's behaviors. Jones and Davis (1965) provide an important clarification of attributional processes when the observer and the target are the same person.

The Theory of Correspondent Inferences

Jones and Davis (1965) make use of the terms "personalism" and "hedonic relevance" to account for attributional processes. These terms describe situations in which the observer has a personal stake in the outcome of the actor's behavior. In these situations, the observer is more motivated to pinpoint the cause of the actor's behavior. The term "personalism" means that the actor's behavior has personal significance to the observer, since the actor's behavior appears to be directed or targeted toward the observer. The behavior has hedonic relevance for the observer if the observer perceives the outcome to have affected her or him in some way, either positive or negative.

Jones and Davis' (1965) attributional framework implies that the more the actor's behavior affects the observer, the more the observer should be motivated to hold the actor responsible for the outcomes or consequences of his or her behavior. The observer should be especially motivated to assign responsibility to the actor if the ultimate effect is strong. Walster (1966) found support for these predictions. She found that observers are more likely to assign personal responsibility to an actor as the consequences of his or her behavior become more serious.

Jones and Davis' (1965) attributional model provides an important perspective on the attributional processes involved in spouse abuse. The act of battering has hedonic relevance in that the actor's behavior negatively affects the observer (i.e., the victim). The battering process also involves personalism, since the battering is especially and *specifically* directed toward the observer. The principles of hedonic relevance and personalism should make the observer/target more prone to attributional biases. The specific direction of these biases (whether toward an internal or external attribution) should be determined by several factors, one of which should be the target's overall evaluation of the relationship she shares with the actor. A positive evaluation of the relationship could lead to *discounting*. However, a negative evaluation might lead the target to quickly and confidently assign blame or responsibility to the actor.

Battering is rarely perceived as being such an unambiguous situation for women that they can easily decide to leave the relationship (Pagelow, 1981). Even in its most severe form, battering frequently is ignored or underevaluated in terms of its severity. The ambiguity of these situations may be partly responsible for the fact that repeatedly abused women frequently resort to the various rationalizations described by Ferraro and Johnson (1983) to justify maintaining their relationship to the abuser. These rationalizations permit the woman to avoid blaming the abuser for this behavior.

Because of their exposure to certain experiences or modes of thinking, some women may be more prone than others to perceive the abuser's behavior as caused by external forces. For example, when women are exposed to media presentations of material which provides explanations or excuses for some men's violent behavior, the women may readily (and prematurely) adapt those explanations to their own needs.

SPOUSE ABUSE AND THE POPULAR CULTURE
OF BLACK WOMEN

The variables that influence a woman's response to family violence are likely to be culture bound (Gelles, 1979). Thus, the factors that are important to one group may not be important for other cultural groups. In order to understand the source of rationalizations that a woman might use for remaining in an abusive situation, the sociocultural environment of the woman must be considered (Cherry & Deaux, 1978; Frieze, Parsons, Johnson, Ruble, & Zellman, 1978). Her decision to remain in an abusive situation might be influenced by variables such as the socialization process, the unique experiences in her family, and the exposure to media sources such as television, newspapers, and magazines.

We propose that minority group and low-income women are especially likely to be exposed to sources that lead them to employ situational explanations of causation for a variety of experiences. We will focus our discussion on Black women and some of the popular literature (newspapers, magazines, and books) that have high readership across social classes within the Black community. An examination of this literature reveals that it often emphasizes the causal role of societal pressures rather than stable dispositional characteristics of the actors. An analysis of some of the social forces that act upon many Black women can provide important insights into the sources of rationalizations that help to keep some women in relationships involving repeated abuse.

EXTERNAL FORCES CONTRIBUTING TO ABUSE
IN BLACK WOMEN

By focusing our analysis on Black women, we are not proposing that all or even most of Black women experience familial violence. Furthermore, those women who do experience abuse are not necessarily unique or different from non-Black women in their experiences or responses. Rather, our analysis is intended to demonstrate how specific features of a given culture can provide powerful combinations of myths, realities, and rationalizations which can keep women in abusive relationships. Similar analyses can and should be performed for women of other cultural groups as well as women of various socioeconomic groups.

Some of the factors which researchers have proposed to be causative factors in conjugal violence are low socioeconomic status, higher wife than husband educational and income levels, and role conflict. These factors are much more likely to be common among minority groups. Some research on the Black family (e.g., Staples, 1973) affirms that these factors frequently occur in Black families. In a popular magazine article, clinical psychologist Anna Jackson is quoted as contending that Black men are particularly sensitive about having their wives earn more money than they do. In the same article, sociologist Alex Swan is quoted as stating that the power and authority traditionally associated with the male partner are challenged when the wife earns more money.

Many researchers and feature writers for popular Black magazines have provided detailed discussions of the adverse economic conditions and negative social and political forces that come to bear upon many Black families. High unemployment rates and systemic racism are two forces widely held to be responsible for the adverse faring of some Black families. In addition, the popular literature is replete with descriptive analyses of the Black family as a matriarchal one in which the female has taken charge, rules with an iron hand, and poses great threat to anyone who challenges her authority.

The view of the Black family as a matriarchal unit is exemplary of the idea of role conflict or role reversal. This premise was advanced to a great extent by Daniel P. Moynihan in his highly controversial report on the Black family (Moynihan, 1965). Despite the controversy associated with this report, Moynihan's conclusions are broadly quoted, and they appear to have garnered a substantial degree of support among the general population. One result of this acceptance is that many discussions of problems within the Black community focus on the mother's influence on these problems. For example, the mother's role is discussed as being uniquely important in the development of "appropriate" sex-role behavior, autonomy and personal functioning among children, and the self-concept of male and female children.

Some researchers of the Black family (Pettigrew, 1964; Young, 1964) have suggested that educational and achievement differences between Black males and females arise because mothers are likely to encourage their daughters more than their sons to attend school and to excel academically. The sons may be more susceptible to competing environmental forces that propel them into dead-end jobs, the military, or even involvement in crime. Much of this susceptibility to environmental force is undoubtedly related to a desire to make immediate financial contributions to the family. Whatever the reasons, the outcome is that greater numbers of Black females than males attend and graduate from college. Their graduation leads to the perception that Black females as a group hold better-paying and more prestigious occupational positions than Black males.

It is a commonly held belief that Black women have always had greater opportunity to advance than Black males. For example, Benson (1981) interviewed psychologist Nathan Hare, who is the publisher of the magazine *Black Male/Female Relationships*. Hare is quoted as stating: "The Black female has always had more access to assimilation to certain aspects of 'White success.'" Benson notes that some writers have also speculated that the Black woman is not as threatening to a White-male-dominated society as is a Black male.

Because the occupational achievement and status of men is generally considered more important than that of women, the perception of the Black woman as exceeding the Black man in educational and occupational status inevitably contributes to conflicts within Black families. An often-made claim is that Black women gain upward mobility at the expense of Black men; articles in popular magazines reflect and contribute to these beliefs. For example, an article in *Ebony* entitled "Are Black Women Taking Black Men's Jobs?" (Marshall, 1983b) provides evidence that many Black men believe the professional and employment gains made by Black women hinder the progress of Black men. However, census data reveal that Black women earn less money than Black men, even when educational levels are matched. Thus, the view that Black women are better off economically than Black men apparently is a myth.

The relationship between family processes and community processes was heavily emphasized in the Moynihan Report. Popular Black magazines also frequently feature articles with this issue as a central theme. Some of those same articles either subtly or blatantly place the blame for many community problems on the Black female. Since she supposedly wields all the power in the home, she is often viewed as the ultimate cause of any problems that arise (see Moore, 1980). Many women may internalize these criticisms and either consciously or subconsciously accept this blame. They may come to believe either that they must take direct responsibility for community processes or that they should make amends and sacrifices for injustices of the past. This perception among women might lead to a conscious attempt to avoid all leadership or rule-making roles in which they might compete with males. Thus, these women may attempt to adopt a submissive role in all interactions involving males.

In this regard, Green (1973) wrote: "The black woman is being forced into a position of not daring to voice her criticism in the struggle [for black liberation] when she sees certain discrepancies for she wants to not emasculate the Black man. She wants not to further the Black/White myth of her as the overpowerful partner." Green also noted that "The problem seems to be that the Black woman's strength has been blown out of proportion, so that now even the slightest degree of aggressiveness or nondependency is regarded as threatening."

The mass media is one important example of the popular culture of all women. We propose that the media (e.g., newspapers, magazines, and television) can influence a woman's interpretation of the "causes" of her own and her partner's abusive behavior. In other words, when the media portrays spouse abuse as being caused by social (external) pressures on the male, the media actually may have played an important role in changing women's attributions about abuse and, subsequently, in convincing some abused women to remain in abusive relationships. These media portrayals imply that women should not hold the husband responsible for his abusive behavior since the behavior results from forces over which he has little control.

Black women are exposed to many social forces that can foster repeated spouse abuse. Moreover, it can be argued that the popular culture of Black women encourages them to make situational attributions for their spouse's abusive behavior. In this section of our chapter we will examine the features of the Black women's culture that predispose them to employ rationalizations such as those described by Ferraro and Johnson (1983).

Appeal to the Salvation Ethic Among Black Women.

The conditions fostering an appeal to the salvation ethic appear to be especially potent among Black women. For example, Black women have learned that some police officers appear to hold Black life in low regard, and that the criminal justice system treats Black males differently than White males.

Many Black females believe that Black males are more likely to be arrested without regard to the strength of evidence linking them to a specific crime, and that once arrested they are likely to be victims of police maltreatment and sometimes fatal beatings (Johnson, 1941; Leavey, 1981; Pettigrew, 1964; Poinsett, 1981; Poussaint, 1972). In addition, media accounts have portrayed numerous fatal confrontations involving Black males with policemen. For example, television, newspapers, and magazines extensively covered the killing by the Miami, Florida, police of a Black insurance salesman, Arthur McDuffie. The brutality of the killing was vividly portrayed by much of the written media (e.g., see Poinsett, 1981), television newscasts and documentaries.

Women exposed to these experiences may decide that they should not call the police in response to marital violence. If a Black woman believes that soliciting police intervention is likely to result in the use of extreme police tactics against the male, she is not likely to turn to the police for assistance. She may instead resort to the salvation ethic as a rationalization on several grounds. First, she may perceive herself as the only "safe" outlet for what she interprets as her mate's expression of his dissatisfaction with his life situation. Certainly, she realizes that drastic ramifications might come about if he expressed either verbal or physical aggression against individuals such as his employer or a co-worker. If he attempts to express his frustrations through aggressive acts within his community, she is aware of the possibility that his acting out will be met with defensive aggression.

She also may be fearful of what might happen to her if she summons the police to intervene in his violence against her. As with women of other ethnic groups, she may fear that the problem may not be taken seriously, and she may be further victimized as a result.

The woman exposed to these circumstances is aptly placed in an avoidance-avoidance paradigm (Lewin, 1948) in which she perceives all possible outcomes of her actions to be equally undesirable. Even if she were not afraid of police violence or retaliation by her mate, she might not want to be responsible for thrusting him into a criminal justice system that she perceives to be both hostile to and crowded with Black males. Thus, the internal perceptions and external realities of Black women may make them more likely than other women to believe that they are saving their mates from an unsympathetic, uncaring society by withstanding their abusive behavior.

Denial of Victimizer Rationalization Among Black Women

Most Black women are aware of the many race-related frustrations that Black men face in the work force or in other aspects of their lives. Some of these women may reason that their husbands are not victimizing them, but that their behavior toward them is merely a reflection of the treatment they receive from the world at large. Whether she is lower-, middle-, or upper-income, much of the popular literature to which the Black female is exposed most often delineates the many ways in which individual and institutional racism is responsible for economic, political, and interpersonal problems within the Black community (see "Black on Black Crime," 1979; "The Black Male-White Female," 1983).

Abundant information exists to indicate that much of the system blame is justified. However, when external entities are held responsible for certain outcomes or events, the Black male may be relieved of the responsibility for his behavior. The perception that external entities are responsible for part of an individual's behavior may be overgeneralized in a way that redefines all of the person's behavior as societally induced and removes the perception that the individual has any control over his/her behavior.

Denial of Injury Among Black Women

The perception of Black women as physically and emotionally stronger than women of other ethnic and cultural groups is the result of the historical context in which the Black woman has evolved in American society. Some authors have suggested, quite reasonably, that the mistreatment and maltreatment of the Black woman by White slaveowners was "justified" by labeling her as something other than a true instance of a feminine character. Nobles (1978) suggests, for example, that those privileges, courtesies, and concessions usually afforded to women in American society could only be withheld from the Black woman in good conscience if she could be labeled as something other than an instance of a woman. By labeling the Black female as tough-bodied and tough-minded, those who mistreated her could escape any guilt feelings that might accompany this mistreatment.

These labels also appear in Black literature, which is replete with references to "strong Black women." Although most of these references to the strength of Black women refer to her emotional strength, this reference was also extended to the physical realm (see, for example, the work of Zora Neale Hurnston, Alice Walker, Maya Angelou, and Ernest Gaines).

In the context of marriage or other intimate relationships, the mate of the "superwoman" might be less inhibited in striking her, reasoning that she is physically tough and can take the abuse. Similarly, having been constantly exposed to this view of herself as an extraordinarily strong woman, the victim might believe herself to be less prone to injury. She may underestimate the seriousness of her injuries or, if the situation allows, ignore her injuries altogether. Failing to seek medical care for injuries sustained in a domestic fight can have at least two important consequences. First, the victim misses out on a chance for professional consultation for her problem. Second, she stands the risk of "affirming" to her abuser that she is indeed tough (Snyder & Swann, 1978). Such an affirmation could lower restraints against violence toward her.

Denial of Options Among Black Women

Black women may be more susceptible to the rationalization that they have a dearth of options than to any of the other rationalizations. Ferraro and Johnson separate options into two categories — economic and emotional. When a women is dependent upon her husband's income for her own livelihood, she may be likely to externalize the causes of his abusive behavior. If the woman were to attribute his behavior to internal causes, she would need to separate herself from her source of income in order to protect herself from further abuse. For many women, this decision would produce serious problems, especially if they had few or no marketable skills or if they had children — especially younger children to be supported.

Ironically, the Black woman's lack of income-producing skills may have been self-encouraged by her fear of pricing herself out of the mating market. If she achieves higher education, occupation, and income levels, she may fear that she is ensuring her social isolation, since only a limited number of Black males have achieved a high level of education and income. In addition, popular feature articles advise that a woman's higher educational achievements are likely to be perceived as a threat to males, especially Black males (Benjamin, 1982; Benson, 1981; Howell, 1979). Other writers propose that working wives make men feel threatened and that men become even more distressed if their wives become successful in their own businesses (Benson, 1981).

A Black woman is often informed by prestigious media sources that she has few emotional options. Much of the literature to which she is exposed suggests to her that she is very unlikely to find another satisfying emotional relationship if she terminates her present one. She is informed by such notable writers as Staples (1970, 1978, 1981) that her lack of options occurs because Black females greatly outnumber Black males (the 1980 census ratio is approximately 180:100). Since the scarcity of Black males is, reportedly, even greater at the high academic achievement levels (see "The Black Male-White Female," 1983; Benson, 1981; Howell, 1979), the lack of options may be an especially strong consideration for middle- or upper-income Black women.

The Black woman is also likely to read or infer from her readings of such authors as Hernton (1979), Staples (1973, 1981), and Wallace (1979) that she has few options for an emotional relationship outside the Black community. This lack of option arises because, supposedly, she does not fit the American standard of attractiveness and desirability. In addition, popular Black magazines such as *Ebony* and *Essence* inform her of the increasing number of Black men who are opting for relations with White or other non-Black women (Howell, 1979; "The Black Woman," 1983).

Denial of Victimization Among Black Women

To the extent that a victim can perceive certain behaviors on his or her part as having precipitated another's actions toward him or her, the victim can effectively remove the burden of guilt from the actor and place it upon himself or herself. Many factors may contribute to a victim's electing to perceive himself or herself as being a causal factor in other's behavior toward him or her. In the context of marital violence, the victimized wife may prefer to perceive herself as having some degree of control or influence upon the partner. Thus, she may construe some action on her part as having caused his behavior. She may prefer to perceive his behavior as having been induced by her rather than by some random force that is unpredictable or uncontrollable (Langer, 1982).

A related possibility is that the wife may have a strong need to perceive her husband's abusive episodes as a *reaction to* her rather than an action *against* her. To the extent that the abused wife makes this attribution, she can avoid the potentially unsettling perception that her husband's behavior is the by-product of a stable internal disposition. She can also persuade herself, however unjustified or self-defeating this persuasion may be, that she has the ability to control his behavior by her own behavior.

The Black female who is familiar with the personality stereotypes surrounding her is at no loss for negative behavioral characteristics she can assign to herself. She learns from media sources that she is "too demanding, too possessive, and too controlling" ("The War Between the Sexes," 1979, p. 39). She might perceive these behaviors as being likely to elicit anger and/or aggression from her partner. These behaviors also may create a negative image in him toward other Black females whom he presumes fit the stereotype as well. As evidence of the potential potency of this perception, Staples (1981) reports that some Black males who exclusively date non-Black females cite as their reason for not dating Black females their belief that Black females are domineering, sexually inhibited, materialistic, and unsophisticated.

Another common stereotypic perception one often finds leveled against the Black female is that she is emotionally unsupportive, especially toward the Black male. Much of this perception may have been fostered by the Moynihan Report (Moynihan, 1965). Cade (1970) proposed that the Moynihan Report (1965) and

Eldridge Cleaver's *Soul On Ice* (1968) provided a backdrop that stimulated many of the Black male activists in the 1960s to actively exclude Black women from all but the most menial tasks. Allegedly, these men "justified" this exclusion on the grounds that Black women had commandeered the family unit (and therefore the Black community) away from concerned male leadership. Cade claimed that many women involved as social and political activists readily accepted the servant-type roles designated to them because these allegations were voiced or alluded to so often that many women began to believe themselves to have been partners in the emasculation of Black males.

The Black woman who perceives the negative stereotypes surrounding her to be true might very reasonably be moved to behave in a way to disprove these stereotypes. If she believes she is perceived as domineering and nonsupportive, she might consciously attempt to alter certain behaviors she believes are connected to this perception. For example, she might make a conscious attempt to become more acquiescent, more nurturing, and less assertive. One possible outcome of these personality alterations is that she may make herself a more susceptible victim to abuse.

Appeal to Higher Loyalties

Black women with strong religious convictions may be particularly likely to use this rationalization. Historically, the Christian church has been one of the strongest organizations in the Black community (Frazier, 1966). As one of the only legal meeting places during slavery, the Black church evolved as a center of social, political, and recreational as well as religious activities. Due to its historical role, the church has amassed a wide appeal and influence among many Blacks. Church officials — particularly ministers — have exerted great influence over members of their respective congregations and communities (Frazier, 1966). In addition to their traditional roles as ministers, church pastors have also served a counseling function for many persons. Among religiously oriented Black women, the pastor has been one important source of advice for dealing with marital problems. Undoubtedly, these pastors frequently give valuable advice.

However, the pastors' religious orientation may predispose them to encourage women to remain married even though the women are being abused. The religion offers little justification for dissolving a marriage. Thus, a minister is likely to encourage the couple to work harder at saving the marriage, to try to be more understanding of each other, or to examine their own behaviors to see if they might be doing things to upset or provoke their partners. In addition, the victim may be advised to think of the children and to try to keep the family together for their sake. Finally, the minister is likely to remind the abused woman that matrimony is a "sacred" responsibility which she should not treat lightly. A spouse-abuse victim encountering this type of counseling is much more likely to believe she should do things to maintain the marriage and try to influence her partner's behavior. Such beliefs are likely to lead her to return to the relationship repeatedly, hoping that she can find the right combination of behaviors to save the marriage.

Thus, the information which is intended to benefit the Black female by presenting her situation in actual rather than mythical terms may have the *negative* side effect of further increasing the salience of the dilemma in which she is trapped. Her dilemma is heightened by the fact that she may have read about, heard about, or actually witnessed enough instances of all the things that could be extenuating circumstances surrounding her condition to render them highly plausible explanations of her condition.

Justified or not, authors in the popular media who emphasize societal (i.e., external) causes of behavior may produce some unintended effects on the audience or reader. Subsequently, by changing the woman's attributions for the "causes" of the abuse, the media may influence her decision to remain in or leave the relationship. For the Black female, her objective reality is a society where she is economically exploited because she is both female and Black.

From an attributional perspective, the repeatedly abused religious woman can be led to believe that she is ultimately responsible for the abusive situation. If she is unable to change her partner's behavior, she may feel that she is at fault. These women may prefer to suffer repeated physical abuse rather than to view themselves as responsible for the failure of their "sacred responsibilities" in the marriage.

Up to this point, we have discussed social and cultural factors which may influence attributional processes in abused women. In the next section, we will describe some personality variables that may also contribute to abused women's attributions.

PERSONALITY VARIABLES RELATED TO
ATTRIBUTIONS ABOUT ABUSE

Type 1/Type 2 Women

According to Benjamin's (1982) typology, the Type 1 woman strongly identifies with the traditional goal of marriage and motherhood and has a greater dependency on men for her identity. The Type 2 woman is nontraditional in that she is generally career-oriented. Although she is not necessarily opposed to marriage, she places major emphasis on her own well-being and personal efficacy. Once she becomes involved in a relationship, the Type 2 woman is less likely to accept sole responsibility for the well-being of the relationship, less likely to accept traditional sex-role behaviors, and less likely to remain in an unsatisfactory relationship than would a Type 1 woman. She also might be more willing to ignore negative stereotypes than the Type 1 woman, who might be intent upon disproving these.

The concept of ego-involvement (Sherif, Sherif, & Nebergall, 1965) helps to explain the responses Benjamin's Type 1 and 2 women would be expected to make in the context of marital violence. According to the ego-involvement concept, the reactions and decisions one makes in situations involving an intimate relationship should be determined by the extent to which one is personally or emotionally invested (ego-involved) in the outcome of that relationship. Intimate relationships such as marriage, dating, or parenting are highly ego-involving. That is, an individual's outcomes in these kinds of relationships should have an immense effect on the person's self-evaluation. These effects should be especially pronounced for persons like the Type 1 woman, whose socialization processes have prepared them for few roles other than that of partner in a marriage. Thus, Type 1 and Type 2 women are likely to react differently to the psychological distress of spouse abuse.

We propose that both Type 1 and Type 2 women should experience cognitive dissonance (Festinger, 1957) when confronted by the fact that they are victims of marital violence. However, due to the different levels of ego-involvement on the part of Type 1 and Type 2 women, the two are likely to use different dissonance-reduction strategies. The Type 1 woman may elect to resolve her dissonance by attributing the cause of her spouse's behavior to environmental factors or to herself, perhaps reasoning that if she were a better partner her spouse would not be motivated to behave violently toward her. The Type 2 woman, although valuing her relationship, would be expected to place much less emphasis on saving the relationship than on ensuring her own well-being. Both cognitive dissonance theory and impression management theory (Hass & Mann, 1976) would suggest that the Type 2 woman, because she has made less of a public commitment to marriage, would be less likely to remain in an abusive relationship. We suggest, therefore, that the Type 2 woman would be less likely to perceive herself to be the cause of her spouse's abusive behavior and more likely to hold him responsible for his behavior, and therefore, more likely to leave an abusive relationship than would be the Type 1 woman. Thus, personality variables such as the Type 1/2 dichotomy might help to explain why some repeatedly abused women terminate their relationships while others remain in them, or return to them.

Type A/Type B Behavior Patterns

Benjamin's Type 1/Type 2 typology appears to have a strong counterpart in the Type A/Type B behavior patterns traditionally discussed in the social science and medical sciences literature. The Type A behavior pattern is characterized by excessive competitiveness, achievement orientation, impatience, and job involvement. The Type B behavior pattern is characterized by the relative absence of these characteristics. According to Turner, Cole, and Cerro (1984), Type A individuals generally attempt to terminate aversive situations with active behavioral strategies such as assertiveness, problem-solving, achievement striving, and aggression. Some of these behavioral characteristics correspond to those we might expect of Benjamin's Type 2 woman in that the Type 2 woman is presumably more achievement-oriented, competitive, involved in work outside the home, and more likely to fight back— either emotionally or physically—than her Type 1 counterpart.

Strube, Turner, Cerro, Hinchey, and Stevens (1984) found that Type B women are more likely to be targets rather than perpetrators of abuse in abusive relationships. The authors suggested that Type B women are likely to employ relatively passive solutions to their husbands' aversive behaviors, showing both a tendency to attribute his behaviors to external or environmental forces rather than to his personality and a tendency to engage in blunting strategies such as reading, watching television, or eating. These blunting strategies serve to psychologically or emotionally "shelter" her from the reality of abusive situation. Although the Type B woman may seek temporary refuge in a spouse-abuse shelter, Strube et al. (1984) propose that she is likely to return to her spouse after the negative environmental forces are perceived to have dissipated. Strube et al. (1984) thus provide evidence that the Type A/Type B personality dimension may help to explain some of the individual differences among women in reaction to violence in their family.

SUMMARY

The present chapter presented a cognitive-attributional analysis of conditions that lead women to remain in repeated abuse situations. We presented evidence that women are more likely to remain in an abusive relationship if they attribute the abusive behavior to uncontrollable environmental forces. We also presented evidence that personality and cultural variables can influence a woman's decision to remain in the abusive relationship. The present analysis focused primarily upon the attributions that Black women might make in repeated abuse situations. We do not contend that all, or even most, Black women accept or believe the cultural influences that we have described as being part of their popular culture. However, if a woman does accept the stereotypes about Black women, we assume that she is more vulnerable to the processes outlined in the chapter. The chapter also presents concepts that can assist individuals who counsel repeatedly abused women.

Much of the evidence we have presented in the chapter is derived from a conceptual rather than an empirical analysis of the media material commonly read by Black women. We cannot be certain that these materials have the effects that we have suggested they do. Further empirical research is required to determine whether the hypothesized attributional effects actually occur in abused women. Additional research is also required to examine the validity of the proposed attribution principles for other ethno-cultural groups. Finally, further research is needed to understand the attributional processes of the males involved in repeated abuse situations. We are currently pursuing these research endeavors.

ACKNOWLEDGMENTS

The authors are indebted to James Alexander, Sally Lloyd, Gordon Russell, Althea Smith, Steve Szykula, Judith Turner, and Holly Waldron for their comments on an earlier draft.

REFERENCES

Averill, J. R. (1982). *Anger and aggression: An essay on emotion.* New York: Springer-Verlag.
Benjamin, L. (1982). Black women achievers: An isolated elite. *Sociological Inquiry, 54,* 141-151.
Benson, C. (1981, January). Do Black women set their standards for marriage too high? *Ebony, 36*(3), 97-102.
Berkowitz, L., & Turner, C. W. (1974). Perceived anger level, instigating agent, and aggression. In H. London & R. Nisbett (Eds.), *Cognitive alteration of feeling states* (pp. 174-180). Chicago: Aldine.
Black on Black crime: The causes, consequences, and cures. (1979, August). *Ebony, 34*(10).
The Black male-White female: An update. (1983, August). *Ebony, 38*(10), 124-128.
The Black woman: A special issue. (1983, September). *Essence, 14*(5).
Cade, T. (1970). On the nature of roles. In T. Cade (Ed.), *The Black woman: An anthology* (pp. 101-110). New York: The New American Library.
Cherry, F., & Deaux, K. (1978). Fear of success vs. fear of gender-inappropriate behavior. *Sex Roles, 4,* 97-101.
Cleaver, E.(1968). *Soul on ice.* New York: Dell.
Coleman, K. H., Weinman, M. L. & Hsi, B. P. (1980). Factors affecting conjugal violence. *The Journal of Psychology, 105,* 197-202.
Dyck, R. J., & Rule, B. G. (1978). Effect of retaliation on causal attributions concerning attack. *Journal of Personality and Social Psychology, 36,* 521-529.
Ferraro, K. J., & Johnson, J. M. (1983). How women experience battering: The process of victimization. *Social Problems, 30,* 325-339.
Festinger, L. (1957). *A theory of cognitive dissonance.* Stanford, CA: Stanford University Press.
Frazier, E. F. (1966). *The Black church in America.* New York: Schocken.
Frieze, I. H., Parsons, J. E., Johnson, P. B., Ruble, D. N., & Zellman, G. L. (1978). *Women and sex roles: A social psychological perspective.* New York: W. W. Norton.
Gelles, R. J. (1979). *Family violence.* Beverly Hills, CA: Sage.
Green, J. (1973). Black romanticism. In T. Cade (Ed.), *The Black woman: An anthology* (pp. 137-142). New York: New American Library.
Hass, R. G., & Mann, R. W. (1976). Anticipatory belief change: Persuasion or impression management? *Journal of Personality and Social Psychology, 34,* 105-111.
Heider, F. (1958). *The psychology of interpersonal relations.* New York: Wiley.
Hernton, C. (1979). The Negro male. In D. Wilkinson & R. Taylor (Eds.), *The Black male in America: Perspectives on his status in contemporary society* (pp. 244-264). Chicago: Nelson-Hall.
Higgins, E. T., Rholes, W. S., & Jones, C. R. (1977). Category accessibility and impression formation. *Journal of Experimental Social Psychology, 13,* 141-154.
Howell, R. (1979, February). What men fear about women. *Ebony, 34*(4), 65-72.

Johnson, G. B. (1941). The Negro and crime. *Annals of the American Academy of Political and Social Science, 217,* 93-104.

Jones, E. E., & Davis, K. E. (1965). From acts to dispositions: The attribution process in person perception. In L. Berkowitz (Ed.), *Advances in experimental social psychology* (Vol. 2, pp. 219-266). New York: Academic Press.

Kelley, H. H. (1967). Attribution theory in social psychology. In D. Levine (Ed.), *Nebraska Symposium on Motivation, 15,* 192-238.

Langer, E. (1982). *The psychology of control.* Beverly Hills, CA: Sage.

Leavey, W. (1981, February). Battered women: Why so many suffer abuse so long. *Ebony, 36*(4), 94-100.

Leavey, W. (1983, August). Is the Black male an endangered species? *Ebony, 38*(10), 41-46.

Lewin, K. (1948). *Resolving social conflicts.* New York: Harper.

Marshall, M. (1983a, March). Can a marriage survive when the wife earns more? *Ebony, 38*(5), 44-48.

Marshall, M. (1983b, August). Are Black women taking Black men's jobs? *Ebony, 38*(10), 60-64.

McArthur, L. Z. (1972). The how and what of why: Some determinants and consequences of causal attribution. *Journal of Personality and Social Psychology, 22,* 171-193.

McArthur, L. Z., & Post, D. (1977). Figural emphasis and person perception. *Journal of Experimental Social Psychology, 13,* 520-535.

Moore, W. (1980, December). Black women, stop criticizing Black men—blame yourselves. *Ebony, 36*(2), 128, 130.

Moynihan, D.P. (1965). *The Negro family: The case for national action.* Office of Policy Planning and Research, U. S. Dept. of Labor, Washington, D. C.

Nobles, J. (1978). *Beautiful, also are the souls of my Black sisters: A history of the Black women in America.* Englewood Cliffs, NJ: Prentice-Hall.

Novaco, R. W. (1979). The cognitive regulation of anger and stress. In P. Kendall and S. Hollon (Eds.), *Cognitive behavioral interventions* (pp. 241-286). New York: Academic Press.

Pagelow, M. D. (1981). *Woman-battering.* Beverly Hills, CA: Sage.

Pettigrew, T. F. (1964). *A profile of the Negro American.* Princeton, NJ: Van Nostrand.

Poinsett, A. (1981, March). Police deadly force: A national menace. *Ebony, 36*(5), 46-52.

Poussaint, A. F. (1972). *Why Blacks kill Blacks.* New York: Emerson Hall.

Pryor, J. B., & Kriss, M. (1977). The cognitive dynamics of salience in the attribution process. *Journal of Personality and Social psychology, 35,* 49-55.

Rule, B. G., & Ferguson, T. J. (1984). Developmental issues in attribution, moral judgement, and aggression. In R. M. Kaplan, V. J. Konecni, & R. W. Novaco (Eds.), *Aggression in children and youth* (pp. 138-161). The Hague: Martinus Nijhoff.

Sherif, C. W., Sherif, M., & Nebergall, R. E. (1965). *Attitude and attitude change: The social adjustment approach.* Philadelphia: Saunders.

Snyder, M., & Swann, W. B., Jr. (1978). Behavioral confirmation in social interaction: From social perception to social reality. *Journal of Experimental Social Psychology, 14,* 148-162.

Staples, R. (1970). The myth of the Black matriarchy. *The Black Scholar, 1*(3-4), 26-34.

Staples, R. (1973). *The Black woman in America: Sex, marriage, and the family.* Chicago: Nelson-Hall.

Staples, R. (1978). Masculinity and race: The dual dilemma of Black men. *Journal of Social Issues, 34,* 169-183.

Staples, R. (1981). *The world of Black singles.* Westport, CT: Greenwood Press.

Straus, M. A., Gelles, R. J., & Steinmetz, S. K. (1980). *Behind closed doors: Violence in the American family.* Garden City, NY: Doubleday.

Strube, M. J., Turner, C. W., Cerro, D. S., Hinchey, F., & Stevens, J. H. (1984). Interpersonal aggression and the Type A coronary-prone behavior pattern: A theoretical distinction and practical implications. *Journal of Personality and Social Psychology, 47,* 839-847.

Tierney, K. J. (1982). The battered women movement and the creation of the wife beating problem. *Social Problems, 29,* 207-220.

Turner, C. W., Cole, A. M., & Cerro, D. S. (1984). Contributions of aversive experiences to robbery and homicide: A demographic analysis. In R. M. Kaplan, V. J. Konecni, & R. W. Novaco (Eds.), *Aggression in children and youth* (pp. 296-342). The Hague: Martinus Nijhoff.

Turner, C. W., Fenn, M. R., & Cole, A. M. (1981). A social psychological analysis of violent behavior. In R. B. Stuart (Ed.), *Violent behavior: Social learning approaches to prediction, management, and treatment* (pp. 31-67). New York: Brunner/Mazel.

Tversky, A., & Kahneman, D. (1974). Availability: A heuristic for judging frequency and probability. *Cognitive Psychology, 5,* 207-232.

Wallace, M. (1979). *Black macho and the myth of the superwoman.* New York: Dial Press.

Walster, E. (1966). Assignment of responsibility for an accident. *Journal of Personality and Social Psychology, 3,* 73-79.

The war between the sexes: Is it manufactured or real? (1979, June). *Ebony, 34*(8), 33-42.

Young, W. (1964). *To be equal.* New York: McGraw-Hill.

Part Two
Personality

INTRODUCTION

Any introduction to a section on personality would be incomplete without at least a passing reference to the "state-trait" controversy of this past decade. Given the topic of this book, aggressive behavior will serve as an example to illustrate the debate. While all of us have the capacity to aggress, many observers of human behavior detect a substantial degree of consistency in the behavior of individuals across day- to-day situations. That is to say, some people seem almost characteristically to react with hostility to any and all provocations; others rarely display aggression in their dealings with others, although they experience the same provocations. However, the view of aggression as a trait has not gone unchallenged. Mischel (1968) has persuasively argued that aggression – along with a number of other behaviors – is not displayed with sufficient consistency by individuals across situations and over time to warrant being regarded as a trait. Rather, he would contend that the behavior is not reliably exhibited by the individual and seems more under the control of situational factors for its expression rather than occurring as the result of some relatively enduring predisposition to aggress. A number of writers have joined the debate and vigorously argued the alternate view.

Perhaps the strongest case for aggression qualifying for something akin to trait status has been made by Olweus (1979). His review of the research bearing on this issue reveals substantial consistency between initial measures of aggression and measures taken again after intervals ranging from a few months to many years. A similar, quite high degree of *behavioral* consistency was also found to occur when the aggression of Norwegian boys was assessed in various settings, i.e., school, home, playgrounds (Olweus, 1979). Although the controversy is unresolved for all facets of "personality," for purposes of this section we will adopt

131

the Olweus view, at least with regard to aggression, and regard it as a major and relatively enduring aspect of personality (see also, Rushton & Erdle, 1987). Estimates of the impact of personality variables may be understated because their measurement is necessarily less precise. For example, Buss (1980) has identified an individual difference variable, private self-consciousness, by which some individuals are more in tune with, more aware of, their internal states, moods and beliefs than others. Self-report measures purporting to tap such internal processes would do so with predictably less success when administered to subjects low on private self-consciousness. Some impressive evidence on this point has been provided by Scheier, Buss, and Buss (1978). The correlation between subjects' scores on a hostility inventory and their performance on an aggression machine was +.34. Analyzing only those who scored high on a measure of private self-consciousness, the correlation jumped to .60. For those low in private self-consciousness, the correlation was virtually zero. Thus, it would appear that for a subset of the population at least, personality variables may be every bit as effective as predictors of interpersonal violence as other complementary approaches. Alternatively, it may be useful instead to regard personality traits as mediators (Baron, 1977), which serve to determine the form, direction, and magnitude of subjects' responses to provocations.

The close interplay between the situation and personality is not always apparent. However, in the historical case studies below, the critical role of inhibitions as an individual difference variable is clearly seen to produce totally different outcomes for those involved with the two male principals. The first anecdote concerns Firmin Abauzit (1679-1767), the Swiss natural philosopher. The story is related to us by S. Smiles (1897) as follows:

> Amongst other things, Abauzit devoted much study to the barometer and its variations, with the object of deducing the general laws which regulated atmospheric pressure. During twenty-seven years he made numerous observations daily, recording them on sheets prepared for the purpose. One day, when a new servant was installed in the house, she immediately proceeded to display her zeal by "putting things to rights." Abauzit's study, amongst other rooms was made tidy and set in order. When he entered it, he asked of the servant, "What have you done with the paper that was round the barometer?" "Oh, sir," was the reply, "it was so dirty that I burnt it, and put in its place this paper which you will see is quite new." Abauzit crossed his arms, and after some moments of internal struggle, he said, in a tone of calmness and resignation: "You have destroyed the result of twenty-seven years of labour; in future touch nothing whatever in this room." (p. 224)

Abauzit's response must surely mark the limits of both human provocation and restraint.

At the other extreme one might consider the turbulent life of the British poet and author, Walter Savage Landor (1775-1864). Landor was expelled from

Rugby and rusticated from Oxford's Trinity College owing to his volatile temper. The event that precipitated his departure from Oxford involved his shooting across at the windows of an undergraduate he despised who was hosting a rival party to his own. His chronically quarrelsome and arrogant nature is most clearly revealed by perhaps the best known of Landor stories. Super (1957) cites one of many versions of the story:

> He had one day, after an imperfect dinner, thrown the cook out of the window, and, while the man was writhing with a broken limb, ejaculated, "Good God! I forgot the violets" (p. 552).

Thus, Landor's typical response to provocations, most of which were fairly inconsequential, was excessive and out of all keeping with the circumstances. Abauzit showed composure in the face of a staggering provocation (one which can perhaps be only fully appreciated by the dedicated scientist). The role of inhibitions would be central to any explanation of these scenarios, as would the part played by anger. Thus, two situations can produce quite unexpected outcomes, outcomes that could only have been predicted by taking one or more individual difference variables into account. While the importance of inhibitions or the lack thereof as a determining factor in aggression is clear in the foregoing, their significance is generally overlooked in investigations of human aggression (Megargee, 1970). It is therefore timely to see a contribution to the present volume (Chapter 11) specifically applying Megargee's model of the chronically overcontrolled hostile individual to wife-battering. Moreover, its application to questions of treatment, emphasizing as it does a seemingly paradoxical *reduction* in excessive inhibitions, holds promise for the treatment of those violent individuals to whom the model applies.

The contributors to this section have necessarily discussed and investigated only a small sample of the full range of personality variables predictive of interpersonal aggression that occurs in the context of intimate relationships. However, those topics that *are* treated point to new directions and provide basic data for the future pursuit of research questions within an individual-differences approach.

REFERENCES

Baron, R. A. (1977). *Human aggression.* New York: Plenum.

Buss, A. H. (1980). *Self-consciousness and social anxiety.* San Francisco: W. H. Freeman.

Megargee, E. I. (1970). Undercontrolled and overcontrolled personality types in extreme antisocial aggression. In E. I. Megargee & J. E. Hokanson (Eds.), *The dynamics of aggression* (pp. 108-120). New York: Harper & Row.

Mischel, W. (1968). *Personality and assessment.* New York: Wiley.

Olweus, D. (1979). Stability of aggressive reaction patterns in males: A review. *Psychological Bulletin, 86,* 852-875.

Rushton, J. P., & Erdle, S. (1987). Evidence for an aggressive (and delinquent) personality. *British Journal of Social Psychology, 26,* 87-89.

Scheier, M. F., Buss, A. H., & Buss, D. M. (1978). Self-consciousness, self-report of aggression, and aggression. *Journal of Research in Personality, 12,* 133-140.

Smiles, S. (1897). *Character.* London: John Murray.

Super, R. H. (1957). *Walter Savage Landor: A biography.* London: John Calder Ltd.

Chapter 7

The Role of Personality in Violent Relationships

Aub Everett

INTRODUCTION

Currently underway at the University of Newcastle, New South Wales, Australia, is a large-scale long-term investigation of the phenomenon of violence in modern-day society. Facets of the investigation include the individual's psychological perception of violence, violence in the schools, in the streets, and cross-cultural comparisons of the psychological dimensions of violence. While still in the early stages, it has become increasingly evident that a very incomplete picture would emerge if one were to ignore the violence that goes on behind closed doors (Straus, Gelles, & Steinmetz, 1980).

The most significant finding to emerge from results to date is that regardless of the state of the objective world (increasing rates of homicide, robberies and muggings, and so on), the crucial data reside in the head of the individual. In psychological terms this translates into the individual's perception of the world (his/her personality, if you like); in sociological terms it is the individual's construction of reality (Berger & Luckmann, 1967). The current research indicates that when two people cohabit in an intimate relationship, they create and maintain their own joint phenomenal world, what has been described as a "private culture" (McCall, McCall, Denzin, Suttles, & Kurth, 1970, p. 15).

Here we are talking about the "personality" of the relationship, unique to the two people involved, and it is this shared, internalized, psychosociological construct that emerges as the crucial consideration in violent relationships.

Such a model has not proved popular among psychologists entrenched in normative methodologies. Its first axiom, the assertion of the uniqueness of the individual personality, the uniqueness being enhanced in permutative fashion when two individuals are involved, means that classifications and typologies of relationships are a waste of time. This point is developed in the current chapter.

OVERVIEW

First we discuss the meaning of violence. The value of an Australian contribution to a collection such as this suggests that the culture makes a difference to the phenomenon under scrutiny — the cultural context is considered from this viewpoint. Moving from the molar level, social and situational factors are examined, culminating in psychological-personality issues. This is followed by a brief consideration of methodological problems and the data base for the current research. Clinical and case study material are presented, followed by a summary statement.

VIOLENCE: PHYSICAL, PSYCHOLOGICAL, AND PROPERTY

Violence in the domestic situation is pragmatically restricted to that involving physical damage to one of the adult partners of the relationship; general consensus prevails among researchers in this area that it does not pay to differentiate between legal and de facto unions — the essential dynamics are similar (Deveson, 1978, p. 100; Dobash & Dobash, 1979, p. 1; O'Donnell & Craney, 1982, p. 52). It is difficult to separate the issues of psychological and physical violence; it is the latter that is more visible and more likely to result in public intervention. Frequently the two aspects of violence go hand in hand. There is some suggestion that some degree of physical violence is not unexpected in working-class relationships which are linked to differential socialization practices (Lewis, 1983, p. 86), while psychological violence is more likely in the middle-class home. Psychological violence by itself is difficult to tap and probably occurs in all relationships to some degree, its prevalence and definition depending very much on the social situation of the victim and what resources are available at the time. There is little doubt that there is a growing awareness among women due to increased publicity (e.g., Women's Coordination Unit, 1983; Women's Advisory Council, 1984) through pamphlets, medical practitioners, media coverage and phone-ins, which increasingly encourage victims to extricate themselves from such situations. The recognition of the problem and its extent in the Australian context closely parallels the establishment of refuges for women who have been beaten; the first one was established in Sydney, NSW, in 1974, with the current number approaching one hundred, Australia-wide (Scutt, 1983). Interestingly, the opening of the first refuge in Sydney places Australia in the forefront of world recognition of the problem of battered women (see Dobash & Dobash, 1979, p. 1).

Such refuges cater primarily to working-class women and their children on a short-term basis, most frequently admitted because of physical violence (Saville, 1982, p. 104). An interesting and unremarked-on correlate of physical and psychological violence was property damage in the current data. From the interview sources it frequently appeared that middle-class spouses would resort to property destruction in order to redress the imbalance of power in the relationship. Property damage has symbolic significance at the psychological violence level — the partner is hurt through the destruction of items deemed to be important by him or her. Such behavior is frequently transformed into bitter property dispute at the institutional-legal level in the middle-class court "resolution" of relationship dissolution, an arena where emotions run high.

THE CULTURAL CONTEXT

Mateship, self-reliance and the pub culture loom large in the folklore of Australia. Convict antecedents, a tradition of the farmer, bushranger, Eureka Stockade and gold (Ward, 1967) emphasize the masculine orientation of the people.* The Australian "prizes leisure above riches or success" and "tends to be more easy-going, cooperative, and enduring, less ebullient, competitive and hard-driving than the American, though both alike are so much more informal and 'democratic' in manner than the Englishman" (Ward, 1967, p. 19). The outdoor bronzed Aussie image needs to be modified by a more realistic viewpoint. Some 4% of males are alcoholics and ischemic heart disease (to which inactivity, obesity, overeating and drinking, and smoking appear to contribute) is the leading cause of death in Australia, accounting for about 30% of all deaths each year since the late 1960s (Edgar, 1980, p. 23). Australian society is currently faced with an unemployment rate of 11%, a falling inflation rate of about 5% and an increase of 10.5% in crime rates in New South Wales from 1981 to 1982 — predominantly in the area of larceny, breaking and entering, and armed holdups.

An interesting comment is added by Lewis: "Male working class chauvinism is a vital cultural defence for men against exploitation in their work environment, which is then carried back to the home" (Lewis, 1983, p. 86). While the working-class male asserts and expects his patriarchal powers to be recognized in the family, the professional male discounts masculine dominance in public yet expects it in his own marriage. This attitude of masculine authority and superiority in the family is very much a central feature of the mores of Australian society, which in general terms relegates the woman to a subordinate position, seeing her

---

* In 1854 in a clash between miners, soldiers and police over licence fees some twenty eight people died - Australia's closest approach to civil insurrection.

more as a possession than a partner – an ideology reinforced by the "Ocker," mateship, and pub cult syndrome.*

The issue of female subordination and possession of the woman by the man stands out as one of the major factors in wife-battering. Dobash and Dobash note that "the first assault was closely related to the husband's growing sense of possession of his wife, authority over her, and the feeling that he had the right to impose his expectations upon her" (1979, p. 14). The same conclusion is reinforced by The Royal Commission on Human Relationships, showing "a picture of men treating their women as possessions, there to provide food and service" (1977, p. 139). In a commentary on women who murder their husbands, Bacon and Lansdowne make the same point: "There is a close link between the husband's possessiveness about his wife's time and conversation generally, and this sexual jealousy and insecurity" (1982, p. 77). The relegation of spouse to the role of a possession is not a uniquely Australian phenomenon. It is differentially distributed across the socioeconomic scale and is obviously changing with increasing education and feminist publicity. We further examine this phenomenon in the section that investigates the personality of the individuals involved in violence.

The final point to be made about violence in the domestic relationship relates to violence in the broader society. On most continua Australia is generally located between the United States and Great Britain, with the Australian way of life more rapidly approximating that of the U.S. Despite the increasing rates of violent crime previously referred to, the streets of the Australian city are safer to walk at night than those of either of the two comparison countries. Although street violence and drug-oriented crime are on the increase, the threat of personal attack is less in Australia. Gun ownership is not seen as a divine right and youth gangs on a weekend football [soccer] rampage are still relatively remote on the Australian horizon.

While the Australian male has a refuge in the pub-mateship environment to some extent, the female usually only has resort to friends in her same situation or to her mother (see Everett & Telfer, 1983). Depending on the socioeconomic status of the female, such arrangements are not regarded as particularly onerous and are in fact an expected facet of life. In the arena of personal relationships, the major investment/commitment is made with respect to the partner with the house/property in conjunction; in the event of relationship dissolution or its threat, emotions and consequent behavior are likely to approach extremes, with the potential for violence running high. The spouse is one obvious recipient of the violence.

A more invidious and uncharacteristic outcome is the attack on the legal/judicial system that has emerged in the past five years. A Family Law Court judge

---

* The pot-bellied, singlet-clad, can-in-hand Australian male.

was shot dead in 1979. The house of another judge was bombed in March 1984. A few weeks later a Family Law Court was bombed in the western suburbs of Sydney. Then again on July 4, 1984 the apartment of a third Family Law Court judge was bombed, seriously injuring him and killing his wife. No one has been apprehended for these offenses; current moves and discussions center around increased security for judges in the area of family law and increasing the degree of formality in sessions of the Family Law Court.

There is no evidence to suggest that there is any direct link between the general (or perceived) level of violence in society at large and violence in the home. There is a suggestion from the above that in areas of domestic dispute, greater extremes of violence may be resorted to by some individuals. Justice Elizabeth Evatt, at the forefront of Family Law Reform, provided a cautionary modifier to extreme responses in the context of violence directed against personnel of the Family Law Court (Australian Broadcasting Commission, 1984). Most individuals in marital dispute situations respond in a rational fashion; the more violent response is resorted to by individuals at the extremes of the normal distribution, here introducing the personality dimension. In terms of the link between perceived level of violence in society and domestic violence, it has been a common finding in the social sciences that when a group finds itself under threat, internal morale tends to be high, suggesting a negative relationship between general societal violence and spouse-battering, other things being equal.

SOCIAL AND SITUATIONAL FACTORS

Any consideration of social factors concentrates on the patterns of relationships that prevail in the group under investigation. From the cultural expose above, it may be seen that such patterns are largely enshrined in existing lifestyles, which in some social circles center around masculine gatherings at the hotel or club, with the female orientation located in friendship and relationship networks, often encompassing young children. Obviously such ongoing social networks are impinged upon by changes of various sorts, including the impact of technology, availability and access to information sources, and demographic and situational shifts.

More pervasive forms of social and economic change are accentuating the prospect of violence in the home. Unemployment, with its consequent insecurity and loss of self-esteem, ranks high in this regard. Frequently this is enshrouded with the stigma of "dole bludger" labels being propagated by public officials and politicians; associated surveillance by the Department of Social Security further isolates the unemployed, placing the unemployed adolescent in the high-risk category. The materialistic emphasis of the media, with the additional lure provided by the "surfie" cult, the drug scene, and the music and disco world can lead to further estrangement of the youth and adult worlds, with accumulated resentment on both sides. All of the foregoing may well operate simultaneously in the one family. Work, in the conventional sense, is becoming increasingly scarce, with some estimates suggesting that the current work force output could be handled by 2% of the working-age population by the turn of the century, with the impact of cybernetics (see Hodgkinson 1967, p. 206).

Such change obviously has effects at the level of the nuclear family, and it is becoming increasingly evident that the nuclear family is only one variant of the options available (see Foster, 1981, p. 147), with the single-parent family accounting for over 30% of enrollments in some schools.

The displacement of the major breadwinner from the work force leads to considerable dislocation and upset in economic and psychological terms. Relocation, retraining, and insecurity are a common consequence. Lack of money leads to a necessary change of life style. Financial commitments are jeopardized, outings are foregone, and constraints on expectations and activities take their toll on relationships, fostering the prospect of family stress.

This is felt in the area of the pub-club culture of the male — there is no money for such indulgence — with accruing frustrations and aggression emerging. When this is coupled with incidental legal change, often associated with political advantage and rising prices, pressures are accentuated in the nuclear family. A recent introduction (December 1982) of the random breath testing (RBT) of motorists has had repercussions at all levels of society. In an effort to reduce the road toll, the pub-club existence has been severely curtailed, with significant effects at the level of individual life-styles. Apart from the results on the economic well-being of the community, RBT was initially successful in reducing the road toll; as the initial impact subsides and fatalities again start to mount, authorities seek out further scapegoats — currently the young, inexperienced driver and the truck operator. Legal change at this level resonates in the family relationship, increasing tensions and the possibility of aggressive responses at the individual level.

It would be remiss to discuss the impact of legal changes in this context without mentioning the impact of the Family Law Act of January 1976, making "irretrievable breakdown" of marriage the only grounds for divorce, following a period of twelve months' separation. During this period of one year, marriage counseling is strongly advocated. This act supplanted the Matrimonial Causes Act of 1959, which had fourteen causes for divorce, "including adultery by husband or wife, on petition of the 'injured' party; drunkenness, cruelty, insanity; desertion for three years and separation for five years" (Scutt, 1983, p. 25). The Family Law Act supplanted some of the darkest days of matrimonial dissent in Australian history — the era of "the divorce raid," when private eyes with off-duty policemen and enraged ex-spouses would endeavor to catch the "erring" partner in a compromising situation through illegal-entry tactics and flash bulbs. This saga has been previously described by the author (Everett 1975), with implications noted at the level of individual privacy. With the introduction of the Family Law Act, divorce rates rapidly escalated but currently appear to have leveled out at about 3 per 1,000 population (Josephian, 1983). The age at first marriage has been gradually falling for males and females (Edgar, 1980, p. 115), with over 50% of divorced people remarrying within ten years. There is little doubt that the safety-valve function of the Family Law Act, in conjunction with information and publicity provided by women's groups, has led, if not to a decrease in the absolute level of spouse abuse, at least to the escape of the victim from the situation.

The overuse of alcohol has long been recognized as a major correlate of spouse abuse. It would appear that the closer the intervening agency is to the domestic dispute, the more important alcohol overuse is seen to be (police, counselors and medical practitioners rank alcohol as one of the central factors). More objective observers tend to disclaim the centrality of alcohol in wife-bashing, tending to regard it as symptomatic of deeper problems. This is the stance taken by Dobash and Dobash (1979, p. 20). A similar cynicism is expressed by O'Donnell and Saville (1982, p. 56) although they note that alcohol was involved in 55% of domestic assaults (N = 145). The same point is reiterated in Scutt (1983, p. 116), where, in a sample of 127 cases of battered wives, only 7% of husbands were drunk; in 37% of the cases, alcohol was not involved. The question of the part played by alcohol as a causative factor must remain in limbo; it is undoubtedly a significant triggering agent in some situations and for some relationships and personalities.

PSYCHOLOGICAL AND PERSONALITY FACTORS

Personality is here defined as an internal predisposition of the individual that gives rise to behavior that tends to be consistent over time and situations. Generally the search for personality under this "hard" definition has not proved fruitful (Mischel, 1968; Everett, 1973). Psychometric measures are not highly predictive of behavior and there is wide variability in the behavior of the individual across situations, despite an intuitive acceptance of the sanctity of the "individual personality." The dimensions being tapped by the test are applicable to the abstract, average person and not the unique individual, except perhaps at the extremes of the normal curve (Vaughan, 1964). The importance of situational determinants has led others to convincingly posit that there is no such thing as personality—only roles exist (Brim, 1966). These are grappling and key issues that must be confronted by the theorist, but they are somewhat peripheral to our current concern—violence in the primary affectional dyadic relationship—between man and woman.

There is no doubt about the existence of consistent behavior, primarily wife-bashing, in this context. The underlying personality factors that prompt such behavior are subject to speculation. From clinical interviews and previous research (Moore, 1979; Scutt, 1983), one of the most frequently cited factors is the low self-esteem of the wife-basher. This, in itself, is not very helpful to the researcher or the individuals involved in the relationship. Low self-regard does not necessarily lead to physical aggression, nor does the violence manifest itself in other situations or in other relationships. Spouse-beating is almost by definition a private occurrence (until it exceeds a certain threshold) primarily restricted in location to bathrooms, kitchens, and bedrooms of the house (Dobash & Dobash, 1979). The secrecy aspect is reinforced by the shame aspect, e.g., "scream quietly or the neighbors will hear" (Pizzey, 1974) and by the respect accorded to domestic self-determination and privacy.

Other personality factors that have been cited in spouse-abuse situations include low frustration-tolerance and jealousy (Gayford, 1975), masochism and guilt feelings on the part of the victim (Scutt, 1983), and aggression (Renvoize, 1978, p. 43). The concentration on normative trait psychology has not been overproductive; not all males high on aggression or low in self-esteem indulge in wife-beating. The tendency of the male to see the woman as a possession, referred to previously, which is frequently an outcome of cultural or subcultural values, has its personality correlates of jealousy and insecurity. Such factors are usually only revealed through projective testing and the clinical interview approach. The point here is that seldom does the investigator have the time, expertise, or inclination to utilize the broad-gamut molar approach that literature suggests is necessary. In order to circumvent the problems inherent in trait psychology and possible biases due to professional socialization and theoretical predilection, a configurational approach to personality has been pursued. Each individual's personality is represented as a configuration of key stimuli/concepts in the situational life space. Furthermore, these stimuli are provided by the individual and are not imposed by the investigator. A key concept is the concept of self. Indices of similarity are derived between the stimuli. The personality configuration is then generated on the basis of the multidimensional scaling maxim that equates similarity to proximity of stimuli in the personality configuration (Torgerson, 1958). There are many multidimensional computer-based scaling techniques that operate on interstimulus/concept similarity indices and give rise to a personality configuration. One of the simplest and most widely used is the Semantic Differential (SD) developed by Osgood, Suci, & Tannenbaum (1957); the methodology is illustrated in the case study cited below.

Methodology

The Semantic Differential questionnaire requires the respondent to rate certain key concepts on a number of bipolar scales. Osgood et al. (1957) claim that there are generally three universal dimensions of meaning: Evaluative (good-bad); Activity (fast-slow); and Potency (strong-weak). These dimensions, with minor variations, tend to emerge regardless of concepts, subjects, and cultures. Since the dimensions are independent it is relatively easy for the practitioner to derive the personality configuration of the subject in three-dimensional Pythagorian space (see Everett, 1971). The major benefits of the SD technique are its economy in terms of subject effort and time and its ease of analysis and interpretation. Since the subject provides the key concepts (elicited through interview) it is individually based; the experimenter is not imposing anything on the respondent beyond the dimensional structure — and this appears to be most valid when rapport is high.

There are substantial methodological problems in the interpretation of previous research and questions of rapport and subject distortion. As mentioned previously, emotions run extremely high, and selective perception and rationalization are common. It is extremely difficult to get equal cooperation from spouses in dispute, and compulsory counseling/testing is not conducive to the elicitation of valid data. Fathers are notoriously difficult to reach (Renvoize, 1978, p. 201), frequently being aggressive and resentful. Women's refuges are the province of the female; male researchers are not welcome. As Scutt comments: "A male researcher would not have been privileged as I was to become a confidant of many strong women who decided that now was the time to reveal the damage suffered in their own homes" (1983, p. 6). The source of the data needs to be closely scrutinized for comparative purposes; totally female samples are biased; telephone samples, phone-ins, counselor, court, and police records are similarly suspect. Door-knock surveys are relatively impossible and the psychological motivation of the women involved can be queried; Renvoize comments on the possessive jealousy of wives who want to keep social workers away from their husbands, and wives who resent the social worker's attention devoted to the child (1978, p. 202). All of these apparently trivial factors do present major problems to the researcher, case-worker, and those who would like to unravel the tangled web of family violence.

The data base in the present study can be questioned on grounds similar to those outlined above. It was derived by interviews and tests with estranged couples with a background of domestic violence leading to separation; in addition interviews were conducted by personnel involved in relevant occupational pursuits, e.g. the Women's Refuge movement, Family Law Court employees, community workers, psychologists, rape researchers, and hospital personnel. Much of the foregoing has been based on information gathered in this way. Owing to the author's predilections, analysis is in nonnormative and qualitative form. To demonstrate the type of analysis involved, the following case study is presented.

Case Study

In order to illustrate the model of personality proposed above, the relationship of Bill and Jenny is worthy of description. They were a middle-class couple who had lived together for eight years before getting married; she had him evicted by the courts one year after the wedding. Both were in their early forties and had been married before; she had three teenage children that lived with her. Their life together had been characterized by violent and heated arguments and several periods of separation. In the three months prior to their final separation, she had called the police to the house on five occasions because of his violent and drunken abuse, leveled at both her and the children.

Bill was a teacher who drank excessively and manifested low self- esteem and considerable insecurity. He was very much part of the male pub culture, spending two or three hours in that environment each day. He resented Jenny's incessant criticism and nagging, which continued regardless of how much he changed his behavior in terms of her demands. He claimed he needed the pub and his mates as a refuge in order to retain his sanity. She resented his spending time and money in that environment. He also stated that when their relationship first started (with high drama as a result of a violent battering by her first husband, with whom she was then living) there had been just the two of them together alone, but she had successively taken her three children back to live with them. He said Jenny had frequently called upon her ex- husband to threaten him.

Jenny was a secretary with a good work record and a close circle of women friends of a feminist persuasion. When she and Bill initially got together, there was considerable separation grief over her children. In the first two years of their relationship she made three attempts at suicide, apparently an attention-getting device, through sleeping pill overdose and wrist-slashing. She claimed Bill had several affairs with other women and bought them expensive presents that he denied her. He had cost her considerable financial loss and his excessive drinking and violence, and particularly the threat they posed for her children's well-being, had made it necessary for her to get him evicted.

In the counseling situation, after consideration of their respective versions of the relationship and total lack of compatability of their personality configurations, they were advised to separate. Both completed Semantic Differential assessments confirming most of the hypotheses generated by the clinical situation. Bill's rating of the concept "Self" was in close proximity to "Mates," "Grog," "Fun," and "Future" and quite remote from "Jenny" and the children. The concept "Jenny" was closely related to "Anxiety," "Tension," "Trouble," and "Argument." Jenny in turn located her self-concept close to "Children," "Future," and "Love" and quite distant from "Bill." For both of them the concept "Resentment" was located with their ex-spouse, and "Financial loss" was similarly located.

Since their separation about a year ago, Jenny has devoted herself to her children and her work. Bill has settled very happily into a new relationship with a younger woman and her two children and the prospects for the future are quite bright.

Several points can be made about the brief case history presented above. The history of the relationship contributed in a unique fashion in determining the personality configuration of the couple involved. The compatability of clinical and test data was confirmed by ipsative (subject-centered) methods, in a highly concise fashion. The use of normative, standardized tests would not provide the same succinctness, breadth of coverage, and economy of effort. Consideration of other case histories lead to similar conclusions. The unsuccessful relationship had developed into a stable conflict-ridden structure over a period of years, the resolution of which could only be achieved through termination. On a more optimistic note, the "personality of the relationship" or construction of reality was shown to be restricted to the particular relationship and not to the personality of the individuals involved. Bill's new relationship is now of seven months' duration and is happy and apparently thriving in a healthy fashion with a total absence of violence. He claims that to this date at least there has not even been an argument.

Similar compatability of interview and personality configuration was demonstrated for several other couples. The major advantage was that each couple has certain key concepts unique to their own relationship, endowing these concepts with their own unique interpretation—even though they may not agree about them. The location of the concept "myself" on the evaluative dimension is an indication of self-esteem; at the time of separation in the above case study, Bill's level of self-esteem was slightly negative, Jenny's somewhat positive. It is intended to follow up such couples in a few years' time to see how the personality configuration has evolved.

CONCLUSION

We have undertaken an examination of wife-beating in the Australian context, with particular emphasis on personality factors that might give rise to this type of behavior. Interviews with participants and professionals in the field have given rise to the viewpoint that personality (internal) factors cannot be viewed in isolation from the cultural and social matrix that give rise to the behavior under investigation. The search for personality traits that cause a man to beat his partner has not been productive or conclusive; maybe low self-esteem, when coupled with environmental factors, is the most significant normative factor that emerges from previous research.

A more fruitful interpretation is provided by the role learning approach suggested by Brim (1966); he posits that personality is nothing more than a learned set of roles, which helps to account for the situational "inconsistencies" of individual behavior. When two people cohabit for a number of years, a common culture is developed—certain issues and concepts emerge as being important—and a set of learned responses evolves into what may be described as the personality of that relationship. This is something that is unique to the dyad, and perhaps to the children involved; it includes a personal linguistic wage and a personal chronology or calender with expectations of a bonding nature that are quite intense, as discussed by McCall et al. (1970, pp. 6-16). When these are threatened by disruption through separation, responses can be quite intense, as suggested by the string of attacks on the institution of the Family Law Court in New South Wales. One hypothesis in this situation is that such disruption was due to a certain individual deemed to be deviant in terms of the normal curve (along the lines suggested by Vaughan, 1964). Yet this individual continues to operate in everyday society without detection, one more confirmation of the learned-repertoire-of-roles approach to personality, in which these attacks would be viewed as a learned situational response of an extreme sort.

This sort of argument can lead to some partial grasp of explaining the problem of the man who bashes his wife. It is a very unsatisfactory and incomplete interpretation to account for this behavior in terms of the man's personality, aggression, low self-esteem, or even in terms of the victim's masochism. Such behavior can only be understood in terms of the full set of role relationships involved, the history of that relationship and its development, and the meaning attached by the incumbents to key symbols in their life together. To measure or assess personality in this situation requires cooperation from both partners (often difficult to obtain) and an instrument that does not force the respondent into fitting the mold of the researcher, psychologist, counselor, or agency involved.

An emergent, ipsative type measure such as the Semantic Differential has been suggested. Yet even this does provide the dimensions of meaning on which the stimuli ("Myself," "Sex," "Children," "Spouse," "Love," "Happiness," "Alcohol," etc.) are located. All that is required for this task is a measure of inter-concept similarity, which can give rise to a personality configuration. The personal-construct theory of Kelly (1955) is another approach that appears promising. The important issue is to derive a configuration that means something in the life of the respondent and not the assessor.

No further light has been shed on the issue of why a man beats his wife. It occurs, using a conservative estimate from Scutt's data (1983), in 15% of Australian homes, though not necessarily on a consistent basis. Alcohol, low self-esteem, financial factors, and peer group pressures are all involved. When the cultural push is towards a "man being a man," defined as someone's coming out on top, such behavior is likely to persist. A redress of power balance in the relationship, accepted at the broadest level, would appear to be the only long-term solution. In the short-term, violent relationships must be terminated; this may have psychological overtones, but is not purely a psychological problem. As Scutt states, "until men themselves initiate change, spouse assault will continue unabated" (1983, p. 140).

REFERENCES

Australian Broadcasting Commission. (1984, March 6). Radio Program *AM*, Sydney N.S.W.

Bacon, W., & Lansdowne, R. (1982). Women who kill husbands: The battered wife on trial. In C. O'Donnell & J. Craney (Eds.), *Family violence in Australia* (pp. 67-94). Melbourne: Longman Cheshire.

Berger, P., & Luckmann, T. (1967). *The social construction of reality.* New York: Anchor Books.

Brim, O. G., Jr. (1966). Personality development as role-learning. In I. Isge & H. W. Stevenson (Eds), *Personality development in children,* (pp. 127-159). Austin: University of Texas Press.

Deveson, A. (1978). *Australians at risk.* Cassell, Australia: Stanmore.

Dobash, R. E., & Dobash, R. P. (1979). *Violence against wives in Scotland.* University of Stirling, Sociology Department Monograph, Scotland.

Edgar, D. (1980). *Introduction to Australian society.* Sydney: Prentice-Hall.

Everett, A. V. (1971). The self concept of high, medium and low academic achievers. *Australian Journal of Education, 15,* 319-324.

Everett, A. V. (1973). Personality assessment at the individual level using the semantic differential. *Educational and Psychological Measurement, 33,* 837-844.

Everett, A. V. (1975). The issue of divorce raids in marital dissolution. Submission to the Royal Commission on Human Relationships (1976).

Everett, A. V., & Telfer, R. (1983). *Some sociological aspects of a Housing Commission Community.* Canberra: Institute of Family Studies, A.N.U.

Foster, L. E. (1981). *Australian education: A sociological perspective.* Sydney, N.S.W.: Prentice-Hall.

Gayford, J. J. (1975). Wife battering: A preliminary survey of 100 cases. *British Medical Journal, 1,* 194-197.

Hodgkinson, H. L. (1967). *Education, interaction and social change.* Englewood Cliffs, NJ: Prentice-Hall.

Josephian, V. (1983). Divorce in Australia: An examination of period analysis. Paper presented at the meeting of the Australian Family Research conference, A.N.U., A.C.T., Canberra, Institute of Family Studies.

Kelly, G. A. (1955). *The psychology of personal constructs* (2 vols.). New York: Norton.

Lewis, G. (1983). *Real men like violence: Australian men, media and violence.* Sydney: Kangaroo Press.

McCall, G. J., McCall, M. M., Denzin, N. K., Suttles, G. D., & Kurth, S. B. (1970). *Social relationships.* Chicago: Aldine.

Mischel, W. (1968). *Personality and assessment.* New York: Wiley.

Moore, D. (Ed.). (1979). *Battered women.* Beverly Hills, CA: Sage Publications.

O'Donnell, C., & Craney, J. (Eds.). (1982). *Family violence in Australia.* Melbourne: Longman Cheshire.

O'Donnell, C., & Saville, H. (1982). Domestic violence and sex and class inequality. In C. O'Donnell & J. Craney (Eds.), *Family violence in Australia* (pp. 52-66). Melbourne: Longman Cheshire.

Osgood, C. E., Suci, G. J., & Tannenbaum, P. H. (1957). *The measurement of meaning.* Urbana: University of Illinois Press.

Pizzey, E. (1974). *Scream quietly or the neighbours will hear.* Hammondsworth: Penguin.

Renvoize, J. (1978). *Web of violence.* London: Routledge & Kegan Paul.

Royal Commission on Human Relationships (1977). *Final Report* (Volume 4, Part 5), *The Family.* Aust. Govt. Publishing Service, Canberra, A.C.T.

Saville, H. (1982). Refuges: A new beginning to the struggle. In C. O'Donnell & J. Craney (Eds.), *Family violence in Australia* (pp. 95-109). Melbourne: Longman Cheshire.

Scutt, J. (1983). *Even in the best of homes: Violence in the family.* Australia: Penguin.

Straus, M. A., Gelles, R. J., & Steinmetz, S. K. (1980). *Behind closed doors: Violence in the American family.* New York: Anchor Press, Doubleday.

Torgerson, W. S. (1958). *Theory and methods of scaling.* New York: Wiley.

Ward, R. (1967). *Australia.* Sydney: Ure Smith.

Vaughan, G. M. (1964). The trans-situational aspect of conforming behaviour. *Journal of Personality, 32,* 335-354.

Women's Advisory Council (1984). *Women and rape.* Sydney: Premier's Department.

Women's Coordination Unit (1983). *Domestic violence: You don't have to put up with it.* Sydney: Premier's Department.

Chapter 8
Hostility Toward Men in Female Victims of Male Sexual Aggression

James V. P. Check, Barbara Elias,
and Susan A. Barton

Research documents that sexual assault has extensive and often long-lasting effects on the victim. Among the more commonly reported effects are fear and anxiety (e.g., Becker, Skinner, Abel, Howell, & Bruce, 1982; Burgess & Holmstrom, 1974, 1977; Kilpatrick, Resick, & Veronen, 1981; McCahill, Meyer, & Fischman, 1979; Medea & Thompson, 1974; Notman & Nadelson, 1980; Sutherland & Scherl, 1977), helplessness and depression (e.g., Atkeson, Calhoun, Resick, & Ellis, 1982; Frank, Turner, & Duffy, 1979; Kilpatrick et al., 1981), and decreased overall social and work adjustment (e.g., Resick, Calhoun, Atkeson, & Ellis, 1981; Sales, Baum, & Shore, 1984). Surprisingly, however, there has been little systematic theorizing and research on the potential impact of sexual assault on women's subsequent hostility toward men, despite the fact that there are a number of indirect indications that women's attitudes and hostility toward men may be affected by sexual victimization. Kirkpatrick and Kanin (1957), for example, found that 35% of their sample of college women who had been offended by male sexual aggression that involved coitus reported feeling anger. Burgess and Holmstrom (1974) also reported feelings of anger and revenge in their rape victim sample, although they did not indicate how frequent or extensive these feelings were. More recently, Wilson (1978) reported that changes "towards males and sexuality generally" (p. 50) were among the most consistent effects observed in their sample of 70 victims of unreported rape. One of the more common of these changes was to avoid men and to not trust them in a wide variety of circumstances. McCahill et al. (1979) found that even as long as 11 months after a rape incident, up to half of the victims still experienced "negative feelings" toward men (including fear), and 39% experienced worsened sexual relations with their partner. Kilpatrick et al. (1981) reported that victims scored significantly higher than nonvictims on both the hostility subscale of the Derogatis Symptom Checklist (Derogatis, 1977) and the anger-hostility subscale of the Profile of Mood States (McNair, Lorr, & Droppleman, 1971), although these scales were no longer elevated at one year post-rape. As well, 17% of Medea and Thompson's (1974) subjects reported feeling hostility toward men, and Feldman-Summers, Gordon, and Meagher (1979) reported decreased sexual satisfaction with a number of sexual activities involving men. Finally, Becker et al. (1982) reported that between 65% and 85% of their sample of attempted and completed rape victims reported feelings of anger and revenge immediately following the assault.

There is also evidence that multiple victimization is associated with higher levels of hostility than single victimization. Ellis, Atkeson, & Calhoun (1982) found that multiple-incident victims "report more suspiciousness and hostility toward others" (p. 223) than single-incident victims, although it is not clear from their research report just how this hostility was measured. As well, McCahill et al. (1979) reported that victims who had been sexually assaulted on a previous occasion experienced more "increased negative feelings" toward men immediately after the current rape than victims who had not been previously sexually assaulted.

One serious problem with the research referred to above is that hostility toward men is not clearly distinguished from general feelings of anger or hostility. Such a distinction is an important one, however, as it may be argued that any hostility felt by female victims of male sexual aggression would in all likelihood be primarily directed toward men. One purpose of the present research, therefore, was to examine the relationship between sexual victimization and *both* general hostility and hostility specifically directed toward men. While there are many measures of general hostility existent in the literature (see Edmunds & Kendrick, 1980, for a review), a problem we faced in this study was the fact that there is no available measure of hostility directed specifically toward men. Therefore, a second purpose of the present research was to develop a preliminary version of a scale of hostility toward men.

A second major problem with the research on the effects of sexual victimization stems from researchers' conceptualization of sexual victimization as legally defined rape. There are a number of problems with this type of approach. First, as Clark and Lewis (1977) and others have amply demonstrated, there are a number of processes at each stage of the legal processing of a rape report that screen out and thus eliminate many actual rape incidents from cases that are legally defined as rape. However, even studies that employ samples other than victims obtained from police files (e.g., studies of rape crisis center clients) still underrepresent the true incidence of rape, as victims often themselves fail to define many instances of forced intercourse as rape (Check & Malamuth, 1982; Koss & Oros, 982). It is also likely that victims who contact a rape crisis center may contact he center precisely because of the effect their experience has had on them, thus providing another source of sample bias.

A third drawback of previous research on the effects of sexual victimization stems from the fact that investigators usually operationally define sexual victimization as having been forcefully raped (as opposed to not having been raped). This operationalization implies a typological approach to sexual aggression, in which a woman is seen as either a victim or a nonvictim. Clearly, such an approach obscures many lower levels of sexual aggression which are not actually rape. In fact, a number of theorists have begun to argue a dimensional view of sexual aggression (e.g., Check & Malamuth, 1983b; Clark & Lewis, 1977; Kirkpatrick & Kanin, 1957; Koss & Oros, 1982), in which rape is seen as only one extreme point on a continuum of forced sexual behaviors. Such a dimensional view led Koss & Oros (1982) to develop their Sexual Experiences Survey, an instrument that measures sexual victimization ranging in severity from being coerced into intercourse by threats of terminating the relationship, to being physically held down and forced to have intercourse. The present study employed the Koss and Oros measure as the criterion measure of sexual victimization, with one modification. Rather than simply asking women whether they had ever been the victim of each of the various acts (see below), they were also asked to indicate *how often* they had been victimized. This multiple-incident measurement procedure was employed because of the earlier-mentioned findings that multiple-incident victims tend to show more hostility than single-incident victims (Ellis et al., 1982; McCahill et al., 1979).

In summary, the present research was designed to assess the relationship between sexual victimization (measured as a continuous variable) and hostility both in general and specifically directed toward men. Female college students were employed as subjects, as previous research had suggested there is a good deal of sexual aggression that occurs on college campuses (Byers & Eastman, 1979; Kanin & Parcell, 1977; Kirkpatrick & Kanin, 1957; Koss, Gidycz, & Wisniewski, 1987; Koss & Oros, 1982). As well, a measure of depression was employed, in order to examine the replicability of previous research suggesting that depression is one of the effects of sexual assault (Atkeson et al., 1982; Frank et al., 1979).

METHOD

Subjects

Subjects were 285 female Introductory Psychology students from the University of Manitoba, who participated for credit in their course. The data from 7 subjects had to be discarded because they had failed to follow instructions properly, or omitted too many items. The analyses reported below are for the remaining 278 respondents. Ninety-four percent of the women were single, and 6% were married. Over half of the women were 18 years of age, with the mean age being 19.7 years (S.D. = 4.12). Ninety percent were Caucasian.

Materials

Sexual Victimization

Koss and Oros's (1982) Sexual Experiences Survey was used as the basic measure of sexual victimization. The women were asked to indicate whether they had experienced each of thirteen different sexual experiences with men, and if so how often. Unfortunately, while this measure has a good deal of face validity (see below), Koss & Oros do not report any other validity or reliability data for their scale.

Hostility Toward Men

For the purposes of the present research, hostility toward men was conceptualized as no different from general hostility, *except that it is directed specifically toward men.* In keeping with this operational definition, the Hostility Toward Men scale was constructed using the following procedure. A total of 118 nonredundant general hostility items was gleaned from the existing literature describing general hostility scales. These included items from the Buss and Durkee (1957), Comrey (1964), Siegel (1956), and Evans and Stangeland (1971) measures, as well as a small number of items written by the senior author (J.V.P.C.). Each of these items was then rewritten so that it referred specifically to men rather than to people in general (e.g., the item "Sometimes people bother me by just being around" was rewritten to read, "Sometimes men bother me by just being around"). All 118 items were then administered and the best 30 items were selected using item-total correlation analysis (see below for further details).

Secondary Measures of Hostility Toward Men

In keeping with Campbell and Fiske's (1959) multitrait-multimethod recommendations, we decided to employ a second measure of hostility toward men. Briefly, subjects were asked to check 5 adjectives from a list of 27 that they felt were most characteristic of *men.* Imbedded in this list were 10 adjectives describing positive attributes (romantic, intelligent, considerate, trusting, confident, trustworthy, sensitive, generous, likeable, and even-tempered), and 10 adjectives describing negative attributes (manipulating, emotional, deceitful, irrational, vain, aggressive, self-centered, vengeful, touchy, and dominating). For comparison purposes, subjects were then asked to check 5 adjectives that they thought were most characteristic of *women.* It was expected that hostility toward men as well as sexual victimization would be related only to the adjectives checked as characteristic of men.

General Hostility

Although the Buss-Durkee (1957) scale has been generally accepted as the most reliable and valid measure of general hostility in the literature (Edmunds & Kendrick, 1980; Megargee & Menzies, 1971), a number of the items used to develop the Hostility Toward Men scale was taken directly from the Buss-Durkee measure. As a consequence, a spurious relationship might exist between the Buss-Durkee scale and the derived Hostility Toward Men scale, simply because of the similarity of their item content. Recently, however, Spielberger, Jacobs, Russell, and Crane (1982) developed the Trait Anger Scale, which seems to be a reasonable measure of general hostility. The scale has a reported alpha reliability of about .90 for college students, and correlates .66 to .73 with the Buss-Durkee hostility scale (Spielberger et al., 1982). The major advantages of the Spielberger et al. measure for the present purposes were that it correlates relatively highly with the Buss-Durkee measure, but at the same time had no overlapping item content with the Hostility Toward Men scale items. Therefore, Spielberger et al.'s Trait Anger Scale was employed as the measure of general hostility.

Depression

The measure of depression that was employed was Radloff's (1977) CES-D scale, a self-report depression scale, which was specifically designed for research in the general population. Radloff reports internal reliabilities for this scale of .85 to .90, and test-retest reliability of .45 to .70 (for intervals up to about one year). As well, the CES-D was found to discriminate psychiatric depression patients from nonpatients, to predict ratings of severity of depression by nurse-clinicians, to correlate well with a number of other self-report measures of depression, and to discriminate individuals who had experienced "negative life events" (e.g., illness/injury, loss of a spouse, etc.) from those who had not.

Procedure

The study was advertised as a study of sexual attitudes and behavior. All measures were contained in one questionnaire, administered in group format by a female experimenter. Relatively large groups were tested (up to 40 individuals), in order to maximize subjects' feelings of anonymity. As well, subjects were told at the beginning of the testing session that they were free to leave at any time during the study with no penalty whatsoever (none chose to do so), and they were assured that their responses were completely anonymous. A small slip of paper with the experimenter's telephone number was given to each and every subject, and they were told that they could telephone her at anytime if there was anything about the study which they would like to discuss with her. Finally, subjects were provided with a written debriefing at the end of the testing session, which briefly explained the nature of the research. They were also asked not to discuss the research with anyone until the study was complete.

RESULTS

The Selection of the Hostility Toward Men Scale Items

As mentioned earlier, the 30 items with the highest item-to-total correlations were selected for the Hostility Toward Men scale. These items are presented in Table 8.1, along with the percentages of subjects responding "true" to each item. The KR 20 reliability of the 30-item scale was .89, and the mean score on the scale was 7.57 (*S.D.* = 6.16).

Factor Analysis of the Hostility Toward Men Scale

In order to determine whether there was in fact only one dimension underlying the Hostility Toward Men scale, a Principal Components Factor Analysis of the 30 Hostility Toward Men scale items was conducted on the matrix of the phi correlation coefficients between the items. An application of the scree test (Cattell, 1966) to the plot of the resulting eigenvalues for each initial factor suggested that only the first factor should be retained. This first factor accounted for 25% of the total variance of the 30 items. Extracting this factor yielded factor loadings above .30 for all items, which was considered to be acceptable. Thus, these results provide support for the assumption that the Hostility Toward Men scale is a unidimensional measure.

The Test-Retest Reliability of the Hostility Toward Men Scale

Since hostility toward men was conceptualized as a relatively stable disposition (although it could be affected by important life events such as sexual victimization), there existed a need to determine the test-retest reliability of the Hostility Toward Men scale. To this end, the 30-item scale was administered to an independent sample of 99 women in two Introductory Psychology classes (for course credit) during class time, followed by a second administration one week later. (During the testing sessions, the men in the class completed a similar questionnaire, for use in other research). Of the original 99 women, 75 were in class during this second administration of the scale. The resulting correlation (test-retest reliability) between the two sets of 75 scores was calculated to be .90. This result suggests that Hostility Toward Men scale scores are stable over a one-week period.

Correlates of Hostility Toward Men

As noted earlier, it was of interest to determine the relationship between the Hostility Toward Men scale and the other measures of hostility. To this end, Pear-

Table 8.1 The Hostility Toward Men Scale

1.	Sometimes men bother me by just being around (39%).
2.	At times I have a strong urge to do something harmful to a man (16%).
3.	Lately, I've been kind of grouchy with men (15%).
4.	I think that most men would lie to get ahead (30%).
5.	It is safer not to trust men (25%).
6.	When it really comes down to it, a lot of men are deceitful (28%).
7.	Men are responsible for most of my troubles (15%).
8.	I think nearly any man would lie to keep out of trouble (34%).
9.	I do not blame a woman for taking advantage of a man who lays himself open to it (22%).
10.	I used to think that most men told the truth, but now I know otherwise (23%).
11.	If you aren't willing to fight, men will walk all over you (39%).
12.	Many time a man appears to care, but really just wants to use you (45%).
13.	Men today don't deserve the breaks they get (21%).
14.	I can easily make a man afraid of me, and sometimes do just for the fun of it (13%).
15.	I am sure I get a raw deal from the men in my life (13%).
16.	I commonly wonder what hidden reason a man may have for doing something nice for me (31%).
17.	My motto is "never trust a man" (16%).
18.	Once in a while I cannot control my urge to harm a man (11%).
19.	When a man is bossy, I take my time just to show him (42%).
20.	I know that men tend to talk about me behind my back (23%).
21.	Most men make friends because friends are likely to be useful to them (22%).
22.	Men always seem to get the breaks (29%).
23.	I can't help feeling resentful when I think of how easy men have it in life (16%).
24.	There are certain men I dislike so much that i am inwardly pleased when they get into trouble for something they have done (42%).
25.	When I look back at what's happened to me I can't help feeling mildly resentful toward the men in my life (27%).
26.	I don't seem to get what's coming to me in my relationships with men (26%). Sometimes men bother me by just being around (39%).
27.	At times I feel I get a raw deal with the opposite sex (41%).
28.	I don't blame women for trying to get everything from men nowadays (12%).
29.	Men irritate me a great deal more than they are aware of (27%).
30.	If I let men see the way I feel, they would consider me a hard person to get along with (18%)

Note: The KR 20 reliability for the Hostility Toward Men Scale was .89, and the mean score on the scale was 7.57 (*S.D.* = 6.16). All items are "true-keyed." The number in parentheses following each item is the percentage of subjects who responded "true" to the item.

Table 8.2. Correlates of Hostility Toward Men

Variable	Correlation with Hostility Toward Men
General Hostility (trait anger):	.32*
Adjectives checked as descriptive of men:	
No. of positive adjectives	-.33**
No. of negative adjectives	.51**
Adjectives checked as descriptive of women:	
No. of positive adjectives	-.03
No. of negative adjectives	.13*

Note: Higher numbers corresponded to, e.g., higher hostility toward men or higher general hostility.
*p<.05.
**p<.01.

son correlations were calculated between the Hostility Toward Men scale and: (a) the Trait Anger Scale; (b) the number of positive and negative adjectives checked as descriptive of men; and (c) the number of positive and negative adjectives checked as descriptive of women. The results of these analyses are presented in Table 8.2.

As can be seen from the first row of Table 8.2, hostility toward men was significantly correlated with the general hostility measure, which is not surprising since general hostility may be assumed to include hostility toward men. Of greater interest are the correlations between hostility toward men and the adjectives that were checked as characteristic of men and women. As can be seen from Table 8.2, the Hostility Toward Men scale was negatively correlated with the number of positive adjectives checked as characteristic of men, and positively correlated with the number of negative adjectives checked. Thus, subjects who scored high on the Hostility Toward Men scale checked fewer positive adjectives and more negative adjectives when describing men than subjects who scored low on the Hostility Toward Men scale. In contrast, there was very little relationship between hostility toward men and the adjectives that were checked as characteristic of women. In this respect, therefore, the Hostility Toward Men scale may be said to have some degree of discriminant validity in predicting only those other measures of hostility that it theoretically is expected to.

Incidence of Sexual Victimization

The percentages of women who reported experiencing at least one incident of each of the 13 Sexual Experience Survey experiences are listed in Column 1 of Table 8.3. For comparison, the percentages of women who responded "Yes" to each item in Koss & Oros' American sample are listed in Column 2 of Table 8.3. It is interesting to note that the aggressive sexual experiences were reported about twice as frequently in the American sample as in the Canadian sample. One possible reason for this difference may be the fact that the American sample was composed of women from all levels of university, whereas the present Canadian sample was composed almost exclusively of first-year students (who, as can be seen from Row 1 of Table 8.3, were less likely to have experienced consenting intercourse). A more likely explanation with respect to the victimization items, however, is that these data are accurately reflecting the fact that Canadians (per capita) are much less likely to be the victims of crime than Americans, as evidenced both by victimization surveys (e.g., Bibby, 1981), and by comparisons of official crime statistics in the two countries (e.g., Doob & Roberts, 1982).

Correlates of Sexual Victimization

In order to determine the relationship between sexual victimization and the various other measures, a sexual victimization score was calculated for each subject by summing (across items 4 through 13) the number of times she reported experiencing each of the aggressive incidents listed in Table 8.3 (up to a maximum of 10 times, in order to minimize the skew of the distribution). Thus the total resulting victimization score reflected not only the number of different experiences a particular subject reported, but also the frequency with which she reported having each experience. Victimization scores were then correlated with each of the other measures, the results of which are listed in Column 2 of Table 8.4. For comparison, the correlations between reported frequency of consensual intercourse and the various other measures are listed in Column 1 of Table 8.4. As can be seen from the table, frequency of consensual intercourse was not related to any of the other measures, thus suggesting that the observed findings with respect to sexual victimization are not simply a function of sexual experience per se.

As can be seen from the first two rows of Table 8.4, the main hypothesis of this investigation was supported. Sexual victimization was found to be associated with hostility toward men, but not with general hostility. As well, sexual victimization was associated with perceptions that men possess many negative attributes and few positive attributes (Table 8.4, Rows 3 and 4). On the other hand, subjects' descriptions of women were unrelated to sexual victimization. Finally, sexual victimization was associated with depression, consistent with previous research (Atkeson et al., 1982; Frank et al., 1979).

Table 8.3.Incidence of Sexual Victimization

Item	Present Sample % Yes	Koss & Oros' % Yes1
Have you ever:		
01. Had sexual intercourse with a man when you both wanted to	52.5%	75.4%
02. Had a man misinterpret the level of sexual intimacy you desired?	54.7%	70.5%
03. Been in a situation where a man became so sexually aroused that you felt it was useless to stop him even though you did not want to have sexual intercourse?	29.9%	32.8%
04. Had sexual intercourse with a man even though you didn't really want to because he threatened to end your relationship otherwise?	2.2%	5.9%
05. Had sexual intercourse with a man when you didn't really want to because you felt pressured by his continual arguments?	8.6%	21.4%
06. Found out that a man had obtained sexual intercourse with you by saying things he didn't really mean?	14.4%	20.4%
07. Been in a situation where a man used some degree of physical force (twisting your arm, holding you down, etc.) to try to make you engage in kissing or petting when you didn't want to?	19.8%	30.2%
08. Been in a situation where a man tried to get sexual intercourse with you when you didn't want to by threatening to use physical force (twisting your arm, holding you down, etc) if you didn't cooperate, but for various reasons sexual intercourse did not occur?	8.3%	18.3%

Table 8.3.Incidence of Sexual Victimization (Continued)

Item	Present Sample % Yes	Koss & Oros' % Yes[1]
09. Been in a situation where a man used some degree of physical force (twisting your arm, holding you down, etc.) to try to get you to have sexual intercourse with him when you didn't want to, but for various reasons sexual intercourse did not occur?	8.3%	8.7%
10. Had sexual intercourse with a man when you didn't want to because he used some degree of physical force (twisting your arm, holding you down, etc.)?	1.4%	3.1%
11. Had sexual intercourse with a man when you didn't want to because he threatened to use physical force (twisting your arm, holding you down, etc.) if you didn't cooperate?	4.3%	8.2%
12. Been in a situation where a man obtained sexual acts with you such as anal or oral intercourse with you when you didn't want to by using threats or physical force (twisting your arm, holding you down, etc.)?	4.0%	6.4%
13. Have you ever been raped?	2.9%	6.0%

Note: These items were taken verbatim from Koss and Oros's (1982) Sexual Experiences Survey.
[1]These percentages were taken from Table 1 of Koss and Oros (1982).

DISCUSSION

The present results provide further confirmation that sexual victimization is associated with depression and hostility. Moreover, these data highlight the importance of studying hostility directed specifically toward men, rather than using measures of general hostility, which may mask the true impact of sexual assault on women's relationships with men. Perhaps if more investigators were to make this distinction, there would be more research toward designing treatment programs that help the victim deal with her negative feelings toward men. Unfor-

Table 8.4. Correlates of Sexual Victimization

Variable	Correlation with:	
	Frequency of Consentual Intercourse	Frequency of Victimiza-tion:2
Hostility toward men:	-.10	.24**
General hostility:	.04	.07
Adjectives checked as descriptive of men:		
No. of positive adjectives	-.02	-.12*
No. of negative adjectives	.02	.16
Adjectives checked as descriptive of women:		
No. of positive adjectives	.00	-.01
No. of negative adjectives	-.06	.02
Depression:	.01	.18**

Note: Higher numbers corresponded to, e.g., higher hostility toward men or higher frequency of victimization.
*p<.05.
**p<.01.

tunately, current treatment programs involving the men in victims' lives seem to focus almost exclusively on men's negative feelings and reactions toward the victim (e.g., Silverman & McCombie, 1980), and thus may fail to recognize the possibility that these feelings might be mutual.

The present findings also provide some preliminary evidence for the reliability and validity of the Hostility Toward Men scale. Thus, the scale is suggested as a potentially useful instrument for future research on sexual victimization, or for other related research on hostility toward men. Researchers are cautioned, however, not to rely heavily on this measure until further validity data are collected. In particular, unlike the construct of male hostility toward women (see Check, 1986; Check & Malamuth, 1983a), there are virtually no theoretical discussions of female hostility toward men in the literature, thus making it difficult to establish the construct validity of any measure of hostility toward men. It is hoped that the present paper will encourage such theorizing and research.

ACKNOWLEDGMENTS

The senior author was supported by a Social Sciences and Humanities Research Council of Canada Doctoral Fellowship #453-82-0118 during the conduct of this research.

The authors would like to thank Daniel Perlman for his helpful comments on an earlier draft of this paper, Neil M. Malamuth for suggesting the adjective checklist procedure, and Hal Wallbridge for constructing the list of positive and negative adjectives that was used in the adjective checklist.

REFERENCES

Atkeson, B. M., Calhoun, K. S., Resick, P. A., & Ellis, E. M. (1982). Victims of rape: Repeated assessment of depressive symptoms. *Journal of Consulting and Clinical Psychology, 50,* 96-102.
Becker, J. V., Skinner, L. J., Abel, G. G., Howell, J., & Bruce, K. (1982). The effects of sexual assault on rape and attempted rape victims. *Victimology, 7,* 106-113.
Bibby, R. W. (1981). Crime and punishment: A national reading. *Social Indicators Research, 9,* 1-13.
Burgess, A. W., & Holmstrom, L. L. (1974). *Rape: Victims of crisis.* Bowie, MD: Robert J. Brady.
Burgess, A. W., & Holmstrom, L. L. (1977). Rape trauma syndrome. In D. Chappell, R. Geis, & G. Geis (Eds.), *Forcible rape: The crime, the victim, and the offender.* New York: Columbia University Press.
Buss, A. H., & Durkee, A. (1957). An inventory for assessing different kinds of hostility. *Journal of Consulting Psychology, 21,* 343-349.
Byers, E. S., & Eastman, A. M. (1979, June). Characteristics of unreported sexual assaults among college women. Paper presented at the meeting of the Canadian Psychological Association, Quebec City, Quebec.
Campbell, D. T., & Fiske, D. W. (1959). Convergent discriminant validation by the multitrait-multimethod matrix. *Psychological Bulletin, 56,* 81-105.
Cattell, R. B. (1966). The scree test for the number of factors. *Multivariate Behavioral Research, 1,* 245-276.
Check, J. V. P. (1988). Hostility toward women: Some theoretical considerations. In G. W. Russell (Ed.), *Violence in intimate relationships.* Great Neck, NY: PMA Publishing.
Check, J. V. P., & Malamuth, N. M. (1982, May). Pornography effects and self-reported likelihood of committing stranger versus acquaintance rape. Paper presented at the meeting of the Midwestern Psychological Association, Minneapolis.
Check, J. V. P., & Malamuth, N. M. (1983a, August). Hostility toward women, rape arousal, and laboratory aggression against women. Paper presented at the meeting of the American Psychological Association, Anaheim, CA.
Check, J. V. P., & Malamuth, N. M. (1983b). Sex role stereotyping and reactions to depictions of stranger versus acquaintance rape. *Journal of Personality and Social Psychology, 45,* 344-356.
Clark, L., & Lewis, D. (1977). *Rape: The price of coercive sexuality.* Toronto: The Women's Press.
Comrey, A. L. (1964). Personality factors Compulsion, Dependence, Hostility, and Neuroticism. *Educational and Psychological Measurement, 24,* 74-84.
Derogatis, L. R. (1977). *SCL-90-R manual.* Baltimore, MD: Clinical Psychometrics Research Unit, Johns Hopkins University.
Doob, A. N., & Roberts, J. (1982). *Crime: Some views of the public.* Ottawa, Ontario: Canadian Department of Justice.
Edmunds, G., & Kendrick, D. C. (1980). *The measurement of human aggressiveness.* Chichester, England: Ellis Horwood.

Ellis, E. M., Atkeson, B. M., & Calhoun, K. S. (1982). An examination of differences between multiple- and single-incident victims of sexual assault. *Journal of Abnormal Psychology, 91,* 221-224.

Evans, D. R., & Strangeland, M. (1971). Development of the reaction inventory to measure anger. *Psychological Reports, 29,* 412-414.

Feldman-Summers, S., Gordon, P. E., & Meagher, J. R. (1979). The impact of rape on sexual satisfaction. *Journal of Abnormal Psychology, 88,* 101-105.

Frank, E., Turner, S. M., & Duffy, B. (1979). Depressive symptoms in rape victims. *Journal of Affective Disorders, 1,* 269-277.

Kanin, E. J., & Parcell, S. R. (1977). Sexual aggression: A second look at the offended female. *Archives of Sexual Behavior, 6,* 67-76.

Kilpatrick, D. G., Resick, P. A., & Veronen, L. J. (1981). Effects of a rape experience: A longitudinal study. *Journal of Social Issues, 37,* 105-122.

Kirkpatrick, C., & Kanin, E. (1957). Male sexual aggression on a university campus. *American Sociological Review, 22,* 52-58.

Koss, M. P., Gidycz, C. A., & Wisniewski, N. (1987). The scope of rape: Incidence and prevalence of sexual aggression and victimization in a national sample of higher education students. *Journal of Consulting and Clinical Psychology, 55,* 162-170.

Koss, M. P., & Oros, C. J. (1982). Sexual Experiences Survey: A research instrument investigating sexual aggression and victimization. *Journal of Consulting and Clinical Psychology, 50,* 455-457.

McCahill, T. W., Meyer, L. C., & Fischman, A. M. (1979). *The aftermath of rape.* Lexington, MA: D.C. Heath.

McNair, D., Lorr, M., & Droppleman, L. (1971). *Manual, Profile of Mood States.* San Diego, CA: Educational and Industrial Testing Service.

Medea, A., & Thompson, K. (1974). *Against rape.* New York: Farrar, Straus, & Giroux.

Megargee, E. I., & Menzies, E. S. (1971). The assessment and dynamics of aggression. In P. McReynolds (Ed.), *Advances in psychological assessment* (Vol. 2). Palo Alto, CA: Science and Behavior Books.

Notman, N. T., & Nadelson, C. C. (1980). Psychodynamic and life-stage considerations in response to rape. In S. L. McCombie (Ed.), *The rape crisis intervention handbook.* New York: Plenum.

Radloff, L. S. (1977). The CES-D scale: A self-report depression scale for research in the general population. *Applied Psychological Measurement, 1,* 385-401.

Resick, P. A., Calhoun, K. S., Atkeson, B. M., & Ellis, E. M. (1981). Social adjustment in victims of sexual assault. *Journal of Consulting and Clinical Psychology, 49,* 705-712.

Sales, E., Baum, M., & Shore, B. (1984). Victim readjustment following assault. *Journal of Social Issues, 40*(1), 117-136.

Siegel, S. M. (1956). The relationship of hostility to authoritarianism. *Journal of Abnormal and Social Psychology, 52,* 368-372.

Silverman, D., & McCombie, S. L. (1980). Counseling the mates and families of rape victims. In S. L. McCombie (Ed.), *The rape crisis intervention handbook.* New York: Plenum.

Spielberger, C. D., Jacobs, G. A., Russell, S., & Crane, R. S. (1982). Assessment of anger: The State-Trait Anger scale. In J. N. Butcher & C. D. Spielberger (Eds.), *Advances in personality assessment* (Vol. 2). Hillsdale, NJ: Lawrence Erlbaum.

Sutherland, S., & Scherl, D. J. (1977). Crisis intervention with victims of rape. In D. Chappell, R. Geis, & G. Geis (Eds.), *Forcible rape: The crime, the victim, and the offender.* New York: Columbia University Press.

Wilson, P. R. (1978). *The other side of rape.* St. Lucia, Queensland, Australia: University of Queensland Press.

Chapter 9
Power Struggles and Intimacy Anxieties as Causative Factors of Wife Assault

Donald G. Dutton and James J. Browning

Since the bulk of published research material on the causes, etiology, and effects of wife assault has been written only in the last ten years, it is not surprising that the level of explanation for this phenomenon is still somewhat rudimentary. Furthermore, since wife assault has been studied by a variety of disciplines, a resulting wide range of possible causes has been posited, from brain damage (Elliot, 1977) and psychopathy (Pizzey, 1974) on the one hand to the "sexist organization of society" (Straus, 1973) on the other.

Indeed, the short history of explanation of causes for wife assault has been dialectical in nature. The first wave of explanation tended to view wife assault as resulting from clinical syndromes existing either in the assaulter, his victim, or both. Hence, wife assaulters have been described as sadistic personalities (Pizzey, 1974), pathologically passive and dependent (Snell, Rosenwald, & Robey, 1964; Faulk, 1974), or as suffering from temporal lobe epilepsy (Elliot, 1977). Some serious empirical problems plagued the studies that explained wife assault as individual pathology. These included: (1) a tendency to generalize from psychiatric case studies (Symonds, 1975) or from prison populations (Scott, 1974; Faulk, 1974); (2) a failure to systematically assess a large sample of wife assaulters; (3) a tendency to rely on descriptive data supplied by the victim (Rosenbaum & O'Leary, 1981); and (4) a failure to analyze acute situational pressures operating in assaultive relationships (Dutton, 1983a). One possible result of these empirical problems may have been the tendency to overestimate the percentage of wife assaulters who did belong to subpopulations with diagnosable individual psychopathology (Dutton, 1983b).

The Diagnostic and Statistical Manual of the Mental Disorders (1981) contains a variety of disorders that share symptomatologies with descriptions of wife assaulters given by their wives (Rounsaville, 1978; Rosenbaum & O'Leary, 1981), by clinicians working with wife assaulters (Ganley & Harris, 1978), or by the men themselves (Gayford, 1975). These would include "conjugal paranoia" with delusions of sexual infidelity by one's spouse; intermittent explosive disorders, including temporal lobe epilepsy (Elliot, 1977), with prodromal acceleration of autonomic activity and post-episode amnesia; and borderline personality disorders with intense mood swings, interpersonal disturbances, anger, and suicidal gestures. Also, Rounsaville (1978) and Gayford (1975) reported substance abuse (typically alcohol) in approximately half of an assaultive population, although Rounsaville reported that only 29% had been drinking at the time of the assault. Furthermore, Rounsaville found that only 6 assaulters (out of 31) had a history of prolonged psychiatric contact and 15 had no prior contact.

Taxonomies are further complicated by violence patterns: both Rounsaville (1978) and Browning (1983) found that about half of wife assaulters were violent outside the relationship, and about 40% were violent in more than one relationship. Clearly, the development of different etiologies for these various violence patterns seems appropriate. In men violent outside the relationship, a learned response of violence to stress or perceived threat (cf. Novaco, 1975) seems likely. In men whose violence occurs only in relationships with women, greater attention might be paid to "content" issues such as jealousy, intimacy-anxiety, etc. In men who are violent in only one relationship, some attention might be paid to structural analyses of interpersonal behavior (cf. Benjamin, 1979; Gottman, 1979). The focus of our research, as we will describe below, is more appropriate to that category of wife assaulter whose violence is specific to relationships with women and whose violence occurs in more than one relationship.

A reaction to this first wave of psychiatric explanation was sociological explanations of wife assault, which viewed it as an extreme example of male attempts to dominate women, prescribed by traditional male sex-role socialization (Straus, 1973; Dobash & Dobash, 1978; Straus & Hotaling, 1980) and fostered by the tacit approval of societal institutions such as the law (Goldman, 1978; Dutton, 1981) and organizations such as the criminal justice system (U.S. Commission on Civil Rights, 1978). However, victim surveys (Straus, Gelles, & Steinmetz, 1980; Schulman, 1979) and surveys of attitudes toward wife assault (Stark & McEvoy, 1970) indicate that it is not considered acceptable behavior by most North American males, nor do most practice it.

Stark and McEvoy (1970) posed the question "Do you approve of a man slapping his wife under appropriate circumstances?" Despite the leading wording of this question, only 20% of the sample agreed. If more extreme forms of violence were substituted such as "hitting," "kicking," or "beating up" and the term "appropriate circumstances" was dropped, the agreement rate on this item might drop precipitously. Wife assaulters themselves provide the clearest evidence that wife assault is not normatively acceptable; they deny, minimize and rationalize their actions at the beginning of therapy (Ganley & Harris, 1978). In our own treatment groups for assaultive males, we routinely take Conflict Tactics Scale (Straus, 1979) reports from the men and their wives and, where possible, compare these reports to police and hospital reports of the incidents leading to the man's arrest and conviction. The men's reports consistently underestimate the amount of violence, its frequency, and severity (Browning & Dutton, 1986). Such minimizing is typically viewed by clinicians as being based on shame and guilt over one's actions. Shame and guilt generally occur because one is aware that one's actions are unacceptable. Furthermore, normative explanations have to explain the absence of wife assault for the majority of North American males. Broad-based victim surveys indicate that even if one took the broadest definition of assault (pushing, slapping or worse), about 80% of males are not assaultive (Straus, Gelles, & Steinmetz, 1980; Schulman, 1979).

To avoid the problems with both the psychiatric and sociological approaches to wife assault, we have adopted a nested ecological model of wife assault that views assaults as multiply-determined by forces in the broader culture (macrosystem), work and peer groups (exosystem), family (microsystem), and the individual himself (Dutton, 1984). Within this framework, we have begun to examine the interaction of ontogenetic and microsystem factors by focusing on the interplay of two potential explanatory variables, power and intimacy.

The selection of these particular concepts for research was based upon the frequency with which power issues and intimacy issues were mentioned by wife assaulters in our treatment groups, and by other clinicians working with wife assaulters (Ganley & Harris, 1978; Martin, 1977; Walker, 1979). Power issues were described through frequent mention of the need to control or dominate the female, descriptions of female independence as loss of male control, and by frequent attempts to persuade or coerce the female into adopting the male's definition of relationship structure and function.

Intimacy issues include sudden increases in the wife's or relationship's demands for greater affection, attention, and emotional support and, at the other end of the continuum, increased demands for greater independence, or freedom from control by the male. Gelles (1975) and Rounsaville (1978) reported that for 40% of repeatedly assaulted wives, the onset of assault coincided with a sudden transition in intimacy, such as marriage or pregnancy. Correspondingly, Daly, Wilson, and Weghorst (1982) describe sexual jealousy as an instigator of wife assault. Jealousy might be viewed as a reaction to perceived relationship loss. We propose that changes in socioemotional distance between the man and his wife can serve as instigators of wife assault. Socioemotional distance can serve as a unifying concept to link reports of wife assault occurring in response to ostensibly opposite instigators such as increases and decreases in intimacy. Our thesis is that an understanding of the interplay of power dynamics on issues of intimacy or socioemotional distance can provide an explanatory framework to deepen our understanding of relationship specific assault.

POWER ISSUES

Although the consequences of the need for control and perception of control have been broadly researched (see for example, Adler, 1966; Baum & Singer, 1980; Perlmuter & Monty, 1979; Bandura, 1977; Langer, 1983; Seligman, 1975), understanding of the need for control in primary relationships is not as thoroughly developed in the psychological literature.

McClelland's (1975) Type III power orientation describes men who satisfy their need for power through having impact on or control over another person. McClelland views power orientations as analogous to Freudian stages of psychosexual development, and accordingly views the Type III as phallically fixated. Winter (1973) applied McClelland's Type III typology to males who compulsively seduce and abandon women. The "Don Juan syndrome" as Winter described it, originates from twin motives to sexually conquer (have impact on) and flee from women. In such a transaction, a male purposively increases intimacy with a female up to the point of sexual seduction, and then decreases intimacy immediately after. Sexual and power motives are intertwined and ambivalence about intimacy produces a repeated approach-avoidance pattern on a continuum of socioemotional distance between the male and the objectified female.

Dutton (1984) extended Winter's analysis to males in monogamous relationships, arguing that the same combination of strong power motivation and ambivalence would operate to create strong needs to control socioemotional distance in order to move alternatively closer (through courtship, conquest and impact) and further away (through emotional withdrawal, verbal criticism, extramarital affairs). Stewart & Rubin (1976) obtained data consistent with this analysis, finding that college-age males who scored high on Thematic Apperception Test (TAT) measures of "n" power were more likely to dissolve premarital monogamous relationships than males scoring low on "n" power. This dissolution was created by high "n" power males in two ways: first, through threatening the primary relationships by forming other romantic attachments (which fulfilled the need for new conquest) and secondly, through the generation of extreme control attempts in the primary relationship. These control attempts took the form of generating conflict through criticism of the female, and constant attempts to modify her attitudes and behavior, in order to have renewed, discernible impact on her. Perceived change of her behavior was tangible evidence of the impact. High scores on "n" power correlate significantly with frequency of arguments

(McClelland, 1975) and with a variety of behavioral indicators of aggression, such as destroying furniture and glassware (Winter, 1973). Also, high scorers write stories with themes reflecting adversarial sexual beliefs (Slovin, 1972), which portray women as exploitive and destructive. Whether these beliefs are a cause or consequence of their adversarial behavioral tendencies toward women is not currently known.

As we report below, however, men in our own research who react with the greatest anger to scenes of husband-wife conflict tend to be men who report high degrees of verbal and physical abuse from their mothers (but not from their fathers). Interestingly, Winter (1973) has proposed that men who developed the conquest-abandonment "Don Juan" syndrome did so in response to maternal mixed communications or double-bind communications (Bateson, 1972), where maternal nurturance was mixed with hostility toward the son. This occurred, Winter speculated, in patriarchal societies where women were repressed and reacted with anger toward the only safe male target, their sons. The ambivalence from the mother created ambivalence toward women in the son. In the study we reported below, self-reports of feelings of both anger and humiliation in response to watching videotaped husband-wife conflicts were significantly correlated to both verbal and physical abuse from the mother.

If a certain amount of transference occurs from the opposite-sex parent to one's spouse, then we might expect sons who were verbally or physically abused by their mothers to feel quite powerless in adult relationships. Male sex-role socialization however, teaches men that powerlessness and vulnerability are unacceptable feelings and behaviors (Pleck, 1981). As a consequence, we might expect exaggerated power concerns in such men, along with mistrust of females and anxiety about intimacy with a female (except when the male feels in complete control over the extent of the intimacy – i.e., able to increase or decrease it as he pleases). Consequently, any perceived threats to male control over the amount of intimacy should produce exaggerated arousal and anxiety in such males.

INTIMACY ANXIETY

Pollak and Gilligan (1982) reported images of violence in TAT stories written by men in response to situations of affiliation. They suggest that, as "fear of success" scores demonstrate reliable gender differences, with women scoring higher, fear of intimacy is a predominantly male anxiety and that males perceive intimate relationships to be dangerous. The working hypothesis we have adopted is that intimacy anxiety has both trait and state properties. The latter involve increases in response to sudden uncontrollable changes in the socioemotional distance between spouses. This distance we assume to be negotiated by both parties to a point that represents an optimal zone. An "optimal zone" for each person is that degree of emotional closeness or distance between themselves and their partner with which they feel comfortable at any given time. This comfort zone may be similar to optimal zones for interpersonal spacing (cf. Patterson, 1976), in that, as with interpersonal spacing zones, "invasions" (too much intimacy) or "evasions" (too little) may produce physiological arousal. Such invasions by the female (from the male's perspective), we term "engulfments;" evasions are called "abandonments." Fear of engulfment can be produced in three main ways: (1) by the female moving emotionally toward the male through increased demands for closeness, attention and affection; (2) by the female remaining static and the male developing an increased need for greater distance than is currently provided; and (3) by shifts in formal role demands such as marriage or fatherhood. Ehrenreich (1983) has incisively described the sociological ramifications of the male "breadwinner" role and of male attempts to flee from the ensuing engulfment. Affective reactions to engulfment may vary but probably carry an admixture of anxiety and resentment, along with a sense of guilt. When coupled with a lack of the man's verbal assertiveness to extricate himself from engulfment, the probability of verbal or physical abuse may increase.

Abandonment anxiety involves perceived uncontrollable increases in socioemotional distance from the male's perspective. Hence, it could be produced by: (1) sexual threat or any other instance of the female moving emotionally further away (or reinvesting her energy outside the primary relationship); or (2) the male's developing an increasing need for intimacy but not successfully expressing it, so that a "stationary" female stays at what was previously an optimal distance but one which is now too far. Also, formal redefinitions produce shifts in intimacy. For example, motherhood redirects female attention toward the child, while simultaneously increasing male "responsibility."

Finally, many clinical reports indicate that males exacerbate abandonment anxieties by behaving in such a way as to maximize the likelihood of abandonment by the female. Walker's (1979) description of the "battering cycle" describes a process whereby assaultive males, having gone through an "acute battering phase," experience guilt, remorse and anxiety that their wife will leave. If she moves to a new lodging, they put her under surveillance, obsess over her, try to convince her to return, and promise they will never be violent again. Men in therapeutic groups who are in an abandonment panic generally behave as though a lifeline were being cut off. They idealize the woman and obsess over her and their mistreatment of her. They reveal the exaggerated dependency they have on her, which was previously masked by their attempts to make her dependent on them or by exaggerated control of her behavior.

Sexual jealousy, especially to the extent it involves delusions or distortions, may represent a form of chronic abandonment anxiety. Jealousy is mentioned frequently by battered women as an issue that incited violence (Rounsaville, 1978; Whitehurst, 1971; Roy, 1977; Daly, Wilson, & Weghorst, 1982). Recent studies (Murstein, 1978; Clanton & Smith, 1977; White, 1980) have viewed jealousy as a mediating construct, produced by anticipated relationship loss, and producing a range of behavioral responses (including aggression and increased vigilance), and affective reactions (including rage and depression).

In many relationships the degree of intimacy or socioemotional distance is a key structural variable that has dramatic impact on individuals in the relationship. Power and control over the degree of intimacy is especially important to the extent that: (a) intimacy with one's spouse satisfies social needs unique to the primary relationship; (b) intimacy represents a major structural variable, and (c) ontogenetically learned anxieties about intimacy transfer onto the spousal relationship. Perceived inability to homeostatically maintain the degree of intimacy within the optimal zone should produce arousal in males. While this arousal may be clinically viewed as a component of state anxiety, a variety of mechanisms operates to induce males to experience the arousal as anger (Novaco, 1976; Dutton, Fehr, & McEwen, 1982). Male sex-role socialization is more compatible with expressions of anger than fear (Pleck, 1981; Fasteau, 1974). Feelings of agency, potency, expressiveness, and determination accompany the expression of anger (but not fear) (Novaco, 1976). Dutton and Aron (in press) found that males viewing interpersonal conflict scenarios demonstrated significant positive correlations between self-reports of generalized autonomic arousal and anger. Females demonstrated significant positive correlations between arousal and anxiety. Also, males experiencing anger as a result of perceived loss of control over intimacy could behave in a variety of ways besides violence, including verbal expression of feelings to the wife, self-abasement, discussion with friends, etc. Behavioral aggression may be more likely for males who (1) have poor repertoires of verbal-expressive skills and (2) believe they should be in a position of coercive power vis a vis their wives. Hence, one way that macrosystem norms may influence violence toward women is through shaping the interpretation of arousal states in males produced by loss of control over intimacy with their wives. A second way is by shaping the behavioral expression of the consequent anger. We have taken some initial steps to empirically investigate some of the relationships suggested by this analysis.

VIDEOTAPE STUDIES

Three groups of 18 men were compared in this study. A Physically Aggressive (PA) group were men who had been convicted of wife assault and were attending a treatment group for spousal violence; a Verbally Aggressive Group (VA) were men attending counselling groups for marital conflict; a Nonaggressive (NA) group was solicited through ads in local newspapers. All three groups were demographically similar (as measured by an index of socioeconomic status by Myers & Bean, 1968). The Straus Conflict Tactics Scale (CTS) Form N (Straus, 1979) was used to assess the men's means of dealing with conflict. Reports from

Table 9.1. Scores on Strauss Conflict Tactics Scales by Group

Group & Item	Reasoning subscale	Verbal subscale	Physical subscale
Physically aggressive (N = 18)			
Man's Self-Ratings	7.9	20.9	9.7
Wife's Ratings of Man	7.6	25.4	16.6
Verbally Aggressive (N = 18)			
Man's Self-Ratings	9.6	15.7	0.7
Wife's Ratings	7.7	13.4	0.9
Nonaggressive (N = 18)			
Man's Self-Ratings	7.0	3.8	0.2
Wife's Ratings	7.5	5.7	0.3

each man and his wife were obtained. Table 9.1 lists the scores on each subscale of the CTS.

The videotape component of the project provided an examination of the emotional impact on wife assaulters of power and intimacy factors in conflict situations. The general strategy was to present the subject with a series of videotaped scenes depicting verbal conflict between a man and a woman, encourage him to imagine himself actually being in the man's shoes, and take measures of arousal and experienced affect. The use of videotape was appealing in that the image could be presented vividly, while shaping a relatively standard image across subjects. It also allowed the roles of both parties in the conflict to be manipulated, whereas such an aim would have been difficult or impossible using a role-play technique.

The videotape component employed a 3 x 2 x 3 factorial design with three levels of subjects (PA, VA, NA), two levels of power (male dominant, female dominant), and three levels of attempted intimacy change (abandonment, engulfment, neutral). Power and intimacy change were manipulated by varying the verbal content of the videotaped scene. The subjects in each group (PA, VA, NA) were randomly assigned to viewing either male-dominant scenes or female-dominant scenes. Each subject then viewed three videotapes, each depicting a different intimacy condition. The order of presentation was counterbalanced.

The scenes were between five and seven minutes in duration, and involved the same man and woman arguing heatedly over an issue. The subjects were told that the man and woman were a couple who had been involved in an "in-depth" study of marriage at the university and had allowed a cameraman to film them at home. In fact, the couple were professional actors.

Relative power was manipulated by having either the man or the woman in the scene dominate the argument verbally. Family interaction researchers (cf. Mishler & Waxler, 1968; Jacob, 1975) have specified a number of discrete behaviors that seem to constitute verbal dominance, including greater talk time, successful interruptions, and winning acquiescence. This information was utilized to manipulate relative power.

Attempted intimacy change was manipulated by varying the issue discussed during the conflict. There were three issues: one for abandonment (woman attempting to move away from the man); engulfment (woman attempting to move closer to the man); and the neutral (no attempted movement) condition. It was decided to have the woman instigate this movement in the tapes (rather than the man) because the dynamic of interest here was the man's attempt to control the woman's behavior. Specifically, the abandonment issue involved the woman stating that she wished to become more independent, spend more time with her friends, and join a consciousness-raising group for women. The engulfment issue involved requests by the woman that the man spend more time talking to her and that he be more open with his thoughts and feelings. Finally, the neutral scene involved an issue that is common to most couples, but does not a priori involve a change in intimacy. The couple argued over whether they would spend their vacation camping or in a city.

Generally, the taped scenes depicted a moderate to severe level of verbal conflict in a realistic home setting. The videotapes were pretested on a small number of married men in their late twenties to provide an estimate of the arousal-producing properties of the tapes as well as a rough check on the power and intimacy change manipulation.

Self-report measures of perceived affect and behavioral response probability were obtained immediately after each videotape scene. A series of 10 adjectives describing affective state was selected from a more extensive list compiled by Russell & Mehrabian (1977). Three of these adjectives (angry, hostile, and aggressive) have been used to assess anger by these authors (Russell and Mehrabian, 1974).

A three-way repeated measures ANOVA was performed on the men's ratings of their anger had they been the man in the scenario. This yielded a significant overall difference amongst groups ($F(2,48) = 4.94$, $p < .01$), which remained significant ($p < .03$) when the anger ratings were corrected for initial levels of anger by using preratings (taken prior to showing the scenes) as a covariate. Observation of the means suggests a linear relationship, with the PA group rating the most anger and the NA group the least. Furthermore, Newman-Keuls comparisons indicated that the PA group reported significantly more anger to the abandonment scene than did the other two groups ($p < .01$).

Table 9.2. Scores, by Group

Group	Relevance of intimacy issue to relationship				Anger self-ratings		
	Aban.	Engulf.	Neut.		Aban.	Engulf.	Neut.
Physically aggressive (PA)	72%	56%	44%	MD*	21.0	16.2	21.1
				FD	21.0	16.4	18.3
					Overall = 119.02		
Verbally aggressive (VA)	39%	72%	56%	MD	17.1	18.4	19.6
				FD	14.4	14.3	16.1
					Overall = 16.67		
Nonaggressive (NA)	29%	56%	0%	MD	12.3	17.2	18.7
				FD	10.9	10.2	12.9

$X^2 = 36.13$, df = 4, p < .001   Overall = 13.70
*male (female) dominant

Novaco's behavioral likelihood scales yielded consistent between- groups differences, with the PA group reporting the least amount of constructive reasoning ($F(2,48) = 8.36$, p < .001), the most verbal aggression ($F(2,48) = 7.93$, p < .001), and the most physical aggression ($F(2,48) = 9.45$, p < .001). Post hoc comparisons revealed the PA group to be significantly different from each of the other two groups on these measures. This was especially true for the abandonment scenes. Finally, the men were asked the relevance of the issues portrayed to their own relationships. The table of percentages generated by this question is contained in Table 9.2. An overall chi-square performed on these data was significant ($X^2 = 36.13$, p < .001). It would appear from observation of the cell frequencies that the abandonment issue was the most relevant for the PA group and least relevant for the other groups.

To generate directions for future research, some "data snooping" techniques were performed. Specifically, an internal analysis that correlated all subjects' anger ratings collapsed across both subjects and videotapes was performed. Composite self-report anger ratings correlated most highly with composite anxiety ratings (+ .86, p < .001) and "humiliation" (+ .60, p < .001). The emergence of humiliation as a key descriptor of affective reactions poses potential heuristic value. Self-reports of humiliation while watching the conflict scenarios correlated + .40, p = .001 with reports of being verbally abused by one's mother in the family of origin and + .40, p = .001 with being physically abused by the mother. Correlations of humiliation with reports of verbal and physical abuse by the father, however, were not significant. This finding suggests support for

Winter's notion of maternal mixed messages contributing to men with strong ambivalence about intimacy and are, in our opinion, deserving of further study.

This study provided tentative support for the hypothesis that assaultive males react more strongly to abandonment scenarios than other males. Data bearing on anger, behavioral likelihood, and relevance to own relationship all indicated stronger reactions from this group. However, within-group variance was great and the sample size was small; hence, our statistical tests lacked power. Our current work is aimed at both increasing the sample size and establishing more pertinent criteria for our Physically Aggressive (PA) group. To this end, men who are also violent outside their primary relationship will be screened out of the PA group, as their violence may be indicative of a broader learned pattern, while our research hypotheses pertain to violence that is relationship-specific.

More work also needs to be done on the status of power-intimacy conjunctions as aversive instigators for assaultive males and the specific relationship of these instigators to behavioral repertoires with violence as a prepotent response. Furthermore, a deeper explanation of the development of humiliation through interactions in the family of origin, and the causal role of humiliation in spouse-specific assault seems warranted.

REFERENCES

Adler, A. (1966). The psychology of power. *Journal of Individual Psychology, 22,* 166-172.

Bandura, A. (1977). Self-efficacy: Towards a unified theory of behavioral change. *Psychological Review, 84,* 191-215.

Bateson, G. (1972). *Steps to an ecology of mind.* New York: Ballantine.

Baum, A., & Singer, J. E. (Eds.). (1980). Applications of personal control. *Advances in Environmental Psychology* (Vol. 2). Hillsdale, NJ: Lawrence Erlbaum Associates.

Benjamin, L. S. (1979). Use of structural analysis of social behavior and Markov chains to study dyadic interactions. *Journal of Abnormal Psychology, 88*(3), 303-319.

Browning, J. J. (1983). Towards a profile of the wife assaulter. Unpublished doctoral dissertation. University of British Columbia, Vancouver, Canada.

Browning, J. J., & Dutton, D. G. (1986). Assessment of wife assault with the conflict tactics scale: Using couple data to quantify the "Differential Reporting Effort." *Journal of Marriage and the Family, 48,* 375-379.

Clanton, G., & Smith, L. (1977). *Jealousy.* Englewood Cliffs, NJ: Prentice Hall.

Daly, M., Wilson, M., & Weghorst, S. J. (1982). Male sexual jealousy. *Ethology and Sociobiology, 3,* 11-27.

Diagnostic and Statistical Manual of the Mental Disorders (3rd ed, 1981). American Psychiatric Association, Washington, DC.

Dobash, R. E., & Dobash, R. P. (1978). Wives: The appropriate victims of mental assault. *Victimology: An International Journal, 2,* 426-442.

Dutton, D. G. (1981). The Criminal Justice Response to Wife Assault. Research Division: Solicitor General of Canada, Ottawa.

Dutton, D. G. (1983a, April). *Masochism as an "explanation" for traumatic bonding: An example of the "fundamental attribution error."* Paper presented at the meeting of the American Orthopsychiatric Association, Boston.

Dutton, D. G. (1983b). A systems approach for the prediction of wife assault: Relevance for criminal justice system policy. In C. Webster & S. Hucker (Eds.), *Probability and prediction: Psychiatry and public policy.* Cambridge: Cambridge University Press.

Dutton, D. G. (1984). A nested ecological theory of male violence towards intimates. In P. Caplan (Ed.), *Feminist psychology in transition.* Montreal: Eden Press.

Dutton, D. G., & Aron, A. (In press). Romantic attraction and generalized liking for others who are sources of conflict based arousal. *Canadian Journal of Behavioural Science.*

Dutton, D. G., Fehr, B., & McEwen, H. (1982). Severe wife battering as deindividuated violence. *Victimology: An International Journal, 7,* 13-23.

Elliot, F. (1977). The neurology of explosive rage: The episodic dyscontrol syndrome. In M. Roy (Ed.), *Battered women: A psychosociological study of domestic violence.* New York: Van Nostrand Reinhold.

Ehrenreich, B. (1983). *The hearts of men.* Garden City, NJ: Anchor, Doubleday.

Faulk, M. (1974). Men who assault their wives. *Medicine, Science and the Law, 14,* 180-183.

Fasteau, M. F. (1974). *The male machine.* New York: McGraw-Hill.

Ganley, A., & Harris, L. (1978, August). *Domestic violence: Issues in designing and implementing programmes for male batterers.* Paper presented at the meeting of the American Psychological Association, Toronto.

Gayford, J. J. (1975). Wife battering: A preliminary survey of 100 cases. *British Medical Journal, 30*(1), 194-197.

Gelles, R. J. (1975). Violence and pregnancy: A note on the extent of the problem and needed services. *The Family Co-ordinator, 24,* 81-86.

Goldman, P. (1978). Violence against women in the family. Unpublished master's thesis, Faculty of Law, McGill University.

Gottman, J. M. (1979). *Marital interaction: Experimental investigations.* New York: Academic Press.

Jacob, J. (1975). Family interaction in disturbed and normal families: A methodological and substantive review. *Psychological Bulletin, 82,* 33-65.

Langer, E. (1983). *The psychology of control.* Beverly Hills, CA: Sage.

Martin, D. (1977). *Battered wives.* New York: Kangaroo Paperbacks.

McLelland, D. (1975). *Power: The inner experience.* New York: Halstead Press.

Mishler, E. G., & Waxler, N. E. (1968). *Interaction in families: An experimental study of family process and schizophrenia.* New York: John Wiley.

Murstein, B. I. (1978). *Exploring intimate lifestyles.* New York: Springer.

Myers, J. K., & Bean, L. (1968). *A decade later: A follow-up of social class and mental illness.* New York: Wiley.

Novaco, R. W. (1975). *Anger control: The development and evaluation of an experimental program.* Lexington, MA: Lexington Books.

Novaco, R. W. (1976). The functions and regulation of the arousal of anger. *American Journal of Psychiatry, 133:*10, 1124, 1128.

Patterson, M. L. (1976). An arousal model of interpersonal intimacy. *Psychological Review, 83*(3), 235-245.

Perlmuter, L. C., & Monty, R. A. (Eds.). (1979). *Choice and perceived control.* Hillsdale, NJ: Lawrence Erlbaum.

Pizzey, E. (1974). *Scream quietly or the neighbours will hear.* London: Penguin.

Pleck, J. H. (1981). *The myth of masculinity.* Cambridge, MA: MIT Press.

Pollak, S., & Gilligan, C. (1982). Images of violence in Thematic Apperception Test stories. *Journal of Personality and Social Psychololgy, 42*(1), 159-167.

Rosenbaum, A., & O'Leary, K. D. (1981). Marital violence: Characteristics of abusive couples. *Journal of Consulting and Clinical Psychology, 41,* 63-76.

Rounsaville, B. (1978). Theories of marital violence: Evidence from a study of battered women. *Victimology, 3,* 11-31.

Roy, M. (1977). *Battered women: A psychosocial study of domestic violence.* New York: Van Nostrand.

Russell, J., & Mehrabian, A. (1974). Distinguishing anger and anxiety in terms of emotional response factors. *Journal of Consulting and Clinical Psychology, 42,* 79-83.

Russell, J., & Mehrabian, A. (1977). Evidence for a three-factor theory of emotions. *Journal of Research in Personality, 11,* 273-294.

Schulman, M. (1979). A survey of spousal violence against women in Kentucky. U.S. Department of Justice: Law Enforcement Assistance Administration, Washington, DC.

Scott, P. D. (1974). Battered wives. *British Journal of Psychiatry, 125,* 433-441.

Seligman, M. E. (1975). *On depression, development and death.* San Francisco: Freeman.

Slovin, M. (1972). The theme of feminine evil: The image of women in male fantasy and its effects on attitudes and behavior. Unpublished doctoral dissertation, Harvard University.

Snell, J. E., Rosenwald, P. J., & Robey, A. (1964). The wifebeater's wife. *Archives of General Psychiatry, 11,* 107-113.

Stark, R., & McEvoy, J. (1970). Middle class violence. *Psychology Today, 4*(6), 107-112.

Stewart, A., & Rubin, Z. (1976). The power motive in the dating couple. *Journal of Personality and Social Psychology, 34,* 305-309.

Straus, M. A. (1973). A general systems theory approach to a theory of violence between family members. *Social Science Information, 12*(3), 105-125.

Straus, M. A. (1979). Measuring intrafamily conflict and violence: The conflict tactics scale. *Journal of Marriage and the Family, 41,* 75-88.

Straus, M. A., Gelles, R. J., & Steinmetz, S. K. (1980). *Behind closed doors: Violence in the American family.* New York: Anchor Press/Doubleday.

Straus, M. A., & Hotaling, G. T. (1980). *The social causes of husband-wife violence.* Minneapolis, MN: University of Minnesota Press.

Symonds, M. (1975). Victims of violence: Psychological effects and aftereffects. *American Journal of Psychoanalysis, 35,* 19-26.

U.S. Commission on Civil Rights. (1978). *Battered women: Issues of public policy.* U.S. Government Printing Office, Washington, DC.

Walker, L. E. (1979). *The battered woman.* New York: Harper & Row.

White, G. L. (1980). Inducing jealousy: A power perspective. *Personality and Social Psychology Bulletin, 6*(2), 222-227.

Whitehurst, R. N. (1971). Violence potential in extramarital sexual responses. *Journal of Marriage and the Family, 33,* 683-691.

Whitehurst, R. N. (1974). Violence in husband-wife interaction. In S. K. Steinmetz & M. A. Straus (Eds.), *Violence in the family.* New York: Harper & Row.

Winter, D. G. (1973). *The power motive.* New York: Free Press.

Chapter 10
A Psychosocial Approach to Family Violence: Application of Conceptual Systems Theory

Carolie J. Coates and Deborah J. Leong

This chapter utilizes a psychosocial approach to conceptualize the dynamics of family violence. The formulation outlined was shaped not only by the research conducted, but also by a base of experiences including interviews with clinical staff treating family violence cases, providing clinical service to family violence victims, and involvement in community advocacy programs addressing the issue.

The conceptual systems approach described herein depicts different personality styles with differential modes of coping with interpersonal conflict. Application of conceptual systems theory to spousal abuse yields profiles of different types of men and women who might become involved in family violence. The intent of this programmatic research effort is to eventually derive differential treatment and intervention implications for individuals with different personality and situational profiles.

LITERATURE REVIEW OF PREVIOUS THEORIES

The Sociological Approach

There are two major approaches to the study of family violence in the literature. The first is a sociological one, which emphasizes the family as a system embedded within the larger society. This approach has relied on quantitative evidence and a macro level of analysis, which ignores the psychological dynamics of individuals within the family. Cultural antecedents of violence, such as historical sanctions or norms supportive of violence against women, and familial background characteristics, including an individual's experience with family violence in childhood, are factors that contribute to the risk of family violence (Davidson, 1977; Giles-Sims, 1983; Martin, 1976; Steinmetz, 1977; Steinmetz & Straus, 1974; Straus, 1976; Straus, Gelles, & Steinmetz, 1979, 1980; Straus & Hotaling, 1980). Isolation of the family unit (Gelles & Straus, 1977) and socioeconomic factors such as unemployment (Gelles, 1974, 1976; Hornung, McCullough, & Sugimoto, 1981) also increase the likelihood of violence. As has been pointed out in a review of the literature by Breines and Gordon (1983), sociological approaches have led to an emphasis on the number of blows rather than the "gestalt of the conflict" (Breines & Gordon, 1983, p. 512). The studies fail to differentiate families in which violence occurs from families in which it does not, because many of the factors studied occur to some degree in most families. The stress induced by unemployment may be experienced by many families, but it does not necessarily lead to violence. Psychological factors that may affect interpretation of stressful situations are not considered in the sociological approach.

Battering is one of the mechanisms used and accepted by a family to control behavior (Gelles, 1981). According to theories of reinforcement, battering behavior would increase over time because the batterer is positively reinforced for his actions. This model serves in part to explain why the maladaptive strategy is maintained, but it fails to explain how the maladaptive strategy originated. It does not explain why battering occurs only once in some families, intermittently in others, and almost continually in still others.

The Clinically Oriented Approach
The second approach represented in the literature on family violence is characterized by clinically oriented studies, typically based on information from clinical interviews. Information about the battered woman, the relationship, and the batterer are often from the point of view of the female victim. Both men and women in violent relationships have been depicted as experiencing low self-esteem, and the dynamic to explain the ineffectiveness of the women in leaving violent relationships has been "learned helplessness" (Walker, 1977-78, 1983). Batterers have been described by their victims as: unpredictable, experiencing low self-esteem, expressing hostility, and having a strong need to control (Martin, 1976; Schultz, 1960; Walker, 1977-78, 1979, 1983).

More recent studies have characterized batterers and proposed treatment plans based on clinical experience in treatment of batterers (e.g., Deschner, 1984; Sonkin, Martin, & Walker, 1985; Star, 1983). These books have provided more enriched clinical descriptions of abusive males and violent couples with the goal of providing treatment to end the violence.

While the clinical approach has yielded richness of detail, the theoretical formulations have been partial, i.e., describing one aspect of the complex phenomena, such as learned helplessness of the victim or the repetitive nature of cycles of violence (Walker, 1977-78, 1979). The results are often overgeneralized, given the methodological limitations of psychiatric samples, and small samples with data from the victim's point of view. In addition, some of the early clinical work was based on an espousal of a feminist ideology highly identified with the victim's point of view. This restricted view of the research of family violence has led to stereotyped depictions of the battered woman and the batterer (Breines & Gordon, 1983).

Both the sociological and clinical explanations have failed to articulate issues such as the following:

1. Why do battering couples and nonviolent couples have similar background characteristics and antecedent experiences?
2. What are the dynamics of battering couple relationships that perpetuate these relationships in the face of physical and emotional pain?
3. What are the motivational attributions and explanations as perceived by the battered women and the batterers themselves?
4. What means other than violence do battered women and batterers have in their repertoires to cope with interpersonal conflicts?

THE PSYCHOSOCIAL APPROACH

In searching for a theory that would provide a framework for pursuit of the above questions, the following criteria were projected. The theory had to:

1. Encompass the interaction between personality characteristics of the individual and situational presses
2. Provide a framework for predicting differential selectivity to highly affectively arousing and motivating situations
3. Provide differential motivational explanations for different personality types
4. Predict different modes of coping with interpersonal conflict.

Conceptual Systems Theory

A social-psychological theory, conceptual systems theory (originally presented in Harvey, Hunt, & Schroder, 1961), was selected. Conceptual systems theory has been utilized in a series of empirical studies, summarized by Harvey (1974, 1986), and it has been applied to human problem areas such as education (Coates, 1971; Coates, Harvey, & White, 1970; Harvey, 1978; Harvey, Coates, Gore, & Prather, 1983; Harvey & Gore, 1979; Harvey, Prather, White, & Hoffmeister, 1968; Harvey, White, Prather, Alter, & Hoffmeister, 1966) and delinquency (Chinn, 1980; Juers & Harvey, 1963). However, it has not been utilized to explain the emotionally charged problem of family violence.

Conceptual systems theory has as its basic premise that an individual's conceptual system, a set of predispositions, serves as a conceptual filter that renders stimuli differentially motivating and ego-involving (Harvey & Felknor, 1970). The theory predicts that under a condition of strong personal involvement (or high ego-involvement) a person's conceptual system will be a salient factor in determining an individual's attributions and affect in response to the involving stimuli or situation, and hence, determine his/her behaviors in that highly involving or possibly stressful situation. Four basic conceptual systems have been deduced, each of which has differential predictions with regard to coping with ego-involving stimuli.

The four principal conceptual systems differ in both the structural dimension of concreteness-abstractness (with abstractness referring to greater cognitive complexity and integration) and in belief content. As a consequence, each is characterized by a unique pattern of interpretive, affective, and behavioral tendencies under conditions of high personal involvement.

Individuals may be classified as representing one of four major conceptual systems depicted by Harvey, Hunt, and Schroder (1961) or an admixture of two or more systems on the basis of their responses to the "This I Believe" (TIB) Test, a semi-projective test designed specifically to measure conceptual systems (Harvey, 1966, 1974, 1986; Harvey et al., 1966). Some experimental work has been completed in an attempt to develop objective scales which can be computer scored and profiled into the conceptual system patterns (Conceptual Systems Test, Harvey et al., 1968; Belief Systems Test, Harvey & Gore, 1980). At this point the computer-scored system classification methodologies are useful for categorization of large samples with backup scoring of the TIB; however, they have methodological problems particularly with respect to identification of System Four individuals.

Many papers have been written from both a theoretical and empirical vantage point about the child-rearing antecedents of the four major conceptual systems (Harvey & Felknor, 1970; Schmidt, 1981), validation with other personality and attitude measures (Harvey, 1966, 1967, 1974), and social perceptions and attributions (Adams, Harvey, & Heslin, 1966; Coates, 1971; Harvey, 1976; Harvey & Ware, 1967; Kritzberg, 1965; Neva, Coates, & Harvey, 1970; Ware & Harvey, 1967; White & Harvey, 1965). A synopsis is presented below for each of the four conceptual system patterns, based on the research cited above and other studies cited in the vignettes.

It should be noted that as the systems depicted move from one to four, higher levels of abstractness and cognitive complexity are indicated; however, the central content of the beliefs and hence the affective reactivity varies with each conceptual system. This intersect of both structure and content of conceptual systems allows for affective and motivational predictions beyond those possible with only the more cognitive dimension of concreteness-abstractness.

System One

System One individuals are characterized as being low on dimensions of cognitive complexity; they tend to think in dichotomous dimensions and to make fewer differentiations than representatives of the more abstract conceptual systems (Adams et al., 1966; Harvey, 1966, 1967). Under stress they generate fewer and less creative solutions to problems (Brown & Harvey, 1968; Harvey, 1966; Harvey & Kline, 1965; Kaats, 1969; Miller & Harvey, 1973). They tend to exhibit a greater intolerance of ambiguity and a higher need for cognitive consistency (Harvey, 1966; Harvey & Ware, 1967; Kaats, 1969; Ware & Harvey, 1967). With regard to judgments in social situations, they have a greater tendency toward extreme judgments, they tend to achieve certainty of judgment with fewer inputs, and they hold their opinions with greater strength and certainty than representatives of more abstract conceptual systems (Harvey & Ware, 1967; Neva et al., 1970; Ware & Harvey, 1967). System One individuals tend to display a strong conviction that there is an extra-personal source of authority. They exhibit a greater reliance on authority and status cues for making decisions than do representatives from the other systems (Desjardins, 1971; Harvey, 1966; Kritzberg, 1965).

In a group situation they are more likely than representatives from other systems to develop a hierarchical social structure with a strong leader and to perseverate with their selected problem solving strategies despite feedback that the strategies are ineffective (Tuckman, 1964). They tend to overgeneralize their social impressions and to utilize stereotypes in depicting others (Coates, 1971; Harvey & Ware, 1967; Ware & Harvey, 1967). They tend to attribute blame to others and to select punitive solutions to social and discipline situations, particularly when the others involved are of lower status (Coates, 1971; Harvey et al., 1966; Harvey et al., 1968; Harvey, Shern, & Brown, 1978).

System One individuals tend to have experienced traditional and authoritarian family structures. The reward and punishment systems were usually predictable, and they may have experienced physical punishment as children. Authority often resided in the father role in the family (Harvey & Felknor, 1970).

System Two

System Two individuals are also on the concrete end of the concreteness-abstractness dimension and so many of the studies cited above for System One individuals with regard to rigidity of conceptual systems also apply to System Two individuals. However, System Two individuals exhibit a belief content which is almost the opposite of that of System One individuals. System Two individuals are anti-authority; many of the traditional societal beliefs about authority are rejected (Harvey, 1966, 1967). In fact, the presence of authority cues can produce poorer performances on creative tasks for System Twos (Harvey & Kline, 1965; Miller & Harvey, 1973). System Two individuals experience strong distrust and often alienation. Self-esteem is often low and they may have an expectation of failure. They are reluctant to disclose about themselves and to share intimacies (Harvey, 1966, 1967, 1974).

While empirical evidence is lacking on the social coping styles of System Two individuals (the education studies, e.g., Harvey et al., 1966; Harvey et al., 1968, found almost no System Twos in teaching positions), the theory would predict withdrawal and capricious punitiveness toward others as consistent with a System Two orientation. System Two individuals have been susceptible to influence attempts which stress low status scores or high expertise (Harvey, 1966, 1967). In group problem solving situations, homogeneous groups of System Two individuals generated interpersonal hostility and lack of agreement (Tuckman, 1964).

System Two individuals reported experiencing childhoods with a high degree of inconsistency and capricious behavior on the part of their parents. They reported feelings of rejection from their parents and they tended to have experienced physical punishment (Harvey & Felknor, 1970).

System Three

System Three and Four individuals have often been combined in previous research on aspects of conceptual abstractness or cognitive complexity. They were also included in previously cited studies for Systems One and Two; in these studies individuals of greater abstractness (Systems Three and Four) were higher on tolerance of ambiguity, creativity under stress, ability to adopt hypothetical sets, and cognitive complexity. System Three individuals have been particularly skilled in role playing situations (Harvey & Kline, 1965) and they relied on their peers in social judgment situations (Harvey, 1967). They tend to wait for appropriate amounts of information before they make judgments about others and they hold their opinions with less certainty than System One individuals (Harvey & Ware, 1967; Neva et al., 1970; Ware & Harvey, 1967). Homogenous groups of System Three individuals generated a group climate of emphasis on process rather than on product (Tuckman, 1964).

System Threes reported experiencing childhood discipline strategies based on explanation rather than on punishment. Often one parent, particularly the mother, may rely on social manipulation in order to control the child, and hence, the child learns this technique as a primary mode of social coping (Harvey & Felknor, 1970).

System Four

The findings of much of the research cited previously for Systems One and Two with regard to cognitive dimensions are just the opposite of the findings for

System Four individuals. System Fours are high on cognitive complexity, tolerance of ambiguity, creativity, independence of judgment, and ability to generate solutions to problems under stress (Harvey, 1966, 1967; Harvey & Kline, 1965; Harvey & Ware, 1967; Miller & Harvey, 1973; Ware & Harvey, 1967). Their teaching styles contain aspects of flexibility, respect for others, and the ability to generate appropriate and creative solutions to cognitive and social problems (Coates et al., 1970; Harvey et al., 1966, 1968). System Four individuals can tolerate hypothetical and dissonant situations, and they do not require stereotypes in order to depict the characteristics of others. System Four individuals can tolerate more information inputs before reaching closure than any of the other conceptual systems (Schroder, Driver, & Streufert, 1967).

In group settings, a homogeneous group of System Fours was more task-oriented and generated more creative and appropriate solutions to problems than other conceptual system groups. Their social configuration was appropriate to task requirements (Tuckman, 1964).

System Fours reported childhoods where exploration of alternatives was encouraged both in the physical world and the world of ideas and values. Parents set standards that were age-appropriate and adjusted them as the children matured and moved toward greater independence. System Fours reported feelings of security about their childhood and that their parents encouraged them to develop as individuals (Harvey & Felknor, 1970).

Application of Conceptual Systems Theory to Family Violence

Given this rationale, conceptual systems should be a valuable predictor of behavior in highly involving interpersonal situations.

What Is at Stake in the Interpersonal Conflict?

Representatives of Systems One and Two would tend to see conflict in terms of power and control. What is at stake is whether or not they maintain or lose control. Because they could not consider a person or an act to be simultaneously "right" and "wrong," they would tend to develop an absolute stance. The need to affirm the antagonist as being wrong and oneself as being right is what concerns representatives of Systems One and Two. Obedience to the rules and authority are important considerations for System One individals, while System Twos might flaunt societal rules and conventions.

Representatives of System Three, on the other hand, would see the crux of the conflict as the threat to the continuance of the relationship. The importance of maintaining the relationship and maintaining the belief that they are kind to others would have higher priorities than proving that one person is right and one is wrong. Representatives of System Four function more abstractly. They would be predicted to treat the conflict as a "problem" to be solved rather than an emotionally charged win-or-lose proposition. Few, if any, representatives from this system would be expected to be involved in family violence.

Which Stressors Trigger the Interpersonal Conflict?

Conflicts would be triggered by different aspects of the environment for different systems. For representatives of Systems One and Two, situations in which they felt that their authority and self-worth were threatened would be stressors. In addition, for System One males, characterized by strong commitment to conventional norms and traditional sex-role orientations, situations where male authority is questioned would be stressful. However, System One females might be passive recipients, uphold a stereotyped sex role for themselves, and submit to violence.

System Two individuals would also be concerned about situations in which too much commitment is expected or demanded. Being smothered or controlled by someone else would be stressful. It is so difficult for System Two individuals to trust that once in an intimate relationship they may feel extremely vulnerable to its potential loss.

Representatives from System Three would be affected by the threat of isolation and estrangement. The perception of an intimate rejecting or leaving them would be stressful. Representatives from System Four would be stressed by overstimulation or an "overwhelming" number of problems, since they generally have a very high capacity for stimulation. In this kind of situation, their ability to cope and problem-solve might be impaired by the sheer number of problems. Only under severe and unusual stress would System Fours be predicted to resort to violence or be involved in violent relationships, if at all.

Who Is to Blame?

The absolute stance of Systems One and Two individuals would lead to a tendency to attribute blame to the other person in a battering situation. Systems Three and Four individuals would not attribute blame in terms of "all" or "nothing," but would tend to perceive multiple causes depending on the situation.

What Are the Styles of Coping with Conflict Situations?

Representatives of Systems One and Two are distinguishable from the more abstract Systems Three and Four by the limited number of responses to conflict situations available to them. Because of the concrete nature of the conceptual systems of One and Two individuals, they would not be able to generate new solutions to problems, but would tend to employ strategies from a limited repertoire.

For males with chauvinistic role conceptions, generally held by representatives of Systems One and Two, the use of force in the form of battering could become acceptable or the "proper" tool to use to correct the "wrong" woman. The use of battering together with verbal assault upon the woman's sense of personal worth may be a desperate effort on the part of the System One or Two male to establish, maintain, or regain in his own eyes superiority over the female partner. This is accomplished by diminishing her sense of personal worth and elevating or reaffirming his own. A System One male would attempt to control from his base of authority while a System Two male might attempt control of his partner by his unpredictability. A System One woman might submit to violence as her duty and out of a belief that she deserved it, while a System Two woman might seek revenge.

Representatives from Systems Three and Four would not be likely to resort to violence because they are able to generate many alternative problem-solving strategies. Under stress, a System Three would prefer to manipulate or induce guilt in another person rather than violate his or her strongly held values of not hurting others. A System Four would prefer to generate an appropriate solution to the problem and would not be invested in "controlling" the behavior of the other person. Negotiation would be a strategy available to Systems Three and Four. However, representatives of Systems Three or Four could become victims of violence and might in that respect become a part of the cycle of violence. One would predict that a System Three or Four woman would generate a solution to her dilemma rather than staying in a violent relationship over time.

Summary
On the basis of the theory the following predictions are made about the types of conceptual systems of men and women in violent relationships:
1. Systems One and Two individuals will be disproportionately represented in samples of batterers.
2. System One individuals will be disproportionately represented in samples of women who have experienced battering over a period of time.
3. Few representatives of Systems Three and Four will be represented either among the batterers or battered women.

UTILIZATION OF THE PSYCHOSOCIAL APPROACH AS A FRAMEWORK FOR AN INITIAL RESEARCH STUDY ON FAMILY VIOLENCE

Research Questions
Our research study (Coates & Leong, 1983; Leong & Coates, 1983) addressed a variety of issues; the questions discussed in this chapter are only those selected from the study that are most relevant to the theoretical framework.* Listed below

* Supported by LEAA, Contract 78-DF-AX-0058, City and County of Denver, monitored by Denver Anti-Crime Council, Denver, Colorado.

are the primary research questions that the study on battered women and batterers addressed:

1. Do the demographic characteristics, the reported incidences of violence, and the involvement of substance abuse appear similar to other samples of men and women involved in family violence reported in the literature?
2. Does the predicted incidence of primarily System One and Two conceptual systems appear in the sample of men and women?
3. What were the men and women's perceptions of the relationship?
4. What were the motivational attributions and control strategies generated by the men and women when responding to videotapes of couples in conflict?
5. Was there any evidence that the incidence of violence, motivational attributions, or control strategies were related to conceptual systems?

Method

Forty-four women and nineteen men involved in family violenc ɔ were subjects in the study (including six men and six women who were couple partners). Clients were referred to the study from crisis centers and safehouses in Denver, Colorado. Administration of the instrument package took an average of two hours and subjects were paid a nominal fee for their participation. Subjects were interviewed by interviewers of their own sex. Only noncrisis clients were accepted for the study and many other safeguards were utilized to protect the clients' identity and safety. Interviews were recorded by interviewer notes and audiotapes.

The interview was divided into three sections (the same order of presentation was used for all subjects):

1. An introduction followed by self-completion measures
2. A semi-structured interview
3. The Simulated Couple Conflict Instrument. (Subject reactions to simulated couple conflicts presented on videotape)

Only those instruments reported upon in this chapter are outlined here. (See Coates & Leong, 1983, for a more detailed methods and instrumentation explanation.) The self-completion measures included a 16-item demographic questionnaire. The conceptual system measure utilized was the "This I Believe" (TIB) Test (Harvey, 1966, 1986; copyright Harvey, 1974). Subjects completed the following stem with the referents listed, "This I believe about _____." The blank space was successively replaced with: "the American way of life," "friendship," "religion," "marriage," "men," "women," and "my power to control the important things in my life." The TIB was scored for the four principal conceptual systems and admixtures.

The semi-structured interview included a semantic differential scale designed to assess perceptions of self and partner and scales designed to assess the pattern of the relationship over time, positive aspects of the relationship, and subject perceptions of the relationship and past conflicts.

The Simulated Couple Conflict Instrument (SCCI) was developed for the study; a series of videotaped scenes of couple disagreements and potential arguments were portrayed by an actor and actress. After viewing a brief, ambiguous conflict scene, the interviewee was asked a number of open-ended questions designed to elicit information about: (1) whether the subject had experienced a similar incident; (2) attributions about the emotions and motivations of the couple on the videotape; (3) the subject's attribution of blame; and (4) how the subject would resolve the situation. Topics for the three videotaped scenes were jealousy, money management, and reconciliation. Interrater reliabilities for the SCCI subject ratings and the interview were .85 or higher. (Additional information about the coding is available in Coates & Leong, 1983.)

The small sample size resulted from limited funding and the difficulty in recruiting batterers. (At that time treatment programs for men were just beginning in Denver). Most of the data are reported in a descriptive fashion. An initial statistical analysis indicated that ethnicity, education, age, and social class variables did not exert significant main effects on the major variables of the study, so data analysis was collapsed across them. There were many significant differences due to sex, reinforcing the obvious conclusion that data for men and women should be reported separately. It was not possible to analyze the data by conceptual systems, due to small cell sizes; however, trends and case studies by conceptual system were provided as guides for further research.

Results

The following section addresses each of the five research questions in turn.

Characteristics of the Sample

Demographic characteristics: A comparison of the sample used in this study with other studies on batterers and battered women yielded similar profiles of demographic characteristics such as age, ethnic composition, educational background, and occupation (Giles-Sims, 1983; Martin, 1976; Roy, 1982; Straus et al., 1980; Walker, 1983). The average age for both men and women interviewed was 28 years. Sixty-three percent of the men and seventy percent of the women interviewed were Anglo. Twenty-six percent of the men and twenty-three percent of the women were Chicano or Spanish-American. Five percent of the men and five percent of the women were Native American. Two percent of the women checked the "other" category and five percent of the men were Black; there were no Black women in the sample.

The level of schooling ranged from ninth grade to college degrees. Seventy-eight percent of the men and forty-two percent of the women reported that they were currently employed. The most prevalent occupations for men were blue-collar trades, and service occupations were the most common occupation for women.

Status and duration of the relationship: At the time of the interview, 37% of the men reported that they were still married to the battered wife, 32% were separated, 16% were living together, and 16% were divorced. In contrast, 20% of the women were married to the batterer, 43% were separated, 4% were living together, 18% were divorced, and 14% marked "other."

For a majority of the men and women, the battering relationship was their first marriage (if they were married); 69% of the men and 61% of the women reported this as their first marriage. Eighty percent of the married men and fifty-seven percent of the women reported this as the first marriage for their partner as well. The mean number of children was 2.6 for the male sample and 2.3 for the female sample. For those subjects who were married, they had been married at the time of the interview for an average of 5.5 years for the men and 6.9 years for the women.

Characteristics of the violence: Subjects were asked both about their history of abuse as well as about the battering relationship. Most of the men and women were reluctant to give details about their experience with abuse in the past. Often subjects who initially said there had been no previous abuse would relate a childhood or adult experience later in the interview or in explaining their reactions to the videotape. Consequently, previous abuse data in this study are unreliable. A higher level of trust would have to be established to gain more accurate data and the questions posed also need revision; however, 15% of the women and 11% of the men did indicate that their parents condoned the violence in the battering relationship.

Subjects were asked to describe current or recent incidents of battering; 86% of the women reported that they had experienced beating, hitting, punching, being held on the ground, and kicking. Furthermore, 75% said they had been hit in the mouth. Smaller numbers reported being hit with an object, violent sexual assault, being shot, or that their partner had attempted to kill them.

Men were asked to describe the types of violent incidents in which they had engaged; 84% of the men said they had beaten their partners, and 58% said they had hit their partners in the mouth. One-fourth said they had attempted to kill their partner. Smaller numbers reported they had engaged in violent sexual assault or that they hit their partners with an object.

Half of the men said they had been hit by their partners and a small percentage said they had been hit with an object by their female partners or had experienced psychological abuse from the women. About a third of the women said they had hit their partners; 16% said they hit their partners with an object, and 2% said they tried to kill their partners with a gun.

The pattern seems to be one of serious physical abuse, with the woman as victim of abuse. On the other hand, about half the men and a third of the women said that the female partners also engaged in hitting. This pattern of physical aggression toward the batterer, as described by the battered woman, is similar to that found in other studies (Straus et al., 1980; Walker, 1983).

Involvement in substance abuse: Drug and alcohol abuse have often been studied in relation to family violence (Giles-Sims, 1983; Rosenbaum & O'Leary, 1981; Roy, 1977, 1982; Walker, 1983), but few studies have examined whether both partners were involved in substance abuse at the time of battering. In response to questions about recent battering incidents, half of the men and a third of the women reported that they had been drinking when the battering occurred; also 37% of the men and 82% of the women reported that their partner had been drinking when violence occurred. A quarter of both the men and women stated they were high on drugs when the hitting occurred; also, 11% of the men and 43% of the women reported that their partners were high on drugs during the hitting. Therefore, a substantial number of men and women reported that at least one of the partners had been using either drugs or alcohol when the hitting occurred.

Conceptual Systems

Listed in Table 10.1 are the results of scoring of the "This I Believe" Test. The designation of a system followed by a zero refers to a relatively clear principal conceptual system. The numbers 2-1, 3-2, etc., refer to admixtures, with the first number representing the primary system and the second number representing the secondary conceptual system. The designations pre-system 1 and pre-system 2 refer to protocols which presented so little integration of basic beliefs that they appeared to be less integrated and defined as personality types than well-evolved System One and Two conceptual systems.

As was predicted from the theory, the majority of batterers in the study could be categorized as having a primary conceptual system of One or Two. However, several were scored as primary System Three orientation.

It was difficult to make conceptual system predictions for the women other than to predict that a woman who now had been in a battering relationship for some time might exhibit a System One orientation. There had been little previous personality information about the female victims, other than to suggest that they had low self-esteem. One could also argue that while there might be personality predispositions that would lead one to remain in a battering relationship, a variety of different types of women unwittingly might find themselves in a battering relationship, especially in light of the information that battering often occurs after marriage.

The results were unanticipated; three basic patterns emerged for the women. There was a group of women who exhibited very primitive and undifferentiated self-presentations and unintegrated beliefs. As conceptual systems theory was designed for intact, normal ego development, our solution was to score the pro-

Table 10.1. Conceptual Systems Distribution

Women		Men	
Conceptual system	Frequency	Conceptual system	Frequency
Pre-System 1	8	1-0	4
Pre-System 2	3	1-2	3
1-0	2	1-3	1
2-0	3	2-0	3
2-1	5	2-1	2
2-3	7	3-0	1
3-1	3	3-1	2
3-2	13	3-2	1
	Total: 44	3-4	1
		Total: 18	

As was predicted from the theory, the majority of batterers in the study could be categorized as having a primary coneptual system of One or Two. However, several were scored as primary System Three orientation.

It was difficult to make conceptual system predictions for the women other than to predict that a woman who now had been in a battering relationship for some time might exhibit a System One orientation. There had been little previous personality information about the woman victims, other than to suggest that they had low self-esteem. One could also argue that while there might be personality predispositions that would lead one to remain in a battering relationship, a variety of different types of women unwittingly might find themselves in a battering relationship, especially in light of the information that battering often occurs after marriage.

tocols as pre-System One or Two. Other developmental formulations, such as the lower stages in Loevinger's ego development theory (Loevinger & Wessler, 1970), may provide more appropriate ways to describe these systems. Another unknown issue is whether these undifferentiated personality types were prone to becoming victims of battering or whether they were produced by the battering.

For the women, another predominant pattern was an admixture of Systems Two and Three. This is a very rare admixture which represents a contradiction of personality systems; one represents cynicism and aggression (System Two) and the other represents a preference for manipulation, passive aggression, and guilt induction as strategies of interpersonal interaction (System Three). A third pattern for battered women involved a primary System Two orientation, which was rigid and hostile.

There is no doubt that the conceptual system distribution for batterers and battered women was skewed in the direction of conceptual concreteness rather than abstractness. The distribution does not resemble the distribution of normal college students reported by Harvey (1966) of 30% System Ones, 15% System Twos, 20% System Threes, 7% System Fours, and the remainder of admixtures. As predicted, no System Fours appeared in the family violence sample either as batterers or as victims.

Perceptions of the Relationship

Initiation of battering behavior: The majority of men and women reported that the relationship in which there was violence (the one being studied) was the only adult relationship in which battering occurred. Upon being asked when the first incident of hitting occurred, half of the men and women said the first violent episode occurred during the marriage, and about a quarter of the men and women indicated that the battering began when the couple started living together. The remainder indicated that battering began during courtship. On the average, both men and women reported that hitting began after they had known each other about two years. These findings are similar to those of other studies (Straus et al., 1980; Walker, 1983).

Cycles of violence: The majority of individuals in the study reported that tensions increased prior to a serious fight and said that they could detect signals that a serious fight was on the way during the week before. The majority of the men and women reported that things got better after a violent episode. Almost none of the individuals indicated that they sought outside help or counseling after the fight. The majority indicated splitting up after a violent fight, but that they got back together again and the relationship improved for a while. These findings at least partially substantiate Walker's (1979) proposal that a cycle is typical.

A majority of the men and women reported that violence became routine over time. Men indicated it was much easier to batter again after they had experienced it once. These findings suggest that inhibitions about violence may lessen over time if there are no negative consequences for the batterer. The results also give support to the notion of the periods of affection and reconciliation after a violent episode serving as intermittent reinforcement to keep the relationship going (Dutton & Painter, 1981). Since System Two individuals (who made up a substantial portion of the sample) also tend to come from child rearing backgrounds that have capricious schedules of reinforcement and punishment, this may be viewed as a "normal" state of family relationships for System Twos.

Frequency of violence: In this sample, "once or twice a month" or every "two or three months" were reported as the most common frequencies for violent physical conflicts for both men and women respondents. However, there were extremes in the sample, from individuals who reported being involved in violent fights every day to those who reported that such conflicts happened once a year or less. These extremes in incidence of violence suggest there needs to be further study of family violence victims and perpetrators in which such variables are systematically controlled (Dutton & Browning, 1983).

Attribution of causal factors: Almost all of the women indicated they knew why the violence occurred, while only 68% of the men reported they knew why it occurred. The reason given by a majority of the women was simply that it was their partner's fault; the remainder of the female sample attributed the event to lack of communication or some outside occurrence. The few batterers who said they knew why the violence occurred attributed it to outside pressures, lack of communciation, or said it was their own fault. The lack of motivational explanations is consistent with predictions that would be made, given the predominately conceptually concrete nature of the respondents.

When the battered woman was asked a more direct question about why she thought her partner hit her, the most frequently cited reasons were: to show who is boss, because he lost his temper, as punishment for being bad, because he was drinking, and to shut me up. When the man was asked why he hit his partner, the principal reasons were: because I lost my temper, to show the wife who was boss, she didn't do what she was supposed to do, and because I was drinking. However, a fifth of the men said they did not know why the hitting occurred. In summary, loss of control and assertion of the male's authority appeared to be the most common reasons cited. Again there was an absence of complex motivational explanations, which one would predict because of the preponderance of conceptually concrete individuals in the sample.

Topics of the serious arguments: When the subjects were asked to respond to a checklist of possible themes (jealousy, money, in-laws, man's work, woman's work, failures, children, drinking, friends, about the argument, or other), half or more of the women checked the topics of jealousy, in-laws, money, children, the man's work, and failures. For the men, the only categories checked by half or more of the men were money, jealousy, and in-laws. Jealousy appeared as a prevalent theme for both men and women; sexual jealousy has been regarded as an important theme of violent conflicts in other studies as well (Dutton & Browning, 1983; Straus et al., 1980; Walker, 1983).

Positive aspects of the relationship: Subjects were asked to describe the positive aspects of the relationship, if any, with the partner involved in the battering in order to provide some insight into the emotional and psychological factors that maintained the relationship. For the men interviewed, shared activities and attention were mentioned as being the most positive aspects for them. In contrast, women rated affectionate feelings, family, and recreation as very important positive aspects of the relationship. A majority of the batterers and battered women stated they were comfortable with their partners most of the time. So much has been written about the negative aspects of battering relationships, it has not been obvious that the participants perceived positive aspects. These rewarding aspects may explain in part why the relationship continues despite the violence.

Responses to the Simulated Couple Conflict Instrument

A new measure developed especially for this study was one in which subjects viewed videotapes of potential couple conflict situations and responded to a series of questions. As the videotapes had not been developed previously and a tight timeline precluded extensive pretesting, there were no pretest norms for selection of scenes for this pilot effort. A high degree of ambiguity (as to who was at fault) and high involvement (topics of high personal involvement) were two conditions needed to maximize differences between conceptual systems. Three topics were developed into videotaped couple conflicts on the advice of counselors who said they were frequently mentioned argument themes on the part of men and women in battering relationships; jealousy, money problems, and reconciliation.

In order to check that the scenes were representative of what the subjects had experienced in their own conflicts, subjects were asked if situations similar to those in the videotapes had occurred between themselves and their partners, with the following results: 68% of the men and 88% of the women reported that the jealousy quarrel was typical; 84% of the men and 64% of the women said they had had similar arguments over money; 77% of the men and 95% of the women said they had experienced a reconciliation similar to the scene in the videotape. Therefore, this seems to validate the relevancy of the videotaped scenes, and possibly the issue of high involvement.

However, the support was not as good for the issue of ambiguity. The money and reconciliation scenes appeared to be lower in ambiguity than was intended, in that most subjects, regardless of conceptual system, tended to view the scenes in very similar ways (i.e., one person on the videotape was clearly at fault). Therefore, there was not much diversity in ratings.

Since only the jealousy videotape seemed to satisfy both conditions of high involvement and ambiguity, only it will be discussed. After the end of each scene, the subjects were asked what the man on the tape was feeling and what the woman was feeling. Responses were coded into three types: (1) gave no motive; (2) labeled the feelings (e.g., "He's mad and so is she"); or (3) Discussed why the person might be angry or attempted to discuss the conflict from different points of view. A clear majority of the batterers and battered women either provided no explanatory motivations for the actor and actress in the conflict or simply labeled feelings. Very few individuals in the sample provided complex, insightful explanations of motivation. These findings would be predicted judging from the concrete conceptual systems of the majority of the sample.

Another factor that was explored was the tendency to attribute blame to the man or the woman portrayed in the videotape. Blame was rated as none (no stated blame of the individual in the videotape), mild blame (some attribution of responsibility), or strong blame (strong, evaluative blaming). Both men and women involved in battering relationships tended to attribute strong blame on the basis of very limited information. This finding is consistent with earlier research with subjects having concrete conceptual systems (Coates, 1971; Harvey & Ware, 1967; Ware & Harvey, 1967). In addition, there did not seem to be any consistent pattern whereby the men tended to blame the woman on the videotape or the women tended to blame the man on the videotape.

Interviewees were asked to describe how they and their partner involved in battering had actually resolved a similar conflict and what they would do if they had been the couple on the videotape. The predominant conflict-resolution strategies reported were yelling, sulking, or violence. Women interviewees and men reporting on their female partners stressed "giving-in" as a common female strategy. Very few subjects reported they would utilize more positive styles such as talking the situation out and resolving the conflict. So, in fact, the majority of the sample reported that no resolution was ever reached for the conflict. These results support findings from an earlier portion of the interview in which individuals reported a very limited repertoire of conflict-resolution styles when describing a recent argument. In addition, a prediction that violence was bound to occur was made by many of the subjects when viewing the videotape.

In general, women and men discussed only their own behavior in the conflict and found it difficult to talk about what their partner would do. When probed about this, a common answer was, "I don't know what he (she) would do." This supports the other data in this study on the lack of insight and egocentric orientation of many individuals involved in family violence. The inability to take the role of the other person would also be predicted from studies of individuals of concrete conceptual functioning (Harvey & Kline, 1965). The majority of respondents had very little insight into causes or motivations of conflict, were quick to use labeling and attribution of blame, and reported they would use very limited and abusive strategies if confronted with a similar situation of potential jealousy.

Relationship Between Conceptual Systems and Other Factors

Due to the small cell sizes when the sample was categorized by conceptual system, these findings must remain suggestive and based on case analysis. There was not much difference between System One and System Two batterers with regard to incidence of violence and attributional and conflict-resolution modes. Both types of batterers tended to be involved relatively frequently in battering, to have little insight into the phenomenon, and to report very limited means of coping with their partners aside from name-calling, hitting, or leaving the scene.

There were some qualitative differences in the cases. System One batterers described engaging in battering because the woman did not do what she was "supposed to do." A lack of insight into what the woman wanted and explanations of battering out of frustration were portrayed. One typical case was a System One young man who reported that he hit his wife in the mouth because "she talked back to him" too much. He stated many times that he did not understand why his wife acted the way she did because it was not the "right" way to act. He reported that his father had beaten his mother to keep her "in line."

The System Two men described extreme feelings of hostility toward other people in addition to their partners. They often said that they could not figure out why their partners made them so mad and that their partners were out to get them. This style of persistent negativity was represented by a System Two man who had such an undercurrent of rage in his voice that the interviewer finally asked him if he were angry. He responded that people often thought he was angry, but that was "just the way he talked."

On the other hand, the batterers classified as having a System Three component clearly presented a different pattern from the System One and Two batterers. In the System Three group, the incidence of violence was very infrequent. One man with a System Three conceptual component reported he hit his wife only once and he could not remember what happened immediately before or after the incident. Prior to the incident, his daughter was in the hospital, he had lost his job, and his wife had become hysterical, according to his account. He reported a very high degree of remorse, stating again and again that it was his fault and it should never have happened.

It appears that the batterer at the moment of battering is highly aroused affectively, is displaying minimal differentiation, and may be unable to disengage from a very compelling set to be violent. According to conceptual systems theory, it would be much easier for an individual of concrete conceptual functioning to regress into this mode given his internal needs for control, quick closure, and being "right." On the other hand, it is possible that under severe stress, some individuals of more abstract functioning would regress into such a state and resort to violence. Dutton, Fehr, and McEwan (1982) have discussed the role of deindividuated violence in severe battering. It also seems plausible that alcohol and drugs may impair judgment and hence make it easier to respond in a concrete/egocentric fashion with a lack of regard for the feelings of the victim.

There were some other differences in pattern between the more abstract, System Three batterers and the more concrete batterers (from Systems One and

Two). The more abstract men assumed more responsibility for the violence, while the more concrete batterers tended to blame the women. The more abstract men were seeking counseling and they could verbalize other strategies for coping with couple disagreements. In the reactions to the videotapes, the batterers with System Three components offered more motivationally based explanations and tended to attribute less blame to the woman on the videotape, and more to the man. Violence was not described by them as a routine solution to conflict.

On a case-by-case basis, there were also differences among the women with respect to conceptual systems. The pre-System One women presented very little self-awareness or expressions of self-esteem. One woman even questioned whether she was a battered woman, because her husband had shot her in the mouth. Another appeared at her interview with broken ribs and had to be taken for medical treatment by the interviewer after the interviewer finally got the woman to admit that she was in pain. Many of these women had been in battering relationships over a period of years, where being beaten had become a way of life. Some were convinced that tolerating the violence was necessary so that their children would have an income. These women would seem to fit the syndrome of battered women of very low self-esteem reported in the literature.

The System Two women were quite hostile and revengeful in their own right. A System Two woman had sought revenge by waiting by her husband's car to shoot him. Violence was a part of their way of relating to others and often they reported fighting back and at times initiating aggressive acts with their partners. Verbal abuse was also one of their strategies for coping with their partners.

The large number of admixture women in the sample with Systems of 2-3 or 3-2 was particularly interesting. These women seemed to have more insight into the conflict than the System One or Two women. They often utilized a primitive manipulative style or a passive-aggressive strategy with their partners. Several explained to the interviewer that they knew that they could "out-talk" their partners, and some of them even reported calculating taking risks of beating to get what they wanted. Their strategies included finding ways to get back at their partners. One woman reported taking her perfume bottles and breaking them into her husband's new suit, grinding the glass into it, to get back at him. These women feel that they can often get their way through manipulation or verbal insults, but their partners can "get out of control" and become violent.

The women as a group tended to have conceptual systems toward the concrete end of functioning, so that there were not discernible differences in patterns of attribution of blame and motivational explanations. However, the case studies did reveal different levels of self-awareness, with the pre-System One women exhibiting very limited self-awareness of even when they were physically hurt. The women of mixed Systems Two and Three were somewhat self-aware in their conscious manipulations of their partners.

The control or self-protection strategies of the women of different conceptual systems were distinctly different. The pre-System One women submitted to the beating and said they thought they had to. When asked if they had found ways to stop the hitting, one responded that she had learned to shield her face with her hands! The System Two women were often violent themselves and sought physical and verbal revenge. The System Two-Three admixture women were much more skillful in explaining their strategies of manipulation to deal with their battering partners, but even they admitted that these strategies did not eliminate the violence.

The six intact couples included in the study were interesting despite the small number. There appeared to be a lack of match in conceptual systems. One pattern was for a woman of admixtures Systems Two and Three to be paired with a System One man. The woman would describe her verbal and manipulative schemes in her interview, while in a separate interview the man would say that he did not know what was going on and that he eventually would get frustrated and hit her. Another pattern was for a more abstract man to be paired with a very concrete woman. Again, the explanations of how the conflict started and the degree of insight into the conflict did not match for the couple partners. In fact, it appeared as if they were talking about totally different people and events. This extreme lack of understanding of the feelings and motivations of the partner, arising either from two partners both having very concrete conceptual systems or from an extreme mismatch of more abstract individuals paired with more concrete individuals, may be a possible cause of violence.

DISCUSSION

The information on conceptual systems of the battered women and batterers provided partial support for the predictions, but also unexpected results for the women. While the batterers tended to be representatives of Systems One and Two as predicted, the battered women demonstrated unpredicted conceptual systems patterns; pre-System One functioning, System Two functioning, or admixtures of Systems Two and Three. This evidence is a departure from and an addition to the personality literature on female victims of battering.

While the study provided evidence that persons of more concrete conceptual systems were overly represented in the sample of individuals involved in family violence, the question remains why only these representatives, and not others of the same conceptual system, were involved in battering. Other personality measures such as locus of control, self-esteem, impulsivity, and clinical pathology, as well as factors such as child-rearing antecedents and sex-role orientation need to be added to the inventory to achieve more complete personality profiles of men and women in battering relationships. Larger samples are also needed in future research so that socioeconomic factors and incidence and prevalence of violence can systematically be addressed in relation to personality profiles. The use of videotaped couple conflicts appears promising as a methodological tool in further studies of the attribution and conflict-resolution strategies of individuals and couples involved in family violence.

The respondents' perceptions of the causes of violence, what keeps the violence going, and the use of violence for control demonstrated very concrete and literal understandings of family violence with minimal evidence of insight. This pattern would be predicted in light of the fact that the majority of the sample was classified as having more concrete, undifferentiated, and less complex conceptual systems. Research is needed on what representatives of different conceptual systems perceive as stressful and how they respond to stress. That respondents could easily cite examples of positive aspects of the relationship and claim feelings of comfort with each other the majority of the time provides evidence for some intermittent interludes of rewarding behavior in the relationship, which probably assist in its maintenance.

While numerous intervention strategies might be generated from the theory (e.g., responses from the legal system, Coates, 1985), the preponderance of concrete conceptual systems seems to provide some evidence for the efficacy of the behavioral and environmental intervention approaches often utilized by battered women's shelters and abusive men's treatment groups. On the other hand, more motivational and insight-therapy-based approaches would be effective with the very few more abstract representatives. One of the long-range goals of this research program is to predict and assess the effectiveness of different treatment modalities for different types of men and women involved in family violence. More research is also needed on the child-rearing practices of the parents involved in spousal abuse in order to design prevention strategies for their children—so they can learn and internalize adaptive and nonviolent modes of interpersonal conflict resolution.

REFERENCES

Adams, D. K., Harvey, O. J., & Heslin, R. E. (1966). Variation in flexibility and creativity as a function of hypnotically induced past histories. In O. J. Harvey (Ed.), *Experience, structure and adaptability*. New York: Springer.

Breines, W., & Gordon, L. (1983). The new scholarship on family violence. *Signs: Journal of Women in Culture and Society, 8*(3), 490-529.

Brown, V., & Harvey, O. J. (1968). Conceptual systems and creativity. Unpublished manuscript, University of Colorado at Boulder.

Chinn, J. C. (1980). A comparison of the conceptual complexity of delinquents and their parents with the complexity of non-delinquents and their parents. Unpublished doctoral dissertation, University of Calgary, Calgary.

Coates, C. J. (1971). The effects of teacher's belief systems and involvement on perceptions of student deviance. Unpublished doctoral dissertation, University of Colorado at Boulder.

Coates, C. J. (1985). The need for an informed response to domestic violence cases. *Canadian Community Law Journal*, 8, 53-66.

Coates, C. J., Harvey, O. J., & White B. J. (1970, February). Observational scales of classroom atmosphere and student behavior: A replication and refinement. Paper presented at the meeting of the American Educational Research Association, Minneapolis, MN.

Coates, C. J., & Leong, D. J. (1983, July). Psychosocial determinants and coping styles of men and women involved in family violence. Paper presented at the North American meeting of the International Society for Research on Aggression, Victoria, B.C.

Davidson, T. (1977). Wifebeating: A recurring phenomenon throughout history. In M. Roy (Ed.), *Battered women: A psychosociological study of domestic violence.* New York: Van Nostrand Reinhold.

Deschner, J. P. (1984). *The hitting habit: Anger control for battering couples.* New York: Collier Macmillan.

Desjardins, L. (1971). A study of authority and attitudes toward authority. Unpublished doctoral disseration, University of Colorado at Boulder.

Dutton, D. G., & Browning, J. J. (1983, July). Violence in intimate relationships. Paper presented at the North American meeting of the International Society for Research on Aggression, Victoria, B.C.

Dutton, D. G., Fehr, B., & McEwan, H. (1982). Severe wife beating as deindividuated violence. *Victimology: An International Journal*, 7, 13-23.

Dutton, D. G., & Painter, S. L. (1981). Traumatic bonding: The development of emotional attachments in battered women and other relationships of intermittent abuse. *Victimology: An International Journal*, 6, 139-155.

Gelles, R. J. (1974). *The violent home: A study of physical aggression between husbands and wives.* Beverly Hills, CA: Sage Publications.

Gelles, R. J. (1976). Abused wives: Why do they stay? *Journal of Marriage and the Family*, 38, 659-668.

Gelles, R. J. (1981, July). An exchange control theory of intrafamily violence. Paper presented at the First National Conference for Family Violence Research, University of New Hampshire, Durham, NH.

Gelles, R. J., & Straus, M. A. (1977). Determinants of violence in the family: Toward a theoretical integration. In W. Burr, R. Hill, I. Nye, & I. Russ (Eds.), *Contemporary theories about the family.* New York: Free Press.

Giles-Sims, J. (1983). *Wife battering: A system theory approach.* New York: Gilford Press.

Harvey, O. J. (1966). System structure, flexibility and creativity. In O. J. Harvey (Ed.), *Experience, structure and adaptability.* New York: Springer.

Harvey, O. J. (1967). Conceptual systems and attitude change. In C. W. Sherif and M. Sherif (Eds.), *Attitude, ego-involvement and change.* New York: Wiley and Sons.

Harvey, O. J. (1974). A partial summary of application of belief systems to education. Unpublished manuscript, University of Colorado at Boulder.

Harvey, O. J. (1976). Belief systems, conservatism, and capital punishment. Unpublished manuscript, University of Colorado at Boulder.

Harvey, O. J. (1978). Belief systems of students and perceptions of teachers. Unpublished manuscript, University of Colorado at Boulder.

Harvey, O. J. (1986). Belief systems and attitudes toward the death penalty and other punishments. *Journal of Personality*, 54, 659-675.

Harvey, O. J., Coates, C. J., Gore, E., & Prather, M. (1983). Students' perceptions of teachers as a function of teachers' belief systems and personological characteristics of the students. Unpublished manuscript, University of Colorado at Boulder.

Harvey, O. J., & Felknor, C. (1970). Parent child relations as an antecedent to conceptual functioning. In R. A. Hoppe, C. A. Milton, & E. C. Simmel (Eds.), *Early experiences in the processes of socialization.* New York: Academic Press.

Harvey, O. J., & Gore, E. (1979). Belief systems of students and behavior problems as rated by teachers. Unpublished manuscript, University of Colorado at Boulder.

Harvey, O. J., & Gore, E. (1980). The belief systems test: An objective measure. Unpublished manuscript, University of Colorado at Boulder.

Harvey, O. J., Hunt, D. E., & Schroder, H. M. (1961). *Conceptual systems and personality organization.* New York: John Wiley.

Harvey, O. J., & Kline, J. A. (1965). *Some situational and cognitive determinants of role playing: A replication and extension.* Technical Report No. 15, Contract Number 1147 (07), University of Colorado at Boulder.

Harvey, O. J., Prather, M., White, B. J., & Hoffmeister, J. K. (1968). Teachers' beliefs, classroom atmosphere and student behavior. *American Educational Research Journal, 5,* 151-166.

Harvey, O. J., Shern, D. L. & Brown, C. (1978). Teacher belief systems, definitions of and response to deviant acts of students. Unpublished manuscript. University of Colorado at Boulder.

Harvey, O. J., & Ware, R. (1967). Personality differences in dissonance resolution. *Journal of Personality and Social Psychology, 7,* 227-230.

Harvey, O. J. White, B. J., Prather, M. S., Alter, R. D., & Hoffmeister, J. K. (1966). Teachers' beliefs and preschool atmospheres. *Journal of Educational Psychology, 57,* 373-381.

Hornung, C. A., McCullough, B. C., & Sugimoto, T. (1981). Status relationships in marriage: Risk factors in spouse abuse. *Journal of Marriage and the Family, 43,* 675-692.

Juers, E. H., & Harvey, O. J. (1963). *Conceptual systems and delinquency.* Technical Report No. 6, Contract Number 1147 (07), University of Colorado at Boulder.

Kaats, G. R. (1969). Belief systems and person perception: Analysis in a service academy environment. Unpublished doctoral dissertation, University of Colorado at Boulder.

Kritzberg, S. F. (1965). *Conceptual systems and behavior styles.* Technical Report No. 13, Contract Number 1147 (07), University of Colorado at Boulder.

Leong, D. J., & Coates, C. J. (1983, July). Personality characteristics and communication styles of batterers. Paper presented at the North American meeting of the International Society for Research on Aggression, Victoria, B.C.

Loevinger, J., & Wessler, R. (1970). *Measuring ego development: 1. Construction and use of a sentence completion test.* San Francisco: Jossey-Bass, Inc.

Martin, D. (1976). *Battered wives.* San Francisco: Glide Publications.

Miller, A. G., & Harvey, O. J. (1973). Effects of concreteness-abstractness and anxiety on intellectual and motor performance. *Journal of Consulting and Clinical Psychology, 3,* 444-451.

Neva, E., Coates, C. J., & Harvey, O. J. (1970). Belief systems and person perception: An extension and replication. Unpublished manuscript, University of Colorado at Boulder.

Rosenbaum, A. & O'Leary, K. D. (1981). Marital violence: Characteristics of abusive couples. *Journal of Consulting and Clinical Psychology, 49,* 63-76.

Roy, M. (Ed.). (1977). *Battered women: A psychosociological study of domestic violence.* New York: Van Nostrand Reinhold Co.

Roy, M. (Ed.). (1982). *The abusive partner: An analysis of domestic battering.* New York: Van Nostrand Reinhold Co.

Schmidt, K. (1981). Relationship between belief systems of students and belief systems of parents. Unpublished doctoral dissertation, University of Colorado at Boulder.

Schroder, H. M., Driver, M. J., & Streufert, S. (1967). *Human information processing.* New York: Holt, Rinehart and Winston.

Schultz, L. G. (1960). The wife assaulter. *Journal of Social Therapy, 6*(2), 103-111.

Sonkin, D. J., Martin, D., & Walker, L.E. (1985). *The male batterer: A treatment approach.* New York: Springer.

Star, B. (1983). *Helping the abuser: Intervening effectively in family violence.* New York: Family Service Association of America.

Steinmetz, S. K. (1977). The use of force to resolve family conflict: The training ground for abuse. *Family Coordinator, 26*(1), 9-26.

Steinmetz, S. K., & Straus, M. A. (Eds.). (1974). *Violence in the family.* New York: Harper & Row.

Straus, M. A. (1976). Sexual inequality, cultural norms, and wifebeating. *Victimology: An International Journal, 1,* Spring, 54-76.

Straus, M. A., Gelles, R. J., & Steinmetz, S. K. (1979). *Violence in the American family.* New York: Anchor Books.

Straus, M. A., Gelles, R. J., & Steinmetz, S. K. (1980). *Behind closed doors.* New York: Anchor Books.

Straus, M. A., & Hotaling, G. T. (Eds.). (1980). *The social causes of husband-wife violence.* Minneapolis: University of Minnesota Press.

Tuckman, B. W. (1964). Personality structure, group composition and group functioning. *Sociometry, 27,* 469-487.

Walker, L. E. (1977-78). Battered women and learned helplessness. *Victimology: An International Journal, 2*(3-4), 525-534.

Walker, L. E. (1979). *The battered woman.* New York: Harper & Row.

Walker, L. E. (1983). Victimology and the psychological perspectives of the battered woman. *Victimology: An International Journal, 8*(12), 82-104.

Ware, R., & Harvey, O. J. (1967). A cognitive determinant of impression formation. *Journal of Personality and Social Psychology, 5,* 38-44.

White, B. J., & Harvey, O. J. (1965). Effects of personality and own stand on judgment and production of statements about a central issue. *Journal of Experimental Social Psychology, 1,* 334-347.

Chapter 11
Men Who Batter Women: From Overcontrolled to Undercontrolled in Anger Expression

Leah Simpson Subotnik

Wife-battering has emerged in recent years as a problem of epidemic proportions. Despite estimates that as many as one-half of all marriages experience violent incidents (Straus, Gelles, & Steinmetz, 1980; Walker, 1979), men who batter have not been studied as systematically as have their victims. The published data on men who batter women come mainly from information reported by their partners (e.g., Roy, 1977; Walker, 1979, 1984) or from clinicians reporting their observations in therapy (e.g., Ganley & Harris, 1978; Symonds, 1978). Faulk (1974) examined 23 batterers in an early study (see also, Barnett & Wilshire, 1987). Other psychological information on some batterers comes from studies of violent men, which only incidentally mention violence against women (e.g., Lion, 1975; Toch, 1969).

The purpose of this study was to increase knowledge about men who batter women by directly interviewing and testing participants in a program for men who are violent to women. Preliminary interviews conducted with six batterers who were patients in an in-patient alcohol and drug treatment unit of a Veterans Administration hospital revealed a constellation of behaviors that appeared to divide the men into two groups, which I designated as "overcontrolled" and "undercontrolled."

The terminology of "overcontrolled" and "undercontrolled" is derived from Megargee (1966). In a study of male adolescent delinquents, he described the "Undercontrolled Aggressive" type as one who responds with aggression to frustration or provocation, showing little inhibition. Megargee also identified the

"Chronically Overcontrolled" type, who has such rigid inhibitions against expressing aggression that he is rarely violent. When aggression by the latter type does occur, according to Megargee, it can be extremely violent.

Although Megargee's terminology apparently had not been applied to wife-batterers before this study, descriptions of batterers by clinicians (Howells, 1976; Madden, 1976; Symonds, 1978) and other researchers (Faulk, 1974; Frieze, McCreanor, & Shomo, 1980) attest to the hypothesis that subgroups exist among batterers. Ideas from these authors and from the preliminary interviews gave rise to the research hypotheses tested in this study.

Symonds (1978) described several types of batterers, some fitting the overcontrolled/undercontrolled typology very well. The type which he called "poorly controlled" actually fits the present definition of "overcontrolled." This man is the "Dr. Jekyll and Mr. Hyde" personality. He appears highly anxious and extremely guilt-ridden when he is confronted with the results of his violent behavior in marriage. He is generally a compliant individual whose aggression is released by alcohol. When confronted with the results of the violent behavior, he generally denies it, or says "I blacked out" (pp. 216-217).

Symonds also described an "undercontrolled" batterer in terminology substantiated by the present research: "He is generally impulsive, irritable, explosive, and immature. He is relatively inarticulate about his feelings. He is a 'short fuse' individual, using his fists rather than his mouth. He is an action-oriented individual, notably deficient in violent fantasies. He has no internally integrated social attitude towards violence, and significantly has little anxiety about expressing it" (p. 216).

In my interviews, the batterers later designated as overcontrolled appeared to feel guilt, not only about their violence, but about anger they felt toward their spouses. Although all the men in the exploratory interviews were alcoholics, those later designated as undercontrolled reported that they had been violent either with or without the use of alcohol, whereas the overcontrolled had been violent only while using alcohol. The undercontrolled men reported that they had been violent with many people as well as their wives, while the overcontrolled were unlikely to have been violent outside their families. The undercontrolled men clearly behaved in ways that exerted control over others and did not want others to exert control over them, as measured by the Fundamental Interpersonal Relations Orientation-Behavior instrument (FIRO-B; Schutz, 1977). The overcontrolled men often claimed they exerted no control at all in their relationships, although they did not like being controlled by others, as measured by the FIRO-B. The interviews showed the overcontrolled men did appear to use nonphysical controlling behavior between their episodes of direct violence. The overcontrolled men exhibited more traditional attitudes toward sex roles and more authoritarian views than the undercontrolled, as measured by Spence & Helmreich's (1978) Attitudes Toward Women Scale (AWS). This traditionalism may have been an artifact of the older ages of the men in the small overcontrolled group, or it may indicate a need by them to have society enforce the control they wish to have but feel helpless to impose. Both overcontrolled and undercontrolled expressed feelings of powerlessness in the situations in which they were violent.

An overcontrolled batterer expressed himself this way: "I'm one for holding everything in...there are times I should get it out of my system – until I'm backed in a corner... Then it comes out lot of times bad ways." His wife said she had to "force" him to talk to her. Both agreed he was usually silent. The husband acknowledged he had been punished as a child for expressing anger – "more than once." He was extremely remorseful about the recent battering incident and was sure another would never occur.

An undercontrolled batterer did not feel guilt about the violence toward the women in his life. Although he regretted that his first wife had suffered a broken jaw when he punched her while they were engaged, he believed the fault was hers because she stood too close: "It was a short punch." This man was violent with others as well as family members. When interviewed, he had already had several weeks of treatment for chemical dependency and was able to label his own behavior as "macho," although he was not ready to change it at this point:

> It was masculine to be in a rough bar and be able to take care of myself... I had to prove I was a man with the group at the bar by kicking a lot of ass, drinking a lot of beer...I thought truck driving was macho, too...I was bragging to family and friends that I'd shoot M. [his wife] when she was jealous of me. I think it [the gun] gives me an upper hand – family and friends won't fuck with me. I like to play with it when drunk. Another macho thing.

THEORETICAL FOUNDATIONS

The view of violence that is the theoretical basis for the current investigation is that violence is a psychosocial phenomenon. My premise is that all individuals are influenced – indeed, shaped – by their social environments, but individuals react out of their own phenomenological awareness. Society's teachings influence and interact with individuals' thoughts, emotions, and visceral sensations to produce violence. The connection is between the interpersonal perspective and the intrapersonal – the interpersonal dealing with relations between individuals and, in a broader sense, between an individual and society; the intrapersonal dealing with the inner experiences, the psychological condition of a person.

The interpersonal perspective of wife-battering can broadly include the role of conflict in marriage, which is affected by cultural attitudes about power in male-female relationships and tolerance of violence to maintain power; the effects of violence and neglect in childhood on later aggression; and sex-role socialization that equates masculinity with dominance. From this perspective came hypotheses for the current study on authoritarian values, attitudes toward aggression, attitudes toward control of others or by others, and attitudes toward sex roles.

The intrapersonal perspective of wife-battering can include a recognition of neurological and biochemical as well as psychological factors. In this study, the overcontrolled and undercontrolled reactions to anger, impulsivity, and feelings of powerlessness were the intrapersonal aspects examined.

Understanding the complexities of violence requires a personality theory that combines a psychodynamic approach to personality with learning theory. Learning theory fits some of the data about wife-batterers. Violent behavior by parents is common in batterers' histories and thus was modeled for their sons (e.g., Barnett, Butler & Ryska, 1987; Ganley & Harris, 1978; Roy, 1977; Schultz, 1960). Aggression in males has been reinforced overtly or subtly in childhood (Bandura & Walters, 1959; Hartley, 1976) and again reinforced in adulthood by societal norms that expect men to be dominant (e.g., Cicone & Ruble, 1978; Walker, 1979).

The learning theory explanation, however, does not seem sufficient to describe the variety of types of men who batter women. Some men clearly react in imitation of earlier models and regard their violence as appropriate behavior. Other men who also had clear models of violence in childhood react in adult life with apparent fear of their angry feelings and even unawareness of their anger until an incident occurs in which they react explosively. They later may exhibit denial or guilt about their violence. The formulations of some psychoanalytic ideas into learning theory terms offer more theoretical possibilities for understanding these various types of violent men (e.g., Dollard & Miller, 1950; Wachtel, 1977).

The formulation by Dollard and Miller (1950) concerning anxiety appears fruitful as an explanation of the batterer. Dollard and Miller described how the helplessness of the human child in his or her dependence on parents for well-being can lead to learning of anxiety and conflict in a variety of situations including those in which the child feels angry. Thoughts and feelings connected with behavior that was punished can become anxiety-laden. Avoidance of such thoughts and feelings is reinforcing.

Apparently, the overcontrolled man who batters women is repressing – or avoiding, in learning-theory terminology – his anger because it is so anxiety-laden for him due to past learning. The undercontrolled batterer is not repressing anger. What both may have in common is that underlying the anger is a feeling of helplessness or powerlessness that is extremely anxiety-laden. The violence is a response to avoid the anxiety of such helplessness. The feeling of powerlessness has been cited as a precipitator of violence by numerous authors who have written on violent individuals (e.g., Lion & Penna, 1976; Madden, 1976; Rothenberg, 1975; Symonds, 1978; Toch, 1969).

With these theoretical formulations in mind, a primary hypothesis was developed to test the questions raised by the preliminary interviews. This hypothesis predicted that, in a sample of men who batter women, the two subgroups identified by raters as overcontrolled and undercontrolled will differ on five variables and be similar on two variables. Twelve subhypotheses predicted expected directions of differences between overcontrolled and undercontrolled subgroups and differences between the subgroups and norm groups reported by the respective test authors.

Subjects who were overcontrolled were expected to have disapproving behavior and attitudes toward aggression as measured by the Aggression scale of the Differential Personality Questionnaire (DPQ; Tellegen, 1978); to be nonimpulsive in behavior as measured by the Impulsivity scale of the DPQ; to hold authoritarian values as measured by the Authoritarianism scale of the DPQ; to maintain that they express little control over other people as measured by the FIRO-B Expressed Control score; and to hold traditional attitudes toward sex roles as measured by the AWS (15-item version, Helmreich, Spence, & Gibson, 1982). Subjects who were undercontrolled were expected to have accepting behavior and attitudes toward aggression as measured by the Aggression scale of the DPQ; to be impulsive in behavior as measured by the Impulsivity scale of the DPQ; to hold unconventional as opposed to authoritarian values as measured by the Authoritarianism scale of the DPQ; to claim they express much control over other people as measured by the FIRO-B Expressed Control score; and to hold nontraditional attitudes toward sex roles as measured by the AWS. Subjects from both subgroups were expected to maintain that they want little control by others as measured by the FIRO-B Wanted Control score, and to exhibit feelings of powerlessness as measured by the Unfriendly World scale of the DPQ.

METHOD

An intake interview, the DPQ, the FIRO-B, and the AWS were administered to incoming clients of the Domestic Abuse Project, an agency in Minneapolis, Minnesota, treating violent men and their families. Three staff members independently reviewed intake interviews and, using a seven-point scale, rated as overcontrolled or undercontrolled all the male clients ($N = 90$) who had completed the full intake procedure between September 1, 1980, and August 31, 1981. Questions on the intake interviews that were examined by the raters for answers that tended toward the overcontrolled or undercontrolled typology were: "With whom have you been violent?," "How often in the last few days have you felt angry?," "How do you usually deal with anger toward others (i.e., people besides partner/spouse and children)?," "Has there been violence when no chemicals were used," and a questionnaire on the nature and frequency of the violence.

Only clients who had been unanimously designated by all three raters as either overcontrolled or undercontrolled were included for further analysis. Ratings were considered in agreement if they were on the same side of the overcontrolled or undercontrolled continuum. Ratings 1, 2, and 3 were regarded as overcontrolled; 5, 6, and 7 as undercontrolled.

There was unanimous agreement by the three raters on 71 subjects and there was disagreement on 19. Raters had been trained earlier on other records, producing reliability coefficients from .75 to 1.00. Some of the raters had had personal experience with some of the clients as they had proceeded through the treatment program. Such experience gave some of the raters additional information on which to base their judgment of whether the clients were overcontrolled or undercontrolled. The raters, however, did not know the results of the other research instruments (AWS, DPQ, and FIRO-B), which were not used in the clinical part of the program. Also, the raters were naive about the research hypotheses concerning the expected directions of scoring on the instruments for the overcontrolled and undercontrolled groups. The experimenter did not see the other research instruments until after the subjects had been rated as overcontrolled or undercontrolled.

Of the 71 subjects on whom raters had agreed, 17 were later eliminated from the statistical analysis because they had not completed all the instruments, leaving 54 protocols to be analyzed, 25 overcontrolled and 29 undercontrolled. Subjects ranged in age from 17 to 52, with a median age of 31. Years in the relationships with the women they were battering ranged from less than a year to 31 years, with a median of 4 years. Of the sample, 49 were white, 2 were black, 2 were American Indian, and 1 was Chicano. Years of education completed ranged from less than 11 to 18-20 or more. A complete description of the sample and a fuller explanation of the method and results may be found in the dissertation on which this chapter is based (Subotnik, 1983).

The discriminant function technique was used to test which variables discriminated between the subgroups. In other words, the question was asked: could the variables predict membership in one or the other criterion group, overcontrolled or undercontrolled? The subgroup means of overcontrolled and undercontrolled subjects were compared with norm groups by z tests. Further analysis was conducted on 18 subjects of the 54 who were closer to the extremes (scores of 1, 2 vs. 6, 7) of the rating scale, with nine in each category of extreme overcontrolled and extreme undercontrolled. A discriminant analysis of that 18 using two variables which were most suggestive of differences in the earlier analysis was run. Z tests were also used to compare these two smaller groups with norm groups (one-tailed tests).

RESULTS

Significant differences between the overcontrolled and undercontrolled subgroups did not appear until the smaller groups of more extreme subjects were analyzed. Since a sample size of 18 could not be tested on all of the hypothesized variables, a discriminant analysis was run using only the two variables which had shown the most discrimination on the analysis of 54 cases: aggression and impulsivity. On the 18-case analyses, the extreme undercontrolled were significantly more impulsive and accepting of aggression than the extreme overcontrolled, Wilks' Lambda = .57, F (1,16) = 12.18, $p < .003$ for impulsivity, and Wilks' Lambda = .66, F (1,16) = 8.81, $p < .01$ for aggression.

In testing the subhypotheses by comparing the large group of 25 overcontrolled subjects with norm groups supplied by each instrument's author, the significant findings were that the overcontrolled men who batter women believe they are not expressing control over others ($p < .0001$), espouse more profeminist attitudes ($p < .001$), and see the world as unfriendly, interpreted by this investigator as a measure of powerlessness ($p < .03$). The more extreme overcontrolled also believe they are not expressing control over others ($p < .05$), espouse profeminist views ($p < .05$), but do *not* see the world as more unfriendly than a norm group. The profeminist scoring on the AWS was in the opposite direction to that predicted.

In comparing the large group of 29 undercontrolled subjects with norm groups, the significant findings were that undercontrolled men who batter women are more impulsive ($p < .007$), believe they are not expressing control over others ($p < .0001$), express more profeminist views than a norm group ($p < .002$), and see the world as unfriendly ($p < .004$). The finding that the undercontrolled men, as well as the overcontrolled, see themselves on the FIRO-B as not controlling others was in the opposite direction to that predicted, but seems logical if this score is also interpreted as a measure of feeling powerless. The more extreme undercontrolled, compared to norm groups, are significantly more aggressive ($p < .001$), more impulsive ($p < .001$), and feel more powerless as reflected by Unfriendly World scores ($p < .0001$). There were no significant results on the subhypotheses on authoritarianism or Wanted Control by others for any of the subgroups.

DISCUSSION

Examination of the results yields several points for discussion. The implications of the finding that extremes of overcontrolled and undercontrolled showed significant differences, the profeminist direction of the AWS scores, the fact that the extreme overcontrolled group did not see the world as significantly more unfriendly than a norm group, and the implications of the powerlessness experience apparently borne out by the study are considered in more detail.

The fact that significant differences between the overcontrolled and undercontrolled subgroups did not emerge until the more extremes of each type were selected indicates that the categories are not truly dichotomous, but are a continuous factor. However, in conducting further research and in planning treatment programs for batterers, it is important to have an awareness of the extremes. Men who batter cannot be regarded as all one type of personality. If a research study ignores or is unaware of these types, results may be ambiguous because the two extremes combined cancel out significant results on some personality variables. Further research would be needed to ascertain whether treatment programs have differential results for overcontrolled or undercontrolled batterers, and, if there are differences, what modifications need to be made to reach the goal of stopping violence.

Different treatment strategies that may be needed for the clearly overcontrolled and undercontrolled can be hypothesized by looking at their characteristic behaviors. The impulsivity of the extreme undercontrolled client will require strong measures to keep him in treatment and responsive to assignments. He will also need to learn nonviolent techniques for tolerating frust ation and unpleasant emotions. The overcontrolled client who denies anger, on the other hand, needs to learn how to recognize and express irritations in an appropriate way before the irritations build up to an explosive point.

All the groups had higher average scores than the norm group on the AWS and all but the extreme undercontrolled group were higher to a significant degree. There are several possible explanations for the apparent conclusion that batterers are more feminist than a population of men not identified as batterers. One possibility is that the scores reflect regional differences in attitudes toward sex roles, the norm group being from Texas and the experimental group from Minnesota. (To test this possibility, a study is currently being conducted to compare batterers with a control group from the same locality in Minnesota).

Another possible cause of feminist direction scores by the batterers in this study is that the clients may have answered the instrument in a manner they thought the Domestic Abuse Project staff would want to hear. The subjects may have endorsed the sex-role they thought was appropriate to the testing situation, but in their own homes the behavior that is really congruent with their self-concept emerged (Horrocks & Jackson, 1972; Spence & Helmreich, 1978).

Still another possible explanation of the AWS scores is that the beliefs expressed were genuine, but that internal pressures intervene in conflict situations and beliefs are forgotten. This last possibility is particularly pertinent to the overcontrolled batterers, whose attitudes about aggression also are ignored in their explosive moments. The powerless feeling, which was both hypothesized and borne out by the results on the DPQ Unfriendly World scale and the FIRO-B Expressed Control scale, could be the internal pressure that overrides values.

The one subgroup that did not show a significant degree of powerlessness on the Unfriendly World — the extreme overcontrolled — nevertheless saw themselves as exerting little control over others on the FIRO-B. This apparent contradiction may possibly be explained by the relative economic success of this particular group compared to the others. Inspection of the descriptive data of the sample showed the extreme overcontrolled men had higher income. Two had incomes over $30,000 and only one in nine had an income below $10,000, compared with six of the nine in the extreme undercontrolled category who had incomes below $10,000. The two instruments may be measuring different aspects of powerlessness.

The primary theoretical basis for this study was that violence is a psychosocial phenomenon, that the interpersonal experiences between individuals and between an individual and society interact with the intrapersonal, inner experiences of an individual. The connection between society's teachings and an individual's violent behavior does not appear to be simple. An interpersonal factor that may lead to intrapersonal conflict is the change in attitudes about men's and women's roles generated by the feminist movement (Spence & Helmreich, 1978; Stewart & Platt, 1982). The results of the AWS in this study appear to indicate that men are aware of the feminist response to men's and women's roles. What happens intrapsychically if this awareness conflicts with earlier teachings about roles and power relationships? Since the men in this study have all been violent against women, a conclusion may be reached that, for these men, the earlier learned permission to use violence superseded beliefs about egalitarian roles.

The intrapersonal experience of a feeling of helplessness, a powerlessness that has been postulated as underlying violence, may itself be mediated by interpersonal factors, which teach that it is terrible to feel powerless, particularly for males, and that such a feeling must be avoided at all costs. Thus, even men who do not usually approve of aggression may become aggressive with the women in their lives.

The feeling of powerlessness and the fear of the feeling could be a personality characteristic developed in childhood or could be a response to difficult economic and social circumstances in later life. An interaction hypothesis would explain the powerless feeling and the use of violence to avoid it as an interaction of difficult circumstances and a personality prone to feeling powerless.

The prevalence of a feeling of powerlessness manifested by so many of the subjects validates the clinical observations of those who have been working with men who batter. Society's values and practices are implicated when such a dynamic is so widespread. Child-rearing practices that define women as the sole source of nurture may produce in sons a life-long ambivalence toward women. The adult male may still experience residual feelings of infant helplessness toward the all-powerful mother image of women (Dinnerstein, 1976). Violence against children, such as slapping and spanking, is accepted in the guise of discipline — only when physical injury results is such discipline labeled as abuse, and even that is epidemic. Such violence can lead to powerless feelings, which are rekindled by stress in adult life (Miller, 1983).

Social values that idealize masculine power in the face of the realities of inter-dependency require challenge, such as that offered by the men's awareness movement. The feminist influence against sex-role stereotypes in child-rearing, early education, and adult self-concept may eventually aid in resolving the contradictions between stereotypes of masculine behavior and the realities of human feeling. Societal practices that encourage a sense of personal power without infringing on others need to be developed. Child-rearing, religious, educational, political, and economic structures should all be examined to determine how they can best foster such a sense of power. Prevention of wife-battering requires seeking changes on a societal level, not only on an individual treatment level.

ACKNOWLEDGMENTS

This chapter is based on a doctoral dissertation submitted to the University of Northern Colorado. I am grateful to Helen Gilbert, Dr. Louisa Howe, Dorothy Samuel, Sandra Gordon Stoltz, and Dr. Leo Subotnik for critical readings of this chapter. I wish to thank the staff of the Domestic Abuse Project of Minneapolis for their cooperation and assistance in collecting the original data.

REFERENCES

Bandura, A., & Walters, R. H. (1959). *Adolescent aggression.* New York: Ronald Press.
Barnett, O. W., Butler, K. E., & Ryska, T. A. (1987, July). *Abuse of batterers and their exposure to violence during childhood (A preliminary report).* Paper presented at the meeting of the National Conference of Domestic Violence Researchers, Durham, NH.
Barnett, O. W., & Wilshire, T. W. (1987, July). *Forms and frequencies of wife abuse (A preliminary report).* Paper presented at the meeting of the National Conference of Domestic Violence Researchers, Durham, NH.
Cicone, M. V., & Ruble, D. N. (1978). Beliefs about males. *Journal of Social Issues, 34*(1), 5-16.
Dinnerstein, D. (1976). *The mermaid and the minotaur: Sexual arrangements and human malaise.* New York: Harper & Row.
Dollard, J., & Miller, N. E. (1950). *Personality and psychotherapy.* New York: McGraw-Hill.
Faulk, M. (1974). Men who assault their wives. *Medicine, Science, and the Law, 14,* 180-183.
Frieze, I. H., McCreanor, M., & Shomo, K. (1980, March). Male views of the violent marriage. Paper presented at the Research Conference of the Association for Women in Psychology, Santa Monica, CA.
Ganley, A. L., & Harris, L. (1978, August). Domestic violence: Issues in designing and implementing programs for male batterers. Paper presented at the meeting of the American Psychological Association, Toronto.
Hartley, R. E. (1976). Sex-role pressures and the socialization of the male child. In D. S. David & R. Brannon (Eds.), *The forty-nine percent majority: The male sex role.* Reading, MA: Addison-Wesley.
Helmreich, R. L., Spence, J. T., & Gibson, R. H. (1982). Sex-role attitudes: 1972-1980. *Personality and Social Psychology Bulletin, 8,* 656-663.
Horrocks, J. E., & Jackson, D. W. (1972). *Self and role: A theory of self-process and role behavior.* Boston: Houghton Mifflin.

Howells, K. (1976). Interpersonal aggression. *International Journal of Criminology and Penology, 4,* 319-330.

Lion, J. R. (1975). Developing a violence clinic. In S. A. Pasternack (Ed.), *Violence and victims.* New York: Spectrum Publications.

Lion, J. R., & Penna, M. W. (1976). Treatment of aggressive behavior. In D. J. Madden & J. R. Lion (Eds.), *Rage, hate, assault and other forms of violence.* New York: Spectrum Publications.

Madden, D. J. (1976). Psychological approaches to violence. In D. J. Madden & J. R. Lion (Eds.), *Rage, hate, assault and other forms of violence.* New York: Spectrum Publications.

Megargee, E. I. (1966). Undercontrolled and overcontrolled personality types in extreme antisocial aggression. *Psychological Monographs: General and Applied, 80*(3), Whole No. 611.

Miller, A. (1983). *For your own good: Hidden cruelty in child-rearing and the roots of violence.* New York: Farrar, Straus & Giroux.

Rothenberg, A. (1975). On anger. In S. A. Pasternack (Ed.), *Violence and victims.* New York: Spectrum Publications.

Roy, M. (Ed.). (1977). *Battered women: A psychosociological study of domestic violence.* New York: Van Nostrand Reinhold.

Schultz, L. G. (1960). The wife assaulter. *Journal of Social Therapy, 6*(2), 103-112.

Schutz, W. FIRO-B, copyright 1967. Palo Alto, CA: Consulting Psychologists Press.

Spence, J. T., & Helmreich, R. L. (1978). *Masculinity and femininity: Their psychological dimensions, correlates, and antecedents.* Austin: University of Texas Press.

Stewart, A. J., & Platt, M. B. (1982). Studying women in a changing world: An introduction. *Journal of Social Issues, 38*(1), 1-16.

Straus, M. A., Gelles, R. J., & Steinmetz, S. K. (1980). *Behind closed doors: Violence in the American family.* New York: Doubleday/Anchor.

Subotnik, L. S. (1983). Overcontrolled and undercontrolled types of men who batter women. *Dissertation Abstracts International* (University Microfilms, No. 83-24360).

Symonds, M. (1978). The psychodynamics of violence-prone marriages. *American Journal of Psychoanalysis, 38,* 213-222.

Tellegen, A. (1978). Differential Personality Questionnaire. Copyright: Tellegen, University of Minnesota.

Toch, H. (1969). *Violent men: An inquiry into the psychology of violence.* Chicago: Aldine Publishing Co.

Wachtel, P. L. (1977). *Psychoanalysis and behavior therapy: Toward an integration.* New York: Basic Books.

Walker, L. E. (1979). *The battered woman.* New York: Harper & Row.

Walker, L. E. (1984). *The battered woman syndrome.* New York: Springer.

Part Three
Situational/External Determinants

The organization of this book provides for a rough distinction between those chapters dealing with the role of "situational" factors and those dealing with "personality" factors in determining interpersonal aggression; however, comparisons of the relative importance of the two foci are inevitable. Where such comparisons are made (e.g., Baron, 1977, p. 176ff), effects arising from the setting are frequently seen to override those attributable to personality variables. However, the preeminence of situational variables is typically demonstrated under conditions of extreme provocation, i.e., intense shock. Under more normal circumstances, both approaches are seen to predict aggressive behavior more equally.

Before one relegates personality variables to a subordinate predictor status, it is important to recognize that most everyday provocations are relatively trivial, producing annoyance- motivated aggression (Zillmann, 1979). The importance of this lies in the conclusions of those who have reviewed the causes of violent crimes. Zahn (1980), for example, notes that the vast majority of homicides originate with disputes involving extremely petty matters. The violence that sometimes follows results from an escalation of hostility through an increasing spiral of exchanged provocations (Goldstein, Davis, & Herman, 1975). Thus, for the general case, an individual-differences approach to understanding aggression holds equal promise alongside that emphasizing the important influence of the situation.

REFERENCES

Baron, R. A. (1977). *Human aggression*. New York: Plenum.
Goldstein, J. H., Davis, R. W., & Herman, D. (1975). Escalation of aggression: Experimental studies. *Journal of Personality and Social Psychology, 31,* 162-170.

Zahn, M. A. (1980). Homicide in the twentieth century United States. In J. A. Inciardi & C. E. Faupel (Eds.), *History and crime* (pp. 111-131). Beverly Hills, CA: Sage.

Zillmann, D. (1979). *Hostility and aggression.* Hillsdale, NJ: Lawrence Erlbaum.

Chapter 12
Alcohol and Spouse Abuse: A Social Cognition Perspective

Barry Corenblum

The Canadian report on wife-battering (Roy, 1982) estimates that in a given year, 10% of women who live with men will be battered, a figure that falls between the results reported in other surveys, e.g., 4% (Straus, Gelles, & Steinmetz, 1980) and 30% (Gelles, 1974). The Canadian report points out a number of issues that remain unanswered: why is the legal system so unresponsive to the needs of the abuse victim; why is there not more provincial and federal support for abuse victims, and — most importantly — why have we ignored a problem that has existed since men and women have been living together? While an answer to these questions is beyond the scope of this chapter, one way in which we can approach these issues is to examine the reasons individuals give for domestic violence. The nature of the attributions people give for an event, especially a negative one, often influences their behavior.

Attribution theory is the study of the explanations people give for their own and others' behavior (Kelley, 1972). The behavior of others is explained by attributions to either external factors (something in the situation, environment or luck) or more likely to internal factors (something about the person or actor). Attributions for our own behavior, however, are attributed externally. There are a number of explanations for this bias (Ross, 1977). Taylor and Fiske (1978) suggest that whatever is perceptually salient in a situation is seen as causal. To observers the actor is more vivid than the background; to the actor, the situation constrains the range of possible behaviors. Jones and Harris (1967), for example, found that students who were told that a debater's pro-Castro speech was an assigned position rated that person as favorable toward Castro as did those who were told that the debater had chosen that position.

The application of these apparently straightforward principles to spouse abuse is not a simple matter. In many cases the observer is asked to make a "retrospective interpretation" (Kituse, 1964) of another's behavior in a situation in which everything about the individual is called into question (Pugh, 1983). Furthermore, attributing responsibility for a rape or an abuse incident has serious evaluative implications. Subjects may be unwilling to make such attributions unless the circumstances clearly point to a particular conclusion. Shotland and Goodstein (1983), for example, gave subjects an elaborate rape scenario in which the degree of protest, force used and timing of the victim's protest were varied. When the man used little force and victim's protest was verbal and late in the interaction, 67% of the subjects thought the man was wrong to force intercourse, but only one-third called the situation rape. When her verbal and physical protests occurred early in the interaction, and he used low force, 92% thought he was wrong, but only 58% called it rape.

There is a zone of uncertainty in sexual activity in which behavior may be excessive but not extreme enought to warrant the label "rape." Nor are such uncertainties limited to rape; as we will see, simply knowing that a man struck his spouse is not sufficient information to hold him responsible. As observers of the event, we want to know more information before causal attributions will be made: was there provocation, who initiated the abuse, who escalated it, is it a recurrent problem, and so forth. These concerns suggest that the factors taken into account are more varied and the processes by which the attribution is made are more complex than is implied by traditional studies of actor-observer differences. Rather than examining variables present in the actor or the observer, a better understanding of the attribution process underlying marital violence can be achieved by adopting a perspective in which factors present in the husband, wife, observers, and the situation interact to produce attributions.

In the three studies reported here, subjects read an abuse scenario in which one, both or neither spouse was intoxicated. Subjects evaluated each spouse and made causal attributions for the incident. In addition, a number of subject characteristics was also examined, e.g., exposure to abuse in the home, subject's own abusive behavior, and personality factors. A multidimensional perspective in which actor, observer, and the situation attributes are combined will give a more complex but more ecologically valid account of the attribution process than one in which these attributes are considered singly.

STUDY I

A number of studies have shown that victims who are described as being low in respectability (Feldman-Summers & Lindner, 1976; Smith, Keating, Hester & Mitchell, 1976), or having an active sex life (Cann, Calhoun & Selby, 1979), or putting themselves at risk (Calhoun, Selby & Warring, 1976) are judged more negatively and are held more responsible for their particular misfortune than those described in more favorable terms. Calhoun et al. (1976), for example, found that females who walked in an area where several rapes had occurred are held more responsible for their own rape, especially when evaluated by female subjects, than those who walked elsewhere. Similarly, offenders who are described as being physically unattractive (Landy & Aronson, 1969) or physically attractive offenders who used their charms to swindle others (Sigall & Ostrove, 1975) are judged more harshly than those without such characteristics or behaviors.

Descriptions of victims and offenders in particular situations allow observers to draw inferences about the character of both victim and offender. As Richardson and Campbell (1980) point out such descriptions may influence attributions of responsibility in two ways: first, such descriptions provide cues as to how such characteristics may have either facilitated or inhibited the interaction between victim and offender; second, the descriptions serve as a nucleus from which other descriptions of the individuals may be generated. Such attributions and evaluations are not independent of the characteristics that observers bring to the situation. Observers judge positive behavior by their friends differently than the same behavior done by a stranger (Regan, Straus & Fazio, 1974; Taylor & Koivumaki, 1976), and an actor's behavior that has personal relevance for an observer is evaluated differently than is behavior that has little relevance (Chaiken & Cooper, 1973). In keeping with the perspective outlined above, characteristics of both actors and observers are necessary for a complete understanding of the attribution process.

One of the characteristics of the victim or offender that has been implicated in marital violence is the degree of intoxication in one or both spouses. In one survey of abused women, Ashley (1978) found that alcohol was implicated in 43% of the cases; Hunter (1983) noted a figure of 35%. Gelles (1974) suggests that intoxication provides a socially acceptable excuse for committing otherwise unacceptable behavior; being intoxicated provides a time out for "out of character" behavior. Gelles hypothesizes that men "who wish to carry out a violent act become intoxicated *in order to carry out the violent act*" (p. 117, italics original). While individuals may harbor such attitudes, observers, who lack access to private thoughts, may entertain a number of different hypotheses concerning alcohol-related violence. On the one hand, observers may indeed believe that alcohol serves to facilitate the expression of aggressive intent; this would lead observers to derogate the abuser and attribute responsibility to him. On the other hand, observers may reason that beating one's spouse while intoxicated is an indication of personal problems; an attribution leading to less responsibility than was the case in the first hypothesis, since the husband may be seen as responding to factors beyond his control. Alternatively, observers may believe that abuse is an unfortunate consequence of drunkenness. The man is not responsible; the alcohol is. Finally, observers may perceive the intoxication and abuse as an example of serious marital problems; if so, attributions of responsibility should fall on both spouses and negative evaluations of the husband would be reduced.

In our society, the reactions to an intoxicated male are often mixed. Sometimes we respond with anger, sometimes with indifference, pity or amusement, but female intoxication is viewed as a violation of female propriety (Johnson & Garzon, 1978). In addition to violating norms of appropriate sex-role behavior, the intoxicated female also violates prevailing social attitudes regarding female drinking. Gromberg (1976) reports that while more females are drinking and rules governing consumption are more permissive than several generations ago "...social attitudes of disapproval toward women's drunkenness are apparently unchanged over time" (p. 126). These ideas suggest that an intoxicated female who is abused should be held more responsible for that abuse than her husband, since he may be seen as justified in punishing his wife (albeit severely) for engaging in antinormative behavior. This hypothesis assumes that observers associate female intoxication with deviance; it is also conceivable that observers may perceive the intoxication as indicative of personal problems. Observers may assume, given no evidence to the contrary, that female intoxication is but one exception to otherwise normative behavior. Under such conditions, observers may search for a number of reasons (e.g., depression, medical problems, poor marriage) which must have been present in varying degrees of severity to elicit the drinking bout. If observers view female intoxication as a response to stress, then a husband who abuses his wife under such conditions will be seen as insensitive and uncaring and responsible for the abuse.

Some of these hypotheses were tested in a study by Richardson and Campbell (1980), who had subjects read an abuse scenario in which one spouse was intoxicated. Subjects then attributed responsibility for the abuse to the man, woman, or the situation. When the husband was intoxicated, more situational attributions were made than when he was sober, but when the wife was drunk, she was blamed more and he was blamed less than when she was sober. These results suggest that observers tend to discount the behavior of an intoxicated husband, pointing to the alcohol as a plausible factor in inducing antinormative behavior. It was noted earlier that an intoxicated female violates both sex-role and drinking norms, and that under such conditions abuse may be seen as justified; ideas that were supported by these results.

These results are intriguing because on the surface they point to yet another example of victim-blaming on one hand and finding a plausible rationale for the assailant on the other. While such attributions have been reported in studies on victimization (Lerner & Miller, 1978), examination of Richardson and Campbell's methodology suggests an alternate explanation. The scenario used in this study involved a verbal disagreement over a bridge party and the woman's failure to prepare a proper dinner; she in turn accused him of not making enough money, the argument escalated into name-calling and ended with her being struck several times. In this study, we have no way of knowing whether or not subjects saw her drinking or the bridge party as recurring problems or as isolated events. Such parties are often held on a regular basis; subjects might have assumed that these issues had been discussed many times before, and that this incident was the last straw. Subjects in the husband-drunk condition on the other hand may have reasoned that spouse abuse is an unfortunate consequence of intoxication. For these subjects there would be little need to look for alternate explanations for his behavior; the booze made him do it.

In the present study, subjects read one of four abuse scenarios in which either the man, woman, both, or neither spouse was intoxicated. The scenarios were adapted from Richardson and Campbell, but care was taken to remove any notion that the problem that led to the abuse had occurred in the past. In addition, the present study also investigated the influence of exposure to abuse on causal attributions. Those exposed to abuse are cognizant of the events that led up to and precipitated an attack upon their mother. This suggests that those who have witnessed abuse would judge the abuser differently than those without exposure. It was argued above that female intoxication may be seen as a sign of personal problems and that a husband who abuses his wife under such conditions would be held responsible. One can argue that subjects who have witnessed abuse in their own home would make this type of interpretation, since their background is one in which problem behaviors may reflect marital discontent. These ideas suggest that subjects exposed to abuse in their own home would attribute greater responsibility to the husband when he abused his intoxicated wife than would those not so exposed.

Method

The subjects were 158 Introductory Psychology students, who participated in a study of person perception. Subjects, who were tested in their regular class period, received on a random basis a booklet which consisted of: a biographical questionnaire, one of four abuse scenarios and questions concerning the scenario, and a questionnaire concerning the causes of alcoholism. The abuse scenario and biographical questionnaire were presented in counterbalanced order, while the alcoholism questionnaire was presented last. Since it is not germane to the present study it will not be discussed further. The biographical section asked whether or not a parent or step-parent had struck (punched or slapped) or otherwise physically abused (pushed or shoved) the other parent, and the frequency (1, never occurred to 5, at least five times) with which the abuse had occurred within the past year. Subjects read one of four abuse scenarios, in which the sex of the intoxicated actor(s) was systematically varied. Subjects in the female-intoxicated condition read, for example,

Mr. H. came home late after work and found his wife lying on the sofa drunk and smelling of alcohol. He yelled at his wife for not preparing a proper dinner. Mrs. H. then yelled at Mr. H. because he didn't earn enough money. The argument grew into swearing and name calling. Mr. H. then struck his wife several times leaving her with a black eye and several large and visible bruises. Mr. H. then walked out.

Subjects made attributions of responsibility to the man, woman, other factors, and assessed the deliberateness of the attack and the likelihood of the abuse recurring. In addition, subjects estimated the likelihood of future intoxication, the degree to which actor's drinking was under the person's personal control, and the likelihood that the drinking reflected marital discontent. All ratings were made on appropriately labeled seven-point scales. In the control condition, in which neither spouse was intoxicated, subjects read an abuse incident that arose from a dispute involving preparation of the evening meal; there was no mention of alcohol and corresponding attributions were removed.

Results and Discussion

Responses to the exposure question were dichotomized into those who had or had not been exposed to abuse and the resulting variable entered into a 4-scenario (man, woman, both, or neither spouse intoxicated) x 2 (exposure) multivariate analysis of variance* with the causal attributions, likelihood of future abuse, and deliberateness of the attack as dependent variables. The analysis revealed a significant scenario ($F(15, 315) = 2.70$, p = .005) multivariate effect, and univariate analyses were significant for attributions to Mr. H. ($F(3, 118) = 4.41$, p = .005) and perceived deliberateness of the attack ($F(3, 118) = 5.50$, p = .002). The man was held less responsible and the act was seen as less deliberate when neither spouse was intoxicated than in the other three conditions. But Mr. H. was held as more responsible and the abuse was seen as more deliberate when Mrs. H. was intoxicated than in any other condition. These main effects were qualified by an exposure by group multivariate interaction ($F(15, 315) = 1.89$, p = .03), with univariate analyses significant for attributions to Mr. H. ($F(3, 118) = 2.71$, p = .04) and marginally significant for perceived intent ($F(3, 118) = 2.40$, p = .07). Post hoc analysis revealed two significant patterns: both exposure groups rated the husband less responsible when neither spouse was intoxicated than in any other condition, and second, those exposed to abuse rated Mr. H. more responsible for the abuse when his wife was intoxicated than in any other condition. Differences between the two exposure groups were due to differences in the wife-intoxicated condition.

---

* Preliminary analysis showed that neither order nor sex of subject had any significant effects.

Attributions of intent indicated that those not exposed to abuse attributed less intent when neither spouse was intoxicated, while those who had been exposed attributed greater intent to injure when Mrs. H. was intoxicated than in any other condition. Comparisons between the groups suggest that those exposed to abuse saw the attack as more deliberate when the wife was intoxicated but less deliberate when both were drunk.

A 3-scenario (man, woman, both intoxicated) x 2 (exposure) multivariate analysis of the alcohol-related questions revealed significant scenario and exposure main effects as well as a significant scenario by exposure interaction ($F(12, 154) = 3.22$, p = .004). Univariate tests indicated a marginal group by exposure effect for perceived control of drinking ($F(2, 82) = 2.65$, p = .07): those not exposed to abuse saw the woman as more in control of her drinking than did those with exposure who were not significantly different in their judgments. A significant group by exposure interaction for the variable likelihood of future intoxication ($F(2, 82) = 7.20$, p = .001) indicated no significant differences within the nonexposed group, while those exposed to abuse rated the female in the female-alone intoxicated condition as less likely to drink again compared to the intoxicated spouse in the other two conditions.

Richardson and Campbell (1980) hypothesized that since an intoxicated female violates appropriate sex role behavior, she should be held more responsible than her husband for her own abuse. Their results supported that notion. The present study argued, and found, that subjects should attribute more responsibility to the man for abusing his intoxicated wife than in any other condition. This hypothesis was predicated on two ideas; first, given no evidence to the contrary, intoxication in a married woman may be seen as a sign of personal distress, and a spouse who abuses his wife under such a state violates a number of marital norms. Second, the results obtained by Richardson and Campbell may have been due to the perception that abuse was the consequence of a recurring and unresolved problem which had reached a breaking point. Generally speaking, subjects in the present study rated the intoxicated woman as more in control of her drinking and less likely to drink again than the male in the intoxicated-husband condition or either spouse in the both-intoxicated condition. These findings suggest that subjects saw her drinking as an isolated incident in otherwise normal behavior. It should also be noted that even though the results were not significant, subjects in the intoxicated-female condition rated Mrs. H. as more discontented with her marriage than similar ratings attributed to Mr. H. in the intoxicated-male condition. This finding corroborates the notion that an uncommon effect, female intoxication, may signify some personal problem.

It was suggested earlier that what an observer brings to a situation often influences the nature of the resulting causal attributions. In this study, the attributions made by those exposed to abuse differed in a number of ways from those not so exposed. When the woman alone was intoxicated, those exposed to abuse attributed more responsibility and greater malevolent intent to the male than did subjects not so exposed; exposed subjects also rated the intoxicated female as less likely to be intoxicated in the future and more discontented with her marriage than those not so exposed. Those exposed to abuse seem to process abuse-relevant information differently than those not so exposed, but such processing appears to be somewhat circumscribed. Only when the female alone was intoxicated did differences between the two exposure groups appear. When the man alone or when both spouses were intoxicated, there were no significant differences between the two exposure groups. One reason for these results may be that when the female alone was intoxicated, her behavior served as a cue for exposed subjects in recalling how bad marital relationships can become. Those exposed to abuse have seen the consequences of their parents attempting to maintain a difficult relationship. In the other three conditions there may have been a number of reasons to explain the abuse, none of which strongly triggered related associations.

When people are confronted with personally relevant events, Higgins and King (1981) suggest the processing, storage, and recall of such events is a function of the degree to which subjects can readily access the relevant cognitive constructs pertinent to the domain of interest. A construct reflects information about some entity derived through experience. This information includes the basic characteristics of category members, the range of category attributes, prototypic examples of the category and the degree to which category attributes vary in their predictive validity. Markus, Sentis and Hamill (1978), for example, found that people who had highly organized, rich, and self-relevant cognitive constructs about body weight (referred to as schematic subjects) made faster judgments and recalled more information about body-relevant issues than those without such structures (referred to as aschematic subjects).

According to construct accessibility theory, the more frequently a given construct has been activated, the more accessible it should become and the more likely a schematic subject will use it to process construct relevant information. Construct accessibility theory would suggest that the different attributions shown by exposed and nonexposed subjects are due to the presence in exposed subjects of particular constructs relevant to the abuse situation, constructs that influence both the processing and evaluation of that information. For example, schematic subjects blamed the man more and attributed more aggressive intent to him than did those without the schema. The relationship between construct accessibility, spouse abuse, and causal attributions has not been actively explored. To further examine some of these relationships, a second study was conducted, in which alcoholics who were either abused or who abused their spouse read one of the four abuse scenarios, and then made causal attributions for the abuse. In comparison to the first study, the second study examined different schemas in a different sample of subjects, where the role of alcohol has different implications than it did for subjects in the first study.

STUDY 2

As part of a larger study on the causal attributions alcoholics make for their own and others' drinking, members of Alcoholics Anonymous (A.A.) read one of the four abuse scenarios used in Study I and then made causal attributions to the man, woman, other factors and, depending upon the scenario, rated the likelihood of future drinking episodes. A.A. philosophy outlines twelve steps through which sobriety can be achieved and maintained (Anon, 1952). Essentially these steps involve an admission that alcoholics have lost control over their drinking and that only through a belief in a "higher power" can sobriety be achieved. These enunciations of faith are accompanied by a personal stock-taking of vices and virtues, followed by an expiation of those vices to both the higher power and to those whom the alcoholic has harmed because of his/her drinking. The process of taking inventory and expiation is followed by the individual serving as a role model (the twelfth step) for new A.A. members.

Alcoholics have a number of excuses for why they drink, and why they continually fail to perform their duties and responsibilities. Beckman (1980) suggests that individuals come to A.A. because these explanations are no longer believed by others. In such a state, the individual may feel helpless, isolated, and without a normative reference group. According to Beckman, A.A. provides an alternate set of causal explanations for the individual's behavior, and these new explanations are validated by the group (Corenblum, 1983). Initially new members attribute their problems to numerous external factors, but as they progress through the twelve steps, they come to attribute their problems to something about themselves and their inability to control their drinking. If A.A. members come to see their own behavior differently as a consequence of group membership, then the behavior of others may be construed differently as a consequence of group membership. This suggests that long-term members may gain insights into the problems of and some sympathies for people involved in alcohol-related violence. As a consequence, these subjects were expected to assign responsibility to a number of different factors, unlike newer members, who were expected to show traditional actor-observer differences.

In addition to indicating length of membership, subjects also indicated whether or not they had been abused in their marital relationship. In the first study, subjects exposed to abuse blamed the husband for the abuse particularly when the wife was intoxicated. Similarly, it might be expected that perceptions of common fate might result in abuse victims showing similar results. On the other hand, the just-world hypothesis (Lerner, 1977) would suggest that abuse victims would attribute more blame to the female than the male. The suffering of an innocent other threatens the perceiver's notion of a fair world, leading perceivers to either derogate the victim's character or to attribute increased responsibility to the victim's behavior. If an innocent other can be victimized as a consequence of alcohol-related violence, then these subjects especially may come to feel that they too can be victimized, despite their attempts to remain sober. By holding the female responsible for the abuse, subjects are suggesting that the victim brought about her own misfortune (cf. Jones & Aronson, 1973). If someone's suffering can be justified, then the perception of a just world is maintained.

Method

During one of the group meetings, 85 members of A.A. (61 males) volunteered to participate in a study on how we "see and react to others." The majority were between 36 and 50 years of age; 50% had at least one year of high school, 21% had completed vocational training or a university degree. As suggested by these figures, 67% were employed in a variety of managerial or trade jobs, and 33% were unemployed. A majority of subjects was married (either legally or common-law) to the same spouse for more than ten years; 62% rated their relationship as satisfactory. Subjects completed a booklet containing a series of biographical questions, spouse abuse scenario and attributions for that abuse, and attributions for own and others' drinking problems. The latter section is not relevant to our discussion and the scenarios have been discussed previously. The biographical section asked for age and sex of respondent as well as the length of membership, and regularity of attendance at A.A. meetings, number of years subjects have had a problem with alcohol, how long they have been sober, and length of and happiness in their current marriage. In addition, subjects indicated the frequency of being abused (e.g., being hit by the other person within the last year) in both their past (if applicable) and current marriage. They also indicated the frequency of abusing their spouses (if applicable) while sober and/or intoxicated. All these questions were answered on a five-point scale, from 1 = none to 5 = more than five times. After completing the biographical questionnaire, subjects read one of the four abuse scenarios and made a number of causal attributions regarding that abuse.

Results and Discussion

Responses to the questions tapping the respondent's own victimization were separated into two groups: (a) never been struck, and (b) struck at least once. Responses to the statement "While sober I have hit my spouse" were separated into two groups, (a) never, and (b) on at least one occasion. Since numbers so warranted, responses to the question, "While intoxicated I have hit my spouse" were separated into three groups: (a) never, (b) a few times (2-3), and (c) more than five times. A chi-square analysis on the responses to the biographical questions showed a positive relationship between spouse-abuse when sober and when intoxicated ($X^2(2)$ = 18.47, p = .0001). Specifically, of those who never struck their spouses while sober, 21.4% did so 2-3 times when intoxicated, and 9.5% did so at least four times when inebriated. Of those who hit their spouses when intoxicated, 9.4% reported doing so at least twice, while 16.5% reported doing so at least five times within the last year. Other results indicated that of those who were not abused in past or current relationships, 29.8% abused their spouses when intoxicated, while 35.19% of those who were abused struck their spouses when intoxicated. Interestingly enough, of those who had never been abused, 40.5% never struck their spouses when intoxicated, while only 3.6% of those who had been abused refrained from doing so when inebriated. ($X^2(2)$ = 16.02, p = .0003).

Contrary to expectations there were no significant relationships between frequency of abuse and either the number of years alcohol has been a problem, length of sobriety or years of group membership. There was, however, a significant relationship between attendance at A.A. meetings and abusing one's spouse while intoxicated ($X^2(2)$ = 8.99, p = .01). Of those who regularly attended, 27.4% did not abuse their spouse when drunk, whereas 17.8% did so on at least two occasions when intoxicated. Of those who attended irregularly, 16.7% never abused their spouse when intoxicated, but 38.1% did so when drunk. A similar trend was observed between attendance and abusing one's spouse while sober: regular attenders were less likely to do so ($X^2(1)$ = 2.52, p = .11).

These data suggest for these subjects that being intoxicated greatly increases the likelihood of their abusing their spouse, particularly if the abuser had been abused in a current or previous relationship. We cannot determine from this data whether the victim became drunk in order to commit abuse, as Gelles suggests, or whether the abuse reflects a pattern of marital interaction. There is some support for this latter notion. A majority of these subjects has been living with the same person for at least ten years and most reported the relationship as satisfactory. While retrospective accounts are always open to bias, and A.A. does promote an attitude of tolerance towards the excesses of intoxication, these data suggest that these individuals have adapted to a particular pattern of existence where periodic beatings are part of the relationship. This should not be taken to mean that this mode of relating to another is unchangeable; those who regularly attended A.A. meetings were less likely to abuse their spouses than those who did not. What may be happening is that such peer support groups as A.A. provide the individual with alternate means of solving not only alcohol-related problems but also other problems as well. Perloff (1983) points out that such peer support groups also help people externalize the locus of the problem and show people that they are not alone in their difficulties. Evidently those who attend regularly are deriving a number of benefits from group discussion in addition to the help they receive with the larger problem of maintaining sobriety.

Attributions for the abuse incident were entered into a three-factor multivariate analysis of variance. In addition to scenario and sex of subject, a number of other variables was also analyzed (e.g., length of membership, frequency of abuse in current marital relationship). Since several analyses were done on the same data, thereby increasing the probability of a Type I error, hypothesis testing was done in two stages: first, a Bonferroni procedure was used to set the multivariate alpha at .01; this in turn was followed (assuming a significant multivariate effect) by a univariate analysis on each dependent variable. Such a procedure ensures that the probability of a Type I error is no greater than the multivariate alpha.

Of the significant multivariate effects, those that concern us here were the scenario x sex x length of membership and the scenario x sex x frequency of current abuse analyses. Except for the variables discussed here, no other variable from the biographical section was significant. Both Mr. H. ($M = 3.95$) and Mrs. H. ($M = 4.05$) were held less responsible for the abuse by long-term (more than five years) than short-term members (less than five years; $M = 4.96$ and 4.13 for Mr. and Mrs. H., respectively).

When the subjects' current level of abuse was taken into account, abuse victims held the woman more responsible ($M = 5.09$) than did nonvictims ($M = 3.70$; $F(1,60) = 13.69$, $p = .001$). A gender x current abuse interaction ($F(1,60) = 3.91$, $p = .05$) indicated that victims of both sexes (male $M = 4.87$; female $M = 5.57$) were more likely to blame the woman than were females and males who were never abused, (female $M = 3.33$; $t(20) = 3.29$, $p = .01$; male $M = 3.85$; $t(52) = 2.26$, $p = .05$).

In the three alcohol-related scenarios, multivariate analyses were conducted on those variables related to drinking. Of the significant effects, those pertinent to this discussion indicated that when the man was intoxicated either alone or with his spouse, subjects rated him as more likely to have been drunk in the past, to drink in the future, and to have the problem under less personal control than was the case when the female alone was intoxicated (F's$(2,44) = 16.43, 3.31, 4.31$; p's $= .001, .05, .02$, respectively).

It was predicted that length of membership in A.A. would be inversely related to attributions of responsibility for a spouse-abuse incident. This idea was supported. Those who belonged to A.A. for more than five years held both the man and the woman less responsible than did those with less than five years of membership. Social comparison theory (Festinger, 1954) suggests that group membership is positively associated with incorporation of group beliefs and values. A.A. posits that alcoholism is a disease over which the individual has no control. Members may come to believe that a person is not responsible for a behavior which stems from uncontrollable factors. Earlier it was noted that those who regularly attended A.A. meetings were less likely to abuse their spouses, but in the present analysis, attendance was not associated with attributions of responsibility. These findings suggest that there are some variables which influence the likelihood of abusing one's spouse and these are different from those which influence the individual's perceptions of another's abuse. While the present data preclude further discussion, these results support the growing awareness (see Miller & Porter, 1983) that the kind of events that need to be explained differs both between the types of victimization (rape vs abuse) as well as within a victim category (own vs other's abuse).

In the present study male and female abuse victims attributed more responsibility to the victim than did nonvictims, results consistent with recent findings on victimization (Perloff, 1983). Before commenting on the possible reasons for such results, it is interesting to note in this sample that the percentage of male abuse victims (28%) is quite comparable to the percentage of female victims (31%) and it is also of interest to note the sex differences in attributions: in all analyses where gender main effects or interactions were found, females attributed more responsibility to the victim than did males.

The subjects in this study are victims in a number of ways, some as a result of their own behavior, others as a consequence of other people's behavior. In attempting to explain the present results, it is important to note that when a person comes to A.A. he or she has usually exhausted all other avenues of help. In a word, the person is desperate. As Beckman (1980) points out, for many it's their last chance for sobriety, and the people know it. Being a victim, regardless of its origins, is an aversive experience involving personal, financial, and psychological loss. It is a state individuals are motivated to leave. A.A. capitalizes on this aversive quality of victimization by altering the individual's attributions for past behavior and supplying new attributions for current and future behavior. But this socialization process takes years (Corenblum, 1983) and it is a moot point whether it is fully effective. When abuse victims read or hear about other victims it brings back to the observers the realization that they are still victims. Such a realization may be threatening to self-esteem, particularly so to those individuals who are trying to rebuild their lives after many years of suffering with alcohol abuse.

Threats to self-esteem that arise from such reminders can be reduced in a number of ways (see Taylor, Wood, & Lichtman, 1983). The just-world hypothesis suggests that when another suffers unjustly, the observer's notion that the world is a fair and just place is threatened, particularly if the suffering is perceived to be extensive, beyond the victim's control, ongoing, and something that cannot be redressed. When the just world has been threatened one can reduce the threat by seeing the victim's behavior as causally important in the abuse (she had it coming) or by derogating the victim's character (she's that kind of person). In this manner the victim is held responsible for the event, thereby restoring the observer's sense of a just world.

An alternate explanation for blaming the victim is suggested by a variant of social comparison theory. A basic tenet of this theory is that individuals compare their outcomes with those who are somewhat better than themselves. Such upward comparisons provide information for improving one's outcomes. When social comparisons involve a threat to self-esteem, however, a number of studies indicates that individuals make downward comparisons; that is, comparisons are made against those who are doing less well than the individual. Such comparisons make one feel good about one's situation relative to the comparison other, but as Taylor et al. (1983) point out, such comparisons, while enhancing self-esteem, provide little information on how to improve one's outcomes. Wills (1981) suggests that downward comparisons are more likely to occur under potentially victimizing situations that threaten self-esteem. The comparison may be a passive process involving a comparison with the unfortunate other or more active, where the person seeks out a target for comparison, thus creating a distance between the self and other. By holding the abuse victim responsible for her victimization, subjects in this study may have been trying to distance themselves from a threatening situation. By seeing Mrs. H. as responsible, subjects may feel somewhat more secure in the face of what appears to be rather similar circumstances to their own. Subjects may reason that after all they are seeking help for their problems, their lives are improving, and so forth. This latter idea points out an important point: while downward comparisons may serve self-esteem needs, the process involves cognitive as well as self-esteem factors. Subjects may have assumed that neither actor is seeking help for his or her problems and perhaps are not motivated to do so. It would be an oversight to regard downward comparisons as reflecting motivational concerns without also realizing that some information processing is also occurring.

In the present study, derogation of the victim may reflect the process of downward comparison or the just-world phenomena. While the present data cannot differentiate between these explanations, future studies may wish to explore the differences by examining the type of information subjects receive about the abuse victim. Just-world concerns are aroused when the innocent suffer unjustly. Information that the victim has been abused many times before or is someone who seeks out that kind of partner should not threaten subject's notion of a fair world, since the victim's behavior brings about her own misfortune. This idea would predict less negative evaluations than when such information was absent. In terms of downward comparisons, such information may threaten the subject's self-esteem, since subjects may have been (or could be) in that situation. Such threats can be reduced by seeing the actor as much worse off than the subject. The answer to these issues awaits further study.

The results of this study differ from those of the initial study. While such differences may have arisen for a variety of reasons, the least of which was the difference in the subject samples, the two studies point to the different types of information that observers and recipients of abuse bring to an abuse situation; the cognitive constructs of the two groups differ. When different constructs are activated or made more accessible (Higgins & King, 1981), the same information will be processed differently. What is activated in one group may be different from what is activated in the other.

The third study was addressed to possible differences in construct accessibility. It differs from the previous studies in two ways: first, a number of personality and cognitive measures was taken so as to better define the underlying constructs; and second, the methodology was similar to that used in research on construct accessibility. Specifically, subjects who had (schematics) or had not (aschematics) been exposed to abuse in their own homes read an abuse scenario where either the man, woman, or neither spouse was intoxicated. Following an interpolated task, to control for memory effects, subjects recalled as much of the story as they could, and then made a series of evaluations and attributions. We were primarily concerned with the influence of exposure, attitudinal and personality factors upon recall and attributions.

STUDY 3*

The subjective factors a person brings to a situation are often more important in the interpretation and recall of what transpired than are the actual occurrences within that situation. Higgins, King, and Mavin (1982) point out that individual differences may be evident not only in the traditional sense of personality factors but also in the kinds of personal constructs people commonly employ to encode, process, and recall construct relevant information. Markus et al. (1978) found that overweight subjects were more knowledgeable about food, fat, calorie intake and other weight-related issues than were normal-weight subjects. Similarly, Kuiper and Derry (1981) found chronic depressives were more likely than nondepressives to recall more accurately and respond faster to negative as opposed to positive personality information. In both studies, those with the schema responded differently to schematic relevant events that did those without. To further examine these ideas within the domain of family violence, a three-part pilot study was conducted in which attitudes, personality factors, and the informational base underlying the abuse schema were explored. Given the rather limited scope of this study, we will present just a general overview of the methodology and the results.

In the first phase, Introductory Psychology students rated their agreement with 45 spouse-abuse statements, which were drawn from a variety of sources (e.g., Burt, 1980). Item analysis resulted in three scales, an attitude scale (alpha = .60) composed of items reflecting a negative attitude toward abusers; a causes scale

* This study was conducted with Gillian King while the author was a Sabbatical Fellow at the University of Western Ontario. This research was supported by a SSHRC Leave Fellowship to the author. 451-81-1152.

(alpha = .78) covered a variety of factors which may lead to abuse; and a sympathy scale (alpha = .68), which suggested a concern for the abuse victim.

In the second phase of the study, a second sample of Introductory Psychology students received a booklet containing six personality scales, the three abuse scales, and three questions designed to determine subject exposure to spouse-abuse. In addition to these scales, subjects completed the Michigan Alcoholism Screening Test (MAST, Selzer, 1971), a measure of drinking-related problems, and a drinking chart which required subjects to indicate how much beer, wine, and spirits they had consumed the previous week. Subjects also indicated how often their parent/stepparent had within the last six months verbally or physically abused the other parent. Verbal and physical abuse were explicitly defined, and subjects were asked to indicate the aggressor and victim. A third question asked subjects to indicate if they knew anyone who was an abuse victim and to state their relationship (if any) to the victim.

Responses to all questions, except the abuse questions, were factor analyzed, and four factors accounting for 65% of the variance were extracted. The varimax rotated structure revealed for factor I a dimension suggesting self-disclosure. The four variables loading on the second factor suggested an authoritarian dimension; the abuse attitude scale and the abuse sympathy scale loaded on the third factor, implying a generalized attitude dimension. The two alcohol questionnaires loaded on the fourth factor, suggesting an alcohol factor.

Several weeks after completing the various scales, subjects were recalled for a study ostensibly in person perception. Each received an envelope containing five tasks; on the first, subjects read a detailed account of a heated argument between a man and his wife, which ended with the husband striking his wife several times. The scenarios were identical except that one-third of the subjects read that either the husband, wife, or neither spouse was intoxicated. To remove any short-term memory effects, the scenario was followed by a twelve-minute nonverbal interference task (Task 2). Following this, half of the subjects recalled word for word, as much of the story as they could (Task 3), while the other half made causal attributions for the abuse and rated each spouse on a variety of bipolar scales (Task 4). For the other half of the subjects, tasks three and four were done in the opposite order. The study ended with a series of manipulation checks (Task 5) and a debriefing session.

Analysis of subject responses to the exposure questions revealed that eleven subjects had been exposed to either verbal or physical abuse or had known an abuse victim, while sixty-four had no exposure. To facilitate data analysis and discussion, this report will focus on the causal attributions. Subjects were asked to estimate the responsibility of the man, woman, or other factors for initiating, arguing, hitting, and escalating the violence as well as to attribute overall responsibility to the man, woman or the other factors. Factor analysis of these attributions revealed three factors: the first reflected a blame-the-woman dimension, while the second factor implied an external dimension; the third factor reflected the husband's responsibility for the abuse. Factor scores were generated for each factor and entered into a 3-scenario (man, woman, neither intoxicated) x 2 (schema present-absent) x 3 (responsibility type: woman, external, husband) analysis of variance with repeated measures on the responsibility factor. The analysis revealed a significant schema x responsibility interaction and a significant scenario x responsibility effect. In the latter interaction, subjects blamed both the husband and the wife when he was intoxicated; when she was drunk, she alone bore full responsibility for the violence. When neither spouse was intoxicated, subjects attributed the violence to external factors.

Analysis of the schema x responsibility interaction indicated that subjects who have been exposed to or know of abuse were more likely (0.465) to attribute responsibility to the woman than to either external factors (-0.247) or the husband (-0.292), whereas those without exposure attributed blame equally across the three categories. Comparisons between the two groups indicated that aschematics were less likely to blame the wife (-0.091) than schematics; the other two comparisons were in the same direction but were not significant. As was the case in study two, those who have had some experience with abuse held the victim more responsible than did those without experience.

Correlations between the personality dimensions and a number of other variables indicated that blaming the victim was positively associated with authoritarianism ($r = .32$) and inversely related to alcohol problems ($r = -.21$), while blaming the husband was inversely related to authoritarianism ($r = -.23$) but positively related ($r = .24$) to sympathetic abuse beliefs. Evaluations of the spouses approached significance in her case but in his case evaluations were inversely related to sympathetic abuse attitudes ($r = -.28$). Interestingly, authoritarianism was inversely related to recall, ($r = -.17$, $p = .06$) and to recall of male-only actions and statements ($r = -.25$). These results suggest that the processing of a spouse abuse incident reflects not only the perceiver's experience with abuse but also personality and attitudinal factors.

The results of this study replicate and extend those of Study Two. Subjects exposed to or who know of spouse abuse held the victim more responsible for her own abuse than did those who were not so exposed. While these results are consistent with the just-world hypothesis, it appears that some individuals are more likely to derogate the victim than are others. Correlational analysis suggests that authoritarians (Cherry & Byrne, 1977) were more likely to derogate the victim than were nonauthoritarians, a finding that has been replicated elsewhere (e.g., Werner, Kaghiro, & Strube, 1982). The current findings suggest that authoritarians may have been responding to the violation of traditional sex roles as displayed by the intoxicated female. As noted previously, characteristics of the actor serve as cues from which other inferences may be generated. In this case, authoritarians may have inferred that she is the kind of person who violates female propriety and deserves what she gets.

The results of this study depart from the results of the first study, where subjects exposed to abuse attributed less responsibility to the victim, particularly when she was intoxicated. There were a number of methodological differences between the two studies, and the one deserving of comment is the impact of time delay caused by the interference task. Such tasks are necessary, since constructs are assumed to be long-term memory structures and their influence upon recall and evaluation must be separated from the effects of short-term memory. Lerner and Miller (1978) suggest that the time sequence involved in the attribution of blame influences the just-world process. They suggest that initially the observer may blame the aggressor, but if nothing happens to end the suffering, or the observer believes the suffering will continue, the observer may blame the victim or both partners. Those exposed to abuse blamed the husband in Study One, where attributions were taken immediately after reading the scenario, but blamed the victim in Study Three, where attributions were delayed. This discussion is post hoc and in need of further study, but the results of Studies One and Three suggest that the time delay between the incident and the drawing of causal inferences influences attributions of responsibility.

GENERAL CONCLUSION

In a recent article, Critchlow (1983) argues that our society has an ambivalent attitude toward the influence of drunkenness upon attributions of responsibility. On the one hand we see alcohol as a disinhibitor, making people do things they would not normally do; on the other, the person is held responsible for becoming intoxicated. Thus they are twice condemned — once for their intoxication and again for any misbehavior. In two studies reported here, such ambivalence was not only evident but was further qualified by the sex of the intoxicated person. Generally speaking, an intoxicated male was held less responsible for wife-beating, while his victim was held more responsible for her own abuse when she was intoxicated. In addition, such attributions were made by both observers and chronic alcoholics. The only exception to these general findings were the results of Study One, where attributions were taken immediately after reading the scenario.

It was noted earlier that descriptions of the offender and victim serve as a nucleus from which other attributions are made. What appears to be happening here is that antinormative behavior committed by an intoxicated male is seen as out-of-character behavior, while such behaviors by an intoxicated female are seen as a stable feature of her personality. She must always be good, for having fallen, she remains condemned.

Attributions of responsibility were influenced not only by characteristics of the spouses but also by characteristics of the observer. Those exposed to abuse as well as abuse victims responded differently to the abuse scenarios than did non-victims and those not exposed to abuse in their own home. It was suggested that both victims and exposed subjects have constructs which facilitate the processing and recall of construct relevant material. Study Three found some support for these notions. In addition, certain personality variables were also shown to influence attributions of responsibility; the results suggested these variables may be independent of the abuse construct. It is evident that a number of factors determine the observer's attributions of responsibility when alcohol is involved, factors which seem also to influence legal process (Critchlow, 1983); small wonder then why efforts to help abuse victims seem so slow in coming.

REFERENCES

Anon. (1952). *Alcoholics anonymous: Twelve steps and twelve traditions.* Alcoholics Anonymous World Service Inc. New York.

Ashley, M. (1978, January). *Shelters: Short term needs.* Battered women: Issues of public policy. Washington, DC.

Beckman, L. (1980). An attributional analysis of Alcoholics Anonymous. *Journal of Studies on Alcohol, 40,* 714-726.

Burt, M. R. (1980). Cultural myths and support for rape. *Journal of Personality and Social Psychology, 38,* 217-230.

Calhoun, L., Selby, J., & Warring, L. (1976). Social perception of the victims causal role in rape: An exploratory examination of four factors. *Human Relations, 29,* 517-526.

Cann, A., Calhoun, L., & Selby, J. (1979). Attributing responsibility to the victim of rape: Influence of information regarding past sexual experience. *Human Relations, 32,* 57-67.

Chaiken, A. L., & Cooper, J. (1973). Evaluation as a function of correspondence and hedonic relevance. *Journal of Experimental Social Psychology, 9,* 257-264.

Cherry, F., & Byrne, D. (1977). Authoritarianism. In T. Blass (Ed.), *Personality variables in social behavior.* Hillsdale, NJ: Erlbaum.

Corenblum, B. (1983, December). Alcoholics causal attributions for their own drinking problems. Paper presented at International Congress of Drugs and Alcohol, Tel Aviv.

Critchlow, B. (1983). Blaming the booze: The attribution of responsibility for drunken behavior. *Personality and Social Psychology Bulletin, 9,* 451-473.

Feldman-Summers, S., & Lindner, K. (1976). Perceptions of victims and defendants in criminal assault cases. *Criminal Justice and Behavior, 3,* 135-149.

Festinger, L. (1954). A theory of social comparison processes. *Human Relations, 7,* 117-140.

Gelles, R. J. (1974). *The violent home.* Beverly Hills, CA: Sage.

Gromberg, E. S. (1976). Alcoholism in women. In B. Kissin & H. Begleiter (Eds.), *The biology of alcoholism: Social aspects of alcoholism* (Volume 4). New York: Plenum.

Higgins, E., & King, G. (1981). Accessibility of social constructs. Information processing consequences of individual and contextual variability. In N. Cantor & J. Kihlstrom (Eds.), *Personality, cognition and social interaction.* Hillsdale, NJ: Erlbaum.

Higgins, E., King, G., & Mavin, G. (1982). Individual construct accessibility and subjective impressions and recall. *Journal of Personality and Social Psychology, 43,* 35-47.

Hunter, J. (1983). Wife-abuse: A survey of relative factors. Unpublished doctoral dissertation, Union of experimenting Colleges and Universities.

236 Alcohol and Spouse Abuse

Johnson, S. & Garzon, S. (1978). Alcoholism and women. *American Journal of Drug and Alcohol Abuse, 5,* 107-122.

Jones, C., & Aronson, E. (1973). Attribution of fault to a rape victim as a function of respectability of the victim. *Journal of Personality and Social Psychology, 26,* 415-419.

Jones, E. E., & Harris, V. A. (1967). The attribution of attitudes. *Journal of Experimental Social Psychology, 3,* 1-24.

Kelley, H. H.(1972). *Causal schemata and the attribution process.* Morristown, NJ: General Learning Press.

Kituse, J.I. (1964). Societal reaction to deviant behavior: Problems of theory and method. In H. S. Becker (Ed.), *The other side.* New York: Free Press.

Kuiper, N., & Derry, P. (1981). The self as a cognitive prototype: An application to person perception and depression. In N. Cantor & J. F. Kihlstrom (Eds.), *Personality, cognition and social interaction.* Hillsdale, NJ: Erlbaum.

Landy, D., & Aronson, E. (1969). The influence of the character of the criminal and his victim on the decisions of simulated jurors. *Journal of Experimental Social Psychology, 5,* 141-152.

Lerner, M. (1977). The justice motives: Some hypotheses as to its origins and forms. *Journal of Personality, 45,* 1-52.

Lerner, M., & Miller, D. (1978). Just world research and the attribution process: Looking back and ahead. *Psychological Bulletin, 85,* 1030-1051.

Markus, H., Sentis, K., & Hamill, R. (1978, September). Consequences of self-schemas for information processing. Paper presented at the meeting of the American Psychological Association, Toronto.

Miller, D., & Porter, C. (1983). Self-blame in victims of violence. *Journal of Social Issues, 39,* 139-152.

Perloff, L. (1983). Perceptions of vulnerability to victimization. *Journal of Social Issues, 39,* 41-61.

Pugh, M. D. (1983). Contributory fault and rape convictions: Loglinear models for blaming the victim. *Social Psychology Quarterly, 46,* 233-242.

Regan, D. T., Straus, E., & Fazio, R. (1974). Liking and the attribution process. *Journal of Experimental Social Psychology, 10,* 385-397.

Richardson, D. C., & Campbell, J. L. (1980). Alcohol and wife abuse: The effect of alcohol on attributions of blame for wife abuse. *Personality and Social Psychology Bulletin, 6,* 51-56.

Ross, L. D. (1977). The intuitive psychologist and his shortcomings: Distortions in the attribution process. In L. Berkowitz (Ed.), *Advances in experimental social psychology* (Volume 10). New York: Academic Press.

Roy, M. (1982, May). Report on violence in the family: Wife battering. Standing Committee on Health, Welfare and Social Affairs, House of Commons of Canada.

Selzer, M. (1971). The Michigan Alcoholism Screening Test: The quest for a new diagnostic instrument. *American Journal of Psychiatry, 127,* 89-94.

Shotland, R. L., & Goodstein, L. (1983). Just because she doesn't want to doesn't mean it's rape: An experimentally based causal model of the perception of rape in a dating situation, *Social Psychology Quarterly, 46,* 220-232.

Sigall, H., & Ostrove, N. (1975). Beautiful but dangerous: Effects of offender attractiveness and nature of the crime on juridic judgments. *Journal of Personality and Social Psychology, 18,* 247-255.

Smith, R. E., Keating, J. P., Hester, R. K., & Mitchell, H. E. (1976). Role and justice considerations in the attribution of responsibility to rape victim. *Journal of Research in Personality, 10,* 346-357.

Straus, M. A., Gelles, R. J., & Steinmetz, S. K. (1980). *Behind closed doors: Violence in the American family.* New York: Anchor Books.

Taylor, S. E., & Fiske, S. T. (1978). Salience, attention and attribution: Top of the head phenomena. In L. Berkowitz (Ed.), *Advances in experimental social psychology* (Volume 2). New York: Academic Press.

Taylor, S. E., & Koivumaki, J. H. (1976). The perception of self and others: Acquaintanceship, affect and actor-observer differences. *Journal of Personality and Social Psychology, 33,* 403-408.

Taylor, S. E., Wood, J. V., & Lichtman, R. (1983). It could be worse: Selective evaluation as a response to victimization. *Journal of Social Issues, 39,* 19-40.

Werner, C., Kaghiro, D., & Strube, M. (1982). Conviction proneness and the authoritarian juror: Inability to disregard information or attitudinal bias. *Journal of Applied Psychology, 67,* 629-636.

Wills, T. (1981). Downward comparison principles in social psychology. *Psychological Bulletin, 90,* 245-271.

Chapter 13
Aggressive Cues and Sexual Arousal to Erotica

Neil M. Malamuth, Seymour Feshbach,
Thomas Fera, and James Kunath

The existence of an intimate relationship between sexual arousal and aggression has often been theorized by psychologists (Freud, 1938; Berne, 1964; Stoller, 1976; Bach & Wyden, 1969) and laymen (Ellison, 1947; Caldwell, 1941) alike. In Freud's seminal paper "Three Contributions to the Theory of Sex," for example, he theorized that "the sexuality of most men shows an admixture of aggression, of a desire to subdue...sadism would then correspond to an aggressive component of the sexual instinct which has become independent and exaggerated" (1938, p. 596). Some psychodynamically oriented investigators have gone as far as suggesting that "...hostility, overt or hidden, is what generates and enchances sexual excitment and its absence leads to sexual indifference and boredom" (Stoller, 1976, p. 903).

Other theoreticians have postulated a rather different link between sex and aggression. According to Fromm (1973) our biology is such that for most individuals hostile aggression is incompatible with sexual arousal whereas self-assertive aggressivity, involving the reduction of inhibition, is mutually facilitative with sexuality. Bach and Goldberg (1974) also argue that our biological heritage has led to forceful, uninhibited, but not hostile or destructive, aggression facilitating sexual responsiveness: "Lovers who exclude aggression from their bedroom cheat themselves of a total and exciting experience, and in fact will probably be unable to achieve genuine erotic fulfillment" (p. 256).

Malamuth, Feshbach, and Jaffe (1977) suggest that learning experiences may link sexual and aggressive responses by virtue of their sharing common "taboo" properties. Encouraging a person to engage in one "taboo" response may disinhibit other inhibited behaviors. Aggressive cues presented by the experimenter are hypothesized as "turn-offs" of inhibition, thus facilitating sexual arousal, rather than as a "turn-on" of sexual feeling. LoPiccolo and Miller (1975a, 1975b) employed a similar proposition in beginning their sexual enrichment programs for normal couples with a session in which participants uttered "taboo" words using vulgar phrases. Experimentally, Feshbach, Malamuth and Drapkin (1974) report that facilitating or inhibiting subjects' aggression in the administration of electric shocks had generalizing effects to sexual responsiveness.

The question arises as to why sexual and aggressive behaviors would be more inclined to be associated than other socially constrained behaviors. There are at least three factors that may contribute to a unique association between these behaviors. First, there are many physiological similarities between sex and aggression (Zillmann, 1984). In the well-known Kinsey studies (Kinsey, Pomeroy, Martin & Gebhard, 1953), it was first noted that in both males and females as many as fourteen of the eighteen physiological changes that occur in sexual responses also accompany aggressive responses. Many other taboo behaviors such as stealing, inappropriate dress, picking one's nose, etc. do not share such physiological similarities with sexual responses. Secondly, there are overt behavioral similarities in features of sexual and aggressive behaviors, e.g., an intense physical embrace and wrestling. Thus, as psychoanalysts have noted, a young child observing adults copulating may mistake the sexual act for an aggressive assault. It may well be that inhibitions associated with engaging in behaviors such as squeezing, screaming, clawing, or grunting in the context of an aggressive act generalize to similar behavioral manifestations within the context of sexual acts. A third element in the relationship between sex and aggression is that they are frequently connected in the public domain. They often are linked together as central themes in literature, drama and the media in general. In many cultures, the extent and degree of societal concern about and suppression of one of these activities parallels the other.

Pornographic* literature seems to contain a high proportion of aggressive material. A *Time Magazine* cover story on pornography reported that the "taboo currently under the heaviest assault is sado-masochism – sexual pleasure derived from domination and inflicting pain on a partner or from being hurt." (April 5, 1976, p. 61).

The present experiments were designed to assess the effect of manipulating aggressive cues within an erotic passage on sexual arousal. This variation was not intended to involve hostile aggression, but rather aggressivity akin to assertive aggression as described by Fromm (1973) and Bach and Goldberg (1974).

---

* The terms pornography and erotica are used interchangeably here without any pejorative meaning necessarily intended.

However, it is recognized that the distinction between hostile and assertive aggression is not always clear-cut. Inasmuch as the aggressive cues inserted in the passage were intended to predominantly reflect assertive, instrumental aggression, it was predicted that the presence of aggressive cues would be associated with increased sexual responsiveness.

EXPERIMENT 1

Materials

A one-page (248-word) description of sexual intercourse between consenting adults was compiled from several novels. A total of ten words was varied to manipulate the aggressive cues and thereby create two versions of the same story. In selecting these words to systematically manipulate, considerable care was taken not to alter the essential meaning of the passage. Some examples of this variation are: (a torrent) vs (an assault) of forceful thrusts; (hugging) vs (forcing) him to her; (intense) vs (hard-locked) embrace; (pressed) vs (slammed) his body; (drove) vs (stabbed) the hardened member.

In order to provide validation for this experimental manipulation, fourteen judges were asked to rate on eight-point scales the connotation of the randomly presented words manipulated in the study. These judges were unfamilar with the purpose of the experiment, but they were informed that the words were taken from an erotic passage and that their ratings should take the context into consideration. The results of these ratings indicated that the "aggressive" words were judged to be significantly more aggressive, antagonistic, and dominant than the "nonaggressive" words, thereby providing support for the intended variation.

Subjects' reactions to the reading materials were assessed by means of a Mood Check List. This form consisted of eleven descriptors of various moods. Two items concerned sexual responsiveness: the first referred to feelings of sexual arousal or being "turned on" whereas the other, appearing at the end of the questionnaire, referred to feeling "sexually tantalized or sensuous." It was reasoned that, while similar, the first item would be more likely to be associated with a clearly discernible response, whereas the latter would reflect a more diffuse state of sexual arousal. Other items concerned feelings such as boredom, anxiety, embarrassment, positive affect, and negative affect. For each mood description, the subject was to check one of nine points on a scale ranging from "none at all" to "extremely."

Since the primary dependent measure of the present investigation consisted of self-reported sexual arousal, some discussion of the validity of these self-reports is warranted. For nondeviant populations, self-reported sexual arousal has been consistently found to correlate highly with genital measures (e.g., Heiman, 1977; Abel, Barlow, Blanchard, & Guild, 1977; Schaefer, Tregerthan, & Colgan,

1976). In general, both with the use of physiological and self-report measures, more confidence may be attached to the validity of indications of sexual arousal than to the absence of such indications, since subjects may be capable of inhibiting as well as hiding arousal (Amorso & Brown, 1973; Abel & Blanchard, 1976; Henson & Rubin, 1971). Typically, discrepancies between self-reports and genital measures are far more likely in the direction of underestimating rather than overestimating arousal via self-reports (Schaefer et al., 1976; Abel et al., 1977). It would seem therefore, that considerable confidence may be attached to self-reports of the existence of sexual arousal.

A separate questionnaire inquired about subjects' backgrounds. Participants were asked to respond to multiple-choice questions concerning their sex, age, occupations, yearly income, marital status, education, and frequency of reading "adult" books.

Subjects and Procedure

Sixty-two male subjects were individually approached in a Hollywood bookstore by the male experimenter.* The data of two subjects was eliminated because of failure to complete the questionnaires.

The bookstore contained both nonerotic and pornographic materials; only those subjects scanning materials in the "adults only" section were approached. The experimenter introduced himself as representing a local publishing company that was interested in obtaining evaluations of erotic materials that might be worthy of publication. He asked the subjects if they would be willing to read a one-page excerpt from an erotic manuscript and anonymously report their reactions. Upon consenting, subjects were given a packet with the front page reading "Fairbanks Publishing Company, Hollywood, California." The second page consisted of either the relatively aggressive or nonaggressive version of the erotic passage, with subjects being randomly assigned to conditions. The third and last page provided an opportunity for the gathering of the background information. After subjects returned the materials, they were thanked for their help and the experimenter answered any inquiries.**

Results

Background data

Analyses of background data provided both a check on the random assignment to experimental conditions and information on characteristics of the

---

* The authors wish to express their gratitude to Mr. Larry Steinberg for permission to conduct the experiment in his bookstore.

** The owner of the bookstore asked that participants not be briefed as to the real purpose of the experiment unless they asked for more information following the completion of the questionnaires. Only one subject did so, and was fully briefed.

sample. Demographic data and related responses in the two experimental conditions were very similar; statistical comparisons with the use of t tests indicated only negligible effects. These background data therefore provided clear support for the intended randomization.

The mean age of the participants was 31, with a standard deviation of 9.9; subjects ranged in age from 18 to 64 years. With respect to yearly income, 13% reported earning $20,000 or more, 39% between $10,000-$20,000, 25% between $5,000-$10,000, and 21% less than $5,000. The majority was single, about 40% indicating that they were currently married. Seventy-one percent reported not having any children. Slightly more than 56% reported having completed or being enrolled in a four-year college; 26% completed or were enrolled in a junior college; the remaining 17% had graduated from high school. With respect to the frequency of reading such materials, 35% indicated once or less a year, 51% on a monthly basis, 8% on a weekly basis, and only 6% on a daily basis.

Mood ratings

A comparison of subjects' mood ratings revealed a significant difference on the item "sexually tantalized or sensuous" t (58) = 2.30, $p < .02$, one-tailed. Subjects who read the story with the more aggressive cues reported feeling more sexually tantalized than those reading the other version of the same story. While those who read the former version also reported considerably higher levels of general arousal and positive affect, these differences did not approach acceptable levels of significance. Differences on other mood items, including that of "sexual arousal," were negligible.

Discussion

The results obtained within the "natural" field setting used provide interesting information regarding the responses of individuals likely to seek out sexually explicit materials. Although subjects' background information generally indicates that this was not a particularly atypical sample of the male population, the reported frequency of reading "adult" books would seem somewhat greater than that in the general population.

The results were partially consistent with the prediction that an increase in aggressive cues would result in enhanced sexual responsiveness. Subjects reading the version of the erotic story containing the more aggressive cues indicated feeling more "sexually tantalized and sensuous" than their counterparts who read the nonaggressive version. No significant differences were found, however, on the item asking subjects how "sexually aroused or turned on" they felt. It would seem that the participants interpreted these items differently, despite the apparent similarities between them. In any case, comparisons of the effects of these two erotic passage versions upon other populations seemed warranted.

EXPERIMENT 2

The second experiment was also designed to assess the effects of aggressive cues in erotica. The subject population studied included both males and females taken from a very different setting than the sample in the first experiment. Since, as described below, the nature of the experiences of males and females differed within this experiment, differences between the genders cannot be attributed to the sex variable per se. However, differences within each gender between reactions to the aggressive vs the nonaggressive passage versions can be meaningfully interpreted.

Method

Subjects and experimental conditions

There were 99 males and 115 female adult subjects, ranging in age from 21 to 60, who participated in the experiment. It was conducted during a guest lecture of a class meeting of two sections of a UCLA extension class entitled: "Pairing — The Search for Intimacy."*

This extension course included one hour of laboratory discussion and one lecture hour. The experiment was conducted during the lecture period. Subjects in the earlier of the two class sections participated in the laboratory discussion prior to the experiment, whereas the other section did not participate in the discussion until after the experiment. This discussion lasted close to an hour and consisted of the female participants revealing what they considered sexual "turn-ons" and "turn-offs" while the male participants listened.

The central manipulation of this study was essentially the same variation of aggressive cues within erotic reading material as that used in the first experiment. Subjects read a slightly revised one page description of the sexual intercourse used in the first study. A total of ten words were once again varied to alter the aggressive cues and thereby create two versions of the same story.

Degree of anxiety about aggression was considered a potentially important variable with respect to the variation in aggressivity. All subjects were administered an Aggression-Anxiety Scale (Feshbach & Singer, 1971; Feshbach, Stiles & Bitter, 1967), in which respondents are presented with thirty true-false items, eleven of which are "filler" items. Scores could range from 0-19, higher scores reflecting greater aggression-anxiety. Scores on this scale were split at the median, 10 for males and 11 for females, so as to separate subjects into high and low aggression-anxiety groups.

---

* The authors wish to express their appreciation to Dr. George Bach, who had invited Dr. Feshbach to his class on "Pairing," for the strong personal support he gave to the idea of a demonstrational study and for his continued encouragement of systematic research in this area.

Procedure

Subjects were seated in a large lecture hall and, as part of a classroom exercise, given three pages. The first page filled out was the Aggression-Anxiety Scale, described to subjects as a personality inventory. Then subjects were asked to read the second page, the erotic passage. Some subjects received the erotic excerpt that contained relatively nonaggressive wording, while others received the more aggressively worded passage. Subjects were instructed that immediately following the passage reading they were to complete the third page, the Mood Check List. When all of the subjects were finished, they were asked to pass the attached pages to the front of the room and, following the collection of these materials, the experiment was explained and discussed in detail.

Results

Randomization of subjects

As a check on the random distribution of subjects in the various experimental conditions, a three-way ANOVA varying the Aggressive Content, Discussion Section, and Sex of Subject was performed on the scores of the Aggression-Anxiety Scale. A significant main effect, $F = 12.36$, $p < .001$ was obtained for subject's sex, with females evidencing higher scores.* The existence of only negligible effects for the other variables suggests that subjects were quite randomly distributed across conditions.

Mood ratings

In this study, the "sexual arousal" and "sexually tantalized" items yielded very similar results; all of the effects that were significant or approached significance with one of the items did so with the other as well. While the effects are stronger if responses to both adjectives are combined, given the results of the first experiment, the analyses for each item were kept separate. For the sake of parsimony, only the data for the "sexual arousal" rating will be presented. It is not clear why, in contrast to the first experiment, subjects in the second study responded very similarly to both of the items dealing with sexual responsiveness.

The mean ratings of the "sexual arousal" item are presented in Figure 13.1. A four-way analysis of variance (Aggressive Content x Discussion Section x Aggression-Anxiety x Subject's Sex) performed on these data indicated a main effect for the Aggressive Content manipulation ($F = 7.46$, $p < 007$), with increased aggressivity resulting in greater sexual arousal. As Figure 13.1 reveals, however, and as indicated by a three-way interaction that approached significance ($F = 2.88$, $p < .10$) between the Aggressive Content, Discussion and Sex of Subject varia-

---

* Unless otherwise indicated, all of the data reported involved 1/198 degrees of freedom.

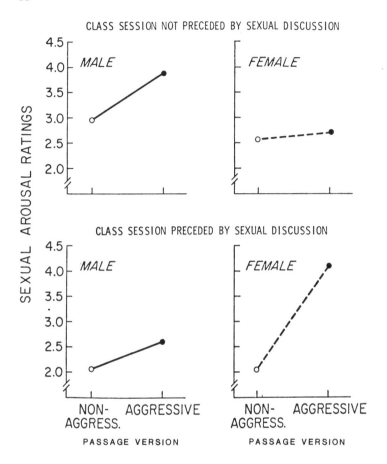

Figure 13.1 A four way analysis of variance

bles, the increased sexual arousal with the aggressive version of the erotic passage occurred mainly and dramatically in females who had earlier participated in a disinhibiting discussion. Simple analyses effects comparing females who read the aggressive vs nonaggressive version within the discussion condition yielded a highly significant effect $F(1,50) = 12.61$, $p < .001$. Males who had not earlier listened to the discussion showed a similar, though nonsignificant effect $F(1,48) = 1.79$, $p < .10$. Females who had not participated in the self-disclosing discussion (Second Class Session) and males who had been observers of the female discussion (First Class Section) evidenced little difference in their responses to the two passage versions.

Similar patterns were observed in other mood items. Subjects who read the more aggressive version indicated feeling more positive, (F = 4.14, p < .05) and frustrated (F = 7.40, p < .01) than their counterparts who had read the less aggressive erotic reading. Interaction effects among the Aggressive Content, Discussion Section and Sex of Subject variables were found for positive affect (F = 9.67, p < .002), negative affect (F = 4.93, p < .03) and on general arousal (F = 4.91, p < .01). These data revealed, in keeping with the sexual arousal data, that females who had not participated in the frank discussion and males who had listened to the discussion showed little differences in their reactions to the two versions of the passage. Males who had not listened to the revealing discussion, and to a greater extent females who participated in the discussion, indicated feeling more generally aroused and positive, and expressed less negative affect after having read the more aggressive as contrasted with the less aggressive version of the passage.

Additional interesting effects emerged that were not related to the aggressivity manipulation. The sexual arousal data also yielded an interaction effect between the sex of subject and discussion variables (F = 4.44, p < .05). This effect revealed that females who had not earlier participated in the discussion reported less sexual arousal than males, irrespective of the version of the story they had read. For those who had engaged in the self-disclosure experience, the pattern is the reverse, with females being the more sexually aroused. Additional data, however, suggest that the effects of the discussion were particularly pronounced for some subjects: an interaction effect between the Discussion and Aggression-Anxiety variables approached significance for sexual arousal (F = 3.54, p < .06), and for the "ability to think clearly" (F = 2.73, p < .10) items and was significant for self-reported anxiety (F = 4.10, p < .05). For those subjects who did not attend the personal discussion prior to the experiment, we find low aggression-anxious subjects reporting somewhat greater sexual arousal and anxiety and lessened ability to think clearly than subjects high in aggression-anxiety. The reverse pattern is found in subjects who had earlier attended the discussion — high aggression-anxiety individuals report being more sexually aroused and anxious and less able to think clearly than low aggression-anxiety subjects.

A second-order interaction between the Discussion, Aggression-Anxiety and Sex of Subject variables that approached significance (F = 3.25, p < .07) further clarifies the first-order interactions in revealing that the discussion particularly affected high aggression-anxiety females. That is, for males there are only slight differences in the sexual arousal reports of low and high aggression-anxious subjects, regardless of whether they did or did not listen to the discussion. For females, among those who did not discuss their sexual preferences, low aggression-anxiety subjects report slightly higher sexual arousal than high aggression-anxious subjects. In contrast, for those female subjects who had earlier engaged in the revealing discussion, we find that it is the high aggression-anxiety subjects who report considerably greater sexual arousal (F (1,50) $= 7.12$, $p < .025$).

DISCUSSION

The findings of the present study are consistent with the expectation that the variation of aggressive content in erotic reading matter will significantly affect its sexual arousal properties. This research was conducted in a nonlaboratory setting with subjects who were older than the usual college samples. Most of the subjects were or had been married and were participating in the course in which the study was conducted primarily for experiential and growth purposes. Many were uninterested in research and some were explicitly antagonistic to "science." Nevertheless, meaningful differences were yielded by the variation of aggressive content.

More specifically, the sexual arousal data of the study may be summarized as follows:

1. For subjects who had not earlier engaged in a self-disclosing sexual discussion, male subjects reported greater sexual arousal than females.
2. The results for subjects who had been involved in a self-disclosing discussion are quite different. It should be again noted that differences between males and females may be a function of their different roles within the discussion as well as their gender (or an interaction between these two factors). After having self-disclosed their sexual "turn-ons" and "turn-offs," female subjects reported more sexual arousal than the male subjects (who had listened to the females' discussion). Moreover, the reading of the more aggressive version of the passage resulted in females reporting much higher levels of sexual arousal, general arousal, and positive affect as compared with those females who had read the less aggressive version; for males, there is only a very slight trend for differences in this direction.
3. Subjects' aggression-anxiety levels, particularly for females, revealed some relationship with the impact of the discussion. High aggression-anxious females who had not participated in the discussion indicated slightly less sexual arousal than low aggression-anxious females. With respect to subjects who had prior to the experiment participated in the discussion, high aggression-anxious females indicated levels of sexual arousal that were considerably higher than those of the low aggression-anxiety females. Somewhat similar but weak trends were noted for males.

While these results need to be very cautiously interpreted in light of the fact that except for the variation in aggressive content the independent variables of the present study were of a correlational rather than an experimental nature (i.e., subjects were not randomly assigned to the Sex of Subject, Discussion, or Aggression-Anxiety conditions), some intriguing possibilities emerge. The data may well be interpreted as implicating the role of inhibitory and disinhibitory factors. The disinhibitory effects of the aggressive cues may emanate from their "taboo" properties and their presentation by the experimenter may serve to communicate a relatively uninhibited, "permissive" attitude that may generalize to sexual responses. Or, perceived physiological and behavioral similarities in features of sexual and aggressive responses may result in the aggressive stimuli being interpreted within the sexual interaction as reflecting intensity of interaction or even passion. It would seem difficult to think of another context in which phrases such as "an assault," "stabbing" or "forcing" would be perceived as anything but purely aggressive. However, within a sexual context, such descriptions may be perceived as uninhibited sexuality.

The fact that heightened sexual arousal tended to be accompanied by increased self-reported anxiety is not necessarily incompatible with a disinhibition interpretation. Firstly, disinhibition may result in greater willingness to acknowledge and report feelings of sexual arousal and of anxiety. Secondly, if one assumes that there is an approach-avoidance gradient in connection with sexual stimuli such that there tends to be greater anxiety with greater sexual arousal, then disinhibition as a function of the inclusion of aggressive stimuli or participation in a sexual discussion may facilitate sexual arousal and result in heightened anxiety resulting from the new level of sexual arousal. Clark's (1952) studies seem compatible with this analysis, in that those disinhibiting experimental conditions that elicited higher levels of sexual motives on the Thematic Apperception Test (TAT) also resulted in increases in sex-guilt themes.

The suggestion that aggressive cues serve as a "turn-off" of inhibition rather than a "turn-on" of sexual arousal did not receive unequivocal support, however, since a significant interaction was not found between subjects' levels of aggression-anxiety and the manipulation of aggressivity. The data may also be interpreted as indicating that aggressive stimuli in the context of erotica have stimulating effects rather than effects mediated by disinhibition. This distinction, though of importance, is operationally difficult to disentangle.

With respect to the discussion, the data suggests that the more inhibited subjects were the most influenced by it. Following the sexual discussion, high aggression-anxiety subjects, particularly females, were more sexually aroused than low aggression-anxious subjects, whereas the differences were in the opposite direction for subjects who had not participated in the discussion. These data are consistent with a study by Fisher and Byrne (1978).

These investigators report that subjects who had relatively phobic reactions to pornography (erotophobes) showed significant behavioral changes in sexual activity following exposure to explicit sexual stimuli. Subjects who had relatively positive reactions to pornography (erotophiles), on the other hand, showed relatively high levels of sexual activity that were unaffected by exposure to pornography. Future research should attempt to analyze some of the cognitive associations that may mediate a sex-aggression link. For example, some subjects may link virility with aggressivity. Similarly, the assertion of dominance through aggression may be associated for some individuals with idealized cultural sex roles. It is necessary to study the effects of varying aspects of erotic literature to determine whether dimensions such as assertive aggression, dominance, or perceived virility can best account for the effects of these stimuli in erotic contexts. The technique employed in the present studies, the systematic subtle variation of the passage content, would seem to readily lend itself to the investigation of a wide range of aggressive stimuli.

REFERENCES

Abel, G. G., Barlow, D. H., Blanchard, E. B., & Guild, D. (1977). The components of rapists' sexual arousal. *Archives of General Psychiatry, 34,* 395-403.

Abel, G. G., & Blanchard, E. B. (1976). The measurement and generation of sexual arousal in male deviates. In M. Hersen, R. M. Eisler, & P. M. Miller (Eds.), *Progress in behavior modification* (Volume 2). New York: Academic Press.

Amorso, D. M., & Brown, M. (1973). Problems in studying the effects of erotic material. *The Journal of Sex Research, 9,* 187-195.

Bach, G. R., & Goldberg, H. (1974). *Creative aggression.* New York: Doubleday.

Bach, G. R., & Wyden, P. (1969). *The intimate enemy.* New York: William Morrow.

Berne, E. (1964). *Games people play.* New York: Grove Press.

Caldwell, E. (1941). *Tobacco road.* New York: Grosset & Dunlop.

Clark, R. A. (1952). The projective measurement of experimentally induced levels of sexual motivation. *Journal of Experimental Psychology, 44,* 391-399.

Ellison, R. (1947). *Invisible man.* New York: Signet Books.

Feshbach, S., Malamuth, N. M., & Drapkin, R. (1974). The effects of aggression inhibition and aggression facilitation on sexual responsiveness. Paper presented at the meeting of the International Society for Research on Aggression, Toronto, Canada.

Feshbach, S., & Singer, R. (1971). *Television and aggression.* San Francisco: Jossey-Bass.

Feshbach, S., Stiles, W. B., & Bitter, E. (1967). The reinforcing effect of witnessing aggression. *Journal of Experimental Research in Personality, 2,* 133-139.

Fisher, W., & Byrne, D. (1978). Individual differences in affective, evaluative, and behavioral responses to an erotic film. *Journal of Applied Social Psychology, 8,* 355-365.

Freud, S. (1938). Three contributions to the theory of sex. In A. A. Brill (Ed.), *The basic writings of Sigmund Freud.* New York: Random House.

Fromm, E. (1973). *The anatomy of human destructiveness.* Greenwich: Fawcett Crest.

Heiman, J. R. (1977). A psychophysiological exploration of sexual arousal patterns in females and males. *Psychophysiology, 14,* 266-274.

Henson, D., & Rubin, H. (1971). Voluntary control of eroticism. *Journal of Applied Behavior Analysis, 4,* 37-44.

Kinsey, A. C., Pomeroy, W. B., Martin, C. E., & Gebhard, P. H. (1953). *Sexual behavior in the human female.* Philadelphia: Saunders.

LoPiccolo, J., & Miller, V. H. (1975a). A program for enhancing the sexual relationship of normal couples. *The Counseling Psychologist, 5,* 41-45.

LoPiccolo, J., & Miller, V. H. (1975b). Procedural outline sexual enrichment groups. *The Counseling Psychologist, 5,* 46-49.

Malamuth, N. M., Feshbach, S., & Jaffe, Y. (1977). Sexual arousal and aggression: Recent experiments and theoretical issues. *Journal of Social Issues, 33,* 110-133.

Schaefer, H. H., Tregerthan, G. J., & Colgan, A. H. (1976). Measured and self-estimated penile erection. *Behavior Therapy, 7,* 1-7.

Stoller, R. J. (1976). Sexual excitement. *Archives of General Psychiatry, 33,* 899-909.

Time Magazine. The porno plague. April 5, 1976, pp. 58-63.

Zillmann, D. (1984). *Connections between sex and aggression.* Hillsdale, NJ: Lawrence Erlbaum.

Chapter 14

At Close Quarters: Personal Space Requirements of Men in Intimate Heterosexual Dyads

Gordon W. Russell, Mary J. Huddle, and
Moreen C. Corson

A select few of our relationships can be described as *intimate,* a term implying at least the potential for moments of endearment and a close physical presence. The close proximity required for intimacy necessarily involves at some point an invasion of another's personal space, defined by one writer as "the area individual humans actively maintain around themselves into which others cannot intrude without arousing discomfort" (Hayduk, 1978, p. 118). Interestingly, the interpersonal distance couples maintain has been shown to predict to the current status of their relationship, i.e., strangers, acquaintances, friends (Haase & Pepper, 1972).

Of course, the status of a relationship seldom remains static. In any developing relationship, occasions necessarily arise when intimacy is tentatively increased by intrusions into one another's personal space. Such advances are typically initiated, although not always, by the male in response to an exchange of implicit and/or explicit signals or cues. Depending upon the setting, the status of the relationship and the internal state of those involved, e.g., moods, intentions, expectations, invasions of personal space may be met with a range of responses from enthusiasm to anger. Thus, welcomed intrusions in one situation may enhance a relationship; unwelcomed intrusions in different circumstances may instead serve as a strong provocation (Kinzel, 1970; Steinmetz, 1977, p. 124). For example, Kinzel (1970) reported that violent prison inmates frequently spoke of their victims as "getting up in my face," although they were at a normal distance for conversation (p. 59).

Inasmuch as the romantic scenario involves a series of discrete decision points (Zimbardo, 1977, p. 93) occurring beyond public view as primary experience — media scripts excepted — any reconstruction of that event must draw from a pool of common knowledge. However, several lines of research provide guides to an understanding of the dynamics present when some developing intimacies suddenly go awry. Schiffenbauer and Schiavo (1976) conducted perhaps the pivotal study in their investigation of the emotional effects arising from invasions of personal space. These researchers have proposed that intrusions into another's personal space produce an *intensification* of the existing mood state(s). That is to say, if an individual is predisposed to affection or liking for the other person, intrusions will serve to heighten such feelings. Otherwise, if one's prior state is that of, for example, mistrust or mild hostility, these feelings too will be intensified, with potentially negative consequences for one or both parties to the relationship. Additionally, the degree of discomfort resulting from an unwelcomed invasion of personal space has been shown to increase with the extent of the incursion (Hayduk, 1981).

A further question concerns the quality of information-processing and/or performance under the stressful conditions that may be created by invasions of personal space (e.g., Curran, Blatchley, & Hanlon, 1978). From the perspective of conceptual complexity theory (Schroder, Driver, & Streufert, 1967), some individuals experiencing sufficiently high levels of stress may revert to a more concrete or simplistic level of information-processing, i.e., decisions involving fewer considerations (dimensions) and tending toward all-or-none distinctions. Moreover, there is typically greater rigidity and a diminished capacity for taking another's point of view. Thus, some persons acutely stressed by intrusions into their personal space may momentarily exercise poor judgment, at least by the standard of their usual behavior. In summary, at least two effects with immediate implications for the course of a relationship can originate with invasions of personal space: the intensification of one's predisposition toward the other party and a deterioration in the quality of judgment.

In those instances where invasions serve as an instigation, one likely outcome is a series of hostile exchanges of escalating intensity (Goldstein, Davis, & Herman, 1975). While the original provocation may seem relatively mild, it must be anticipated that the victim will retaliate, indeed retaliate somewhat more forcefully than her/his "assailant." The retaliation itself is apt to be perceived as another attack, calling for yet a further response, the sequence producing a spiral of increasingly violent exchanges. Once underway, such disputes take on a life of their own with neither party able to easily extricate himself from the hostilities. Baron (1973) has shown that even the threat of a further hurtful retaliation does not deter individuals from aggression against someone once they have been angered by that person. Whereas the outcome is often serious, occasionally fatal, the original provocation is usually trivial. Studies have consistently revealed that homicides involving intimates frequently begin over petty issues (see review by Zahn, 1980).

Our ability to accurately read and infer one another's state from nonverbal cues is at best imperfect (Argyle, 1975). However, the difficulty is further compounded when one brings to intimate situations a deeply held and culturally reinforced set of beliefs, beliefs which can override contrary evidence and which can cause, for example, the male to discount or misinterpret a female's plea to desist in his advances. Thus, men who believe that women both invite and enjoy the use of force in sexual relationships would predictably disregard a woman's statements that she wished no further intimacy. For women involved with men subscribing to these rape myths, or with men who regard violence as appropriate to a normal relationship (Burt, 1980), the implications for their well being are as serious as they are obvious. Recent experimental evidence is quite convincing on this point (Malamuth, 1983; Malamuth & Check, 1982). Men who are accepting of rape myths and interpersonal violence in relationships with women were found to direct more aggression against a female confederate and express a greater desire to hurt her than others not sharing such attitudes.

Reviews of studies on personal space (e.g., Hayduk, 1978, 1983) have provided general support for the hypothesis that violent individuals maintain a larger personal space than nonviolent persons. Furthermore, these same individuals and others requiring greater interpersonal space characteristically react more strongly to intrusions (Hayduk, 1981). Studies that have addressed questions related to the *shape* of personal space have generally reported that frontal distances are slightly greater than those tolerated at the rear (Hayduk, 1983). However, investigations using prison inmates and/or delinquents as subjects typically report larger rear areas.

Insofar as aggression against women is a central theme (Burt, 1980) and likely consequence of rape myths (e.g., Malamuth, 1983), those men holding such beliefs and/or those whose attitudes normalize the role of violence in their relations with women would predictably seek to establish greater interpersonal distances in potentially intimate situations. Moreover, when the social skills that might facilitate intimate experiences are also deficient, greater interpersonal distances will again be established, with anger, frequently a concomitant of shyness (Zimbardo, 1977), remaining as a negative element in their relationships. Thus, the present investigation sought to test the hypotheses that males who are shy, assaultive, or regard aggression as welcomed by females and a normal feature of heterosexual relations share a common need to distance themselves from the all-too-frequent targets of their wrath—women.

The external physical attributes of a person may also influence the interpersonal distance that one establishes. The occurrence of distancing or approach effects is further presumed to be mediated by an arousal mechanism, a view consistent with evidence (Curran et al., 1978) showing that intrusions of personal space produce heightened physiological arousal. This heightened state of arousal then mediates either a response of intimacy or compensatory adjustments of interpersonal distance, depending upon the evaluative label (positive or negative) that one applies to her/his internal state (Patterson, 1976). For example, Nesbitt and Steven (1974) had an attractive female confederate stand in lines at an amusement park dressed either in a conservative blouse and skirt or in "an ankle-length dress of gold jersey with a high lustre." Men established greater distances in the latter condition. While the researchers chose to interpret their findings in terms of a "stimulus intensity" concept, their procedure provided for an equally valid representation of "arousal."

The present design attempts to draw a sharper distinction between levels of arousal in operationalizing a normal state as a conservative dress condition and an aroused state as a more revealing "swimsuit" condition. The present investigation provides for testing the relationships between the individual-differences variables described above and men's personal space needs in dyadic interactions with women; these same variables also predict to sexual assault (e.g., Check & Malamuth, 1983; Zimbardo, 1977).

Numerous experiential variables originating during formative periods in the socialization process might also be expected to influence the quality of men's interactions with women. For example, Goldstein (1973) has reported that rapists— dispositionally shy (Zimbardo, 1977) and by definition assaultive — had less exposure to erotica during adolescence than control subjects. Similarly, the frequency of reading *Playboy* and *Penthouse* magazines has been linked to the self-reported likelihood of raping (Malamuth & Check, 1981). Thus, in the interests of expanding the nomological net, exposure to erotica was explored in relation to the major variables by means of a supplemental item.

METHOD

Subjects
The experimental subjects (N = 73) were male volunteers recruited from Introductory Psychology sections at the University of Lethbridge. The men averaged 20.26 years of age (SD = 3.61), 88% of whom were single, 11% married and 1% other. Their participation earned a bonus research credit in the course.

Measures
Measures of the four independent variables were administered individually to treatment and control subjects. Included in the battery was a six-item scale of social anxiety, i.e., shyness, presented as part of the entire 23-item Self-Conscious-

ness Scale (Buss, 1980). Subjects provided self ratings of shyness e.g., "I get embarrassed very easily," on 5-point scales anchored by "Extremely Characteristic" to "Extremely Uncharacteristic."

Burt's (1980) Acceptance of Interpersonal Violence (AIV) scale (6 items) measures attitudes endorsing coercion as a legitimate tactic in gaining compliance in intimate and sexual relationships. An example of an item from the scale is: "Sometimes the only way a man can get a cold woman turned on is to use force." Subjects are asked to indicate the extent of their agreement on 7-point scales ranging from "Strongly Agree" to "Strongly Disagree."

The 19-item Rape Myth Acceptance (RMA) scale (Burt, 1980) was designed to assess the extent to which males endorse a set of beliefs involving the use of force and the role of females in inviting sexual advances. The items include: "When women go around braless or wearing short skirts and tight tops, they are just asking for trouble."

The Assault subscale of the Buss-Durkee (B-D) Hostility Inventory (Buss & Durkee, 1957) contains ten true-false items and purports to assess the extent to which one characteristically resorts to physical aggression when provoked. A typical item is: "I have known people who pushed me so far that we came to blows." Unlike most other subscales of the B-D inventory, the assault measure has been found to be unrelated to the biasing effects of a social desirability response style among males in the present student population (Russell, 1981). As with the AIV and RMA scales, the assault items were embedded among a substantial number of filler items.

Inasmuch as circumstances required that subjects complete the paper-and-pencil measures following their participation in the treatment conditions, a control group (N = 17) was constituted of subjects who were not exposed to the experimental procedures. This allowed a check on the possibility of scores being affected by influences arising from the experimental experience itself rather than reflecting a presumably stable set of beliefs and traits.

Procedure

The experiment was conducted in a large white room (35 x 23 feet) devoid of furnishings except for a table, chair and cabinet along a side wall. Several variables, e.g., odor, color, previously shown to influence personal space (Gilmour & Walkey, 1981; Nesbitt & Steven, 1974) were specifically controlled in the present design. A professional model, whose role is described below, wore the same hairstyle and faint perfume at all experimental sessions. She was clad in either a burgundy wool knit dress (unaroused condition) or a one-piece swimsuit of the same color (aroused condition).

Each subject was met in a reception area by a male experimental assistant who directed him through a door and down a corridor to the laboratory. There the principal investigator thanked the subject for keeping his appointment and in-

Figure 14.1   Model approaches subject as judges record closest distance between them

troduced him to the model and the two co-investigators, who stood at some distance, clipboards in hand. Subjects in the dress and swimsuit conditions (randomly assigned) were instructed as follows:

> What we would like you to do in a moment is to stand in the center of the room facing the far wall with your feet together and your hands at your sides. Then Peggy will slowly approach you from different angles and you are to say: "Stop!" when you start to feel uncomfortable or when you think she is too close. Is that fairly clear? Now, if you would rather not continue it is perfectly okay. You will still be given your research participation credit [none withdrew]. Okay then, Peggy will...[the specifics from above were repeated]. Keep your shoulders square to the front, i.e., don't swing around

when she approaches from the back angles, but by all means turn your head to watch her from the corner of your eye. Do you have any questions?

As can be seen in Figure 14.1, the model approached the subject from each of eight randomly ordered directions. The distance tolerated by a subject was taken as the distance between the toe of the model's leading foot and the nearest point on the perimeter of the subject's body when he said "Stop!" The distances were independently judged and recorded by the female co-investigators, who were aided in their task by inconspicuous tabs placed along each line of advance. Throughout her measured approaches, the model fixed her gaze on the subject's shoulder area, avoiding eye contact. When subjects failed to check her advance, she stopped just short of a collision, the distance being recorded as zero.

Subjects were thanked and directed back to the reception area, where the experimental assistant had them complete a questionnaire that included the battery of measures described above. The men were first asked to rate the model's physical attractiveness on a 10-point scale just as they, in turn, had been rated during the experimental session by the two female researchers. Next, subjects completed self-report measures of their mood states during the experiment proper. These ratings were made on a set of 7-point, bipolar adjective scales anchored by: nervous — not nervous; pleasant — unpleasant; aroused — unaroused; tense — relaxed; embarrassed — not embarrassed; guilty — not guilty. Subjects then completed the principal measures of shyness, the AIV and the RMA scales, the B-D assault subscale, and the supplemental question asking about their earliest exposure to erotica. Specifically, subjects were asked the age at which they first "read" *Playboy* and/or *Penthouse* magazines. Those men assigned to the control condition were not exposed to the experimental treatment and completed only the battery of principal measures in the reception area.

RESULTS AND DISCUSSION

A preliminary assessment of the measures and the effectiveness of the procedures was undertaken. Subjects rated the model as equally attractive in the dress (M = 8.42, SD = 1.07) and swimsuit (M = 8.62, SD = .98) conditions (t < 1). Apparently, more revealing attire does little to enhance men's appreciation of a beautiful woman. However, it is equally plausible to suggest that differences in their ratings of attractiveness may have been masked by a ceiling effect. The judges' independent ratings of each subject's physical attractiveness yielded a reliability coefficient which was unacceptably low (r = .69) and, consequently, several planned analyses were not pursued. In contrast, the reliability of their interpersonal distance estimates was .996. Finally, subjects in the treatment and control conditions did not differ significantly in their scores on the shyness, AIV, RMA, and assault scales.

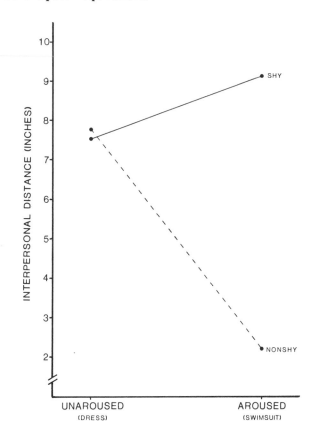

Figure 14.2 Interpersonal distance requirements of shy vs. nonshy men under two levels of arousal.

The principal analyses produced an interesting pattern of results.* A 2 (unaroused vs aroused) x 2 (high vs low shy) ANOVA, the results of which are presented in Figure 14.2, yielded differences on shyness, $F(1,51) = 5.66$, $p < .05$, and a significant arousal x shyness interaction, $F(1,51) = 6.61$, $p < .02$. Although shy subjects were expected to keep the model at a greater distance than nonshy subjects regardless of her attire (Zimbardo, 1977), they did so only in the swimsuit condition. Nonshy men allowed closer approaches by the model in the swimsuit condition than those with the model in the dress condition, $t(25) = 2.99$, $p < .005$, whereas shy men kept her at the same distance in both conditions, $t < 1$.

---

* Median scores on each measure of the four independent variables were excluded from their respective analyses to create two more homogeneous groups.

Finally, analyses of the shapes of personal space failed to reveal any significant differences between the frontal and rear distances of either shy or nonshy subjects.

An explanation emphasizing their interpretation of the situation perhaps offers the most parsimonious account of the dynamics underlying the behaviors of shy and nonshy subjects. The presence of three older experimenters in a formal laboratory setting virtually ensured that the subjects' behavior would be circumspect in regard to the model, i.e., "appropriate" distances maintained. Most likely, these demand characteristics act more to restrain the approach tendencies of nonshys than to encourage closer approaches by shy subjects. However, the model's appearance in a swimsuit signaled a less decorous, more permissive atmosphere with unmistakable sexual overtones. Shy men typically experience sexually toned encounters as threatening, inasmuch as they possess relatively fewer social skills, have less sexual experience, and feel anxious in novel situations (Zimbardo, 1977, p. 94). Indeed, the present supplemental ratings indicate that shys in the swimsuit condition were more aroused, t (27) $=$ 1.85, $p < .05$; nervous, t (27) $=$ 2.07, $p < .025$; tense, t (27) $=$ 4.41, $p < .0005$; and embarrassed, t (27) $=$ 3.07, $p < .005$ than their nonshy counterparts. In the dress condition, shy subjects described their state only as more nervous, t (24) $=$ 2.53, $p < .02$ and tense, t (23) $=$ 2.39, $p < .05$. However, despite the shys' need to distance themselves from the model and the more extreme emotional states they experienced in her presence, there is no evidence to suggest that they underwent a negative experience. To the contrary, shy and nonshy subjects alike rated their states in all conditions as extremely pleasant and virtually free of guilt.

The failure of the shys to match the approach responses of the nonshys to the scantily clothed model may in large measure be attributed to the greater stress they subjectively experienced in the high arousal condition. Situations that are stressful or threatening to people have previously been shown (Dosey & Meisels, 1969) to be associated with needs for greater interpersonal distances. Shys seemingly experienced levels of stress that simply overrode the effects of any approach tendencies countenanced by the informality of the swimsuit condition. For nonshys, who experienced relatively little stress, the presence of permissive cues (Leonard & Taylor, 1983) effectively weakened inhibitions against the attractive prospect of engaging the model at very close quarters.

Interestingly, the high "stimulus intensity" condition of Nesbitt and Steven's (1974) study resulted in greater interpersonal distances, whereas men in the present investigation consistently allowed *closer* approaches in the comparable swimsuit condition. That is to say, separate overlapping analyses of the trait and attitudinal variables yielded generally significant main effects on arousal (swimsuit condition) for AIV, F (1,57) $=$ 5.01, $p < .05$; RMA, F (1,53) $=$ 4.85, $p < .05$; assault, F (1,51) $=$ 3.86, $p < .10$; and, as noted above, shy subjects. A resolution of these discrepant findings is likely to be found in the two totally different re-

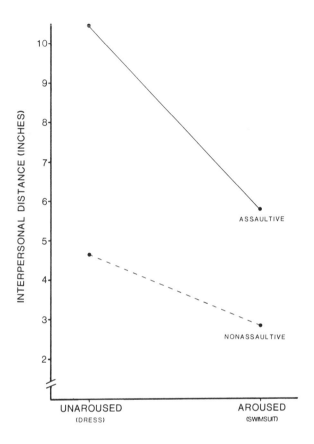

Figure 14.3   Interpersonal distance requirements of assaultive vs. nonassaultive men under two levels of arousal.

search settings and the men's attributions regarding the role and/or status of the respective confederates.

In marked contrast to the laboratory with its special set of demand characteristics, Nesbitt and Steven (1974) conducted their study in the naturalistic setting of an amusement park, using an unobtrusive measure of personal space. It could be safely assumed that their subjects arrived at a different interpretation of the unescorted and unfamiliar female in the park's concession lines than that reached with regard to the present laboratory confederate, to whom subjects were initially introduced. In the former circumstance, approaches to the female confederate carry the ever-present risk of a bungled involvement, whereas in the latter situation there are fewer unknowns, with close interpersonal distances clearly sanctioned in the preliminary instructions to subjects. Taken together, these two findings highlight the critical importance of contextual influences in determining whether approach or distancing behavior will occur.

As presented in Figure 14.3, analysis of the assault data resulted in significant main effects for assault, $F (1,51) = 7.34$, $p < .01$, and again, marginal effects in the case of arousal. The interaction term was nonsignificant. In addition to maintaining a larger personal space, assaultive men described themselves as more nervous, $t(25) = 2.77$, $p < .02$, in the presence of the model although, unlike shys, they tolerated somewhat closer approaches in the swimsuit condition. Finally, the analyses of shape failed to reveal significant differences between the frontal and rear distances established by our subjects in either the assaultive or nonassaultive conditions. The need for a larger rear zone appears to be largely confined to deviant populations.

Previous findings that violent offenders require greater personal space (e.g., Curran et al., 1978; Gilmour & Walkey, 1981; Kinzel, 1970) are thus supported and, additionally, are extended by the present investigation to include assaultive male students in their interactions with women under different levels of arousal. However, unlike our shy subjects, these men are predisposed to resort to physical aggression when provoked.* Thus, inasmuch as individuals requiring greater personal space, shy and assaultive males in the present circumstance, generally react more strongly toward intruders (Hayduk, 1981), the consequences of an unwelcomed intrusion would be predictably more serious in the latter case. In all likelihood, such victims frequently misjudge their partner's motive for reacting violently insofar as it occurred at distances commonly regarded as appropriate to the ongoing activity or status of the relationship.

Neither AIV nor RMA scores was successful in predicting those who have needs for greater personal space, $F (1,57) < 1$; $F (1,53) = 1.38\ ns$, respectively. The interaction terms were also nonsignificant. However, as previously noted, men in the swimsuit conditions of both analyses tolerated closer approaches by the model than their counterparts assigned to the dress conditions. The failure of men scoring high on AIV and RMA to establish greater interpersonal distances seemingly contradicts the present analyses of assault data and considerable evidence (Hayduk, 1983) that violent individuals generally require greater personal space. However, the AIV and RMA scales, themselves related $r = 0.53$, $p < .005$, tap a domain of attitude/beliefs in which aggression and coercion are normalized or used as a tactic specifically in relations with women. In contrast, the B-D assault items assess generally aggressive behaviors that are nonspecific as to situations or the sex of targets. It may be that men who are accepting of vi-

---

* Assaultiveness and shyness were unrelated in the present investigation, $r = .09, ns$.

olence in relations with women and/or adhere to rape myths are not overly aggressive in other situations. This suggestion has previously been put forward by Malamuth and Check (1982) with reference to the AIV scale. However, the present pattern of intercorrelations offers little support for the suggestion. Although assault scores were unrelated to RMA (r = .12, *ns*) they were significantly correlated with AIV (r = .25, p < .025). It might also be noted, but only parenthetically, that an ex post facto analysis involving the Zaks and Walters (1959) aggression scale used as a source of filler items yielded significant relationships with AIV (r = .33, p < .005) *and* RMA (r = .32, p < .005).

Thus, violent men may have needs for greater personal space in most day-to-day situations, situations where their aggression is likely to meet with disapproval. However, if some of these same men have learned that coercion and force are approved or even welcomed as tactics in encounters with females, then their apparent aloofness, their tendency to physically distance themselves from others, may well vanish in the special circumstance of their interactions with women.

An exploration of the correlates of early exposure to erotica resulted in several interesting relationships. Subjects' ages and the ages at which they first read *Playboy* and/or *Penthouse* were significantly related, r = .36, p < .005. The magnitude of the correlation was somewhat surprising considering the limited age range (17 to 31 years) of our subjects. In all likelihood, the relationship reflects a decade of rapidly increasing public acceptance of these magazines and an expanded market among younger consumers. Early exposure to erotica was also associated with more favorable ratings of the model's attractiveness (r = -.23, p < .05) and, most importantly, higher scores on the B-D assault scale (r = -.33, p < .005). However, age of first exposure was unrelated to AIV (r = .03, *ns*); RMA (r = .07, *ns*); and shyness (r = .03, *ns*). The strong association between early exposure and general assaultiveness should be viewed alongside earlier findings (see review by Check & Malamuth, 1982; Goldstein, 1973) showing relationships between deviant sexual practices and extensive exposure to pornography at younger ages. In a related study, Malamuth and Check (1981) reported that the *frequency* of reading *Playboy* and *Penthouse* was strongly correlated with the use of sexual coercion and men's self-reported likelihood of raping. Overall, these findings accord well with those of Zillmann and Bryant (e.g., 1982, 1986), whose work calls into question a common assumption that no ill effects are produced by extended exposure to the more benign, standard erotic fare.

In consideration of a related issue, Prescott (1977) has advanced the plausible suggestion that increasing physical contact may serve as an effective means of reducing aggression between individuals and between nations. Based upon findings that those cultures that are characterized by greater interpersonal distances also tend to be more authoritarian, punitive, and aggressive, the suggested strategy of lessening taboos against touching or intimate distances holds promise for reducing conflict. Programs intended to foster intimacy and reduce shyness at the individual level (e.g., Whitman & Quinsey, 1981; Zimbardo, 1977) have already shown success. However, it is a further question whether a reduction in aggressivity necessarily follows on the heels of an improvement in social skills. It is suggested that the effectiveness of social skills programs specifically addressing the needs of men in assaultive relationships with women stands to be increased by a recognition of several recent lines of research.

Firstly, programs should be carefully tailored to take into account the *meanings* that intimate situations hold for men. For example, analysis of Thematic Apperception Test stories written in response to affiliative situations has led Pollak and Gilligan (1982) to conclude that men's fear of intimacy may underlie their violence in social relationships. Indeed, one could reasonably interpret the self-reports of heightened nervousness and tenseness by the present shy and assaultive subjects as reflecting a state of fear. Pollak and Gilligan further observe that women seeking safety in relationships with men, relationships that some men, in turn, perceive as dangerous and potentially explosive, may often be inadvertently placing themselves in even greater peril.

Secondly, it would seem important to capitalize on recent evidence (Check, 1984) attesting to the fragile nature of rape myths in the design of social skills programs for the treatment of violent offenders. Successful treatment is much more likely to follow from multifaceted programs incorporating variables demonstrated to be *causally* related to the unwanted behavior. Such is likely the case with rape myths (Malamuth, 1983) and, if so, they may prove relatively easy to dispel even among an offender group. While a worthwhile goal in its own right, it would be naive to assume that improving social skills will necessarily result in a lower incidence of assaults against women. One result could see friendlier rapists!

The effectiveness of programs fostering the development of social skills and/or intimacy with a view to reducing antisocial behavior will ultimately have to be judged against an appropriate behavioral criterion, e.g., a subsequent lowered rate of recidivism for sexual assault. This same evaluation is, of course, also required of other therapeutic approaches to the treatment of men who are violent in their dealings with women. Success in these efforts will only be realized with the most thoughtful application of research findings, a recognition of the heterogeneous composition of offender categories, and provision for the continuing evaluation of programs against valid criteria.

ACKNOWLEDGMENT

The authors wish to thank Peggy L. Schramm, who served as our experimental confederate with grace and competence. Dr. Leslie A. Hayduk kindly offered comment on an earlier version of the manuscript. Thanks also to Professor David G. P. Spinks and John G. Baker for their assistance to the project.

REFERENCES

Argyle, M. (1975). *Bodily communications.* London: Methuen.

Baron, R. A. (1973). Threatened retaliation from the victim as an inhibitor of physical aggression. *Journal of Research in Personality, 7,* 103-115.

Burt, M. R. (1980). Cultural myths and supports for rape. *Journal of Personality and Social Psychology, 38,* 217-230.

Buss, A. H. (1980). *Self-consciousness and social anxiety.* San Francisco: W. H. Freeman.

Buss, A. H., & Durkee, A. (1957). An inventory for assessing different kinds of hostility. *Journal of Consulting Psychology, 21,* 343-349.

Check, J. V. P. (1984, June). Counteracting the effects of violent pornography: An application of the attitude change research. Paper presented at the meeting of the Canadian Psychological Association, Ottawa, Canada.

Check, J. V. P., & Malamuth, N. M. (1982, August). Pornography and sexual aggression: A social learning theory analysis. Paper presented at the meeting of the International Society for Research on Aggression, Mexico City.

Check, J. V. P., & Malamuth, N. M. (1983). Sex role stereotyping and reactions to depictions of stranger versus acquaintance rape. *Journal of Personality and Social Psychology 45,* 344-356.

Curran, S. F., Blatchley, R. J., & Hanlon, T. E. (1978). The relationship between body buffer zone and violence as assessed by subjective and objective techniques. *Criminal Justice and Behavior, 5,* 53-62.

Dosey, M., & Meisels, M. (1969). Personal space and self protection. *Journal of Personality and Social Psychology, 11,* 93-97.

Gilmour, D. R., & Walkey, F. H. (1981). Identifying violent offenders using a video measure of interpersonal distance. *Journal of Consulting and Clinical Psychology, 49,* 287-291.

Goldstein, J. H., Davis, R. W., & Herman, D. (1975). Escalation of aggression: Experimental studies. *Journal of Personality and Social Psychology, 31,* 162-170.

Goldstein, M. J. (1973). Exposure to erotic stimuli and sexual deviance. *Journal of Social Issues, 29,* 197-219.

Haase, R. S., & Pepper, D. T. (1972). Nonverbal components of empathic communication. *Journal of Counseling Psychology, 19,* 417-424.

Hayduk, L. A. (1978). Personal space: An evaluative and orienting overview. *Psychological Bulletin, 85,* 117-134.

Hayduk, L. A. (1981). The permeability of personal space. *Canadian Journal of Behavioural Science, 13,* 274-287.

Hayduk, L. A. (1983). Personal space: Where we now stand. *Psychological Bulletin, 94,* 293-335.

Kinzel, A. F. (1970). Body-buffer zone in violent prisoners. *American Journal of Psychiatry, 127,* 59-64.

Leonard, K. E., & Taylor, S. P. (1983). Exposure to pornography, permissive and nonpermissive cues, and male aggression toward females. *Motivation and Emotion, 7,* 291-299.

Malamuth, N. M. (1983). Factors associated with rape as predictors of laboratory aggression against women. *Journal of Personality and Social Psychology, 45,* 432-442.

Malamuth, N. M., & Check, J. V. P. (1981). The effects of exposure to aggressive pornography: Rape proclivity, sexual arousal, and beliefs in rape myths. Paper presented at the meeting of the American Psychological Association, Los Angeles.

Malamuth, N. M., & Check, J. V. P. (1982, June). Factors related to aggression against women. Paper presented at the meeting of the Canadian Psychological Association, Montreal, Canada.

Nesbitt, P. D., & Steven, G. (1974). Personal space and stimulus intensity at a Southern California amusement park. *Sociometry, 37,* 105-115.

Patterson, M. L. (1976). An arousal model of interpersonal intimacy. *Psychological Review, 83,* 235-245.

Pollak, S., & Gilligan, C. (1982). Images of violence in Thematic Apperception Test stories. *Journal of Personality and Social Psychology, 42,* 159-167.

Prescott, J. (1977). Body pleasure and the origins of violence. In P. G. Zimbardo & C. Maslach (Eds.), *Psychology for our times* (pp. 336-344). Glenview, IL: Scott Foresman.

Russell, G. W. (1981). A comparison of hostility measures. *Journal of Social Psychology, 113,* 45-55.

Schroder, H. M., Driver, M. J., & Streufert, S. (1967). *Human information processing.* New York: Holt, Rinehart & Winston.

Schiffenbauer, A., & Schiavo, R. S. (1976). Physical distance and attraction: An intensification effect. *Journal of Experimental Social Psychology, 12,* 274-282.

Steinmetz, S. K. (1977). *The cycle of violence.* New York: Praeger.

Whitman, W. P., & Quinsey, V. L. (1981). Heterosocial skill training for institutionalized rapists and child molesters. *Canadian Journal of Behavioural Science, 13,* 105-114.

Zahn, M. A. (1980). Homicide in the twentieth century United States. In J. A. Inciardi & C. E. Faupel (Eds.), *History and crime* (pp. 111-131). Beverly Hills, CA: Sage.

Zaks, M. S., & Walters, R. H. (1959). First steps in the construction of a scale for the measurement of aggression. *Journal of Psychology, 47,* 199-208.

Zillmann, D., & Bryant, J. (1982). Pornography, sexual callousness, and the trivialization of rape. *Journal of Communication, 32,* 10-21.

Zillmann, D., & Bryant, J. (1986). Shifting preferences in pornography consumption. *Communication Research, 13,* 560-578.

Zimbardo, P. G. (1977). *Shyness.* Reading, MA: Addison-Wesley.

Chapter 15
Intra-Familial Violence: Training Police For Effective Interventions

J. Edwin Boyd*

INTRODUCTION

It has been the experience of most North American police departments within the past few decades that the demands placed on police time and resources have expanded beyond the traditional law enforcement role. In particular this increase has become noticeable in the domain of domestic crises and intrafamily conflict (Bercal, 1970; Cummings, 1970; Gammon, 1978; Loving, 1980). Domestic disputes cover a wide range of phenomena including wife-beating, child abuse, landlord-tenant disputes, and child custody arguments. When the level of violence and/or disturbance becomes sufficiently great, the police are often called, either by one of the disputants, or perhaps a neighbor, to intervene and settle the dispute.

Police agencies represent the major and perhaps most universally available social service agency with a mobile capacity (service goes to client) to respond to crises on a 24-hour basis. They further represent the power and authority required to have a significant impact upon individuals who become involved in such domestic crises.

A distinction is frequently made between "peacekeeping" activities of police and "law enforcement" activities. Police agencies sometimes see these activities as being in conflict. The law enforcement role has in the past been considered

* This research was carried out at Royal Canadian Mounted Police Depot Division, Regina, Saskatchewan, and The University of Calgary, under DSS contract No. OSU 80-00265 under the auspices of the Solicitor-General of Canada. The views expressed in this report are those of the author and do not reflect the views or policies of the R.C.M.P. or the Solicitor-General.

the traditional or important activity for police, with peacekeeping getting much less attention. Police have not always been comfortable with their peacekeeping role in domestic crisis interventions, (Bard, 1969; Zacker & Bard, 1973; Barocas, 1973; Novaco, 1975) and have preferred instead to pursue the law enforcement route.

Another factor adding to police ambivalence about domestic disputes relates to the sanctity of the private household. The attitude in our society has been that whatever happens within the family confines ought not to be interfered with by outsiders. The domestic dispute situation focuses attention on the dilemma inherent in the two police roles. On the one hand, police agencies reflect our attitude of family privacy and are reluctant to intervene. On the other hand, violent behavior can constitute assault and can be the object of law enforcement activity.

The domestic dispute represents a conflict amongst a number of sets of rights: the rights of the individual family member, the rights of the family as a unit, and the rights and obligations of society at large. The policeman is regularly asked to decide on the spot which parties' rights should prevail. Whether the situation is talked out, referred to a counseling service, or proceeds on to court is dependent on the decision of the individual police officer.

The increasing involvement of police agencies in domestic conflict as a result of changing attitudes has been thoroughly documented (Levens & Dutton, 1977; Liebman & Schwarz, 1972; Martin, 1976; Straus, 1977). In addition, police injuries and deaths have resulted during attempts to resolve domestic disputes. The skills and knowledge required to resolve these disputes successfully have therefore become of great importance in police training programs.

Domestic Conflict Intervention Training

A pioneering work by Bard and Berkowitz (1967) examined the effectiveness of domestic crisis training for police officers. It included a series of hypotheses centered on the reduction and prevention of recurring domestic violence through a synthesis of mental health skills and police manpower. The question addressed was whether or not teaching mental health skills to police interveners would increase police effectiveness and hence form a new source of mental health manpower. It was anticipated that if the training were effective, there would be a reduction in domestic complaints across the target area (a precinct of New York city slums), there would be a reduction in the homicide rate, and the number of repeat calls would diminish. The independent variable manipulation involved 160 hours of instruction delivered to 18 self-selected and experienced policemen.

In spite of a great deal of publicity, many of the hypotheses in this study were unsubstantiated. The expectation – that 18 experienced patrolmen, given 160 hours of training, could effect a significant decrease in domestic complaints across an entire precinct of New York slums, that repeat calls would be reduced, or that family homicide rates would go down – is recognized today as little more than wishful thinking. In retrospect it would seem that the potency of the training was greatly overestimated. Alternatively, perhaps the task was underestimated and the resulting set of criterion variables were largely insensitive to the manipulation of the training conditions.

This initial study did, however, set the tone of future research on the strength of two important issues. First, death and injury to police officers involved in domestic interventions in the previous year represented 32% of the total fatality rate and 40% of the injury rate. The reduction of these deaths and injuries amongst the group of trained officers was an impressive, even if somewhat indirect or limited confirmation of training effectiveness. Within the police community, the strength of this finding alone gave instant credibility to the notion of training policemen to manage domestic conflict.

The second major issue that emerged as a result of the Bard and Berkowitz study was related to the method of training. Experiential learning in the form of live acted simulations of domestic conflicts were utilized in the training program. This method capitalized on a major theme in police training, which was that of growing dissatisfaction with the traditional didactic or cognitive approach to training (McNamara, 1967). McNamara, also working in conjunction with the New York Police Department, published a study identifying a lack of interpersonal skills as a major source of uncertainty and ineffectiveness in police work. He wrote:

> We have seen that the academy's attempt to prepare recruits for the problems associated with face to face interaction was problematic with respect to the appropriateness of content...and with respect to the pedogogical methods used to transmit this knowledge, that is, the classroom lecture. Further the reluctance of the academy to develop a comprehensive series of field training exercises was particularly problematic in regard to the development of interpersonal skill of the recruits. (p. 250)

McNamara's emphasis on the reduction of casualties and on more innovative teaching methods made this study a milestone in its field. It precipitated a rapid proliferation of training programs in police departments throughout North America (Levens, 1978).

In support of this trend, Zacker and Bard (1973) observe that a cognitive or didactic training format representing the "passive" mode of learning is best for procedural training which does not require the exercise of individual judgment to the extent that is required of police officers. Information received in a passive mode hinders an individual who must translate it into the active mode required in his daily functioning (Zacker & Bard, 1973, p. 207).

The difference between *experiential* (active) and *classroom* (passive) learning are of central importance in determining the optimal set of activities through which a training establishment can promote maximum skill in conflict management with minimum investment of time and resources. The experiential mode of training in the form of live, acted dramatization of domestic conflicts has been incorporated almost universally in such training (Bard & Berkowitz, 1967; Zacker & Bard, 1973; Doornink, 1975; Driscoll, Meyer, & Schanie, 1973; Schrieber, 1977; Schwalb, 1976).

The popular appeal of the experiential mode is not unique to police training (Raser, 1969; Schulz & Sullivan, 1972). Entire journals pertaining to simulation and to simulation gaming have recently appeared. However, a recent review of this literature (Bell, Boudreau, Fish, Killip, & Milloy, 1981) demonstrated that, despite profuse numbers of publications and tremendously diverse applications, simulation techniques have not been adequately evaluated. Those efforts that have been made have not produced much support for the effectiveness of simulation learning (Palys, 1978; Parasuraman, 1981; Pierfy, 1977). The exception is the use of simulation training in relation to learning psychomotor tasks, such as driving a car and flying an airplane. The incorporation of this training strategy in a variety of educational and training milieus appears to be fostered more by its own intrinsic appeal and face validity than by empirical substantiation of its worth.

The relevant functions of simulation identified by Bell et al. (1981) appear to be "simulation as research" and "simulation as training/education." Many police agencies use simulation in training, and assume that its impact is significant. The design of research using simulation methods attempts to test hypotheses related to the training function. A test of the correspondence of the training function with the research methods in the same performance domain would be a first step in substantiating the ecological validity of simulation methods. If simulation in training produces significant results in research tests, our confidence in simulation methods is thereby increased.

A reasonable argument can be set forth describing the rationale through which experiential learning ought to be included in domestic training. With few exceptions, experiential learning creates believers of those who utilize it judiciously. The appeal of simulation techniques appears so strong that we have forgotten to ask whether we engage it for the "sake of the game" — because it has pleasurable, stimulating, and dramatic properties — or in fact if it has utility in achieving the training objectives that pertain to domestic conflict management.

None of the major works which has been discussed thus far has examined exactly what any of these different training strategies actually achieves. We can conclude on the basis of these early studies that performance changes, which occur as a result of the various training approaches, are for the most part beneficial and useful, both to the police officers and the public (Bard, 1969; Bard & Berkowitz, 1967; Zacker & Bard, 1973; Driscoll et al., 1973), but specificity in regard to the effects of training is lacking in these earlier studies.

A first step in furthering the knowledge base in this domain is the establishment of a full range of performance skills which are deemed necessary for optimal police management of domestic conflict. The creation of a valid and reliable behaviorally anchored rating scale (Smith & Kendall, 1963) explicating the objectives of training and at the same time facilitating the establishment of performance standards can thus be achieved. Objective ratings can be made regarding the officer's use of external safety techniques, physical control procedures, interviewing ability, and so on.

If such an instrument can be developed, then pertinent questions regarding optimal training conditions can be examined. The interaction between experiential, didactic and observational learning methods can be investigated. The contribution of general police training with and without specific training in conflict management can be assessed. The important variable of amounts of practice can be evaluated for rates of return and transfer of training effects across different sets of intervention skills. Skill levels of officers with varying amounts of service can be investigated and yield data regarding the need for, and type of, in-service training that may be required. From the training perspective, answers to the foregoing questions are imperative to future development in domestic conflict training.

In order to address some of the foregoing questions, a field experiment was conducted at the Depot Division R.C.M.P. Police Academy in Regina, Saskatchewan. A sensitive and reliable performance measure was created to assess the quality of domestic interventions done by recruit trainees on a variety of actor-simulated domestic situations involving some violence. The subjects for this experiment consisted of four separate groups of R.C.M.P. trainees. These four groups of recruits (N = 32 each), with different types and amounts of training, intervened in a series of domestic disputes.

The hypotheses to be tested in this field experiment are stated as follows:
1. Fully trained recruits whose training includes a crisis-intervention and conflict-management (CICM) package will display greater skill in managing simulated domestic conflict than fully trained recruits whose training excludes crisis intervention and conflict management.
2. Naive recruits with no training except crisis intervention and conflict management will exhibit greater intervention skill than naive recruits with no training whatsoever.
3. All groups will exhibit increased levels of skill over practice trials.
4. Fully trained recruits with crisis intervention and conflict management training will exhibit greater gains over practice trials than will other groups.

CRITERION DEVELOPMENT

The Domestic Intervention Performance Scale
In order to assess the impact of various independent variable conditions, it was necessary to develop a sensitive measure of performance skills pertaining to all aspects of domestic conflict management. For this purpose the Domestic Inter-

vention Performance (DIP) Scale was developed. It was necessary to address the issues of external validity in regard to establishing optimum outcome criteria. A clear definition of the set of optimum skills regarding how policemen ought to handle "domestics" was required. The result was intended to represent the most effective set of strategies that could be devised; and further that these strategies be perceived not only as effective but as acceptable to the police community in this country [Canada].

The perception of "optimum" performance criteria for a domestic intervention may, of course, vary somewhat across the various interest groups concerned. These different groups may hold differing assumptions regarding both cause and remedy of a domestic dispute. Some, for example, will feel that proactive arrest policy in cases of wife-battering will function as the best remedy and argue for more stringent laws (Hanneman & Lystad, 1975). Others will argue that existing legal frameworks are adequate and that the problem lies in partisan application of the law by predominantly male police services (Loving, 1980). Still others may shun the legal outcome as a viable remedy, preferring counseling and mediational alternatives instead. In approaching the development of the DIP Scale, it was recognized that such controversies existed and that each case is unique. Generalizations, however, are possible and enable the creation of standards and procedures that are almost always applicable. Loving (1980) proposed a methodological procedure which provided the officer "…with a range of successful intervention techniques for handling any criminal violation, protecting the victim, and ensuring officer safety, including: The alternatives available for dealing with a given situation; the factors to consider in choosing among the available alternatives; and the relative weight each factor should have" (p. 81).

The present research has created a set of standards that represent procedures and processes within which "…officers can respond in a manner that will prove useful and effective; be free as possible of personal prejudices and biases; and achieve a reasonable degree of uniformity in handling similar incidents in the community" (Goldstein, 1977, p. 112).

The measurement technique toward which these methods were aimed was the behaviorally anchored rating scales. Police performance in other domains has previously been assessed using these methods (for example, Boyd, 1976; Boyd & Riddell, 1973; Landy, Farr, Saal, & Freitag, 1976).

The development of the definition of criterion performance and scales of measurement began with the use of Flanagan's (1954) critical incident technique. Experienced Mounted Police officers were asked to simply recount both a positive and then a negative intervention in as much detail as possible regarding what they did. It was recognized that the officers participating in the process may not have claim to "superior" ability but they did represent the best approximation, as well as the most likely group, to be able to generate the range of discrete behavioral elements which were being sought. This process generated several hundred discrete behaviors. These behaviors were then presented to a group of instructors at the training depot, who were asked to place these behaviors in categories such that behaviors in each category represented similar aspects of domestic intervention performance. They were asked to limit the number of groups to not more than 15 and then to label each group.

The resulting sub-scales, minus their assigned behaviors, were then presented to 60 recruits, who utilized Smith and Kendall's (1963) retranslation approach to scale construction. Those behavioral items which 80% of the recruits reliably placed back into the original sub-scale were subsequently used by our research committee in developing the first draft of the DIP Scale. Although this first draft was more detailed and contained in its manual a much higher level of specificity than previous work, most of its major categories were found to be in harmony with efforts of police services in Canada.

Finally, to insure further that all aspects of policing were represented, each section within the training division at Depot (e.g., Firearms, Self-defense, Law, Drill staff, Management, etc.) was invited to send one member to sit on a committee to review, evaluate, and learn to employ the DIP Scale. A nine-member committee spent two days learning, discussing, and recommending changes to the DIP Scale and manual. The resulting version of the scale was subsequently pilot-tested by live-rating on three separate occasions with troops of 32 members, who were engaging in simulated domestic interventions as a normal part of their training. Interrater reliability following debriefing sessions between each phase (some 300 live-rated interventions later) yielded estimates of +.87 using Winer's (1962) variance estimation procedure.

The resulting version of the DIP Scale is composed of nine subscales with 57 separate judgments (items) overall. The scale itself is printed on two optical scanning sheets and can be computer-scored. Scales are sequentially ordered so that whether one is live- or video-rating, each subscale is scored as that phase of the intervention is concluded, thus minimizing potential halo effects. Positive points are assigned for correct procedures and negatives are subtracted for incorrect procedures. A range of scores from less than 0 (a highly unlikely performance) to a maximum of 137 points is possible. Although no comprehensive norms are available, total scores are of limited interest, since performance reflected on each subscale is more revealing. Standards of performance required to score individual interventions were incorporated into a scoring manual (Boyd & Bell, 1981). Table 15.1 presents the scale titles and a brief definition of the associated behaviors.

Training of Judges

The choice of raters was influenced by the experience in training a pilot group of staff members from each of the sections at Depot to use the DIP Scale reliably. It became evident that the most sensitive ratings could be attained by in-

Table 15.1. Subscales of the Domestic Intervention Performance (D.I.P.) Scale
and Their Associated Behaviors

	Scale Name	Behaviors
I.	Phone Information	obtaining significant information about the complaint, e.g. name, address, weapons
II.	Approach & Entry	planned, safe approach to the dwelling, gain safe, legal entry
III.	Gaining Physical Control	physical separation of disputants, de-escalation of emotionality
IV.	Understanding the Problem	use of interviewing skills to define the problem and generate acceptable alternative solutions
V.	Seeking Agreement	assisting the clients to come to agreement as to the best solution
VI.	Structure	overall management of episode in cooperation with partner
VII.	Concluding the Intervention	assisting clients to implement solution, then leave safely
VIII.	Police Techniques	proper information-recording, knowledge and explanations of law
IX.	Attitudes	confidence and assertiveness without excess force, with freedom from bias; emotional control and empathy towards problem

dividuals who had two particular bases of knowledge. One was a sound understanding of police procedure and the law. The second was a sensitive understanding of what good interviewing and relationship skills involve. Schwalb (1976) also stresses that these were important knowledge bases for the raters used in her videotape ratings.

Raters were obtained by securing the services of members of the staff at Mobile Family Service Society in Regina, Saskatchewan, Canada. These individuals are professional crisis-interveners who work in conjunction with the Regina City Police, as well as the social service and health network of the city in providing 24-hour immediate mobile response to all manner of crises in the city. These people were, however, naive with respect to the purposes of this experiment.

Twelve members of the mobile staff entered the training sessions. These sessions were held with 6 members at a time, due to the 24- hour staffing needs of their agency. Earlier pilot work which employed staff members at Depot achieved a reliability of .87 using the instrument on live interventions. The use of videotape in rating proved much less taxing than the live ratings. A two-day study session was held with raters using the actual practical training setup and scoring each other via the DIP Scale. Subsequent training was handled by the judges discussing sections of the DIP Scale training manual and rating a series of training tapes. Additional descriptions were provided in the training manual to eliminate potential ambiguities and enhance interrater reliabilities. Interrater reliability estimates were generated using Winer's (1962) variance estimation procedures to generate the coefficient (pp. 124-132). The resulting estimates for the nine subscales ranged from + .84 to + .93, with a median of + .89.

INDEPENDENT VARIABLE CONDITIONS

The three independent variables in the experiment were labeled "Theory," "Training," and "Practice." All three factors represent methods or types of training whose relative contribution in resolving domestic conflict is being assessed in this research. Although these factors were discussed earlier in this chapter, they can now be operationally defined for use in this research.

Theory Condition

Theory, when referred to as one of the independent variable conditions in this research means that set of information which is routinely presented to recruits in a traditional "classroom learning" situation. The predominant style of presentation is the "didactic" form discussed previously. The theory condition consisted of twenty 50-minute periods of lecture material. This material and the manner in which it was taught will be referred to as "CICM Theory." CICM Theory is synonymous with the acute-stage crisis-intervention model proposed earlier. The "no-theory" condition defines the absence of the aforementioned 20 instructional periods.

Training Conditions

The independent variable called "Training" in this research refers to basic police training as it is normally conducted at the Royal Canadian Mounted Police basic training academy. It includes all of the subject areas regularly taught during the 26-week basic training course, with the exceptions of those areas which were part of the experimental manipulation to be discussed shortly. Examples of typical subject areas taught are: firearms training, driver training, physical training, self-defense, operational training, law and court procedure, as well as human relations training.

Practice Condition

The third independent variable condition employed actor-simulated domestic conflicts and was called the "Observation/Practice Factor." This factor was composed of both an active (intervene) and a passive (observe others intervene) dimension. An important element in this condition was debriefing. Debriefing refers to a 15-minute group discussion/lecture, which reviews the elements of each simulated episode according to the principles of CICM (crisis intervention and conflict management), which were taught as part of the Theory condition.

Those groups who did not receive Theory instruction were "pseudo-debriefed." That is, participants discussed their own performance for 15 minutes with the trainer and the rest of their troop, but in this condition the trainer provided no theoretical interpretation. He did not comment on adequateness of performance or offer either praise or criticism that might influence subsequent performance. The Theory groups did experience theoretical interpretation from the instructor during debriefing. Both debriefing and pseudo-debriefing were conducted for their respective groups by the same instructor, who taught the Theory package.

Observation/Practice took place in two full training days (seven 50-minute periods each). The professional actors who staged the improvisations were supplied by Regina's Globe Theatre. Each of these "Globe" days took place in the portion of the practical training complex that contains a simulated residence. During each Globe day, every recruit in the troop (N = 32) intervened in one simulated domestic dispute with a partner and observed 15 other simulated interventions performed by his troopmates. A Globe day therefore contained simulations, each with its own debriefing.

Test Conditions

Live, professionally acted dramatizations of three preselected and standardized situations served as the test circumstances. Three pairs of professional actors were hired, trained, and pretested in their roles to ensure reliable replication of scenarios and a uniform degree of difficulty across actor pairs. The scenarios were modeled on actual cases and chosen on the basis of their representation of police work. Each scenario was modified so as to include the necessity for each intervening officer to display a wide range of required techniques and behaviors. For example, a weapon was not directly involved in all scenarios, but one was at least present in each scene, necessitating that it be removed.

Test simulations differed from the simulations normally employed in training primarily in that their content was confidential and that they were standardized, as referred to earlier. During a test simulation, no troopmates observed and the fourth wall (of movable partitions) enclosed the house. Extraneous influences were thus minimized during testing sessions. Each testing session was videotaped for later rating.

Experimental Assignments

Four groups of subjects were involved in a major experiment to test the impact of the independent variable conditions described earlier. Two of the four groups were in the Training condition and experienced a normal course of basic training to the 20-week, and the 23-week periods respectively. The 20-week group at this stage had received all its basic training with the exception of the human relations section, given from weeks 21 through 23. The other group in the Training condition had received the additional information contained in the human relations package of training and was only two weeks from graduation. The 23-week group is referred to as the Training plus Theory group and the 20-week troop is the Training No Theory condition. The difference between these two groups, then, was that one had received CICM Theory and the other had not.

The two No Training groups on the other hand had no previous training whatsoever. Each arrived at the training division and became involved in the experiment during a one-week period prior to its induction day into training. Hence the training environment had no formal impact on these recruits prior to the research. The first of these groups was a No Training No Theory group while the second group received two days of Theory in lectures, which contained the acute-stage crisis-intervention material identical to that received by the "Training plus Theory" group at the twenty-third week of its training. The Theory condition consisted of 20 periods of lecture material.

Both the foregoing theory and practice areas were taught by a randomly selected member of the human relations teaching staff at Depot. The only consideration in the choice was that he be in his second year as a Depot instructor. That individual was kept blind as to any of the details concerning the nature of the research. Professional non-police lecturers taught two subject areas to each group which received CICM Theory. These two subject areas were the section on juveniles and the section on the legal aspects of family violence.

As described earlier, the observation/practice dimension consisted of experiential learning and had both an active (intervene) and a passive (observe) dimension. All of the groups in the experiment were exposed to both the "Globe" training days.

The observation/practice sessions took place on two separate days; the first, on the day following the first experimental test scenario (T1) and the second, two days later following test number 2 (T2). On each of the three testing days (T1,T2,T3), pairs of recruits reported to the practical training complex as needed throughout the day (approximately 1 hour/pair). Scores were obtained by rating the videotapes made during these testing days.

PROCEDURES

Materials and Apparatus

In order to preserve a high degree of isomorphism between the studio design and the field conditions which were being simulated, some stringent technical obstacles had to be overcome. A studio was created inside the practical training building. It consisted of a two-roomed house with a fully furnished living room and kitchen, which had movable partitions representing the fourth wall. When these partitions were in place they concealed two main cameras, which were operated continuously by camera persons. Two additional cameras were fixed strategically to view the approaches to the home from the outside. Video information was fed into the control room, where a pretrained video technician was in charge of selecting the appropriate monitor to feed into the master tape. A backup recording deck was operated at all times to avoid loss of data through technical error. Split-screen taping ensured that each officer was visible on one-half of the screen at all times, to ensure independent ratings. Dual channel audio pickup permitted separate conversations to be isolated throughout.

Another room, which came to be known colloquially as the "nerve center" contained a master monitor, which allowed an immediate viewing of what was actually going onto the master video tape. A 2-way communication between the nerve center and the control room enabled the video technician to correct for both video and audio shortcomings or malfunctions. In addition, the nerve center was equipped with two closed-circuit telephone lines. One line was hooked directly to the set and enabled the recruits and the actors to make a phone call to anywhere they desired. The phone was actually answered and technical advice supplied if requested (e.g., points of law, referrals, appointments, etc.), according to specified rules for each scenario. The second telephone in the nerve center was equipped with an audio tape to record complaint calls made from the nerve center to another room designated as "Buffalo Detachment RCMP." Each officer independently answered a time-limited phone complaint made by one of the actors prior to each intervention.

An additional room was equipped with a full range of sizes of mounted police uniforms, boots, Sam Browns, etc. (as well as specially "plugged" revolvers) so that all recruits and officers wore an identical uniform during the intervention. Since some groups of subjects had not yet been issued uniforms and others had rank clearly marked on them, a common uniform reduced these potential sources of confound for the actors. This room was also used for recruit questionnaires after each intervention was complete, and for debriefing purposes.

Experimental Test Procedure

The recruit subjects had been randomly assigned to their troops before their arrival for training. Each of the four troops was then assigned to one of the four experimental treatment conditions. Testing was performed on three different days for each troop, separated by the observation/practice days.

Recruits performed interventions in pairs. Each recruit worked only once with each partner, and was exposed to each of the three actor pairs only once. The test simulation scenarios were the same throughout any one testing day. Day 1 was a child custody dispute, day 2 was an abortion conflict and day 3, a wife-battering. This was done to minimize confounds from information that might pass amongst the recruits.

Testing began at 6:30 a.m. each day. On entering the facility, each pair was directed to the dressing area, fitted for a uniform, dressed, and equipped with a specially welded pistol. No participants were permitted to take their own weapons into a simulation, for obvious reasons. Once outfitted, each officer in turn was placed into the simulated detachment office, where he received a phone call from a complainant. The phone call was standardized at 60 seconds duration in order to encourage the recruit to do most of his fact finding in person during the intervention. After each officer had independently handled the same complaint call, they both were allowed a five-minute discussion period before a red studio light signaled that they should leave the building and proceed to the "house" at "69 Depot Street." They were instructed to handle the situation they encountered in the same manner they felt it should be done in the field. On completion of the intervention, recruits returned to the dressing area, where they were seated and asked to respond to a questionnaire dealing with both factual and attitudinal response to the situation.

Altogether 128 interventions were enacted by the recruits and recorded for rating. The tapes of the interventions were assigned randomly amongst the raters. Each rater made an independent assessment of only one of the two officers on each tape. A color-coded arm band ensured that each officer was uniquely identified.

Results

The DIP Scale had 9 subscales designed to tap different aspects of Domestic Intervention Performance. A three-way factorial analysis of variance was conducted for each of the subscale scores to identify specific effects of the various behaviors examined. The factors were: Training-No Training (2) x Theory-No Theory (2) x Practice Trials (3).

Alternative analyses would have been a multivariate analysis of variance, or an analysis of variance of total scores. However, these analyses might well serve to obscure the very subtle effects that the design of the study was intended to highlight. For that reason, separate analyses of variance were performed. Because multiple analyses of this sort tend to increase the experiment-wise error rate, a significance level of .001 (Kirk, 1968) was adopted to reduce the likelihood of Type I error.

The summary table of significant main effects and interactions displayed in Table 15.2 indicate the F tests which reached the .001 level of significance for both the total score and all the DIP subscale scores. Table 15.2 summarizes the major findings of this research.

The comparison of F ratios for the total score analysis against the F ratios for each subscale suggests that either (a) the total score showed significance due to

Table 15.2. Summary Table of Significant Main Effects and Interactions

UNIVARIATE F RATIOS

Variables

Source	Degrees of Freedom	Total	Phone Information	Approach and Entry	Gaining Control	Under-standing the Problem	Seeking Agree-ment	Structure	Con-cluding	Police Techniques	Attitudes
Training	1,116	.63	24.12*	6.95	2.50	0.34	2.25	11.01*	2.07	0.79	2.89
Theory	1,116	121.28*	0.50	218.78*	30.32*	50.89*	41.55*	33.46*	12.03*	19.82*	63.91*
Practice	2,232	53.27*	57.34*	4.36	62.17*	28.94*	21.75*	18.10*	7.70*	5.21	12.45*
Training x Theory	1,116	.86	4.85	10.98*	1.93	0.99	3.89	0.26	0.27	12.06*	0.76
Training x Practice	2,232	9.92*	1.51	2.07	4.66	2.42	4.43	1.29	5.19	10.49*	10.13*
Theory x Practice	2,232	2.09	1.15	10.23*	3.60	3.58	1.43	4.41	0.58	0.58	1.09
Training x Theory x Practice	2,232	.96	4.74	0.93	1.73	0.62	2.68	1.25	0.13	2.39	0.39

*p ≤ .001

specific subscale effects, or (b) effects on some subscales were obscured by lack of effects on others. For none of the analyses was there any 3-way interaction. There were five two-way interactions of interest.

DISCUSSION

The purpose of this research was to glean information regarding the utility of classroom, or didactic instruction, labeled as Theory, and experiential, or active learning, called Practice. Information regarding different amounts of Practice was also sought. These instructional modules were tested experimentally for their contribution to performance as measured by the DIP Scale, both with and without the impact of basic police training, referred to as Training. More generally, information was required to determine if the instructional approaches improved trainee performance in domestic interventions. If so, to what extent would performance be enhanced, by how much instruction, and which skills would be most responsive to which instructional methods? This information would be critical in shaping future content and methodological development in police training establishments.

As with any study of this nature, the findings have answered some questions and raised others. The use of a sensitive outcome measure has revealed that no single training condition is equally effective for all individuals, and conversely, that not all the dependent variables were equally influenced by the independent variable conditions. In retrospect, early concern over establishing a stringent statistical significance level has proven not to be problematic. For the most part, instructional methods produced either highly significant changes or almost no change at all.

It is not possible within the scope of this chapter to discuss all possible significant results. Rather, two major findings will be emphasized: (a) the impact of Theory and Practice and (b) the interaction of Training with Theory.

The Impact of Theory and Practice

The most powerful finding of this study is that CICM Theory and experiential Practice each contribute a specific set of skills and knowledge that basic police training (Training) does not otherwise provide. Recruits exposed to the teaching approaches examined in this research demonstrated significant improvement in their performance, as defined by the DIP Scale, of intervention skills required for successful handling of domestic disputes. The data of Table 15.2 attest to both of these statements.

The results of this study stand in contrast to the conclusion reached by Schwalb (1976). She states:

The high consensus amongst trainers regarding type of training needed is supported by the current study. Training need not involve didactic lectures, reading assignments, nor written homework, if the goal of training is objective behaviors change. The necessary skills are learned in only one way, *through active practice.* [emphasis added] (p. 96)

It appears that Schwalb has been seduced by the popular trend in this literature to downplay didactic learning in favor of experiential training (Zacker & Bard, 1973; McNamara, 1967).

The data of this study support the hypothesis that the CICM Theory package tested represents an extremely important factor in shaping performance in domestic interventions. Theory was the factor which accounted for significance on more subscales than any other. Theory contributed significantly on eight of the nine DIP scales. The only subscale to which it did not contribute by either main effect or interaction was "telephone information," a skill area not taught in the Theory package.

In addition to the foregoing main effects, Theory was involved in interactions on the subscales for Approach and Entry and Police Techniques. For the Approach and Entry scale, Theory interacted significantly with Training. Theory makes a significant contribution on this subscale, whereas Training makes no significant difference to the result. On this same variable, Theory interacts significantly with Practice. The presence of Theory accounts for a significant increase in mean scores across trials, while its absence results in a significant decrease by trial 3.

The confirmation of CICM Theory as an important teaching method is welcome, given the advantages of lower cost, reduced time, and effort which Coleman (1977) earlier attributed to the information-assimilation mode of learning. It appears that the concern regarding the limits for transfer of information from the assimilation to the experiential mode is not entirely warranted. On the other hand, despite the potency of this Theory, the evidence suggests that it should not be used as the sole method of instruction. Certain of the required skills are either not learned, or fail to transfer into the active mode. While didactic instruction appears the most effective method of beginning this task, it did not alone produce maximum attainment of the desired training objectives.

Experiential learning, in the form of simulated interventions, established itself in this study as an important teaching method, with or without the benefit of CICM Theory. Seven of nine DIP scales showed significant main effects for the practice factor.

On those subscales where Practice main effects did not emerge, significant interactions with Practice were present. In all, Practice was involved in four significant interactions, three with Training and one with Theory. The Training interactions involved the Police Techniques, Attitude, and Total score variables. Practice, even without Training, resulted in significantly higher trial 3 mean scores for Police Techniques and Total score variables.

The issue of the effectiveness of simulation as a teaching method was one important concern within the domestic conflict literature reviewed earlier. The present design, from the point of view of both independent and dependent variables employed, is believed to represent a more rigorous test of the hypothesis that "Practice would improve performance across all groups" than has been achieved to date.

These data would support the expansion of this training. Also one may consider the application of the experiential training mode to achieve training objectives in related areas.

Although there are no normative data regarding expected peak performance under increased instruction, there is ample room for continued mean score improvement. Only two of the nine subscales showed any indication of approaching their maximum attainable score. This raises the question of how much additional experiential learning would be beneficial before the learning curve would peak.

The present results pertaining to the Practice factor demonstrate that as an instructional method it can, particularly along with didactic material, significantly improve performance toward the required standards. The utilization of simulation methodology as both a teaching and a research method has, as others who have used simulation techniques have indicated (Palys, 1978; Parasuraman, 1981), been beneficial in creating a better understanding of the requirements involved in competently using Domestic Intervention skills.

The Interaction of Training with Theory

Training as defined in this research reflected the basic police training (e.g., law, physical education, small arms) included in the "conventional" syllabus with CICM Theory and practice excluded.

The data from this study relate to the issue of the impact of Training on the outcome measures, and have been derived from recruits without field experience. Most previous research on the question has relied upon comparisons between experienced officers. Typically some of these patrol officers received special instruction in conflict management while others served as a control group.

Relative to the other two factors examined in this research basic police training is a less powerful teaching approach in enhancing DIP Scale performance. Inspection of Table 15.2 indicates that Training is significant on only two of nine DIP scales whereas Theory and Practice contribute significantly on nine and eight DIP scales respectively. The two subscales which were significantly influenced by the Training factor are variable I Telephone Information and variable VI Structure of Intervention.

Training interacted with other factors on five occasions, twice with Theory and three times with Practice. Contrary to prediction, these Training interactions did not serve to enhance DIP Scale performance.

In each instance where Training has had a significant interaction it did not elevate performance relative to those without the Training as was expected. In fact there is a general pattern throughout the data. Comparisons indicate that the groups with Training begin at a significantly higher level of performance than those without training. However at Trial 3 the group without Training is performing significantly better than those with Training. All of these data suggest that those with training start at a better level of performance but for some reason tend to improve at a slower rate with Practice. This of course is contrary to the hypothesis that Training in combination with the other factors would facilitate greater improvement for the same amount of Practice.

Given the relative lack of impact demonstrated by the Training factor overall it would be convenient to dismiss Training as not relevant to domestic intervention or conversely to dismiss conflict management as not relevant to policing. Such dichotomous, even simplistic thinking, is not unknown but does not fit the data. While Training was not significant for the Total Score as a main effect, it did interact significantly with Practice. One seemingly parsimonious explanation as to why an initially significant benefit is not sustained over Practice is found in the issue of specificity. It might be hypothesized for example that knowledge derived from Training is general as opposed to specific knowledge. Consequently when performance for untrained groups is relatively low (such as at Trial 1) Training has a contribution to make.

As the opportunity for the observation and practice of specific skills increases, the untrained groups increase in their performance of these skills. However, the more global or general information derived from training no longer serves to enhance performance.

This explanation would be consistent with the high degree of significance obtained for the more specific or specialized instructional components of CICM Theory and Practice. However this hypothesis alone cannot be seen as a sufficient explanation of why the No-Training group should surpass the Training group at Trial 3 as it did, for example, on the total DIP Scale mean score. It would appear that some additional factors must be identified in order to more fully account for these interaction findings.

Among the plausible explanations for the data involving Training interactions is the possibility of a primacy effect of Training. CICM Theory is received near the end of a recruit's Training program. The possibility exists that attitudes and information received prior to CICM Theory may limit the effectiveness of subsequent instruction. If such a factor is operative here it may occur in a variety of ways. One hypothesis may be that the sheer volume of information received by recruits in the short time period of training may contribute to reduced retention of information received in the latter stages of this training. This process could be exacerbated, given the heavy schedule of physical training which is interspersed throughout the program (eg., swimming, self-defense, P.T., foot drill, noon-hour parade, and recreational sports) by physical fatigue interfering with the didactic learning process. This factor might be termed simply "fatigue" or "information overload."

In addition to the possibility of accounting for these interaction data through an "information overload" hypothesis one should consider not only the volume of information but also the motivational properties attendant upon the information. It is possible that Trained groups who were nearing graduation carried a sense of "fait accompli" and consequently were less motivated or harbored something of a "know it all" attitude, which could account for the data.

Another hypothesis that is plausible is that a motivational difference between the trained and untrained groups might originate from a more fundamental divergence than the simple motivational difference. Speculation therefore extends beyond concern with primacy effects into possible role incompatibility or incongruency between the different aspects of instruction. Training may emphasize elements within the police role such as law enforcement in such a way as to inhibit performance on the outcome criteria measured by the DIP Scale. CICM Theory itself may be directly or indirectly advocating methods of dealing with the public that are not consistently reinforced in other parts of the program. There has long been concern within training establishments that the various segments of police instruction may be offering messages to recruits which are at cross purposes.

SUMMARY

This research addressed the impact of police training on domestic crisis interventions, i.e., interventions into intrafamilial violence. The setting for this investigation was the training academy of the Royal Canadian Mounted Police, at Regina, Saskatchewan. The experiment was designed to test the impact of various components of training. More specifically, groups of trainee constables were tested against specific performance criteria on domestic interventions, depending on phase of training, type of training, and amount of practice. The Domestic Intervention Performance (DIP) Scale was developed and standardized as a sensitive measure of a number of dimensions of performance.

The following general conclusions can be drawn about the effects of training:

1. R.C.M.P. training, excluding the CICM module, does not generalize to domestic crisis situations. Domestic crisis problems seem to require skills other than those of the traditional law-enforcement role of police.
2. The presentation of CICM Theory noticeably enhances the performance of skills required in the resolution of domestic crises.

3. The opportunity for structured practice in domestic interventions increases the performance skill level of constables.

4. On some measures of performance, "traditional" police training, other than CICM and human relations, seem to set a limit on optimum performance. Where Training interactions are significant, the No-Training recruits conclude with higher mean scores than the Training group.

The results of this research suggest that current training methods in CICM have a strong impact on performance in domestic crisis interventions. These results have implications for further domestic conflict management instruction, the use of simulation in training and research, the role of field trainers in this area, and of in-service training for serving policemen.

REFERENCES

Bard M. (1969). Family intervention police teams as a community mental health resource. *Journal of Criminal Law, Criminology and Police Science, 60,* 247-250.

Bard, M., & Berkowitz, B. (1967). Training police as specialists in family crisis intervention: A community psychology action program. *Community Mental Health Journal, 3*(4), 315.

Barocas, H. A. (1973). Urban policemen: Crisis mediators or crisis creators. *American Journal of Orthopsychiatry, 43*(4), 632.

Bell, G., Boudreau, B., Fish, T., Killip, S., & Milloy, D. (1981) Simulation methods in applied psychology: A critique. Unpublished project for Doctoral Seminar in Psychology, University of Calgary.

Bercal, T. E. (1970). Calls for police assistance: Consumer demands for governmental service. In H. Hahn (Ed.), *Police in urban society.* Beverly Hills, CA: Sage Publications.

Boyd, J. E. (1976). Longitudinal comparison of factor structures in a police performance appraisal system. Paper presented at the meeting of the Canadian Psychological Association, Toronto.

Boyd, J. E., & Bell, G. L. (1981). Domestic Intervention Performance (D.I.P.) Scale: Manual and scoring procedures. Unpublished manuscript.

Boyd, J. E., & Riddell, B. J. (1973). *Performance appraisal manual.* City of Calgary Police Service, Calgary.

Coleman, J. S. (1977). *Experiential learning: Rationale, characteristics and assessment.* San Francisco: Jossey-Bass.

Corley, J. B. (1970). College of Family Physicians of Canada. Evaluation Oral Examination. Presentation to the 66th Annual Congress on Medical Education, Chicago.

Cummings, M. (1970). Police and service work. In H. Hahn (Ed.), *Police in urban society.* Beverly Hills, CA: Sage Publications.

Doornink, J. D. (1975). Collaborative planning of family crisis intervention training by police trainees and mental health personnel. Unpublished doctoral dissertation, Kent State University, Kent, Ohio.

Driscoll, J., Meyer, R., & Schanie, C. (1973). Training police in family crisis intervention. *Journal of Applied Behavioral Science, 9*(1), 62-82.

Flanagan, J. C. (1954). The critical incident technique. *Psychological Bulletin, 51,* 327-358.

Gammon, M. A. B. (1978). *Violence in Canada.* Toronto: Methuen Publications.

Goldstein, H. (1977). *Policing a free society.* Cambridge, MA: Ballinger Publishing Co.

Kirk, R. E. (1968). *Experimental design: Procedures for the behavioral sciences.* Monterey, CA: Brooks/Cole.

Landy, F. J., Farr, J. L., Saal, F. E., & Freitag, W. R. (1976). Behaviorally anchored scales for rating the performance of police officers. *Journal of Applied Psychology, 61,* 750- 758.

Levens, B. R. (1978). Domestic Crisis Intervention: A literature review of domestic dispute intervention training programs (Part 1). *Canadian Police College Journal, 2,* 215-247.

Levens, B. R., & Dutton, D. G. (1977). *The social service role of police: Domestic crisis interventions.* Research Division: Ministry of the Solicitor General of Canada.

Liebman, D. A., & Schwartz, J. A. (1972). Police programs in domestic crisis interventions: A review. In J. R. Snibbe & H. M. Snibbe (Eds.), *The urban policeman in transition.* Springfield, IL: Charles C. Thomas.

Loving, N. (1980). *Responding to spouse abuse and wife beating. A guide for police.* Police Executive Research Forum, Washington, D.C.

Lystad, M. H. (1975). Violence at home: A review of the literature. *American Journal of Orthopsychiatry, 45*(3), 328-341.

Martin, D. (1976). *Battered wives.* San Francisco, CA: Glide Publications.

McNamara, J. H. (1967). Uncertainties in police work: The relevance of police recruits' background and training. In D. J. Bordua (Ed.), *The police: Six sociological essays.* New York: John Wiley.

Novaco, R. W. (1975). *Anger control: The development and evaluation of an experimental treatment.* Toronto, Lexington Books.

Palys, T. S. (1978). Simulation methods and social psychology. *Journal of the Theory of Social Behavior, 8*(3), 341-368.

Parasuraman, A. (1981). Assessing the worth of business simulation games: Problem and prospects. *Simulation and Games, 12,* 189-200.

Pierfy, D. A. (1977). Comparative simulation game research: Stumbling blocks and stepping stones. *Simulation and Games, 8,* 255-268.

Raser, J. R. (1969). *Simulation and society: An exploration of scientific gaming.* Boston, MA: Allyn and Bacon.

Schrieber, F. B. (1977). Design, implementation and evaluation of a twenty-four-hour crisis intervention training program for police. Unpublished doctoral dissertation, University of Colorado.

Schulz, R. L., & Sullivan, E. M. (1972). Developments in simulation and social and administrative science. In H. Guetzkow, P. Kotler, & R. L. Schulz (Eds.), *Simulation in social and administrative science: Overviews and case examples* (pp. 3-47). Englewood Cliffs, NJ: Prentice-Hall.

Schwalb, G. (1976). Police-specific communication training: A practice approach to family crisis mediation. Unpublished doctoral dissertation, University of Houston.

Smith, P. C., & Kendall, L. M. (1963). Retranslation of expectations: An approach to the construction of unambiguous anchors for rating scales. *Journal of Applied Psychology, 47,* 149-155.

Straus, M. A. (1977). A sociological perspective on the prevention and treatment of wife-beating. In M. Roy (Ed.), *Battered women.* New York: Van Nostrand-Reinhold.

Winer, B. J. (1962). *Statistical principles in experimental design.* New York: McGraw Hill.

Zacker, J., & Bard, M. (1973). Effects of conflict management training on police performance. *Journal of Applied Psychology, 58,* 201-208.

Index

Acceptance of Interpersonal
Violence (AIV), 57-58, 257, 259,
261, 263-264
Acquaintance rape (*see also,* rape,
sexual assault), 43-63, 80
epidemiology-men, 46-47
epidemiology-women, 44-46
hidden rapes, 44
offender characteristics, 51-55
research
critique, 61-63
future directions, 61-62
victim characteristics, 47-51
Aggression (*see also,* hostility)
annoyance-motivated, 215
as a trait, 131-132
male to female, 29-30, 68, 93-103
and family types, 95-99
developmental determinants,
91-103
extremely aggressive boys, 93,
100-103
conditions producing female
victimizer, 103
sex differences, 91-93
similarities to sexual behavior,
239-240
Alcohol, 137, 141, 164, 189, 195, 204,
217-235
Alcoholics Anonymous, 225-229
social comparison theory, 228-230
twelve steps to sobriety, 225

authoritarianism, 233-234
in Victorian England, 17
Michigan Alcoholism Screening
Test (MAST), 232
Anxiety, 206
and aggression, 245-249
associated with abandonment,
168-169
Arousal
sexual, 240-243, 245-249, 256,
260-263
measures of, 241-242
Attitudes Toward Women Scale
(AWS), 204, 207-211
Attributions, 107-110, 113-116,
217-235
theory, 107-110, 113-116
Just-world hypothesis, 225-226,
229-230, 234

Battering cycle, 168, 191
Buss-Durkee Hostility Inventory, 32,
152-153, 257, 259

Child abuse, 68-73
criteria of, 77-79
Cobbe, Francis Power, 7-8, 12-26
"An Act to Amend the
Matrimonial Causes Act," 24-25
her career, 12-14
most important writings, 13
Conceptual Systems theory, 177,

179-198, 254
coping styles, 184-185
distribution of conceptual systems,
189-191
Crisis-Intervention and Conflict
Management Package (CICM),
273, 277-279, 283-288
Critical Incident technique, 274-275

Differential Personality
Questionnaire (DPQ), 207-211
Domestic conflicts
police role in, 269-270
police training for interventions,
270-273
arrest option, x
experiential vs classroom
learning, 271-272
simulation of, 271-273, 275, 278-283
Domestic Intervention Performance
Scale (DIP), 273-277, 281-287
Don Juan syndrome, 166-167

Erotica
aggressive cues, 240-244
Playboy/Penthouse, 256
age of earliest exposure, 259, 264
Escalation effects, 215, 254-255

Fundamental Interpersonal
Relations Orientation-Behavior
instrument (FIRO-B), 204, 207-211

Hostility (see also, aggression)
and private self-consciousness, 132
as a construct, 31-32
as a trait, 29
Hostility Toward Men, 149-160
by female victims, 149-151
Hostility Toward Men Scale, 154-156
factor analysis of, 154
reliability, 154-155

validity, 156, 160
Hostility Toward women, 29-40
definition, 39-40
manifestations, 37-39
theoretical perspectives, 32-37
feminist theory, 34-37
psychiatric theory, 32-34
Hostility Toward Women Scale,
39-40

Inhibitions, 132-133, 239-240, 249
International Society for Research
on Aggression (ISRA), vii
Intimacy, 165-166
mens' fear of, 167, 265

Jealousy, 17, 168-169, 192-194

le Vice Anglais, 10

Machismo, 35, 205

Ocker, 138
Overcontrolled hostile individual,
133, 203-212
definition, 203-204

Personal space, 167-169
definition, 253
invasion, 168, 253-254, 260-263
shape, 255, 263
Physical attractiveness
and personal space, 256
reliability of ratings, 259
Punch and Judy show, 21

Rape (see also, sexual assault,
acquaintance rape)
definitions, 37-38, 43-44
incidence, ix, 30, 43-46, 86-87, 151,
157-159
rape culture, 52

types, 38
Rape myths, 54-58, 255, 265
  Rape Myth Acceptance Scale
    (RMA), 57, 257, 259, 261, 263-264
Royal Canadian Mounted Police
  (R.C.M.P.), 273, 277, 280

Scripts
  intimate relationships, 254
  sexual, 58-59
Self-esteem, 50, 142, 146, 178, 182,
  197, 229-230
Semantic Differential, 142-146,
  186-187
Sexual assault (*see also,* rape,
  acquaintance rape)
  and depression, 151, 157
  in acquaintance relationships, 43-63
Sexual Experiences Survey, 151-152
Sexual intercourse
  expectations in dating relationship,
    58-60
Shyness, 255, 257, 259-261, 264-265
  and assault, 263
  and guilt, 261
Simulated Couple Conflict
  Instrument (SCCI), 186, 187,
  193-194
  reliability, 187
Spousal violence (*see also,*
  wife-beating)
  and power, 166-167
  and property damage, 137, 167
  Assessing Environments III (AE
    III) Questionnaire, 70-88
  Black women, 117-125
  and mass media, 109-110
  and the popular culture, 117-120,
    127
  causes, 68-69, 163-166, 177-179,
    192, 205-206
  clinical approach, 178-179

in Australia, 135-147
  a case study, 143-145
  attacks on legal/judicial system,
    138-139
  unemployment, 139-140
incidence of, 30, 67, 203, 217
issues, 179
powerlessness, 209-212
power motives, 166-167
punitive childhood experiences,
  68-88
rationalizations for remaining,
  110-112, 120-125
religion, 112, 124-125
sociological approach, 177-178
subordinate status of women,
  137-138
Type 1/Type 2 women, 125-126
Type A/Type B behaviors, 126-127
wives as possessions, 138, 142
Straus Conflict Tactics Scale (CTS),
  169-170

This I Believe Test (TIB), 180, 186,
  189-191

Wife-beating (*see also,* Spousal
  violence)
  as humorous, 1-4, 20-21
  assumptions of "experts", x
  causes of, 7-8, 17-20, 25-26, 68-69,
    192, 205-206
  in Victorian England
    Caroline Norton, 9
    causes of, 7-8, 17-20, 25-26, 68-69
    Charles Dickens, 8-9
    crowding, 17
    English law, 10-12, 21-23
    examples of domestic torture,
      14-15
    incidence, 16-17
    John Stuart Mill, 9-10

proverbs, 10
reasonable chastisement, 11-12
religion, 21
subordinate status of women,
    18-20
wives as property, 18
international reporting of, ix
legal system, ix-x
Parlimentary (in)action on, 1-5
    British parliament, 1-2, 21-25
    Canadian parliament, 1, 3-5, 217